De Gruyter Handbook of Organizational Conflict Management

De Gruyter Handbook of Organizational Conflict Management

Edited by
LaVena Wilkin and
Yashwant Pathak

DE GRUYTER

ISBN 978-3-11-152922-6
e-ISBN (PDF) 978-3-11-074636-5
e-ISBN (EPUB) 978-3-11-074650-1
ISSN 2748-016X
e-ISSN 2748-0178

Library of Congress Control Number: 2022938298

Bibliographic information published by the Deutsche Nationalbibliothek
The Deutsche Nationalbibliothek lists this publication in the Deutsche Nationalbibliografie;
detailed bibliographic data are available on the internet at http://dnb.dnb.de.

Contents

Section 1: Interpersonal Conflict Management

Section 2: Organizational Conflict Management

Section 3: **Intercultural, International, and Ethic Conflict Management**

Section 4: **Methods for Managing Organizational Conflicts**

Section 5: **Special Topics in Organizational Conflict Management**

Contributors

Costanza Alessio, University of Miami

Costanza Alessio is a post-baccalaureate research associate in the laboratory of Dr. Amishi Jha in the Psychology Department at the University of Miami. She received her B.A. in Psychology at Florida International University. In Dr. Jha's lab, she has been investigating the impact of mindfulness training on cognitive and psychological wellbeing in high-demand/high-stress professional settings. Her research interests are focused on the intersection between social cognition and goal pursuit, with an emphasis on understanding the cognitive mechanisms that support and hinder prosocial behavior and social collaboration under challenging circumstances.

Barb Allen, Nova Southern University

Barb Allen, PhD is an independent consultant who works in the field of organizational development and change management. Barb assists groups in practicing new communication and interaction patterns as they lead change together. Her inclusive participatory approach gives voice to and leverages the diverse talent from all parts of the organization towards creatively solving complex problems. She holds an MBA from the University of Arkansas in Little Rock and a PhD in Conflict Analysis & Resolution with a concentration in organizations from Nova Southeastern University in Ft. Lauderdale, Florida.

Jordan Barry, University of Miami

Jordan Barry is a post-baccalaureate research associate in Dr. Amishi Jha's lab at the University of Miami. He received his B.A. in Psychology and in Philosophy at the University of Connecticut. In Dr. Jha's lab, he works on projects with active-duty military service members, as well as other high-demand/high-stress groups, to study attention and working memory and the impact of mindfulness training on those systems.

Charity Butcher, Kennesaw State University

Charity Butcher, PhD is currently Professor of Political Science and Interim Director of the School for Conflict Management, Peacebuilding and Development at Kennesaw State University. She is the recipient of the 2021 American Political Science Association Distinguished Teaching Award. She teaches courses in American Politics, International Relations, American Foreign Policy, Global Security, Peacebuilding and Peacekeeping, and Theories of Conflict. She has authored or co-authored three books, including NGOs and Human Rights (University of Georgia Press, 2021), Understanding International Conflict Management (Routledge, 2020), and The Handbook of Cross-Border Ethnic and Religious Affinities (Rowman and Littlefield, 2019), and has numerous peer-reviewed articles on issues related to war, religion, ethnicity, human rights, terrorism, peacebuilding, and the Scholarship of Teaching and Learning. She is part of the editorial team for the Journal of Peacebuilding and Development is on the editorial boards of International Studies Perspectives and PS: Political Science & Politics.

https://doi.org/10.1515/9783110746365-203

Kenneth Cloke, Author, Speaker, Mediator
Ken Cloke, JD, PhD is a world-recognized mediator, dialogue facilitator, conflict resolution systems designer, teacher, trainer, author, and public speaker. He holds a B.A. from the University of California, Berkeley; a JD from U.C. Berkeley's Boalt Law School; a PhD from U.C.L.A.; and a LLM from U.C.L.A. Law School. He did post-doctoral work at Yale University School of Law and is a graduate of the National Judicial College in Reno, Nevada. He has been a pioneer and leader in the field of mediation and conflict resolution for the last 37 years. He is co-founder of Mediators Beyond Borders, based in Washington D.C. The organization supports individuals, organizations, communities, and governments around the world in building conflict resolution capacity and conflict literacy, focusing on under-served communities. He has done international work in conflict resolution in over 25 countries, including Armenia, Australia, Austria, Brazil, Canada, China, Cuba, Denmark, England, Georgia, India, Ireland, Japan, Latin America, Mexico, Netherlands, New Zealand, Nicaragua, Pakistan, Puerto Rico, Scotland, Thailand, Ukraine, the former USSR, United Kingdom, and Zimbabwe. As Director of the Center for Dispute Resolution, Kenneth Cloke works as a mediator, arbitrator, attorney, coach, consultant, and trainer, specializing in resolving complex multi-party conflicts which include community issues, grievance and workplace disputes, collective bargaining negotiations, organizational and school conflicts, sexual harassment and discrimination lawsuits, environmental and public policy disputes. Ken is the author of numerous books about mediation, organizational issues, and conflict resolution, including Mediating Dangerously: The Frontiers of Conflict Resolution (2007); The Crossroads of Conflict: A Journey into the Heart of Dispute Resolution (2012); Conflict Revolution: Mediating Evil, War, Injustice, and Terrorism; and The Dance of Opposites: Explorations in Mediation, Dialogue and Conflict Resolution Systems (2013). His latest book is Conflict Revolution: Designing Preventative Systems for Chronic Social, Economic and Political Conflicts. He is co-author with Joan Goldsmith of Thank God It's Monday! 14 Values We Need to Humanize the Way We Work; Resolving Conflicts at Work: 10 Strategies for Everyone on the Job (3rd Edition); Resolving Personal and Organizational Conflicts: Stories of Transformation and Forgiveness; The End of Management and the Rise of Organizational Democracy; and The Art of Waking People Up: Cultivating Awareness and Authenticity at Work. He speaks internationally on a wide range of topics. Ken is currently an Adjunct Professor at Pepperdine University's School of Law, Strauss Institute. He is also an Adjunct Professor at Southern Methodist University, Saybrook University, and the University of Southern California. He has been an Adjunct Professor at Harvard University School of Law's Program on Negotiation, Insight Initiative; Albert Einstein College of Medicine, Cape Cod Institute; Massey University (New Zealand); and the University of Amsterdam's ADR Institute, among others.

Robin Cooper, Nova Southeastern University
Robin Cooper, PhD is Assistant Dean for Strategic Initiatives and Program Development and Associate Professor of Conflict Resolution and Ethnic Studies at Nova Southeastern University's Halmos College of Arts and Sciences (HCAS). Her scholarship reflects her strong research interests in identity-based conflict, cross-cultural conflict resolution, collaborative practices in organizational contexts, qualitative research, and student learning. She is Co-Editor of the Peace Education Book Series for *Information Age Press*, Senior Advisory Editor of *Peace and Conflict Studies*, Senior Editor

of *The Qualitative Report*, Associate Editor of *Forum: Qualitative Social Research*, and an Associate of the Taos Institute, a community of scholars whose practice reflects the principles of social constructionism. She is also on the Executive Board of the Peace and Justice Studies Association.

Teresa A. Daniel, Sullivan University

Teresa A. Daniel, JD, PhD serves as Dean & Professor-Human Resource Leadership Programs at Sullivan University (www.sullivan.edu) based in Louisville, KY. She is also the Chair for the HRL concentration in the university's PhD in Management program. Dr. Daniel has a significant body of research in HR with an emphasis on two primary areas of inquiry: (1) *counterproductive work behaviors* (focused on workplace bullying, sexual harassment, and toxic leadership), and (2) *HR's unique role and its impact on individual and organizational effectiveness* (focused on the management of toxic workplace emotions, responding to situations of workplace bullying and harassment, dealing with toxic leaders, and the management of people during mergers and acquisitions). Her work has been actively supported by the national Society for Human Resource Management (SHRM) through the publication of her research in numerous articles, interviews, and two books: *Guardrails: Taming Toxic Leaders and Creating Positive Workplace Cultures* (SHRM, 2021) and *Stop Bullying at Work: Strategies and Tools for HR, Legal & Risk Management Professionals* (SHRM, 2016). She is also the author of Organizational Toxin Handlers: The Critical Role of HR, OD, & Coaching Practitioners in Managing Toxic Workplace Situations (Palgrave Macmillan, 2020). Dr. Daniel was honored as an Initial Fellow of the *International Academy on Workplace Bullying, Mobbing, and Abuse* in 2014 and received the *Distinguished Alumnus Award* at Centre College in 2002. Most recently, she was the *2019 Grand Prize Winner* of the national SHRM HR Haiku contest.

Ekaterina Denkova, University of Miami

Ekaterina Denkova, PhD is a Research Assistant Professor in the Division of Cognitive & Behavioral Neuroscience in the Department of Psychology at the University of Miami. She serves as the Assistant Director of the Neuroimaging Facility & Assistant Director of Research for the UMindfulness Initiative. She received her PhD from the University of Strasbourg after which she joined the University of Alberta as a CIHR Fellow. She serves as Co-investigator on several federally funded grants with Dr. Amishi Jha. Dr. Denkova is a cognitive and affective neuroscientist. Using brain and behavioral methods, she broadly studies the neural basis of cognitive and affective processes and their trainability with mindfulness training. More specifically, Dr. Denkova's work has two intertwined lines of research. The first line of research focuses on the interplay between cognitive and affective processes underlying personal memories and thoughts, such as mind-wandering, ruminations, and intrusions. The second line of research examines the impact of mindfulness training on these cognitive and affective processes in high-stress/high-demand professionals.

Brittany Foutz, Salisbury University

Brittany Foutz, PhD is a faculty member of the Department of Conflict Analysis and Dispute Resolution at Salisbury University. She teaches International Law and various United Nations courses with the Salisbury University Department of Political Science and the Honors College. In addition, she has been recently awarded an Honors College Faculty Fellowship. She serves as the Faculty

Advisor for Salisbury University's Model United Nations, the United Nations Millennium Fellowship, and the United Nations Association Chapter. At the university, Dr. Foutz is a Fulton School of Liberal Arts Remote Teaching Specialist. Dr. Foutz is, also, a Senior Research Fellow and Trained Mediator at the Bosserman Center for Conflict Resolution in Salisbury, Maryland. Dr. Foutz's research interests include international law, transitional justice, reparations, the International Criminal Court, and human rights and the rule of law. Her dissertation addresses how the implementation and use of reparation mechanisms affects the satisfaction of child soldier and sexual violence victims of the International Criminal Court (ICC), the world's court. Dr. Foutz is the Co-Director of Salisbury Regional Centre of Expertise, a location acknowledged by the United Nations Educational, Scientific and Cultural Organization and United Nations University. This United Nations location focuses on conflict prevention and creative problem-solving. Dr. Foutz has been elected to be on the United Nations Americas Governance Committee and United Nations Americas Strategic Planning Support Committee, and Leader of the United Nations Americas Task Force on Education. She serves as a formal consultant for the United Nations Human Rights Council's Working Group on the Use of Mercenaries, the United Nations Regional Centre of Expertise Global Network, and the United States Institute of Peace Africa Program. Furthermore, she has fluency in six languages and has received over a million dollars in grants. Dr. Foutz has her PhD in International Conflict Management from Kennesaw State University's School of Conflict Management, Peacebuilding and Development. Her dissertation is entitled "Victim Satisfaction with Reparations from the International Criminal Court: An Examination of Child Soldier Cases from Kenya and Sexual Violence Cases from the Democratic Republic of Congo" and is currently a manuscript in publication with Oxford University Press.

Alexia Georgakopoulos, Nova Southeastern University
Alexia Georgakopoulos, PhD is a Professor in the Department of Conflict Resolution Studies at Nova Southeastern University (www.hcas.nova.edu), where she teaches masters and doctoral students in one of the nation's earliest conflict resolution programs. She is the Director of the Institute of Conflict Resolution and Communication (www.ICRCtraining.com), a mediation and conflict resolution training and consulting firm specializing in delivering educational training and mediation certification to professionals. She is an approved primary trainer from the Florida Supreme Court and delivers model Florida Supreme Court Mediation Certification Programs and continuing mediation education to the public. She is the Editor of The Handbook of Mediation: Theory, Research, and Practice published by Routledge Publishers. The handbook is the most contemporary handbook of mediation in the field, and it features nearly 60 thought leaders, forefront authorities, and notable practitioners in the fields of mediation, peace studies, justice, human rights, and conflict resolution. Dr. Georgakopoulos is a practicing mediator in diverse forms of mediation (family, commercial/ corporate, environmental, and multinational mediation) as well as a facilitator, arbitrator, dispute systems designer, conflict coach, and peacebuilder in both domestic and international contexts. She served as part of the Middle East Initiative Group of the Mediators Beyond Borders, worked as a facilitator with a House Representative who was charged by the White House to address policy issues concerning Climate Change and National Security, and she continues to train thousands of mediators throughout the world in classroom and training contexts. She received the reputable Quality of Life Grant and designed a Youth Peace Leadership Mentorship Program that supports

youth peace education and youth literacy. A world-class scholar and practitioner in conflict resolution, she was featured on NBC's Today Show to discuss peace in the diverse world. Her great grandmother experienced the sights of genocide in her small village in Epirus Greece, her grandfather served in the US military for three years abroad during WWII, her mother worked for U.S. Department of Defense overseas, her parents worked abroad and experienced Revolution in the Middle East, and Alexia Georgakopoulos has devoted her life work and career to conflict transformation and peacebuilding.

Joan S. Goldsmith

Dr. Joan Goldsmith has been an organizational consultant, coach, and educator for the past thirty-five years, specializing in leadership development, organizational change, conflict resolution, and team building. Joan has authored several books on leadership including (with Warren Bennis) Learning to Lead, and the soon to be published Women Leaders at the Grassroots: 9 Stories and 9 Strategies. She has served on numerous boards of directors and been an advisor to the Woman's International Health Coalition, Disney Institute for Women Entrepreneurs, Women's Lens on Global Issues, and Women International League for Peace and Freedom, and a speaker at national and local conferences on issues of women in leadership. As a family therapist, coach, and consultant, she has specialized in supporting individuals in improving their skills, life and work patterns and organizations. She has been a consultant to faculty and administration in U. S. and international universities. In the non-profit sector and in educational reform, she has been an advisor on organizational issues, school change, curriculum development and teacher education. She is an Associate of the Synergos Institute, which builds international, collaborative partnerships to end poverty in the Southern Hemisphere. She has had professional engagements in Mexico, Brazil, Cuba, the Bahamas, Japan, China, India, the Netherlands, and Great Britain. She is a founder of Cambridge College, a former member of the faculties of the Harvard University, UCLA, Antioch University, and holds a Master of Arts in Social Sciences and a Doctorate of Humane Letters.

Hyacinth Guy, Hyacinth Guy, Coaching for Success Consulting Firm

Hyacinth Guy, PhD has been a Practitioner of Organizational Development and Strategic Human Resource Management for over thirty (30) years. Dr. Guy is the Principal Director of Hyacinth Guy Human Resource Company a Leadership and Organizational Development Company with a focus on building Personal and Organizational Competencies. Dr. Guy is particularly passionate about helping to establish the workplace systems and culture that facilitate the achievement of organization goals. Dr. Guy has a PhD in Conflict Analysis and Resolution from Nova Southeastern University, Fort Lauderdale, an MBA from Andrews University, Michigan, an MA from The Institute of Social Studies, Erasmus University, Netherlands, and a BSc, Social Science from the University of the West Indies. Dr. Guy is a certified Human Resource Management Practitioner with certifications from the Human Resource Certification Institute, the Society of Human Resource Management, and she is a certified Workforce Planner from the Human Capital Institute. She is also a trained personal and organizational development LifeSuccess Coach and Facilitator of the Proctor Gallagher Institute and a certified Wellness Teacher with the Chopra Education Center. She has integrated her LifeSuccess and Wellness training with her other competencies to help individuals and organizations unearth latent potential and move into action to achieve their goals. Dr. Guy is a past Chairman of the Teaching Service Commission and the Regulated Industries Commission and is the present Chairman of the Industrial Relations Advisory Committee and the Cipriani College of Labor and Cooperative Studies.

Maia Carter Hallward, Kennesaw State University

Maia Carter Hallward, PhD is a Professor of Middle East Politics in the School of Conflict Management, Peacebuilding and Development at Kennesaw State University and Executive Editor of the Journal of Peacebuilding and Development. She is author or co-author of seven books, including NGOs and Human Rights (University of Georgia Press, 2021), Understanding International Conflict Management (Routledge, 2020), Global Responses to Crisis and Conflict in Syria and Yemen (Palgrave 2019), and Understanding Nonviolence (Polity, 2015), with over 20 peer-reviewed articles on topics including nonviolence, peacebuilding, human rights, the role of religion in politics, women's leadership, and civil resistance in Israel/Palestine. She has led or co-led multiple learning experiences to Israel/Palestine that have explored the interplay of religion, culture, and religion, and she has participated in faculty delegations to Morocco, Turkey, and Oman. Maia is on the Fulbright Specialist Roster for Conflict Resolution and a Fulbright Scholar in Jordan (2022).

Gayle Hardison, Nova Southeastern University

Gayle Hardison is a graduate of the University of Virginia and Dowling College and holds degrees in Sociology and Business Administration. She has 35 years of experience in the insurance industry, 30 of which have been in leadership training, developing and leading successful teams. Presently Gayle is a Doctoral candidate in the practice of Conflict Resolution at Nova Southeastern University.

Leah P. Hollis, Rutgers University

Dr. Leah P. Hollis is the Founder and President of Patricia Berkly, LLC, a healthy workplace advocate, and diversity trainer. Her recent book, Human Resource Perspectives on Workplace Bullying in Higher Education Understanding Vulnerable Employees' Experiences, was released by Routledge (2021), examining the structural problems and inadequate policies that allow workplace bullying to hurt vulnerable employees. She has continued her research with Intersecting Distress (forthcoming 2022), which examines intersectionality, Black women, and workplace bullying. Serving as Lead Consultant of Workplace Bullying, Equity, Access, and Diversity, Hollis speaks nationally and internationally, including appearances in Milan, Italy; Athens, Greece; Oxford, England; New York, New York; Los Angeles, California, Texas, and Pennsylvania. Her work has been covered by University Business, Nature, The Chronicle of Higher Education, higheredjobs.com, and Forbes Magazine. Hollis has an exemplary career in higher education administration, where she has held senior leadership and faculty posts. Currently an Associate Professor at Morgan State University, Dr. Hollis has taught at Northeastern University, the New Jersey Institute of Technology, and Rutgers University. Dr. Hollis received her Bachelor of Arts degree from Rutgers University and her Master of Arts degree from the University of Pittsburgh. She received her Doctor of Education in Administration, Training, and Policy Studies from Boston University, as a Martin Luther King, Jr. Fellow. Also, Dr. Hollis continued her professional training at Harvard University through the

Graduate School of Education, Higher Education Management Development Program. She earned certification in Project Management and Executive Leadership at Stanford University and Cornell University, respectively. Further, she has earned certifications in EEO Law/Affirmative Action and Conflict Resolution and Investigation from the American Association for Affirmative Action. She also serves as an expert witness regarding workplace bullying, harassment, and discrimination. She is also the author Unequal Opportunity Fired without cause, Filing with the EEOC, which focuses on workplace discrimination.

Amishi P. Jha, University of Miami
Dr. Amishi Jha, PhD is Director of Contemplative Neuroscience and Professor of Psychology at the University of Miami. She received her B.S in Biological Psychology from the University of Michigan, her Ph.D in Psychology (Cognitive Neuroscience) from the University of California–Davis, and her post-doctoral training at the Brain Imaging and Analysis Center at Duke University in functional neuroimaging. With grants from the Department of Defense and several private foundations, she leads research on the neural bases of attention and the effects of mindfulness-based training programs on cognition, emotion, resilience, and performance in education, corporate, elite sports, first-responder, and military contexts. In her laboratory at the University of Miami, she uses functional MRI, electrophysiological recordings and behavioral techniques to understand why our attention sometimes fails us, and if it can be trained for greater focus and less distractibility.

Haleh Karimi, Bellarmine University
Haleh Karimi, PhD is an assistant professor of management at the W. Fielding Rubel School of Business at Bellarmine University. She received her PhD in Management from Sullivan University, an executive MBA from Bellarmine University, and her Bachelor of Science in Management and Computer Information Systems from Central Missouri State University. Dr. Karimi has extensive industry experience working in fortune 500, mid-size, startup, and non-profit organizations. She has over a decade of experience teaching and administering at higher-education institutions, specifically at Sullivan University, the University of Louisville, and Bellarmine University. This combination has given her the vision to use high-impact pedagogies in her classroom for achieving students' long-term success. She has been recognized and received numerous awards for her teaching styles by her management and her students. Her research focuses on strategies to improve personal, professional, and organizational goals. She believes this leads us to a win/win outcome for all key stakeholders and ultimately for our communities.

Neil H. Katz, Nova Southeastern University
Neil H. Katz, PhD is a graduate of the University of Maryland. He is in his 50th year as a professor, former chair, or director of training at several universities. He currently serves as professor in the Department of Conflict Resolution Studies at Nova Southeastern University (NSU) and professor emeritus at the Maxwell School of Syracuse University. He operates his consulting firm, *Neil Katz and Associates*, specializing in organizational leadership and workplace conflicts .He is the author or co-author of over 50 books, book chapters and articles including the third edition of the popular *Communication and Conflict Resolution Skills*, Kendall/Hunt 2020. Throughout his career, Neil has

been the recipient of several prestigious awards including the Marlin Luther King Human Rights Award from the Syracuse community for his leadership in nonviolent conflict resolution, the William Kreidler Award for Distinguished Service to the field of Conflict Resolution from the Association of Conflict Resolution, and the President's Distinguished College Professor of the Year Award from NSU.

Loraleigh Keashly, Wayne State University
Loraleigh Keashly, PhD is a graduate of the University of Saskatchewan, Canada). She is currently Professor in the Department of Communication at Wayne State University, Detroit. Her research, teaching and consulting focus on conflict and conflict resolution at the interpersonal, group, intergroup and organizational level. Her main research focus is the nature, effects, and amelioration of uncivil and bullying behaviors in the workplace with a particular interest in the role of organizational structure and culture in the facilitation or prevention and management of these behaviors. She has focused her recent attention on the academic environment and works with universities on these issues. She has developed and conducted trainings in building bystander efficacy to take constructive action in challenging situations. Her works in progress focus on 1) the power of relationships at work and 2) civility in academia. She has published over 40 articles and book chapters. She has been a consultant to organizations and an expert witness on cases of workplace bullying and hostility.

Ralph H. Kilmann; CEO, Kilmann Diagnostics LLC
Ralph H. Kilmann, PhD is CEO of Kilmann Diagnostics (KD) in Newport Coast, California. In this position, he has created all of KD's online courses and assessment tools on the four timeless topics of conflict management, change management, expanding consciousness, and quantum transformation. Ralph's online products are used by such high-profile organizations as Amazon, Bank of America, DuPont, ExxonMobil, FedEx, GE, Google, Harvard University, Microsoft, NASA, Netflix, Philips, Twitter, the U.S. Department of State, Verizon, Wal-Mart, the World Health Organization, and Zoom Video. Ralph earned both his B.S. in graphic arts management and M.S. in industrial administration from Carnegie Mellon University in 1970, and a Ph.D. degree in the behavioral sciences in management and social systems design from the University of California, Los Angeles, in 1972. After Ralph left UCLA, he immediately began his professional career as an Assistant Professor at the Katz School of Business, University of Pittsburgh. In 1991, the faculty awarded him the George H. Love Professorship of Organization and Management, which he held until 2002, when he relinquished his tenured faculty position. Instead of staying in Pittsburgh, Ralph moved to the West Coast, since he wanted to fulfill his California Dream, which eventually led to the creation of Kilmann Diagnostics. Ralph has published more than twenty books and one hundred articles. In 2021, Ralph wrote and published his "legacy book," which integrates everything he's ever created and presented across all his previous books and articles: Creating a Quantum Organization: The Whys & Hows of Implementing Eight Tracks for Long-Term Success. He is also the coauthor of more than ten assessment tools, including the Thomas-Kilmann Conflict Mode Instrument (TKI) and the Kilmann Organizational Conflict Instrument (KOCI). To learn more about the author and his work, visit his website: www.kilmanndiagnostics.com.

Michele Lemonius, University of Manitoba

Michele Lemonius is Human Rights and Conflict Management Advisor at the University of Manitoba. She is a doctoral candidate in Peace and Conflict Studies at the University of Manitoba and holds an MA in Conflict Analysis and Manage from Royal Roads University, and a Master's in Adult Education from St. Francis Xavier University. She has ten years of experience in the field of conflict management.

Barbara Sunderland Manousso

Barbara Sunderland Manousso, PhD, M.P.H., CEO and founder of Manousso Mediation and Arbitration, LLC and Solution2Conflict, has taught and practiced mediation and arbitration worldwide, since 1993, as a family and civil mediator, arbitrator, ombudsman, facilitator, negotiator, conflict resolution coach, as well as author of articles and book chapters, related to her research and practice. In addition, for many years, she has been a professor in Global Conflict Management at the University of St. Thomas in Houston, TX, training foreign-service officers. She has worked for years closely with many professional conflict management organizations, the Houston Better Business Bureau's ADR programs, the Small Business Administration, and American and Texas Bar Associations. Her baccalaureate was from Brown University; Master of Public Health, from the University of Texas School of Public Health; and PhD, from Nova Southeastern University. She also holds a graduate certificate in Healthcare and Conflict. She attended South Texas College of Law and chaired the Healthcare Society and holds many ADR certificates, those required by statute and numerous conflict certificates and hours beyond statute requirements. A former president of the Association of Conflict Resolution Houston chapter, she is internationally recognized as a leader and mentor in the field of mediation and arbitration. From 2015 to 2018, she chaired the international Association for Conflict Resolution International's Education, Research, and Training Section and from 2012 to 2015, she chaired the ACR international Health Care Section. She has lectured in Shanghai, China, Bangkok, Thailand, Goa, India, Halifax, Canada, Ireland, Mexico, and New Zealand. Students come from around the world to take her trainings in Houston. In 2019, she received the Suzanne Adams Award from the Texas Association of Mediators, as the top dispute resolution practitioner in Texas. In 2018, she was recognized for a Lifetime Achievement Award in mediation and arbitration from the Association for Conflict Resolution Houston Chapter, A Houston Business Journal Mentor, and A Woman Who Means Business by the Houston Business Journal. In 2010, she was recognized as One of the Fifty Most Influential Women in Houston by Houston Women's Magazine. In 1992, she was recognized by the Egyptian Suez Government. In 1972, she was recognized by the White House as Rhode Island's Outstanding Small Business. She is currently the president of Brown University's Class of 1977.

Katsiaryna Matusevich, Barry University

Katsiaryna Matusevich, PhD is an Associate Professor of Human Resource Development at Barry University in Miami, where she is also leading the Human Resource Development graduate program. Her research focuses on exploring a link between organizational environment and employee well-being, and, specifically, on the role that situational factors such as organizational culture, leadership, social support, and team psychological safety play in promoting peak experiences known as flow. On the practitioner side, Dr. Matusevich uses her expertise to partner with organizations to co-create solutions to improve communication, leadership, and performance through science-based interventions. She holds a certificate in Brain-Based Coaching through the Neuroleadership Institute and has a credential of a Results Coaching System trained coach. She also holds an Associate Certified Coach (ACC) credential from the International Coach Federation. She has provided executive coaching, leadership development, and communication solutions to national industry-leading companies in homebuilding, healthcare, financial services, and fashion.

Pavel Mischenko, Leader Talent Consulting
Pavel is the Managing Partner of Leader Talent, LLC with 25 years of experience in International Business Consulting, Human Resources Development, and Administration. Originally from Russia, he holds graduate degrees in Engineering (M.S., Moscow State University) and Family Therapy (M.A., Syracuse University). He designs and facilitates performance-based development programs in the area of leadership, management, communication, conflict resolution, and teamwork. Mr. Mischenko is a Faculty Member of Management Centre Europe / American Management Association and an Adjunct Faculty with the Syracuse University. With a strong international background, he has delivered consulting projects worldwide with more than 5000 executives, managers, and technical professionals from mid-size to large Fortune 500 companies. Pavel is a Founder of the BOTH® Method helping organizational leaders to build highly productive teamwork while effectively managing conflict and stress.

Alisa V. Moldavanova, Wayne State University
Alisa V. Moldavanova is Associate Professor and MPA program director at The Joseph R. Biden, Jr. School of Public Policy and Administration at the University of Delaware. She previously served as Associate Professor and Coordinator of the graduate certificate in nonprofit management at Wayne State University (Detroit, Michigan). Her current research investigates organizational sustainability in the context of public service organizations, the role of inter-organizational networks and other forms of social connectedness in enabling sustainable organizations, as well as how nonprofits and other public service organizations foster sustainable development in their local communities. She is also conducting research on the role of civil society and nonprofit sector organizations in advancing democracy. Dr. Moldavanova's work has been published in leading public administration and urban studies journals, as well as in numerous edited book collections. She is also an editor of the 2018 book, "The Nonprofit Sector in Eastern Europe, Russia, and Central Asia: Civil Society Advances and Challenges" (Brill Publishers).

Christopher T. H. Miners, Queen's University, Smith School of Business
Christopher T. H. Miners is an Associate Professor of Organizational Behavior at the Smith School of Business at Queen's University in Canada. He received his B.Sc. in Psychology from McGill University, and his PhD in Organizational Behavior and Human Resource Management from the University of Toronto. Christopher's research investigates abilities, personality traits, and intra- and interpersonal processes that facilitate job performance and promote well-being. The focus of his first line of research is on emotional intelligence. Christopher's current research examines the relations between

emotional intelligence and negotiation performance, moral decision-making, and social influence. A second line of his research investigates the antecedents and consequences of counternormative behavior in group contexts. He has published papers on these topics in a variety of journals, including Administrative Science Quarterly, Leadership Quarterly, and Journal of Experimental Social Psychology, as well as a number of book chapters. His research is funded by the Social Sciences and Humanities Research Council of Canada, and has been featured on the Discovery Channel, in The Economist, and by the Government of Canada and the Institute of Electrical and Electronics Engineers. He is an award-winning teacher who delivers courses in organizational behavior and emotional intelligence in the workplace for undergraduate, graduate, and executive audiences. Christopher enjoys mentoring students, and has supervised and served on many M.Sc. and PhD committees.

Jack Nasher, Munich Business School

Jack Nasher, PhD is a negotiation advisor and academic. Oxford educated, he is currently a professor at Munich Business School and teaches at Stanford University. He founded the NASHER Negotiation Institute, training and advising companies all over the world. Alongside his studies in Philosophy (PhD), Psychology (MA), Management (MSc), and Law (German State Exam), he earned his stripes at the European Court of Justice, at the United Nations in New York City, and at Wall Street's leading law firm Skadden. Jack's books became multiple bestsellers and appeared in the US, China, Russia, and dozens of other countries, reaching bestselling status in many. Articles from and about him appeared in publications such as Harvard Business Review, The Wallstreet Journal, ZEIT, and the China Times. Jack writes the annual Forbes list of "Top 10 World Changing negotiations". Professor Jack Nasher is a Principle Practitioner of the Association of Business Psychology and regularly speaks at management conventions, where his research has been awarded with a gold medal. He is an avid mentalist and regularly demonstrates mind mysteries at Hollywood's Magic Castle.

Terry Morrow Nelson, Nova Southeastern University

Terry Morrow Nelson, PhD is currently the Associate Dean of Student Affairs and Associate Professor at Nova Southeastern University's College of Health Care Sciences. Her work focuses on identifying opportunities to leverage human potential for the greater good through her practice and research efforts. Morrow Nelson is a Florida Supreme Court Mediator, Certified Christian Conciliator and President of the Morrow and Associates Partnership for Leadership and Transformation. She serves on the editorial review boards for the Journal of Leadership Education, Internet Journal of Allied Health Sciences and Practice, Journal of Peace and Conflict Studies, and The Qualitative Report.

Yashwant Pathak, University of South Florida

Yashwant Pathak, PhD earned his doctorate in Pharmaceutical Sciences. Later he also completed his Executive MBA and Master of Science in Conflict Management from Sullivan University in Louisville, KY. He is presently working as Associate Dean for Faculty Affairs, College of Pharmacy, University of South Florida Health, Tampa Florida. He is actively involved in many nonprofit organizations including the International Center for Cultural Sudies which organized a conference at Tampa on eastern and indigenous perspectives on conflict resolution. He has edited several books in the field of nanotechnology, drug delivery systems, Nutraceuticals, conflict resolution, and cultural studies.

Frederic S. Pearson, Wayne State University

Frederic S. Pearson, PhD is Professor of Political Science, and Gershenson Distinguished Research Faculty Fellow at Wayne State University in Detroit, USA; for the past 30 years he has served as Director of the University's Center for Peace and Conflict Studies. He is also Distinguished Service and Teaching Professor. He was previously professor and research fellow at the University of Missouri-St. Louis and twice a Fulbright scholar in the Netherlands and U.K. His Ph.D. dissertation was on Middle East conflict systems, and his numerous books include: Civil War: Internal Struggles, Global Consequences (with Marie Olson Lounsbery); Arab Approaches to Conflict Resolution (with Nahla Hamdan); Arms and Ethnic Conflict (John Sislin) and Arms and Warfare, Negotiation. An authority on international military intervention, arms transfers, conflict resolution and peacemaking, Dr Pearson was editor of the 2001 special issue of the Journal of Peace Research on Identity-based Disputes and Conflict Management, and governmental consultant on US National Security, 21st Century, in Washington, DC, as well as at the UN. Other relevant recent articles have included studies of post-hostilities stability in civil wars, as well as intervention and the prospects for democratization and peaceful protest successes, inter-organizational collaboration, nuclear arms control, and conflict exit strategies.

Eileen Petzold-Bradley, Nova Southeastern University

Eileen Petzold-Bradley is a Learning and Development Specialist, Certified Coach, and Conflict Resolution Practitioner that works with diverse teams and executives in the facilitation, moderation, and transformative guidance through complex individual and organizational conflicts. She supports leaders and organizations alike to grow and enhance their conflict resolution skill toolkit and trains them to become more agile, resilient, and able to handle change and organizational challenges. Eileen is a doctoral candidate specializing in Organizational Conflicts at NOVA Southeastern University's Department of Conflict Resolution Studies and served as a Graduate Teaching Assistant for senior faculty for three years. She is a Dispute Resolution Fellow 2021 for the American Bar Association's Dispute Resolution Section (ADR Practice Management and OMBUDS Committees) and an active member of the International Council for Online Dispute Resolution, The International Ombudsman Association, and Association for Conflict Resolution. Currently, Eileen is the Educational Development and Outreach Director at BRDGES Academy, a leading educational institution offering conflict resolvers intercultural skills training and professional certifications in mediation. Most recently, Eileen worked with academics, leaders, and professionals from various industries and sectors, providing career and conflict coaching at EP Bradley and Ingeus. Eileen also ran an English Language Center and was the Master Franchisor for the Helen Doron Educational Group in Berlin, Germany. In her early career, Eileen was a foreign policy consultant carrying out relevant research on pressing environment and security themes to enhance dialogue and influence policy decision-makers and military leadership in Europe and the US for various governmental and international institutions. Eileen is an American and Panamanian and has lived in Europe, USA, and Panama. Eileen holds several coaching certifications (Marshall Goldsmith Stakeholder Centered Coaching and Systemic Coaching from European Coaching Association), a master's degree in Urban & Environmental Planning from the University of Virginia, and a dual Bachelor of Arts degree in International Studies & Spanish from George Mason University.

Brian Polkinghorn, Salisbury University

Brian Polkinghorn, MS, MA, MPhil, PhD is a Distinguished Professor of Conflict Analysis and Dispute Resolution at Salisbury University. In 1994 Brian was the co-founding faculty member of the Department of Conflict Analysis and Resolution (DCAR), Nova Southeastern University. In 2000 he designed in launched the Department of Conflict Analysis and Dispute Resolution (CADR) and became the Executive Director of the Bosserman Center for Conflict Resolution (BCCR), a United Nations University Regional Center of Expertise, at Salisbury University. He has worked in the conflict intervention field since 1985 as a mediator, arbitrator, facilitator, trainer, researcher, academic program and curriculum developer, conflict coach, dispute systems designer and ombudsman. He has published over 50 articles, book chapters and books and has been the (co)principle investigator on several dozen research projects. Brian has also been the recipient of more than 80 research and program grants. He has practiced in a dozen countries primarily in the areas of environmental policy dispute intervention, labor-management, cross border cooperative enterprises, leadership development and support of peace talks. Brian is an alum of the Carter School for Peace and Conflict Resolution (CSPCR), George Mason University, the Program on the Analysis and Resolution of Conflicts (PARC), Syracuse University and was a Fellow with the Program on Negotiation (PON), Harvard University Law School. Brian was a National Fellow with the US Environmental Protection Agency, a United States Presidential Fellow, the University System of Maryland Wilson Elkins Professor and a Senior American Fulbright Scholar with the Evens Program in International Conflict Resolution and Mediation at Tel Aviv University. Brian is currently a Fulbright Alumni Ambassador with the Council for the International Exchange of Scholars (CIES) the scholar division of the Institute of International Education (IIE).

Neal J. Powless, Syracuse University

Neal J. Powless, MS, NCC, and PhD Fellow at Syracuse University's S.I. Newhouse School of Public Communications, is a traditional member of the Onondaga Nation and Eel Clan. Three years ago, he became the University Ombuds at Syracuse University, transitioning from the Office of Multicultural Affairs and Career Services Center. Neal has a Masters's degree in Counseling from Syracuse University and a BS in Psychology from Nazareth College. He has taught courses and presented internationally for over 25 years about Indigenous culture and value systems and is the Co-Founder/Co-Owner with his wife, Michelle, of Indigenous Concepts Consulting. His professional accomplishments include the production of multiple movies and films, 3'x All-American, 2002 All-World, Professional World Championship and numerous Hall of Fame's for lacrosse and coach of the Netherland's national team since 2014.

Laura Rees, Queen's University, Smith School of Business

Laura Rees, PhD is an Assistant Professor of Organizational Behavior, recently joining the College of Business at Oregon State University (USA) from the Smith School of Business at Queen's University (Canada). She received her A.B. in Economics from Harvard University, and her PhD in Organizational Behavior from the University of Michigan. Laura's research focuses on emotions and related cognitive and interpersonal influences that often arise spontaneously and without much conscious thought, but profoundly shape decision-making, negotiations, performance, persuasion and cooperation, interpersonal perceptions and interactions, and well-being at work. Her first line of research examines the antecedents and consequences of complex emotion-influenced experiences – including ambivalence and authenticity – for both individuals and groups. Her second line of research investigates ethical and other implications of both complex and simple emotional experiences. Her third line of research explores voice habit, a new theoretical construct developed by Laura and her colleagues that proposes an automatic perspective of voice behavior. Her research has been published in journals such as Academy of Management Review, Journal of Business Ethics, Academy of Management Annals, Journal of Applied Psychology, Journal of Experimental Social Psychology, and Journal of Experimental Psychology: Applied, among others, as well as numerous book chapters. Laura has taught courses on negotiations, organizational behavior and leadership, and ethics to undergraduate, MBA, and other master's students. She has written several negotiation cases and leads negotiation workshops for a variety of university and executive audiences. She is currently developing two podcast series focused on the application of cutting-edge scholarship in negotiation and conflict management, found at www.NegotiationandConflictTeam.com.

Scott L. Rogers, University of Miami
Scott Rogers, M.S., J.D., is founder and director of the University of Miami School of Law's Mindfulness in Law Program and co-founder of UMindfulness, the University's Mindfulness Research & Practice Initiative. Since 2010 Professor Rogers has been collaborating on neuroscience research exploring the enduring brain and behavior changes that may accompany mindfulness-training programs. A nationally recognized leader and columnist in the field of mindfulness, Professor Rogers has taught mindfulness to tens of thousands of people including accountants, athletes, business and community leaders, financial advisors, educators, firefighters, judges, lawyers, law and medical students, law and medical school faculty, negotiators, parents, physicians, pilots, soldiers, and therapists. His training programs have been integrated into numerous corporate and academic settings. Professor Rogers is author of "The Six-Minute Solution: A Mindfulness Primer for Lawyers," "Mindfulness for Law Students," "Attending: A Physician's Introduction to Mindfulness," "Mindful Parenting," the "The Elements of Mindfulness," and the forthcoming textbook, "The Mindful Law Student." He lectures across the country, speaks at law, medical, and scientific conferences, and been interviewed in newspapers and magazines for his work on mindfulness. His work at the University of Miami School of Law has appeared in the Wall Street Journal and his research has been written about in the New York Times.

Kuryakin C. Rucker
Kuryakin (KC) Rucker, JD, PhD is a human resources and management consultant, Michigan-licensed attorney, and entrepreneur with over 15 years of human resources and labor relations experience with multiple Fortune 500 companies, large municipalities, and government contractors. Dr. Rucker is a native of Detroit, Michigan and earned his Bachelor of Arts in Speech Communication, Master of Arts in Industrial Relations and Juris Doctor in Employment and Labor Law from Wayne State University in Detroit. He earned his Doctor of Philosophy (PhD) in Management with a focus in Human Resources Leadership from Sullivan University in Louisville, Kentucky. He is also certified as a Senior

Professional in Human Resources (SPHR) by the Human Resources Certification Institute and Senior Certified Professional (SHRM-SCP) by the Society for Human Resources Management. Since 2019, Dr. Rucker has been the President and Senior Consultant of Rucker Management Consultants, LLC, located in Huntsville, Alabama. RMC is a full-service human resources and management consulting firm focused on partnering with small- and medium-sized organizations to provide practical solutions to HR and management issues. Dr. Rucker is also an adjunct professor in the Department of Management, Marketing and Logistics at Alabama A&M University, where he teaches courses in management and human resources management.

Jessica Senehi, University of Manitoba

Jessica Senehi, PhD is Professor of Peace and Conflict Studies at the University of Manitoba. She is a co-editor of the Routledge Companion to Peace and Conflict Studies (2019), the Routledge Handbook on Ethnic Conflict and Peacebuilding (2022). She holds a PhD in Social Science and an MS in Biopsychology from Syracuse University.

Creighlynn D. Thoele, RAISE Beyond Consulting

Creighlynn Thoele, PhD is the Chief Executive Officer for RAISE Beyond, a consulting company in Shreveport, LA. Dr. Thoele founded RAISE Beyond after identifying a critical need for positive culture change within local communities throughout the country. Centered on the beliefs that one person can make a difference and that a team of people can change the world, Dr. Thoele leads a team of Reliable, Authentic, Innovative, Solutions-based Experts (RAISE) who work together to make powerful, positive, inclusive, and innovative changes throughout various organizations and communities. Dr. Thoele previously served as the Command Culture Advisor for the U.S. Air Force Global Strike Command Headquarters and as a Human Intelligence Officer for the U.S. Army. Dr. Thoele specializes in human behavior. She has developed numerous community-based initiatives, ranging from strategic to tactical-level, which address a variety of local community challenges, including social innovation, racial and socio-economic disparities, community development, rising youth crime rates, innovating public education, and more. Dr. Thoele has also been pivotal in the development of four new non-profit organizations within northwestern LA in an effort to spearhead change efforts within the area's under-resourced communities. Dr. Thoele has developed and facilitated courses on a variety of topics, including culture, leadership, strategy, performance, change management, and conflict resolution. Her growing body of research focuses on the impact of individual and collective behavior on organizational and operational effectiveness. Dr. Thoele has an MBA from Cameron University in Lawton, OK and a PhD. in Strategic Management from Sullivan University in Louisville, KY.

Leigh Thompson, Kellogg School of Management

Leigh Thompson, PhD is the J. Jay Gerber Distinguished Professor of Dispute Resolution and Organizations at the Kellogg School of Management, Northwestern University. An acclaimed researcher, author, and speaker, Thompson's research focuses on negotiation, creativity, and teamwork. Thompson's books include Negotiating the Sweet Spot: The Art of Leaving Nothing on the Table, Creative Conspiracy: The New Rules of Breakthrough Collaboration, Making the Team,

The Mind and Heart of the Negotiator, The Truth about Negotiations and Stop Spending, Start
Managing. Thompson directs several executive education programs, including Negotiation Mastery
Class, Leading High-Impact Teams, High Performance Negotiation Skills, Constructive Collaboration,
and Negotiating in a Virtual World. Thompson created several publicly available teaching videos:
Negotiation 101, Teamwork 101, High Performance Collaboration: Leadership, Teamwork, and
Negotiation (MOOC series with Coursera), as well as Is Your Team Slacking?, Managing Virtual
Teams, High-Performance Negotiation Skills for Women, and How Brainwriting can Neutralize the
Loudmouths.

Michael A. Wahlgren

Michael A. Wahlgren is a Doctoral candidate at Nova Southeastern University with the Department
of Conflict Analysis and Resolution. His background is in education and organizational culture with
a dissertation focus on assessing and improving organizational cultures through workplace conflict
resolution training. Michael is a graduate of Florida Institute of Technology and Central Michigan
University and earned degrees in Communication and Administration. He is a military veteran and
has held numerous leadership positions with the Department of Defense over the past 10 years.

LaVena Wilkin, Sullivan University

LaVena Wilkin, PhD is the Dean of PhD Programs at Sullivan University. Before joining Sullivan,
she spent twenty-six years in the construction industry, and three of those years she co-owned a
masonry sub-contracting company. She started teaching as an adjunct instructor in 1999. After
selling the construction company in 2001, she came to work at Sullivan full-time as the Associate
Director of the Evening and Weekend Division. She has also served as the Dean of the College
of Business Administration and the Dean of Conflict Management programs for Sullivan. Dr.
Wilkin has facilitated workshops on communication, conflict, emotional intelligence, forgiveness,
P.E.A.C.E. from Conflict, and workplace bullying for the Center for Non Profit Excellence, The
Archdiocese of Louisville, Integrating Women Leaders, FireKing, Governor's Equal Employment
Opportunity Annual Conference, the Academic Leadership Academy, the Society for Strategic
Human Resources Managers, Unity of East Louisville, Duke Energy, The Archdiocese of Louisville,
and several other organizations. She also created a basic conflict management course for the
Collaborative Institutional Training Initiative (CITI). She also conducted a Webinar for Collaborative
Institutional Training Initiative (CITI) entitled Managing Conflicts With Your Dissertation Chair.Dr.
Wilkin published an article on workplace bullying in the International Journal of Business and Social
Science, and for several years she wrote a quarterly column for Business First.She contributed a
chapter in The Handbook of Mediation: Research, Theory, and Practice. She is also co-editor of a
book entitled Organizational Conflicts: Challenges and Solutions. She is the Editor for the Journal of
Conflict Management, a scholarly journal that publishes research in many of the multidisciplinary
areas of managing conflicts. She co-edited a book, entitled "From Discord to Harmony: Making the
Workplace Hum", which was published in March 2020. She is a certified mediator, conflict coach
and employee engagement facilitator. Dr. Wilkin earned her bachelors and master's degrees from
Sullivan University. She earned her PhD in Conflict Analysis and Resolution from Nova Southeastern
University in Ft. Lauderdale, Florida. Her dissertation topic was workplace bullying in academe.

Dr. Wilkin is the Vice-President emeritus for the Board of Directors at Unity of East Louisville. Additionally, she previously served on the Board of Directors for the Society for the Prevention and Aggression Among Adolescence (SPAVA).

Anthony P. Zanesco, University of Miami
Anthony Zanesco, PhD is a cognitive neuroscientist who studies attention and mind wandering, the dynamics of electrophysiological brain states, and how meditation and mindfulness training affect one's ability to focus and regulate distraction. He completed his PhD at the University of California, Davis, in 2017. He is currently a postdoctoral associate in the laboratory of Dr. Amishi Jha in the Psychology Department at the University of Miami.

Sandore (Sandy) Zehr
Sandore (Sandy) Zehr, PhD serves as the Director of Congressional & Public Affairs for Naval Surface Warfare Center, Crane Division (NSWC Crane) and is the Division Manager for the Corporate Communications Division. In this role, he serves as the principal advisor to NSWC Crane regarding policy decisions, courses of action, and ramifications related to internal and external communication. Dr. Zehr also plays an active role with the Naval Sea System Command (NAVSEA) Propel Leadership Development Program. In this role, he designs course content and leads training courses for both new and experienced leaders across the NAVSEA enterprise. Prior to joining NSWC Crane, Dr. Zehr spent over 27 years in private sector corporate leadership. During this time, he served as Vice-President and Shareholder for Artistic Media Partners, which was Indiana's largest radio broadcasting corporation. In this role, Sandy was primarily responsible for organizational leadership and operational oversight for part of the organization's portfolio. Dr. Zehr serves as a Key Adjunct and Research Chair with the DeVoe School of Business, Indiana Wesleyan University, and is a Distinguished Lecturer with Sullivan University. Dr. Zehr's educational background includes a Bachelor of Science degree in Chemistry from the University of Indianapolis, Public Management Certificate from Indiana University, Master of Business Administration (MBA) from Ball State University, and a Doctorate (PhD) in Management from Sullivan University. He has been married for 37 years and has three children and seven grandchildren. Sandy is an avid fan of baseball (New York Yankees) and college soccer (Indiana Hoosiers). He enjoys travel, and spending quality time with his family.

Acknowledgements

One of my favorite quotes is Mahatma Gandhi's "Be the change you wish to see in the world". My little section of the world is brighter, and I can live by Gandhi's words because so many people encourage me, support me, and cheer me on. I have the most wonderful colleagues, amazing family, the dearest friends, and the perfect husband. I am truly grateful.

LaVena Wilkin

To the loving memories of my parents and Dr Keshav Baliram Hedgewar, who gave proper direction to my life. My beloved wife, Seema, who gave positive meaning and my son, Dr. Sarvadaman Pathak, who gave a golden lining to my life. I would like to dedicate to the memories of my wonderful mentors Ma Lakshmanrao Bhidejee, Ma Chamanlaljee and Ma Madhujee Limaye for my social life and Prof Gregory Gregoriadis London, Professor Robert Levy and Professor Simon Benita as my postdoctoral mentors.

Yashwant Pathak

https://doi.org/10.1515/9783110746365-204

Preface

Workplace conflict is inevitable when organizational leaders and employees with diverse backgrounds, knowledge, and experiences work together. Their overarching goal is to accomplish the mission and goals of the firm. Yet, conflict can blur their vision and prevent them from working together for the good of the organization. It may appear as though they are pulling on opposite ends of the rope, and the day-to-day operations can be overwhelming, tiring, and stressful.

Part of the problem is that most people have not been taught how to productively manage conflicts, and when they do what they have always done they are getting the same negative results. Absenteeism, presenteeism, turnover, wasted time, loss of reputation, decreased productivity, and lower profitability are just some of the costs associated with unmanaged or mismanaged conflicts.

Conflict management is an ever-evolving area in organizational affairs. Organizations are microcosms of society, and as society evolves and changes, leaders will benefit from understanding typical root causes of conflicts (both interpersonal and organizational), appropriate methods for managing conflicts, and unique concepts that contribute to conflict situations. Although many people believe that conflict is either something to be avoided or something to fight to win, when managed appropriately, conflicts can be the lifeblood of an organization. Conflict can be the impetus that sparks creativity and innovation and leads to positive organizational policy and culture changes.

The goal of this handbook was to offer organizational leaders, employees, and conflict management scholars a deeper understanding of what causes conflicts and provide them with solutions for turning unproductive conflicts into positive opportunities for growth. This handbook offers insights into emotional intelligence, conflict styles, mindfulness, gender issues, employee engagement, and microaggressions as causes of organizational conflicts. It also provides practical solutions to resolving these situations, including learning about the importance of soft skills, creating collaborative practices, and designing conflict systems to reduce the likelihood of mismanaged conflicts. In addition, organizational leaders can help resolve them through negotiation, mediation, coaching, and employing ombudspersons. Finally, this handbook delves into topics that have been given less attention, such as human resources role in resolving conflicts, workplace bullying, political conflicts, ethno religious conflicts, birth order, and forgiveness.

It has been a labor of love and a true privilege to work with the amazing authors and contributors who made this handbook a reality, and we would like to express our deepest appreciation to all the chapter authors for their excellent contributions to the different dimensions of organizational conflict management. We also would like to express our gratitude to DeGruyter Publishing and especially to everyone there who provided support to us from the beginning as we wrote the book proposal, worked on

https://doi.org/10.1515/9783110746365-205

the suggested edits, and helped us get the book published. Finally, we appreciate our universities as they provided moral support throughout the entire process.

If you find gaps or areas of conflict you would like to learn more about, please let us know, and we will work to include those in the next edition.

LaVena Wilkin
Yashwant Pathak

Section 1: **Interpersonal Conflict Management**

LaVena Wilkin
Chapter 1
Shining a Light on Organizational Conflict

Abstract: When it comes to managing organizational conflicts, leaders often either try to avoid the situation or attempt to force a solution. While both avoiding and forcing may occasionally be an effective conflict management approach, when used consistently, they simply exacerbate the conflict. There is a good reason leaders use these approaches; they have not learned conflict management skills, so they adopt the approach they learned in their families of origin. This chapter offers insights into root causes of conflicts and offers practical tools to help leaders manage inevitable conflicts that arise when people work together.

Keywords: perceptions, diverse ideas, generate solutions, emotional reactions, mindfulness

Conflicts happen. Simply stated, life generates conflict situations. As individuals we have different experiences, values, beliefs, perceptions, and assumptions. In our relationships, personal and professional, we often compete for scarce resources; we have different communication styles; and we have different perceptions about life. Then, consider that we develop our conflict management styles early in life based on our families' views of conflicts, and that these styles can be difficult to change, even when they are not productive. In a constantly changing world, leaders are managing diverse workforces that include more women, minorities, and ethnicities. Once taboo religious and sexual orientation conversations are now openly discussed. In some cases, people are not tolerant about differences, and they are vocal about that intolerance. All these factors contribute to a world and a workplace that is bubbling over with conflicted people and situations (Wilkin, 2020).

Conflict situations are exacerbated when leaders have not been taught how to productively manage them. Yet, teaching these skills is not part of most primary or post-secondary school curriculums. As a result, when the inevitable conflicts occur, it is easy for leaders to try to dismiss them or tell the affected employees to "go work it out." The fallacy is that if the employees knew what to do, they would not seek help from their organizational leaders. Instead of avoiding or forcing a solution to conflicts, it is helpful learn and utilize skills for resolving them. The outcome can be a win/win for the organization and the employees (Wilkin, 2020).

https://doi.org/10.1515/9783110746365-001

Illuminate the Conflict

Conflict is an inevitable part of organizational life and by its very nature, it generates change. Although the word "conflict" has a negative connotation, when managed productively, it is an opportunity for growth because it provides a spark that ignites creativity, innovation, and improvements in a dynamic organization. In fact, since conflict is the manifestation of discontent with an interaction, process, product, or service by either the firm's employees or its customers, viewing it as a productive and ongoing process will help organizations thrive in a competitive environment. Disputes, competition, sabotage, inefficiency, low morale, and withholding information are all warning signs that conflict is about to halt or slow organizational progress (Costantino & Merchant, 1996).

While unmanaged or mismanaged conflicts increase the chances for entrenchment and resistance, a paradigm shift towards appreciating healthy, productive conflict will keep organizations on the cutting edge. On the other hand, if an organizational culture encourages an attitude of either avoidance or arrogance, the well-oiled machine becomes an empty vehicle that sputters and dies on the side of the road. The aversion to conflict and the resultant change encourages complacency. While those firms are spending time and resources in litigious warfare, they miss out on opportunities to adapt to the vibrant, ever-changing competitive environment. Meanwhile, their proactive competition is enjoying the fruitful results of its conflict management efforts, the durability of those efforts, and the impact on both internal and external relationships (Costantino & Merchant, 1996).

Although it sounds counter-intuitive, the first step in productively managing conflicts is to acknowledge that they are not always damaging. Generally speaking, conflicts are neither positive nor negative. Rather, how we manage the conflicts determines if the outcomes are productive or destructive. When productively managed, conflicts provide opportunities for us to shine our lights on the situations, develop more effective processes, and build collaborative relationships. To illuminate the conflict, we can incorporate the following concepts into our strategic conflict management practices:
- Listen to perspectives
- Invite Diverse Ideas
- Generate a psychologically safe workplace
- Hone a mindfulness consciousness
- Think about emotional reactions

When leaders *LIGHT* the way, they model these strategies for others. They build positive working relationships that result in improved communication, respect, productivity, collaborative problem-solving, and empathy. Employees are more motivated and productive because they can focus on the organization's vision, mission, and goals, rather than being sidetracked and consumed by the conflicts. Additionally, they are strategies everyone can use when they are faced with a conflict situation.

Listen to Perspectives

Communication and perceptions are underlying components of all conflict (Wilmot & Hocker, 2011), so listening to various perspectives is the basis of managing organizational conflicts. Meanings, perceptions, and responses to conflicts are created based on an individual's social realities and experiences. Often people act competitively or cooperatively depending upon the lens through which they view the communication, the perspective of the situation, and the perception of the people involved in the situation. Instead of compassionately listening to others, we tend to filter our communication through our own lens of assumptions and biases (Wilkin, 2020). It is too easy to judge others as selfish, lazy, or close-minded when we do not understand why they act or interact in certain ways, or when we have not taken the time to understand their perspectives. We may think that our viewpoint is the only correct one.

We have been taught to believe that if we see it with our own eyes, it is reality. The truth is that the lens through which we view the world can skew what we see. The following image (Figure 1.1) is a powerful depiction of why it is important to clarify the perspective of not only what we see, but also what the other person sees.

Figure 1.1: What do you see? (Mi, 2013).

No matter how they tilt their heads or how long they look at the image, some people only see the young lady, while others only see the old one. The picture, of course, contains an illusion of both. Even when the participants only see one or the other, it does not change the reality that both are there.

Opening our hearts and being willing to listen and understand why others have a different perspective can shine a LIGHT on opportunities to learn, grow, expand our understanding, and resolve conflicts. We can gain a new and different perspective (Wilkin, 2020).

Invite Diverse Ideas

One might think that since communication and perceptions are at the root of most conflicts, if we master listening to perspectives, we could extinguish conflicts. While that is a good beginning, it is also important to build on that concept and to invite people to present diverse ideas for problem-solving. People are more likely to buy-in to solutions when they helped generate them. In fact, one of the pillars of facilitation as a conflict management method is creating ideas, and although that is a more formal problem-solving process, inviting diverse ideas and solutions is something we can all do when faced with a conflict. Schwarz (2002) contends that when we brainstorm ideas, it is important to refrain from evaluating them, include the wildest ideas, and generate as many solutions as possible.

Generate a Psychologically Safe Workplace

It is vital that leaders create a psychologically safe space for employees to offer these diverse ideas because if they do not believe they can trust the leader or the process, they will not share their ideas or engage in the brainstorming practice. As a result, leaders may make unilateral decisions that only exacerbate the conflicts, which could cause the problem to fester, grow, and eventually spiral out of control.

Edmondson and Mortenson (2021) offer guidance for leaders to begin these conversations and create a culture of psychological safety. The first step to begin the conversation and recognize creative resolutions to conflicts is more effective when everyone feels safe, and they are willing to generate creative ways to resolve the issues. Leaders who are candid, humble, and vulnerable lead by example, and their employees are more willing to share their own concerns and ideas (Wilkin, 2022).

Sharing ideas may take some time because employees may not feel safe, or they may not trust that what they say will not be used against them in some way (Wilkin, 2022). However, leaders who are mindful about their responses to shared information, who model respect for their employees, and who are genuine and honest can begin to build a psychologically safe workplace (Edmonson & Mortenson, 2021).

Many years ago, when I purchased the construction company where I had worked for over twenty years, I needed to hire someone to take care of the payroll and bookkeeping. After interviewing several people, I hired a person who had absolutely no experience in either of these areas. My sense was that she was genuine, trustworthy, and smart. I could teach her how to do the tasks, but those were qualities I could not teach. Her previous employer was critical of her performance, which was why she left that organization. I tried to impress on her that there were no mistakes, just lessons she would learn.

Our first few weeks, I did the payroll, and she watched me input everything into the software. After that, she did the payroll while I watched her and offered guidance.

Then, it was time for her to try on her own. She was afraid. She did not want to make a mistake. I reassured her that anything that went wrong could be fixed. Mistakes were made; we fixed them. She eventually gained her confidence in the job. She offered ideas and suggestions for ways to improve processes because she knew I valued her and her ideas. She became one of my most valuable employees, and years later, even after I sold the company, she and I are still in touch. I not only created a psychologically safe workplace for her, but she also trusted me, and she blossomed.

Hone a Mindfulness Consciousness

Until recently, mindfulness was viewed as a nebulous or new age concept that had nothing to do with the workplace (Wilkin, 2022). However, mindfulness is a valuable tool that will help leaders resolve organizational conflicts and make better decisions (Riskin & Wohl, 2015; Yu & Zellmer-Bruhn, 2018). Mindfulness is defined as focusing our attention and bringing our awareness to experiences without judging them or being attached to a specific outcome (Brown et al., 2007). In today's work environment, where busyness, multitasking, and virtual meetings are normal ways of being, it can be difficult for leaders to focus their attention on what is happening in the moment. Consequently, when conflicts arise, it is easy to slip into mindlessness, act on autopilot, and do whatever we have done before to resolve conflicts, even if we know those methods are ineffective (Riskin & Wahl, 2015). Practicing mindfulness gives us more control over the conflict. If we can be fully present in the moment, we may be more compassionate towards others, ourselves, and the situation. As a result, conflicts are less likely to escalate and lead to unproductive outcomes (Yu & Zellmer-Bruhn, 2018).

Think About Emotional Responses

Every conflict is connected to some emotion because if we did not care there would not be any conflict. Emotions are the windows to people's inner core, and they provide leaders with information that words alone do not offer. Becoming more mindful of emotions is one way to listen and learn without any exchange of words (Wilkin, 2022). Goleman's (2005) model of emotional intelligence provides five concepts that help leaders think more about their emotional responses to conflict situations. His model focuses on self-awareness, self-regulation, empathy, motivation, and social skills.

Self-awareness and self-regulation are at the core of thinking about emotional responses to conflicts. Self-awareness is the ability to understand your own emotions and determine why you feel a certain way. Self-aware leaders acknowledge their emotions, but do not make decisions solely based on feelings. Self-regulation, the second component of emotional intelligence, is the ability to monitor your emotions; emotionally intelligent leaders do not allow others to push their hot buttons. In addition, emotionally intelligent leaders are motivated to accomplish goals.

Empathy is a significant characteristic of emotional intelligence. In fact, Wilkinson (2019) says empathy is the glue that holds society together. Empathy is the channel that connects people and provides a view of the world through the other person's lens (Wilkin, 2020). Empathetic people are open and honest, and as a result, they easily cultivate relationships. Through self-reflection and self-awareness, empathetic people create and live life authentically without being too quick to judge or stereotype others (Wilkin, 2022).

The final concept of Goleman's model (2005), social skills, encompasses the other four concepts. People with good social skills are team players, and they enjoy mentoring others and helping them grow within the organization. They understand that an organization is most successful when people play well together and communicating and building relationships are key factors in the way they interact with others.

Although the five concepts are presented as linear, they are interconnected. For example, it is challenging to be self-regulated and motivated if you are not self-aware. Likewise, empathy for others is difficult if you are not aware of your own emotions and what triggers them (Wilkinson, 2019). Empathetic people develop and manage good relationships with others, which is also a part of the concept of social skills.

Conclusion

Conflict will always happen. The determining factor as to whether the conflict will be constructive or destructive to your organization is how you deal with it. Avoiding or ignoring the conflict will inevitably cause it to come back and cause harmful effects. Learn how to manage it and your organization will benefit more than if it had never happened. So, shine a light on conflict and begin productively managing it.

References

Brown, K. W., Ryan, R. M., & Creswell, J. D. (2007). Mindfulness: Theoretical foundations and evidence for its salutary effects. *Psychological Inquiry, 18*(4), 211–237.

Costantino, C.A., and Merchant, C.S. (1996). Designing conflict management system. San Francisco: Jossey-Bass.

Edmondson A. (1999). Psychological safety and learning behavior in work teams. *Administrative Science Quarterly, 44*, 350–383. https://doi.org/10.2307/2666999

Edmonson, A., & Mortenson, M. (2021). What psychologicall safety looks like in a hybrid workplace. Harvard Business Review Digital Articles, 1–7.

Fisher, R. & Shapiro, D. (2006). Beyond Reason: Using Emotions as you Negotiate. NY: Viking-Penguin Group.

Goleman, D. (2005). Emotional intelligence: Why it can matter more than IQ. New York, NY: Bantom Books.

Mi, C. (2013, April 12). *old-lady-young-woman11*. Coach Mi Motivate Inspire. https://coachmi.com.au/why-men-dont-listen-and-women-cant-read-maps/old-lady-young-woman11/

Riskin, L.L. & Wahl, R. (2015). Mindfulness in the heat of conflict: Taking STOCK. *Harvard Negotiation Law Review*, *20*, 121–155. https://ssrn.com/abstract=2754646.

Schwarz, R. (2002). The Skilled Facilitator: A comprehensive resource for consultants, facilitators, managers, trainers, and coaches. San Francisco, CA: Jossey-Bass.

Wilkin, L. (2020). From discord to harmony: Five skills for keeping your workplace humming. In L. Wilkin and T. Belak (Eds.) *From discord to harmony: Making your workplace hum* (pp. 319–332). Charlotte, SC: Information Age Publishing. Charlotte, NC: Information Age Publishing, Inc.

Wilkin, L. (2022). From disruption to connection: How mindful conflict management builds bridges during the pandemic and beyond. In s. Malka and R. Tiell (Eds.) *Back to a New Normal: In search of stability in an era of pandemic disruption* (pp.85–96). Charlotte, SC: Information Age Publishing. Charlotte, NC: Information Age Publishing, Inc.

Wilkinson, I. G. (2019). In praise of empathy: The glue that holds caring communities together in a fractured world. *Canadian Journal of Family and Youth*, *11*(1), 234–291.

Wilmot, W. & Hocker, J. (2011). Interpersonal Conflict (8th ed.). New York, NY: McGraw-Hill.

Yu, L., & Zellmer-Bruhn, M. (2018). Introducing team mindfulness and considering its safeguard role against conflict transformation and social undermining. *Academy of Management Journal*, *61*(1), 324–347.

Christopher T. H. Miners, Laura Rees

Chapter 2
Emotional Intelligence in Workplace Negotiations

Abstract: In this chapter, we discuss the emotional issues that warrant consideration before, during, and after negotiation and conflict management situations to help people successfully use emotional intelligence (EI) abilities at each stage. As considerations before negotiating, we discuss the interplay of expectations versus reality, including the risks as well as benefits of high levels of EI, the importance of context in shaping how helpful or harmful specific emotions can be, and the fact that emotions and cognitions jointly influence each other. During negotiation, we highlight the importance of understanding how even authentic emotional signals can be (mis)interpreted, the complexity of perceptions and differences in perception based on individual ability and contextual factors, and the myriad of other intrapersonal, interpersonal, organizational, and broader cultural factors that can influence these processes. We then review the need to consider subjective outcomes and long-term and potential ripple effects for both interpersonal and organizational relationships following conflict. Finally, we briefly discuss important emerging trends involving EI in workplace negotiations, including communication channels and artificial intelligence. Overall, our aim is to highlight some of the most critical issues at each stage of negotiation, to provide (necessarily) broad, overarching advice, and to share references that facilitate a deeper dive into the role of EI in negotiations. To conclude, we include a tear-away page of guiding questions for each stage to help you effectively adapt to any given situation.

Keywords: emotion expression, emotional intelligence, emotional (mis)communication, emotion perception, emotions as information, negotiation, conflict management

Our emotions have evolved to help us address the challenges of individual survival and, relatedly, navigate the complexities and embrace the opportunities of collective, social co-ordination (Keltner & Haidt, 1999). Emotions direct our attention, predispose us to process information in particular ways, and prepare us to take specific actions that can help us protect our interests and realize our ambitions (Inzlicht et al., 2015; Keltner & Horberg, 2015). The benefits of emotions can be amplified if we have the ability to perceive our own and others' emotions accurately, to understand the patterns of thought and behavior that follow from the experience of a particular emotion, and to shape the emotional landscape that we

Note: The authors made equal contributions to this chapter and therefore are listed in alphabetical order.

https://doi.org/10.1515/9783110746365-002

inhabit, individually and collectively, so that we can move ourselves and others in the direction of our goals.

In this chapter we focus on emotional intelligence in conflict management and negotiation at work. Emotional intelligence (EI) is a set of inter-related abilities that enable people to use emotions, and the informational value of them, to facilitate goal-oriented actions (Côté, 2014; Salovey & Mayer, 1990). Historically, researchers have argued that four abilities together constitute EI: the abilities to perceive, use, understand, and manage emotions (e.g., Mayer et al., 1999). Currently, the constituent parts of EI are under debate (Elfenbein & MacCann, 2017; Maul, 2012; Mayer et al., 2016). Its broad definition, however, remains unchanged. Furthermore, it is widely agreed that EI exists as a distinct form of intelligence, and that it is separate from personality traits, motivational attributes, and other types of characteristics (Côté & Miners, 2006; MacCann et al., 2014). We focus on EI as a set of inter-related abilities, and on its role in conflict management and negotiation, in the following pages.

At first glance, the extant literature on EI and negotiation and conflict management (hereafter the broader term "negotiation") appears to be sparse and often contradictory. The evidence ranges from EI helping people to obtain desirable outcomes in negotiations (e.g., Elfenbein et al., 2007), to its absence in determining the outcomes of negotiations (e.g., objective value; Elfenbein et al., 2008), to facilitating desirable outcomes for the other parties in negotiations at the expense of people with a high level of EI (e.g., Schlegel et al., 2018). However, by examining research on the facets of EI (e.g., emotion recognition ability), only a part of which overlaps with the mainstream research on EI, and research on discrete emotions (e.g., anger), we are better able to delineate the benefits and potential costs that are likely to accrue to those higher in EI. More often than not, EI can help people to improve the process of negotiation, the subjective experience of it, and its consequences for themselves and their counterparts.

In this chapter, we discuss the emotional issues that warrant consideration before, during, and after negotiations. We also look into the future of negotiations, as technology continues to redefine the way in which people interact with one another. Our aim is to highlight some of the most critical issues at each stage of negotiation, to provide (necessarily) broad, overarching advice, and to share references that facilitate a deeper dive into the role of EI in negotiations.

Emotional Intelligence Before Negotiation

We now turn to important considerations before entering into a negotiation. More specifically, we highlight common misconceptions about the emotional landscape of negotiations, describe the actual emotional landscape, and identify the most effective ways to navigate it.

Expectations Versus the Reality of EI and Emotions. A person may encounter a number of potential emotional challenges while preparing to negotiate. First, unless the person has completed a validated ability measure of EI and received feedback on their performance, the person's beliefs about their level of EI are likely to be inaccurate. There is substantial evidence that people's beliefs about their abilities, in general, are only weakly associated with their actual levels of the abilities (Dunning et al., 2004). EI is no exception (Brackett et al., 2006). It therefore makes sense, first, for a person to heighten their self-awareness about EI by completing the Geneva Emotional Competence Test (Schlegel & Mortillaro, 2019), Mayer-Salovey-Caruso Emotional Intelligence Test (Mayer et al., 2002), Situational Tests of Emotional Understanding and Management (MacCann & Roberts, 2008), or other similar measures.

Second, while a high level of EI can facilitate a successful negotiation, by itself, it will fall (far) short of guaranteeing a positive outcome. In some respects, Goleman (1995) popularized EI by presenting it as a panacea to personal, interpersonal, organizational, and societal problems. EI is not a panacea, however, and the scientists who introduced EI to the world never claimed it to be (Mayer, 2004). It is simply another important individual difference, along with cognitive intelligence, the Big Five personality traits, and many other abilities and personality traits (Côté & Miners, 2006; Joseph & Newman, 2010; Mayer et al., 2016). No more, no less. Furthermore, there is some evidence that EI can be harmful. For example, intrapersonally, people with a high level of emotion recognition ability can be overly sensitive to others' subtle expressions of negative emotions and, in turn, allocate too many cognitive resources to these expressions at the expense of a higher level of job performance (Bechtoldt & Schneider, 2016; Elfenbein & Ambady, 2002). Interpersonally, EI can be used to pursue antisocial goals, such as deception and interpersonal deviance, just as fruitfully as it can be used to pursue prosocial goals (Côté et al., 2011; Gaspar et al., 2021; Kilduff et al., 2010). Finally, expertise in the emotional aspects of negotiations is much narrower than EI and requires extensive practice. EI can serve as a strong foundation from which to build this context-specific expertise, but it cannot serve as a substitute for it (Potworowski & Kopelman, 2008).

Third, people are not particularly good at accurately predicting their emotional reactions to events (see Wilson & Gilbert, 2003, for a review). Two of the most robust findings in this area of research are that people routinely overestimate the intensity of positive emotions associated with a desirable event (e.g., achieving a goal) and of negative emotions associated with an undesirable event (e.g., failing to achieve a goal). For the former, people often engage in "focalism," whereby they concentrate on the anticipated desirable event to the neglect of other concurrent events that will limit the positive emotional resonance of the anticipated event (Wilson et al., 2000). For the latter, people often engage in "immune neglect," the tendency to overlook the (considerable) extent to which people can adapt to, and recover from, even the most dramatic, severe negative experiences (Gilbert et al., 1998). This information should be kept in mind so that one is neither disconcerted nor disoriented by the absence of a sea of joy during or after a successful negotiation, or a flood of misery during or after an unsuccessful one.

Emotions Can Be Helpful and Harmful. Similarly, people often hope or even expect to experience specific emotions during negotiations that they believe will facilitate positive outcomes. For example, an individual may believe that they will remain calm at first, then show glimpses of happiness to help build trust and encourage cooperation, and finish with a flourish of anger to instill anxiety and fear in others and, ultimately, to benefit their own outcomes. The problem, however, is that no emotion is uniformly helpful or harmful; context is everything. For example, the expression of anger can be perceived as an appropriate manifestation of high power and a sign of toughness and, in turn, help a person to obtain additional resources from the other parties, or it can be seen as an inappropriate reaction by a person with less power and, in turn, place pressure on the person with less power to make concessions to appease the other parties for the outburst (Tiedens, 2001; Van Kleef & Côté, 2007). The key, of course, is to know what emotion to express, and at what intensity, at a particular time during a negotiation. This consideration brings us neatly to the importance of an individual's ability to manage emotions and to its behavioral manifestation, emotion regulation.

Emotions and Cognition Exert Reciprocal Influence. By helping individuals to manage and regulate emotions, EI offers a valuable means by which to refine or reshape the emotional landscape of negotiations. Gross (2015) provides a multistage model through which emotions emerge: an event occurs, a person pays a certain amount of attention to the event, the event is appraised in terms of its impact on, and meaning with respect to, personal goals that are currently active, and this context-based evaluation (e.g., Is this event controllable? Who is responsible? Does this facilitate or thwart progress towards my goals?) yields the changes in cognition, behavior, physiology, and subjective experience that define a particular emotion. For example, anger follows an appraisal that an event is controllable, that another party is responsible for the outcome, and that the outcome inhibits progress towards one or more goals of personal significance (Keltner & Horberg, 2015; Smith & Ellsworth, 1985). The experience of anger will then shape the thoughts and actions of the person in question by instigating a sense of injustice (cognition), action tendencies that support restorative justice (behavior), an increased heart rate that prepares the person for this behavior (physiology), and the ability to consciously label the experience (subjective experience; "I am angry").

Importantly, at every stage of the model, there is an opportunity to consciously or subconsciously intervene to determine the specific emotion(s) that emerge and their intensity. For example, people may sometimes have control over the events to which they are exposed: by electing to negotiate a contract with a service provider when an inexperienced, kind sales representative is available and a veteran, hardened sales representative is on holiday, a person can maximize the chance of experiencing calm and happiness and minimize the chance of experiencing anxiety and fear. Similar flexibility is available even at later stages of the model when emotions are closer to being fully formed. For example, reappraisal involves altering the way in which an event is framed to change its emotional impact (Gross & John, 2003): if a person has to negotiate with the veteran, hardened sales representative who angrily shouts about their dissatisfaction with an offer, it could be viewed as the precursor to a personal, professional disaster (resulting in anxiety), or reframed as an opportunity to respond calmly and confidently (resulting in happiness) and to introduce additional evidence of the appropriateness of the offer that, together, may disconcert the sales representative (who was expecting embarrassment and appeasement instead).

Overall, EI enables accurate mapping of the emotional landscape of negotiations moment to moment and heightens understanding of how individuals' and others' emotions are likely to influence their thoughts and actions. In fact, most contemporary psychologists would argue that emotions and cognition are so tightly intertwined that it is pointless to consider either in isolation (Inzlicht et al., 2015; Keltner & Horberg, 2015). By translating their abilities to read, understand, and manage their own and others' emotions into useful, actionable information, those high in EI can make strategic decisions that productively refine and reshape the emotional landscape and outcomes of negotiations. In the next section, we explore the role of EI in managing the processes and relationships in negotiations and, in turn, contributing to the outcomes of them.

Emotional Intelligence During Negotiation

In this section, we highlight three key points to keep in mind about the signals you send and how they can be (mis)interpreted, the (mis)perceptions you might form, and the myriad of other, often overlooked factors that influence all parties' emotional expressions and perceptions, and ultimately their decisions and actions during negotiations.

Emotional Signals Can Be (Mis)interpreted. Emotions during negotiations – and therefore intelligent use of them – rely on a dynamic process of signals and perceptions based on the perceived signals (Bühler, 1934; Scherer, 1988). In their simplest form, these signals can be understood as an intuitive and evolutionarily adaptive means of communication (Fridlund, 1994). Put simply, emotional expressions serve as cues of the expresser's goals, intentions, and motivations (Keltner & Haidt, 1999; Oatley & Jenkins, 1992; Van Kleef, 2009, 2010)

Expressers face at least three choices during negotiations that can dramatically shape the conversation: how authentically to express, how intensely to express, and through what medium to express their emotions. First, authentic emotions are true reflections of felt emotions rather than feigned (Hochschild, 1983). Although it is tempting to think that authentic emotional displays are always preferable, they are a double-edged sword: anger, for example, can lead both to increased concessions from the perceiver as well as increased chances of impasse and reciprocal anger (Friedman et al., 2004), especially if the anger is inauthentic (Campagna et al., 2016; Côté et al., 2013; Tng & Au, 2014). In the long run, forcing expressions can also lead to serious psychological and physiological distress for the expresser (Hühlsheger & Schewe, 2011).

Moreover, even expressions of authentic emotions do not always accurately reflect the expresser's intentions, for multiple reasons. Expressions may not be clearly displayed, or there may be no clear way to express what one is feeling, as when people feel complex or multiple emotions (e.g., Rothman, 2011). Expressions of the same authentic emotion may differ based on cultural differences in emotional expressivity and intensity (see Rees & Kopelman, 2019, for a summary), or when there are interpersonal differences in the emotions or expressions expected in a given context (Tsai et al., 2007; see also Mesquita & Boiger, 2014). For example, in the case of a frowning counterpart, the frown may be the result of (authentic) confusion rather than displeasure and may be more surprising (and thus potentially riper for misunderstanding) in contexts in which this kind of expression is non-normative.

Second, the intensity of emotional expressions influences negotiations beyond the basic idea that more intense expressions send stronger signals. Cultural and individual differences in prototypical expressivity can influence the meaning and the reception of any given signal (Adam & Shirako, 2013). An intense expression from a more expressive individual may be a less helpful cue than one from a reserved individual. Beyond the individual, how appropriate that expression is should also be considered. Expressions that are considered less appropriate – for example, based on the context or a characteristic of the expresser (e.g., the expresser's status; Callister et al., 2017) – or are too intensely expressed can lead to less favorable outcomes for the expresser (Adam & Brett, 2018; Cheshin et al., 2018; Geddes & Callister, 2007; Glikson et al., 2019).

Third, how expressions are communicated – verbally and/or nonverbally, and through what channel – also impacts their effects. Although some research has argued that a wide range of media, including pictures, videos, text, and emoticons (Van Kleef et al., 2015) influence perceivers similarly (Rees et al., 2020; Van Kleef et al., 2011), other work has shown that voice and face-to-face communications are perceived more accurately than text-only messages for conveying a variety of messages, including sarcasm, sadness, anger, and seriousness (Kruger et al., 2005). Although research exploring the differences in emotional communication in digital versus face-to-face interactions is ongoing (e.g., Erle et al., 2021), overall, people with a high level of EI are more likely to recognize how the idiosyncrasies of particular communication modalities (verbal and/or nonverbal) and channels (face-to-face, video conference, chat, text, etc.) may independently and jointly influence emotional signals and, in turn, signal perception.

The Complexity of Perceptions. Interpersonal perceptions are based on signals from an expresser that are received and translated into mental representations of the expresser by the perceiver that subsequently guide the perceiver's reactions (Blau,

1962; Bodenhausen & Hugenberg, 2009; Jones, 1990). Although perceptions happen very quickly and can be based on thin slices of information, they have important consequences for the relationship (Ambady, 2010; Ambady & Rosenthal, 1992; Berry, 1990; Krumhuber et al., 2007; Willis & Todorov, 2006).

Perceivers naturally vary in their emotion recognition ability and in their emotional granularity in particular; that is, in their ability to feel and differentiate between relatively more (higher granularity) versus fewer (lower granularity) emotions (Barrett et al., 2001). Perceivers are also likely to vary in terms of their ability to feel and recognize complex emotions such as ambivalence (Bagozzi et al., 1999; Grossman et al., 2016). However, when attention or processing capacity is constrained, such as when under time pressure, even highly skilled perceivers' abilities to receive and respond thoughtfully to emotional signals can be similarly inhibited (Van Kleef et al., 2004). More generally, perceivers also differ in terms of how motivated they are to understand the situation (Kruglanski, 1989), which can dramatically shift how different perceivers respond to even the same emotional signal. For example, perceivers higher (versus lower) in motivation to understand their counterpart's emotions may concede more to an angry opponent than to a happy one (Van Kleef et al., 2004), because they recognize the counterpart's anger as a negative signal that all is not well and behavioral change is needed (Cacioppo & Gardner, 1999; Weiner, 1985).

Second, the specific nuances of the signal also shape how perceivers respond. For example, disappointment, worry, guilt, and regret could be considered similar emotions to encounter in a conflict – all convey that the expresser believes the ratio of outcomes between the counterparts is unacceptable. However, disappointment and worry differ from guilt and regret. The former convey that the expresser believes they have received too little, whereas the latter convey that the expresser believes they have taken too much (Baumeister et al., 1994; Clark et al., 1996). Although subtle, such differences matter for perceivers' responses. For example, compared to non-emotional counterparts, perceivers tend to make more concessions to expressers showing disappointment or worry rather than guilt or regret (Van Kleef et al., 2006).

Many Factors Influence Emotional Expression and Perception. Effectively resolving conflict also requires consideration of the intrapersonal, interpersonal, organizational, and broader cultural factors at play. For example, beyond the effects of external time constraints noted above, how tired, emotional, and free to express emotion people feel will influence what and how they express as well as what and how well they perceive others' expressions (e.g., Grandey et al., 2012; Marcus & Schuler, 2004; Muraven & Baumeister, 2000). Interpersonally, higher EI in general and higher levels of the ability to manage emotions in particular can help prevent task-based conflicts from bleeding into relationship conflict (Curseu et al., 2012; Yang & Mossholder, 2004). Organizationally, people who feel more psychologically safe are more likely to admit mistakes and believe that others do not intend to harm them compared to people who feel less psychologically safe (Edmondson, 1999). Feeling safe to express emotions authentically with coworkers helps forestall negative outcomes for employees such as burnout (Grandey et al., 2012), and could help employees feel able to raise and resolve conflicts earlier and more effectively. Culturally, matching one's expressions and expressivity to the expectations of the context can help increase effective communication and perception of emotion and reduce potential misperception (Mesquita & Boiger, 2014; Rychlowska et al., 2015). Overall, the key is to recognize that signals are information, and that adequate consideration must be given to the various factors impacting their intelligent translation into strategic, actionable information.

Emotional Intelligence After Negotiation

Beyond objective outcomes such as who gets what and how value was allocated between parties, subjective outcomes, long-term effects, and ripple effects should also be considered. First, although most research focuses on objective outcomes, recent work has begun exploring the meaning and value of subjective outcomes. Subjective outcomes include how individuals feel about the objective outcomes, themselves, the negotiation process, and the relationship (Curhan et al., 2006). These four components are important: subjective value is positively associated with better final outcomes for the individual in the current negotiation (Curhan et al., 2010) and in future negotiations with the same counterpart (Curhan et al., 2006). Furthermore, research shows that EI facilitates higher levels of subject value and positive, strong relationships with others in general (Brackett et al., 2006; Elfenbein et al., 2008; Foo et al., 2004; Mueller & Curhan, 2006).

Second, beyond the complexity of actually implementing an agreed conflict resolution – which is too-often ignored in assessments of outcomes – long-term implications for the parties and potential ripple effects beyond the parties must be considered. Interpersonally, people form expectations of counterparts' "enduring patterns of anticipated behavior" (Burgoon, 1993: 31), which in turn shape how future interactions are likely to unfold. Thus, patterns of conflict can become self-fulfilling prophecies if not effectively resolved in the moment. Organizationally, a study of long-term job negotiation outcomes demonstrated that the subjective value of negotiated job offers can predict satisfaction and relationship well-being one year later (objective economic outcomes had no effect; Curhan et al., 2009). In the same way that people develop expectations of interactions with others, they also develop expectations of interactions with organizations (Rousseau, 2004). Overall, just as emotional expressions serve as information that may be (mis)communicated and (mis)perceived, objective and subjective outcomes are likely to have longer-term effects between the disagreeing parties and potential ripple effects beyond them. Successful use of EI in conflict situations relies on attention to these broader factors.

Conclusion

We have focused on summarizing a few key aspects of the effective deployment of EI before, during, and after negotiations. Although not exhaustive, we hope that this analysis helps to inform and encourage the strategic use of emotions during negotiations in the workplace. Thus, rather than provide an inflexible and prescriptive list of emotions, thoughts, and behaviors for using EI, which necessarily would not be helpful in all situations, we have highlighted key considerations to help you navigate through the stages of negotiation. We have also created a tear-away page of guiding questions for each stage to help you effectively adapt to any given situation. As a final resource, below, we highlight the role of EI in a number of emerging trends in workplace negotiations.

First, email and other non-face-to-face channels of communication are becoming increasingly common in negotiations. This trend introduces at least three additional complexities that constrain and enable the benefits of EI to varying degrees: differences in media richness across channels, variance in (a)synchrony across channels, and an increase in the likelihood of using multiple channels in a single negotiation and/or across time. Non-face-to-face channels limit the richness of information (Daft & Lengel, 1986), and therefore can inhibit the clear expression and accurate perception of emotions (Kruger et al., 2005). However, as less synchrony introduces delays between ideation, emotions, expressions, perceptions, and reactions, less synchrony along with leaner channels may be helpful to those lower in EI, at least initially. For example, speaking impulsively (Graham & Herberger, 1983), unintentionally leaking emotions (Ekman & Friesen, 1969), and processing perceived information from one's counterpart quickly and simplistically rather than systematically (Chaiken et al., 1989) become less of a concern when communication is less synchronous. However, according to channel expansion theory (Carlson & Zmud, 1999), as familiarity with a particular channel and a particular person grows, the channel becomes effectively richer. Similarly, the use of multiple channels in a single negotiation and/or across time can also constrain and enable the benefits of EI in a number of ways. For example, adding non-face-to-face channels to an in-person negotiation decreases the likelihood of helpful emotional contagion (see Barsade et al., 2018, for a review) and expression mimicry (Hess & Fischer, 2013), but also decreases the likelihood of harmful negative emotional spirals.

Finally, an exciting yet underexplored area of research resides at the intersection of EI, negotiations, and artificial intelligence (AI). AI in general, and computer agents designed to negotiate with people in particular (e.g., https://jtmell.com/iago/), will be no more or less effective than their underlying algorithms. Although significant progress has been made in developing emotionally expressive AI (e.g., DeSteno et al., 2012), research on software that can accurately detect basic human emotional expressions (e.g., https://imotions.com/) and predictive human-computer negotiation models (e.g., Mell et al., 2021) remains nascent. These developments are captivating, given our general readiness to anthropomorphize non-human entities (e.g., Ashforth et al., 2020) and to ascribe human characteristics such as trustworthiness to robots (DeSteno et al., 2012). Although the full implications of AI in negotiations remain unknown, we encourage negotiators with all levels of EI to pay careful attention in the coming years to how AI – which is likely to seem progressively more human – influences and is influenced by the emotional landscape of negotiations. Overall, additional research is needed to understand the role of EI in negotiations as new technologies alter the nature and timeline of interpersonal interactions.

Guiding Questions for Effective Use of EI in Negotiation

Before Negotiation	– How capable are you in terms of EI? Be honest about your abilities in general, and in this particular situation. How capable is your counterpart?
	– What other abilities and/or characteristics of you and/or your counterpart can help, or potentially harm, you or others in this situation? Is there a risk of either party using EI in a harmful way, and if so, how can this be mitigated?
	– How are your and your counterpart's predictions for what emotions are likely to arise potentially incorrect? How can you proactively plan to manage the emotions (yours, others') in the situation to maximize their positive effects and minimize their negative effects?
	– At what stage – cognition, behavior, physiology, subjective experience – does intervention need to happen, if at all, if a particular emotion were to arise at a certain point in the negotiation? What should the intervention look like, and how can you facilitate its successful implementation?
During Negotiation	– What emotional signals is each party sending, and how do they (in)accurately reflect the expresser's internal state? Are the signals authentic? Expressed with appropriate intensity? How is the medium influencing the signals?
	– How are your and your counterpart's perception abilities (e.g., granularity) influencing both parties' perceptions and inferences? What about other constraints such as time pressure or other factors shaping both parties' motivation to understand the signals in this situation?
	– How are the unique nuances of the particular emotional signal(s) influencing both parties' perceptions and responses? Are the signals being perceived with appropriate granularity?
	– What other factors, such as psychological safety to make mistakes or express authentically, could be influencing the situation? Are there any individual or cultural expectations or differences at play?

(continued)

After Negotiation	– What aspects of the subjective outcomes are particularly likely to be salient in this situation to each party? How can both parties maximize the subjective outcomes for each other and themselves? – What long-term ramifications should be considered, such as how this situation may set a precedent for future patterns of behavior between the parties? What kinds of tradeoffs, if any, should be made between short-term vs. long-term objective and/or subjective outcomes? – What are the potential ripple effects beyond this relationship that should be considered? How will our negotiation process and/or outcomes influence others, the organization, and/or individuals' relationship to the organization?
Emerging Trends	– How are the media richness, (a)synchrony, and number and type of communication channels used influencing the emotions in the negotiation? How are they influencing both parties' abilities to effectively deploy EI? – Is AI involved, even in seemingly simple ways? If so, how is it influencing emotions and the role of EI in the situation? For example, predictive text algorithms may inadvertently alter the course of the negotiation. – How might more extensive integration of AI (e.g., via avatars or using AI agents to act on one's behalf) influence emotions and use of EI? How can these effects be harnessed to maximize benefits and minimize harm?

References

Adam, H., & Brett, J. M. (2018). Everything in moderation: The social effects of anger depend on its perceived intensity. *Journal of Experimental Social Psychology, 76*, 12–18.

Adam, H., & Shirako, A. (2013). Not all anger is created equal: The impact of the expresser's culture on the social effects of anger in negotiations. *Journal of Applied Psychology, 98*(5), 785.

Ambady, N. (2010). The perils of pondering: Intuition and thin slice judgments. *Psychological Inquiry, 21*(4), 271–278.

Ambady, N., & Rosenthal, R. (1992). Thin slices of expressive behavior as predictors of interpersonal consequences: A meta-analysis. *Psychological Bulletin, 111*(2), 256–274

Ashforth, B. E., Schinoff, B. S., & Brickson, S. L. (2020). My Company is Friendly, Mine's a Rebel: Anthropomorphism and shifting organizational identity from "What" to "Who". *Academy of Management Review, 45*(1), 29–57.

Bagozzi, R. P., Wong, N., & Yi, Y. (1999). The role of culture and gender in the relationship between positive and negative affect. *Cognition & Emotion, 13*(6), 641–672.

Barrett, L. F., Gross, J., Christensen, T. C., & Benvenuto, M. (2001). Knowing what you're feeling and knowing what to do about it: Mapping the relation between emotion differentiation and emotion regulation. *Cognition & Emotion, 15*(6), 713–724.

Barsade, S. G., Coutifaris, C. G., & Pillemer, J. (2018). Emotional contagion in organizational life. *Research in Organizational Behavior, 38*, 137–151.

Baumeister, R. F., Stillwell, A. M., & Heatherton, T. F. (1994). Guilt: An interpersonal approach. *Psychological Bulletin, 115*(2), 243–267.

Bechtoldt, M. N., & Schneider, V. K. (2016). Predicting stress from the ability to eavesdrop on feelings: Emotional intelligence and testosterone jointly predict cortisol reactivity. *Emotion*, *16*(6), 815–825.

Berry, D. S. (1990). Taking people at face value: Evidence for the kernel of truth hypothesis. *Social Cognition*, *8*(4), 343–361.

Blau, P. M. (1962). Patterns of choice in interpersonal relations. *American Sociological Review*, *27*(1), 41–55.

Bodenhausen, G. V., & Hugenberg, K. (2009). Attention, perception, and social cognition. In F. Strack & J. Förster (Eds.), *Social Cognition: The Basis of Human Interaction* (pp. 1–22). New York, NY: Psychology Press.

Brackett, M. A., Rivers, S. E., Shiffman, S., Lerner, N., & Salovey, P. (2006). Relating emotional abilities to social functioning: a comparison of self-report and performance measures of emotional intelligence. *Journal of Personality and Social Psychology*, *91*(4), 780–795.

Bühler, K. (1934). *Sprachtheorie*. Jena: Fischer.

Burgoon, J. K. (1993). Interpersonal expectations, expectancy violations, and emotional communication. *Journal of Language and Social Psychology*, *12*(1–2), 30–48.

Cacioppo, J. T., & Gardner, W. L. (1999). Emotion. *Annual Review of Psychology*, *50*, 191–214.

Callister, R. R., Geddes, D., & Gibson, D. F. (2017). When is anger helpful or hurtful? Status and role impact on anger expression and outcomes. *Negotiation and Conflict Management Research*, *10*(2), 69–87.

Campagna, R. L., Mislin, A. A., Kong, D. T., & Bottom, W. P. (2016). Strategic consequences of emotional misrepresentation in negotiation: The blowback effect. *Journal of Applied Psychology*, *101*(5), 605–624.

Carlson, J. R., & Zmud, R. W. (1999). Channel Expansion Theory and the experiential nature of media richness perceptions. *Academy of Management Journal*, *42*(2), 153–170.

Chaiken, S., Liberman, A., & Eagly, A. H. (1989). Heuristics and systematic information processing within and beyond the persuasion context. In J. S. Uleman & J. A. Bargh (Eds.), *Unintended Thought: Limits of Awareness, Intention, and Control* (pp. 212–252). New York, NY: Guilford Press.

Cheshin, A., Amit, A., & Van Kleef, G. A. (2018). The interpersonal effects of emotion intensity in customer service: Perceived appropriateness and authenticity of attendants' emotional displays shape customer trust and satisfaction. *Organizational Behavior and Human Decision Processes*, *144*, 97–111.

Clark, M. S., Pataki, S. P., & Carver, V. H. (1996). Some thoughts and findings on self-presentation of emotions in relationships. In G. J. O. Fletcher & J. Fitness (Eds.), *Knowledge Structures in Close Relationships: A Social Psychological Approach* (pp. 247–274). Hillsdale, NJ: Erlbaum.

Côté, S. (2014). Emotional intelligence in organizations. *Annual Review of Organizational Psychology and Organizational Behavior*, *1*, 459–488.

Côté, S, DeCelles, K. A., McCarthy, J. M., Van Kleef, G. A., & Hideg, I. (2011). The Jekyll and Hyde of emotional intelligence: Emotion-regulation knowledge facilitates both prosocial and interpersonally deviant behavior. *Psychological Science*, *22*(8), 1073–1080.

Côté, S., Hideg, I., & Van Kleef, G. A. (2013). The consequences of faking anger in negotiations. *Journal of Experimental Social Psychology*, *49*, 453–463.

Côté, S. & Miners, C. T. H. (2006). Emotional intelligence, cognitive intelligence, and job performance. *Administrative Science Quarterly*, *51*(1), 1–28.

Curhan, J. R., Elfenbein, H. A., & Eisenkraft, N. (2010). The objective value of subjective value: A multi-round negotiation study. *Journal of Applied Social Psychology*, *40*(3), 690–709.

Curhan, J. R., Elfenbein, H. A., & Kilduff, G. J. (2009). Getting off on the right foot: Subjective value versus economic value in predicting longitudinal job outcomes from job offer negotiations. *Journal of Applied Psychology*, *94*(2), 524–534.

Curhan, J. R., Elfenbein, H. A., & Xu, H. (2006). What do people value when they negotiate? Mapping the domain of subjective value in negotiation. *Journal of Personality and Social Psychology*, *91*(3), 493–512.

Curseu, P., Boros, S., & Oerlemans, L. (2012). Task and relationship conflict in short- term and long- term groups: The critical role of emotion regulation. *International Journal of Conflict Management*, *23*, 97–107.

Daft, R. L., & Lengel, R. H. (1986). Organizational information requirement, media richness, and structural design. *Management Science*, *32*(5), 554–571.

DeSteno, D., Breazeal, C., Frank, R. H., Pizarro, D., Baumann, J., Dickens, L., & Lee, J. J. (2012). Detecting the trustworthiness of novel partners in economic exchange. *Psychological Science*, *23*(12), 1549–1556.

Dunning, D., Heath, C., & Suls, J. M. (2004) Flawed self-assessment: Implications for health, education, and the workplace. *Psychological Science in the Public Interest*, *5*(3), 69–106.

Edmondson, A. (1999). Psychological safety and learning behavior in work teams. *Administrative Science Quarterly*, *44*(2), 350–383.

Ekman, P., & Friesen, W. V. (1969). Nonverbal leakage and clues to deception. *Psychiatry*, *32*(1), 88–106.

Elfenbein, H. A., & Ambady, N. (2002). Predicting workplace outcomes from the ability to eavesdrop on feelings. *Journal of Applied Psychology*, *87*(5), 963–971.

Elfenbein, H. A., Curhan, J. R., Eisenkraft, N., Shirako, A., & Baccaro, L. (2008). Are some negotiators better than others? Individual differences in bargaining outcomes. *Journal of Research in Personality*, *42*(6), 1463–1475.

Elfenbein, H. A., Foo, M. D., White, J., Tan, H. H., & Aik, V. C. (2007). Reading your counterpart: The benefit of emotional recognition accuracy for effectiveness in negotiation. *Journal of Nonverbal Behavior*, *31*, 205–223.

Elfenbein, H. A., & MacCann, C. (2017). A closer a look at ability emotional intelligence (EI): What are its component parts, and how do they relate to each other? *Social and Personality Psychology Compass*, *11*, no pagination specified.

Erle, T. M., Schmid, K., Goslar, S. H., & Martin, J. D. (2021, August 5). Emojis as social information in digital communication. *Emotion*. Advance online publication.

Foo, M. D., Elfenbein, H. A., Tan, H. H., & Aik, V. C. (2004). Emotional intelligence and negotiation: The tension between creating and claiming value. *International Journal of Conflict Management*, *15*(4), 411–429.

Fridlund, A. J. (1994). *Human Facial Expression: An Evolutionary View*. San Diego, CA: Academic Press.

Friedman, R., Anderson, C., Brett, J., Olekalns, M., Goates, N., & Lisco, C. C. (2004). The positive and negative effects of anger on dispute resolution: Evidence from electronically mediated disputes. *Journal of Applied Psychology*, *89*(2), 369–376.

Gaspar, J. P., Methasani, R., & Schweitzer, M. E. (2021). Emotional intelligence and deception: A theoretical model and propositions. *Journal of Business Ethics*. Advance online publication.

Geddes, D., & Callister, R. R. (2007). Crossing the line(s): A dual threshold model of anger in organizations. *Academy of Management Review*, *32*(3), 721–746.

Gilbert, D. T., Pinel, E. C., Wilson, T. D., Blumberg, S. J., & Wheatley, T. P. (1998). Immune neglect: A source of durability bias in affective forecasting. *Journal of Personality and Social Psychology*, *75*(3), 617–638.

Glikson, E., Rees, L., Wirtz, J., Kopelman, S., & Rafaeli, A. (2019). When and why a squeakier wheel gets more grease: The influence of cultural values and anger intensity on customer compensation. *Journal of Service Research*, *22*(3), 223–240.

Goleman, D. (1995). *Emotional Intelligence*. New York, NY: Bantam.

Graham, J. L., & Herberger, R. A. 1983. Negotiators abroad – do not shoot from the hip. *Harvard Business Review, 61*(4),160–168.

Grandey, A., Foo, S. C., Groth, M., & Goodwin, R. E. (2012). Free to be you and me: A climate of authenticity alleviates burnout from emotional labor. *Journal of Occupational Health Psychology, 17*(1), 1–14.

Gross, J. J. (2015). Emotion regulation: Current status and future prospects. *Psychological Inquiry, 26*(1), 1–26.

Gross, J. J., & John, O. P. (2003). Individual differences in two emotion regulation processes: Implications for affect, relationships, and well-being. *Journal of Personality and Social Psychology, 85*(2), 348–362.

Grossman, I., Huynh, A. C., & Ellsworth, P. C. (2016). Emotional complexity: Clarifying definitions and cultural correlates. *Journal of Personality and Social Psychology, 111*(6), 895–916.

Hess, U., & Fischer, A. (2013). Emotional mimicry as social regulation. *Personality and Social Psychology Review, 17*(2), 142–157.

Hochschild, A. R. (1983). *The Managed Heart: Commercialization of Human Feeling.* Berkeley, CA: University of California Press.

Hülsheger, U. R., & Schewe, A. F. (2011). On the costs and benefits of emotional labor: A meta-analysis of three decades of research. *Journal of Occupational Health Psychology, 16*(3), 361–389.

iMotions Software. (n.d.). Retrieved from https://imotions.com/.

Inzlicht, M., Bartholow, B. D., & Hirsh, I. B. (2015). Emotional foundations of cognitive control *Trends in Cognitive Science, 19*(3), 126–132.

Jones, E. E. (1990). *Interpersonal Perception.* New York, NY: W. H. Freeman.

Joseph, D. L. & Newman, D. A. (2010). Emotional intelligence: An integrative meta-analysis and cascading model. *Journal of Applied Psychology, 95*(1), 54–78.

Keltner, D., & Haidt, J. (1999). Social functions of emotions at four levels of analysis. *Cognition and Emotion, 13*(5), 505–521.

Keltner, D., & Horberg, E. J. (2015). Emotion-cognition interactions. In M. Mikulincer & P. R. Shaver (Eds.), *APA Handbook of Personality and Social Psychology* (Vol. 1, pp. 623–664). Washington, DC: American Psychological Association.

Kilduff, M., Chiaburu, D. S., & Menges, J. I. (2010). Strategic use of emotional intelligence in organizational settings: Exploring the dark side. *Research in Organizational Behavior, 30*, 129–152.

Kruger, J., Epley, N., Parker, J., & Ng, Z. W. (2005). Egocentrism over e-mail: Can we communicate as well as we think? *Journal of Personality and Social Psychology, 89*(6), 925–936.

Kruglanski, A. (1989). The psychology of being "right": The problem of accuracy in social perception and cognition. *Psychological Bulletin, 106*(3), 395–409.

Krumhuber, E., Manstead, A. S. R., Cosker, D., Marshall, D., Rosin, P. L., & Kappas, A. (2007). Facial dynamics as indicators of trustworthiness and cooperative behavior. *Emotion, 7*(4), 730–735.

MacCann, C., Joseph, D. L., Newman, D. A., & Roberts, R. D. (2014). Emotional intelligence is a second-stratum factor of intelligence: Evidence from hierarchical and bifactor models. *Emotion, 14*(2), 358–374.

MacCann, C., & Roberts, R. D. (2008). New paradigms for assessing emotional intelligence: Theory and data. *Emotion, 8*(4), 540–551.

Marcus, B., & Schuler, H. (2004). Antecedents of counterproductive behavior at work: A general perspective. *Journal of Applied Psychology, 89*(4), 647–660.

Maul, A. (2012). Examining the structure of emotional intelligence at the item level: New perspectives, new conclusions. *Cognition & Emotion, 26*(3), 503–520.

Mayer, J. D. (2004). Be realistic. *Harvard Business Review, 82*, 28.

Mayer, J. D., Caruso, D. R., & Salovey, P. (2016). The ability model of emotional intelligence: Principles and updates. *Emotion Review*, *8*(4), 290–300.

Mayer, J. D., Caruso, D. R., & Salovey, P. (1999). Emotional intelligence meets traditional standards for intelligence. *Intelligence*, *27*(4), 267–298.

Mayer, J. D., Salovey, P., & Caruso, D. R. (2002). *Mayer-Salovey-Caruso Emotional Intelligence Test*. Toronto, ON: Multi-Health Systems.

Mell, J. (n.d.). https://jtmell.com/iago/. Retrieved on August 12, 2021.

Mell, J., Beissinger, M., & Gratch, J. (2021). An expert-model and machine learning hybrid approach to predicting human-agent negotiation outcomes in varied data. *Journal on Multimodal User Interfaces*, *15*(2), 215–227.

Mesquita, B., & Boiger, M. (2014). Emotions in context: A sociodynamic model of emotions. *Emotion Review*, *6*(4), 298–302.

Mueller, J. S., & Curhan, J. R. (2006). Emotional intelligence and counterpart mood induction in a negotiation. *International Journal of Conflict Management*, *17*(2), 110–128.

Muraven, M., & Baumeister, R. F. (2000). Self-regulation and depletion of limited resources: Does self-control resemble a muscle? *Psychological Bulletin*, *126*(2), 247–259.

Oatley, K., & Jenkins, J. M. (1992). Human emotions: Function and dysfunction. *Annual Review of Psychology*, *43*, 55–85.

Potworowski, G., & Kopelman, S. (2008). Strategic displays and responses to emotions: Developing evidence-based negotiation expertise in emotion management (NEEM). *Negotiation and Conflict Management Research*, *1*(4), 333–352.

Rees, L., Chi, S. C. S., Friedman, R., & Shih, H. L. (2020). Anger as a trigger for information search in integrative negotiations. *Journal of Applied Psychology*, *105*(7), 713–731.

Rees, L., & Kopelman, S. (2019). Logics and logistics for future research: Appropriately interpreting the emotional landscape of multicultural negotiation. *Negotiation and Conflict Management Research*, *12*(2), 131–145.

Rothman, N. B. (2011). Steering sheep: How expressed emotional ambivalence elicits dominance in interdependent decision making contexts. *Organizational Behavior and Human Decision Processes*, *116*(1), 66–82.

Rousseau, D. M. (2004). Psychological contracts in the workplace: Understanding the ties that motivate. *Academy of Management Perspectives*, *18*(1), 120–127.

Rychlowska, M., Miyamoto, Y., Matsumoto, D., Hess, U., Gilboa-Schechtman, E., Kamble, S., et al. (2015). Heterogeneity of long-history migration explains cultural differences in reports of emotional expressivity and the functions of smiles. *Proceedings of the National Academy of Sciences*, *112*, E2429–E2436.

Salovey, P., & Mayer, J. D. (1990). Emotional intelligence. *Imagination, Cognition and Personality*, *9*, 185–211.

Scherer, K. R. (1988). On the symbolic functions of vocal affect expression. *Journal of Language and Social Psychology*, *7*(2), 79–100.

Schlegel, K., Mehu, M., van Peer, J. M., & Scherer, K. R. (2018). Sense and sensibility: The role of cognitive and emotional intelligence in negotiation. *Journal of Research in Personality*, *74*, 6–15.

Schlegel, K., & Mortillaro, M. (2019). The Geneva Emotional Competence Inventory (GECo): An ability measure of workplace emotional intelligence. *Journal of Applied Psychology*, *104*(4), 559–580.

Smith, C. A., & Ellsworth, P. C. (1985). Patterns of cognitive appraisal in emotion. *Journal of Personality and Social Psychology*, *48*(4), 813–838.

Tiedens, L. Z. (2001). Anger and advancement versus sadness and subjugation: The effect of negative emotion expressions on social status conferral. *Journal of Personality and Social Psychology*, *80*(1), 86–94.

Tng, H.-Y., & Au, A. K. C. (2014). Strategic display of anger and happiness in negotiation: The moderating role of perceived authenticity. *Negotiation Journal*, *30*, 301–327.

Tsai, J. L., Louie, J. Y., Chen, E. E., & Uchida, Y. (2007). Learning what feelings to desire: Socialization of ideal affect through children's storybooks. *Personality and Social Psychology Bulletin*, *33*(1), 17–30.

Van Kleef, G. A. (2009). How emotions regulate social life: The Emotions as Social Information (EASI) model. *Current Directions in Psychological Science*, *18*(3), 184–188.

Van Kleef, G. A. (2010). The emerging view of emotion as social information. *Social and Personality Psychology Compass*, *4/5*, 331–343.

Van Kleef, G. A., & Côté, S. (2007). Expressing anger in conflict: When it helps and when it hurts. *Journal of Applied Psychology*, *92*(6), 1557–1569.

Van Kleef, G. A., De Dreu, C. K. W., & Manstead, A. S. R. (2004). The interpersonal effects of emotions in negotiations: A motivated information processing approach. *Journal of Personality and Social Psychology*, *87*(4), 510–528.

Van Kleef, G. A., De Dreu, C. K. W., & Manstead, A. S. R. (2006). Supplication and appeasement in conflict and negotiation: The interpersonal effects of disappointment, worry, guilt, and regret. *Journal of Personality and Social Psychology*, *91*(1), 124–142.

Van Kleef, G. A., van den Berg, H., & Heerdink, M. W. (2015). The persuasive power of emotions: Effects of emotional expressions on attitude formation and change. *Journal of Applied Psychology*, *100*(4), 1124–1142.

Van Kleef, G. A., Van Doorn, E. A., Heerdink, M. W., & Koning, L. F. (2011). Emotion is for influence. *European Review of Social Psychology*, *22*(1), 114–163.

Weiner, B. (1985). An attributional theory of achievement motivation and emotion. *Psychological Review*, *92*(4), 548–573.

Willis, J., & Todorov, A. (2006). First impressions: Making up your mind after a 100-ms exposure to a face. *Psychological Science*, *17*(7), 592–598.

Wilson, T. D., & Gilbert, D. T. (2003). Affective forecasting. In M. P. Zanna (Ed.), *Advances in Experimental Social Psychology* (Vol. 35, pp. 345–411). San Diego, CA: Elsevier Academic Press.

Wilson, T. D., Wheatley, T., Meyers, J. M., Gilbert, D. T., & Axsom, D. (2000). Focalism: A source of durability bias in affective forecasting. *Journal of Personality and Social Psychology*, *78*(5), 821–836.

Yang, J., & Mossholder, K. (2004). Decoupling task and relationship conflict: The role of intragroup emotional processing. *Journal of Organizational Behavior*, *25*, 589–605.

Sandore (Sandy) Zehr

Chapter 3
Psychological Safety: Creating a Healthy Conflict Culture

Abstract: The concept of fearless feedback can be an especially effective technique for the conflict management practitioner seeking to help a group or organization manage interpersonal conflict. Fearless feedback is grounded in the principles of psychological safety, the latter of which is defined as a "belief that one will not be punished or humiliated for speaking up with ideas, questions, concerns, or mistakes" (Edmondson, 1999, p. 354). When group members realize that they can fearlessly share their perspectives, conflicts can be resolved in an efficient and rapid manner. With this approach, individuals are encouraged to ask questions and feel safe in voicing respectful disagreement because positive intent is ascribed to all parties. An equally important term for the practitioner of conflict manager is culture, which describes the unique personality of a group and illustrates the way things are done within the organization. The way organizational members approach conflict management and resolution is inextricably linked to organizational culture. For the conflict management practitioner, effective strategies to leverage psychological safety to enhance corporate culture and resolve conflict include emphasizing employee engagement, creating favorable conditions, and monitoring/measuring progress. When faced with a conflicting situation, employees have three choices: ignore the conflict, escalate the issue, or utilize fearless feedback to address it immediately. Organizations whose employees' needs for safety are met experience the development of an overall sense of trust within the group. A person who trusts the team to be psychologically safe will be more willing to take a risk by offering their personal perspective (fearless feedback) when faced with interpersonal conflict, thereby addressing the conflict in an immediate, healthy manner.

Keywords: psychological safety, employee engagement, culture, trust, social exchange, fearless feedback

As we begin an examination of psychological safety and its impact on conflict resolution, we will open the discussion with a brief anecdote. Often, an illustration can be a meaningful way to describe a concept. Before relating the short tale, some context is necessary. It is important for the reader to know that I am an aficionado of dad jokes. I like to hear them and, often to the chagrin of my family, I like to share them. In defining the dad joke, Merriam-Webster (n.d.) uses the phrase "endearingly corny" and I find this to be an apt description of these witticisms. However, as the introductory story will clearly identify, even the seemingly innocuous dad joke can be a source of conflict.

https://doi.org/10.1515/9783110746365-003

Dad Joke Creates Conflict: A Story

It was a beautiful, bright fall morning in the Midwestern United States. As I drove to my office just after daybreak, I marveled at the beauty of the trees, as the leaves were changing colors, just as they do every autumn in the Midwest. The oppressive, sometimes unbearable humidity that is a part of the summer season in the Midwest was gone, and the air was now crisp and clear. Most importantly, the baristas at the local coffee shops were again crafting Pumpkin Spice Lattes, a seasonal favorite. Indeed, all was right with the world on that morning as I drove into my office parking lot.

As I proceeded to walk from my car to my office, briefcase in one hand and Pumpkin Spice Latte in the other, an autumn-related dad joke popped into my head and in a most undignified manner, I literally snorted as I laughed aloud. One simply cannot drink Pumpkin Spice Latte while engaging in raucous laughter. Sadly, I have no recollection of the witty thing that popped into my head that morning and can only recall my overzealous and unsophisticated response.

As I continued to traverse toward my office, I passed one of my employees in the hallway. Still chuckling to myself, I determined that I should share this pearl of a dad joke that was rolling around in my head. I figured my employee would also find my joke funny, and we could have a few laughs together to start the workday. Unfortunately, I could not have been more wrong in my assessment of the situation and the relative humor, or lack thereof, in my new joke. From the reaction on the employee's face, it was abundantly clear that my funny quip did not have the desired outcome and apparently, was not so funny after all. I remained undaunted, confident in my ability to be humorous, and simply assumed that it would just take the person a few minutes to "get it" as I continued down the hallway to my office.

I stepped into my office and began settling in for the day. Within a few seconds, I distinctly heard the sound of my office door closing. Upon turning around, I saw this same person standing in front of me. Of course, my initial thought was that they had figured out the joke and had come to my office so we could share a few laughs together. Again, I could not have been more wrong. Instead, the individual looked me directly in the eye and said, "Boss, here is what you said, but this is how I heard it" and I knew instantly that I had unintentionally said something offensive and created conflict. It was a dad joke gone wrong!

I am delighted to report that, in literally one minute, we were able to resolve the conflict and go on our way. By addressing the issue in the moment, the employee set the stage for us to deal with the conflict instantly and work together on a joint resolution. Further, I took the opportunity to apologize for my blunder. In the process, I also learned the valuable lesson that I need to filter my dad jokes before sharing with others.

Conflict Response Behavior

As practitioners of conflict management, it is instructive to focus on the behavior of the offended employee and the conscious choice they made at that moment in the hallway, when my joke did not land as I had intended. The offended party had several alternatives in reacting to the conflict. Of the myriad of available options, three such choices included ignoring the conflict altogether, escalating the issue by involving others, or addressing the conflict immediately by offering fearless feedback.

Ignoring the Conflict. The employee could have easily adopted the approach of doing and saying nothing, thereby ignoring the conflict altogether and leaving it unaddressed. In this scenario, the conflict would have been avoided and the employee's concerns would have likely remained internalized and unresolved. Ignoring the conflict would also have had negative implications for me, as I would remain unaware that my joke had offended. I could have easily continued sharing the joke with others and run the risk of creating additional unintended conflict.

Escalating the Issue. Another response alternative available to the offended employee was that of involving fellow employees and amplifying the conflict. Arguably, the issue would have escalated rapidly had the employee continued to the group's office cubicle area and proceeded to share with fellow employees the details of the hallway conversation. One can imagine that the offended individual could have regaled colleagues and others in the general vicinity with a colorful description of the incident. Recounting the incident in this manner would have ensured the entire team, except me, was well aware of my transgression. In this response scenario, the issue would have likely intensified very quickly as the team spent the remainder of the day in "drama mode" talking about my insensitive joke. Meanwhile, I would remain unaware of the conflict and left to wonder why my team was behaving in such a manner. Escalating the conflict would have had deleterious effects on the team's performance and on my interpersonal relationships with not only the offended employee, but their colleagues as well.

Fearless Feedback. Instead of choosing to ignore or escalate the conflict, the employee adopted an approach our workgroup has labeled as "fearless feedback" and chose to address the issue immediately. The approach took courage on the part of the employee, but I posit that it did not take as much courage as one might expect. Why? Because our workgroup has been intentional to create a culture that not only makes it safe, but also encourages employees to speak up and raise issues or concerns.

The concept of fearless feedback, as practiced in our group, is grounded in the principles of psychological safety, and it has been especially effective at helping the group manage interpersonal conflicts. Psychological safety is a "belief that one will not be punished or humiliated for speaking up with ideas, questions, concerns, or mistakes" (Edmondson, 1999, p. 354). When employees realize that they can fearlessly share their perspectives, conflicts can be resolved in an efficient and rapid manner.

Criteria for Scenario Resolution Success

Reflecting on the scenario described, one can see fearless feedback in action. The employee demonstrated this by fearlessly coming to my office to offer feedback in real time. It should be noted here that for this approach to be effective, positive intent must be ascribed to all parties. It was critical that the employee assume good intent associated with my actions in sharing the joke. This was indeed the case as I had simply not spent enough time thinking about the ramifications and alternative interpretations that might result from sharing the quip. Likewise, I had to assume that the employee had the best of intentions in taking the time to address the matter within seconds of the conflict occurring. Indeed, my understanding of the employee's fearless feedback in that moment was that it was based on a desire to "care enough to share." The employee simply wanted to improve the situation and help me, rather than create drama.

The workgroup described in the opening story continues to evolve and become increasingly adept at resolving conflict through sharing fearless feedback. The remainder of this chapter will offer the theoretical underpinnings for the approach, provide details as to the research-based development of the approach, and detail strategies for the conflict resolution practitioner desiring to leverage psychological safety to enhance corporate culture and resolve conflict.

Social Exchange Theory

The development of the conflict management approach illustrated in the scenario was grounded in the principles of social exchange theory. Homans (1958) described social exchange theory as one of reciprocity in the relationship between the employee and the organization. As part of the exchange relationship, employees tend to be in a mode of constant assessment, evaluating the "gives" and "gets" to compare what is being provided the organization with what is being returned in exchange (Homans, 1958). This give and get relationship, and the constant evaluation of the balance thereof, is the basis for social exchange theory.

A starting point for leaders and conflict management practitioners seeking to increase organizational acumen around healthy conflict resolution is to establish conditions that contribute to favorable social exchange. Simply stated, employees should perceive that the balance of the reciprocal social exchange with the organization is advantageous. A key outcome of favorable social exchange conditions is the creation of psychological safety within the organization. Frazier et al. (2017) described the connection between social exchange and psychological safety by stating "the entirety of the social exchange system influences psychological safety" (p. 119). As such, psychological safety becomes a mechanism through which beneficial outcomes of the give and get relationship between the employee and the organization are demonstrated. Both sides receive benefits. A practical example of the benefits of psychological safety through the lens of social exchange theory is with employee acceptance of organizational change management initiatives. Rimm-Kaufman (2016) found that in an environment characterized by psychological safety, employees demonstrate an increased willingness and acceptance of organizational change. Likewise, Kahn (1990) noted that when satisfactory social exchange creates a perception of increased psychological safety, employees respond with increased employee engagement.

The creation of a favorable social exchange environment was an essential component in developing the conflict management approach described in the opening story. Employees are more willing to engage in offering fearless feedback in the face of conflict when they know that organizational leadership will reciprocate with an openness to receiving the feedback. This positive exchange environment enables all parties to work collaboratively to resolve the issue.

Culture

Culture describes the unique personality of the group and helps to explain the way things are done within the organization. Writing for Harvard Business Review, Groysberg et al. (2021) describe culture as "the tacit social order of an organization: It shapes attitudes and behaviors in wide-ranging and durable ways." A more expansive definition that encompasses the indoctrination of newcomers to the organization was offered by Schein (2010), who defined culture as:

A pattern of shared basic assumptions that was learned by a group as it solved its problems of external adaptation and internal integration, which has worked well enough to be considered valid and, therefore, to be taught to new members as the correct way to perceive, think, and feel in relation to those problems (p. 17).

As we contemplate the definitions of culture, it is noteworthy that we can observe the manifestation of the group's culture, or personality, in many ways. We can readily identify both visual and verbal cues that better help us define a group's culture. Culture can be witnessed through watching teammates interact and observing the levels of trust and employee engagement within the group. We can even ascertain culture based on what people place on their desks or choose to include in the background of a virtual team meeting. Most importantly for the conflict management practitioner, we can observe culture in the way group members handle interpersonal conflict.

The phrase "Culture eats strategy for breakfast" is credited to renowned management expert and author, Dr. Peter Drucker (as quoted in Campbell et al., 2011). Indeed, culture is an important factor within the organization. The Society for Human Resource Management (SHRM) determined that nearly 25% of employees in the United States are unhappy with their workplace culture (Alonso, 2019). Further,

Alonso (2019) noted that nearly 20% of employees reported seeking a new job based on culture in their present workplace, and approximately 33% of employees attributed workplace culture to making them irritable at home. These statistics make a compelling case for the potential impacts of a negative organizational culture and support Drucker's assertion as to the importance of culture.

Conflict and Culture

An additional implication of Drucker's statement about the importance of culture is that it becomes a powerful endorsement for the value of an organizational conflict culture characterized by productive conflict handling. Relative to the linkage between conflict and culture, Katz and Flynn (2013) suggested that "culture is key to influencing conflict management systems and strategies" (p. 398). It is important to note that organizations can have an overall conflict culture in which employees adopt a similar, consistent style when resolving an interpersonal conflict (Gelfand et al., 2012). In such organizations, group members share a set of basic tenets about decision-making and the way conflicts should be resolved (Schein, 2010). When seeking to equip the organization to better handle interpersonal conflicts, practitioners are well-advised to ensure that organizational culture is made a key consideration. An argument can be made, based on the comment attributed to Drucker, that a productive conflict culture is even more important than a well-designed organizational conflict management strategy.

Reflecting on the earlier anecdote about conflict resulting from a dad joke, one can identify the principles of a productive conflict culture within the subject organization. The offended party adhered to the established cultural norm of being fearless in providing timely feedback to address the conflict. Likewise, when the feedback was delivered, my intentional response to honor and accept the perspective offered was in accordance with the tenets of the organization's conflict culture. The beneficial outcome of the fearless feedback approach was that the parties involved in the interpersonal conflict were able to collaborate and reach a timely and efficient resolution.

Employee Engagement

The establishment of the positive conflict management approach was facilitated by an overall organizational leadership philosophy that emphasizes a culture of employee engagement. A key benefit of this employee-centered approach is that engaged employees are more likely to participate in collaborative behavior with their colleagues (Anitha, 2014). Conflict management practitioners will readily agree that establishing a workplace environment in which employees are prone to collaborate offers a platform for healthy conflict resolution behavior. In addition to collaboration, employee engagement research results further indicate that an engaged workforce exhibits beneficial employee behavior and produced an increase in organizational performance (Albrecht et al., 2015; Anitha, 2014; Chughtai & Buckley, 2008).

In his foundational treatise on the topic, Kahn (1990) defined employee engagement as "the harnessing of organizational members' selves to their work roles" (p. 694). The definition of employee engagement offered by Shuck and Wollard (2010) describes the construct as "an individual employee's cognitive, emotional, and behavioral state directed toward desired organizational outcomes" (p. 103). Both descriptions of employee engagement offer a connection with an employee's psychological state. In fact, when initially describing employee engagement, Kahn (1990) proposed psychological meaningfulness, psychological availability, and psychological safety as antecedents of employee engagement. Psychological meaningfulness is defined as "a feeling that one is receiving a return on investments of oneself in a currency of physical, cognitive, or emotional energy" (Kahn, 1990, p. 703). Describing psychological availability, Kahn (1990) used the phrase "the sense of having the physical, emotional, or psychological resources to personally engage at a particular moment" (p. 714). Kahn (1990) described employees who are psychologically safe as "able to show and employ oneself without fear of negative consequences to self-image, status, or career" (p. 708).

Empirical Research Results

When one considers the connection between employee engagement and psychological safety, the rationale for the leadership focus on employee engagement as an enabler to developing a healthy conflict management culture becomes apparent. The results of a quantitative research study on the subject organization presented further impetus for the focus on employee engagement. This study measured levels of employee engagement, psychological meaningfulness, psychological availability, and psychological safety (Zehr, 2017). When normalized to a 10-point scale, the research indicated that employee engagement, psychological meaningfulness, and psychological availability each yielded a respectable score of 8.2 out of 10 (Zehr, 2017). However, the organizational results for psychological safety measured 5.2 out of 10, indicating that employees did not describe themselves as working in a culture characterized by psychological safety (Zehr, 2017).

The interdependence between employee engagement and psychological safety was also demonstrated in the study. In alignment with previous research on the topic (e.g., Kahn, 1990; May et al., 2004), psychological safety was found to be a predictor of employee engagement (Zehr, 2017). Interestingly, the study also demonstrated that as employee engagement increased, so did psychological safety, thereby creating a virtuous cycle (Zehr, 2017). According to Frazier et al. (2017), the reciprocal condition whereby employee engagement serves as a predictor of psychological safety, while theorized by some, had not previously been demonstrated. For the conflict management practitioner, an awareness of the critical connection between employee engagement and psychological safety can be a powerful tool in the development of a robust and healthy conflict culture.

Psychological Safety. In defining psychological safety, Kahn (1990) placed an emphasis on the individual and highlighted the ability to be oneself "without fear of negative consequences to self-image, status, or career" (p. 708). Edmondson's (1999) definition of the construct focused on the team culture and emphasized the perception that the team is safe for raising questions or concerns without the fear of admonishment or humiliation. Within both definitions is the implication that a person assessing the team as psychologically safe will be more willing to take a risk by offering personal perspective when faced with interpersonal conflict. Research on the topic supports this notion and indicates that team members are more willing to engage in collaborative behaviors and freely share suggestions when they believe the organizational culture to be psychologically safe (Carmeli & Gittell, 2009; Edmondson & Lei, 2014; Kahn, 1990). It is through the willingness and ability to collaborate and share viewpoints related to interpersonal issues that that healthy conflict management and resolution can occur.

Psychological Safety and Trust. Psychological safety is a critical element in the workplace. In fact, research indicates that employees have an "underlying psychological need for safety" (Lyu, 2016, p. 1360). When employees' needs for safety are met, an overall sense of trust can develop within the group. Edmondson (1999) suggested that trust is a necessary precursor at both the individual and team level for the employee to feel that the team is safe for risk-taking and speaking up. In a high-trust team environment characterized by psychological safety, "people are comfortable being themselves" (Edmondson, 1999 p. 354).

Stephen MR Covey suggested that trust is built upon the principles of character and competence, and further asserted that trust is a vital component of communication (2006). Covey described trust as a glue that holds relationships together (2006). When team members trust each other, there is "an expectation or a belief that the other person is well intended" (Vaida & Ardelean, 2019). When individuals assume good intent from each other, fearless feedback can produce a healthy conflict culture within the team.

Applications for Conflict Management Practitioners

Informed by results of initial research (Zehr, 2017), principles of social exchange theory, employee engagement, and psychological safety were synthesized to support the intentional creation of the conflict management culture described in the opening story. Understanding that employees likely had neither the time nor the inclination to avail themselves to the theoretical research on the topic, an attempt was made to synthesize the body of information to a few simple premises to make the concepts more accessible and comprehendible. To accomplish this, psychological safety was described simply as "fearless feedback" and employees were asked to embrace principles of trust related to assuming each person is competent (Covey, 2006) and well intentioned (Vaida & Ardelean, 2019).

Embrace Fearless Feedback. Feedback can be offered in many forms, some of which include both declarative statements and exploratory questions. When an organization is intentional about embracing fearless feedback, group members are encouraged to ask questions. Often, this can run counter to one's social conditioning, which inhibits a person from speaking up or asking questions. To illustrate, consider a small child who incessantly asks "why" and the reaction of the curious youngster's parents. Often, adults react by discouraging the child from asking so many questions. Ultimately, individuals become conditioned to not speak up and ask questions. Intentionally embracing fearless feedback can create a culture in which individuals, despite any conditioning to the contrary, can feel more open to asking questions of one another and collaboratively exploring potential solutions to interpersonal conflict. Through fearless feedback, group members are comfortable in voicing questions and respectful disagreement because positive intent is ascribed to each group member.

What About Poor Performance and Poor Behavior? It should be noted that embracing fearless feedback and psychological safety does not mean that poor performance and poor behavior are tolerated. On the contrary, when a team member observes a colleague underperforming, fearless feedback challenging the underperformer can be offered in real time by a trusted colleague. Likewise, if someone on the team is being disrespectful and creating conflict, the behavior can be confronted by a teammate. Fearless feedback implies that individuals are free to voice dissent, but in doing so, should display an attitude by which they "care enough to share" and demonstrate positive intent.

Creating Conditions. Setting the stage for the development of a healthy conflict culture is a vital step for the conflict management practitioner. When an organization focuses on psychological safety, the inclusion of a wide range of viewpoints and diverse perspectives becomes an important condition for successful implementation. While working to resolve conflict, leadership must ensure that the viewpoints of all parties to the conflict are included and considered. As the organization becomes more adept at conflict management, the diversity within the group can offer a distinct advantage.

Employees should be taught to celebrate differences and the organizational growth that can be accomplished from learning from one another as conflicts are managed. Within the subject organization, we use the mantra "embrace your inner weirdness" to signal to employees that it is safe to be yourself. When employees are less concerned about how they might appear to others, they feel freer to offer constructive feedback, good ideas, and even share potential dangers that others may not see.

Measure and Monitor. The ability to periodically assess progress and make changes to the direction can be a powerful tool for the practitioner. As the fearless feedback initiative matured and evolved in our organization, I found that employees were comfortable with self-reporting when a mistake had been made. I considered this an unexpected benefit of fearless feedback and an indicator of the program's efficacy in resolving conflict in a timely manner. Often, employees would come to me and share mistakes that likely may have never been uncovered. Interestingly, employees stated that they felt compelled to be transparent and forthcoming about mistakes because an environment was created in which they felt safe to do so. I assert that when employees begin to self-report and openly talk about learning from their mistakes, positive progress in creating a constructive conflict management culture has occurred.

A more direct way to measure team psychological safety is with a seven-question survey instrument developed by Edmondson (1999). As designed, the survey uses a seven-point scale in which individuals answer questions using a range of choice from one (Very Inaccurate) to seven (Very Accurate). It is important to note that some of the items within the survey are reverse scored.

For the practitioner wishing to complete a quick, non-quantitative assessment of team psychological safety, the survey can be administered with team members answering each question with a simple yes or no. The seven questions from the Edmondson (1999) survey as follows:

1. If you make a mistake on this team, it is often held against you.
2. Members of this team are able to bring up problems and tough issues.
3. People on this team sometimes reject others for being different.
4. It is safe to take a risk on this team.
5. It is difficult to ask other members of this team for help.
6. No one on this team would deliberately act in a way that undermines my efforts.
7. Working with members of this team, my unique skills and talents are valued and utilized.

Conclusion

In conclusion, the conflict management approach illustrated in the opening anecdote has become ingrained as a cultural norm in our workgroup. During a recent discussion with the employee involved in the story, they indicated having no memory of the incident. On the other hand, I remember many details of the conflict, except for the actual content of the dad joke. The employee and I both surmise that the lack of recollection is an indicator that fearless feedback has become our normal mode of interpersonal conflict management within the group and that fearless feedback has become second nature. Once this conflict was quickly addressed and resolved, the employee felt satisfied with the outcome and did not give the issue further thought. I suggest that, for the practitioner seeking to foster a healthy conflict culture, this is a compelling endorsement of the described approach.

References

Albrecht, S. L., Bakker, A. B., Gruman, J. A., Macey, W. H., & Saks, A. M. (2015). Employee engagement, human resource management practices and competitive advantage: An integrated approach. *Journal of Organizational Effectiveness: People and Performance, 2*(1), 7–35.

Alonso, A. (2019). Workplace Culture Matters. *HR Magazine, 64*(4), 89.

Anitha, J., (2014). Determinants of employee engagement and their impact on employee performance. *International Journal of Productivity and Performance Management, 63*(3), 308–323.

Campbell, D., Edgar, D., & Stonehouse, G. (2011). *Business Strategy: An Introduction*. New York, NY: Palgrave Macmillan.

Carmeli, A., & Gittell, J. H. (2009). High-quality relationships, psychological safety, and learning from failures in work organizations. *Journal of Organizational Behavior, 30*(6), 709–729

Chughtai, A. A., & Buckley, F. (2008). Work engagement and its relationship with state and trait trust: A conceptual analysis. *Journal of Behavioral and Applied Management, 10*(1), 47–71.

Covey, S. R., & Merrill, R. R. (2006). *The speed of trust: The one thing that changes everything*. New York, NY: Simon and Schuster.

Edmondson, A., (1999). Psychological Safety and Learning Behavior in Work Teams. *Administrative Science Quarterly, 44*(2), 350–383.

Edmondson, A. C., & Lei, Z. (2014). Psychological safety: The history, renaissance, and future of an interpersonal construct. *Annual Review of Organizational Psychology and Organizational Behavior, 1*(1), 23–43.

Frazier, M. L., Fainshmidt, S., Klinger, R. L., Pezeshkan, A., & Vracheva, V. (2017). Psychological safety: A meta-analytic review and extension. *Personnel Psychology, 70*(1), 113–165.

Gelfand, M. J., Leslie, L. M., Keller, K., & de Dreu, C. (2012). Conflict cultures in organizations: How leaders shape conflict cultures and their organizational-level consequences. *Journal of Applied Psychology, 97*(6), 1131.

Groysberg, B., Lee, J., Price, J., & Yo-Jud Cheng, J. (2021, July 8). *The Leader's Guide to Corporate Culture*. Harvard Business Review. https://hbr.org/2018/01/the-leaders-guide-to-corporate-culture

Homans, G.C. (1958). Social behavior as exchange. *American Journal of Sociology, 63*(2), 597–606.

Kahn, W.A. (1990). Psychological conditions of personal engagement and disengagement at work, *Academy of Management Journal, 33*, 692–724.

Katz, N. H., & Flynn, L. T. (2013). Understanding conflict management systems and strategies in the workplace: A pilot study. *Conflict Resolution Quarterly, 30*(4), 393–410.

Lyu, X. (2016). Effect of organizational justice on work engagement with psychological safety as a mediator: Evidence from China. *Social Behavior and Personality: An International Journal, 44*(8), 1359–1370.

May, D. R., Gilson, R. L., & Harter, L. M. (2004). The psychological conditions of meaningfulness, safety and availability and the engagement of the human spirit at work. *Journal of Occupational and Organizational Psychology, 77*(1), 11–37.

Merriam-Webster. (n.d.). Dad joke. In *Merriam-Webster.com dictionary*.

Rimm-Kaufman, S. E. (2016). Applications of psychological safety to developmental science: Reflections and recommendations for next steps. *Research in Human Development, 13*(1), 84–89.

Schein, E. H. (2010). *Organizational culture and leadership* (Vol. 2). San Francisco, CA: John Wiley & Sons.

Shuck, B., & Wollard, K. (2010). Employee engagement and HRD: A seminal review of the foundations. *Human Resource Development Review, 9*(1), 89–110.

Vaida, S., & Ardelean, I. (2019). Psychological safety and trust. A conceptual analysis. *Studia Universitatis Babes-Bolyai, Psychologia-Paedagogia, 64*(1), 87–101.

Zehr, S. L. (2017). Safe to be Engaged or Engaged to be Safe? A Quantitative Examination of the Relationship Between Employee Engagement and Psychological Safety Within the Federal Workforce. (Doctoral dissertation). Retrieved from ProQuest Dissertations database.

Ralph H. Kilmann
Chapter 4
Thomas-Kilmann Instrument (TKI) and the Kilmann Organizational Conflict Instrument (KOCI)

Abstract: It is a great pleasure to share with you the evolution of my work in conflict management and change management, which, of course, includes what I have learned from using the Thomas-Kilmann Conflict Mode Instrument in many different situations since the early 1970s.[1] That evolution of my work with the TKI instrument eventually led me to develop the Kilmann Organizational Conflict Instrument almost 50 years later, which I call KOCI for short. In essence, the KOCI explicitly assesses how an organization's systems and processes, represented by the eight tracks of quantum transformation, powerfully influence how effectively organizational members can resolve their most challenging conflicts and problems. Knowing one's conflict style can assist individuals and their organizations with creating productive outcomes to conflict situations.

Keywords: conflict style, competing, collaborating, compromising, avoiding, accommodating, conflict assessment

Before I share more about the KOCI assessment tool, let me put my work on conflict management in a historical perspective, which will convey why it became so necessary for me (hence, the driving "purpose") to explicitly assess how members approach – and attempt to resolve – their systems conflicts.

A Brief History of the TKI

In the early 1970s, Ken Thomas and I developed the TKI assessment tool to assess how individuals respond to interpersonal conflicts in general, without specifying any particular situation. In fact, directly below are the standard TKI instructions printed on every TKI paper booklet, and these same exact instructions are also shown on your computer or mobile screen when you take the online version of the TKI assessment tool: "Consider situations in which you find your wishes differing from those of another person. How do you usually respond to such situations?"

---

[1] Adapted from of Dr. Kilmann's legacy book: *Creating a Quantum Organization* (2021). All text and figures are Copyright © 2021 by Kilmann Diagnostics LLC. All rights reserved.

https://doi.org/10.1515/9783110746365-004

The respondent is then shown thirty pairs of statements that describe different behavioral responses to any interpersonal conflict. For each pair of A/B choices, the person is asked to select the statement that best characterizes his or her behavior, which represent those five different conflict-handling modes: collaborating, competing, compromising, and so forth. After a person completes her responses to these thirty items, the results reveal which conflict modes that person might be using too much or too little, as compared to a large normative sample.

It is important to re-emphasize this key point: Respondents to the TKI are not presented with any specific interpersonal situation. Instead, respondents are asked to provide their typical responses to conflict across all such situations. In fact, when a trainer or facilitator reviews the TKI's instructions for a group of participants, there is always someone in the audience who asks this question: "Since I respond to conflict differently, depending if I am at home or at work, which setting should I keep in mind while responding to the items on this instrument?"

The facilitator who is administering the TKI to these participants is expected to provide this standardized answer: "Do not think of any situation when you respond to the thirty items on the TKI. Just provide your typical response, your average response to conflict, across all the situations in your life."

By 1974, just before the TKI was officially published, Ken and I already knew that some people had a little difficulty responding to the TKI by mentally averaging, so to speak, their typical response to conflicts across all situations, rather than focusing only on their behavior in the workplace or focusing only on their behavior in their home with family or friends, or in some other specified social setting. But despite this dilemma, we still worded the TKI instructions to illicit the typical or average behavioral response a person has to interpersonal conflict in general, since our exclusive use of the TKI at that time (as young assistant professors) was in teaching college students who either were unemployed or held jobs in altogether different organizations.

Modifying the Standard TKI Instructions for a Specific Conflict Situation

By the late 1970s, I became regularly involved in conducting management training workshops and implementing various consulting programs inside organizations. Not surprisingly, I made considerable use of the TKI assessment, since almost everyone needed to be more comfortable with conflict and learn how to manage workplace conflict much more effectively. I do not recall exactly when I first tried modifying the TKI for a specific conflict situation, but I began experimenting with modifying the TKI's standard instructions so that member responses to the assessment would be specific to how conflicts were being addressed inside the organization. So instead of using the standard TKI instructions, which implicitly ask people to consider ALL situations in their life, I began asking participants to respond to the TKI's 30 A/B items along these lines: "In this organization, or in this group, or in this department . . . how do you usually respond when you find your wishes differing from those of other members?"

When I modified the TKI instructions in this manner, respondents never again asked me whether they should respond to the TKI in terms of their conflict experiences at home or at work. I had now provided them with a specific situation that they could easily keep straight in their minds as they responded to all 30 A/B items on the TKI assessment tool.

Using Two TKI Assessments to Explore the Inside and Outside Organizational Perspective

After having modified the standard TKI instructions for many organizations and work situations in the 1970s and 1980s, by the early 1990s, it occurred to me to ask each member to take TWO TKIs, each with modified instructions. This approach seemed radical at the time, but revealed some valuable information that one TKI, by itself, could never provide.

To make a long story short, when I conduct management training programs or provide consulting services to an intact group or organization, I ask the members to take their first TKI from the perspective of inside their group, department, or organization (however they wish to focus on conflict at work), and then, right afterwards, I ask those same members to take a second TKI from the perspective of outside their group (meaning, how they respond to conflict in all other settings of their life, excluding their current group or department). In essence, this second TKI is much like the original TKI, since it asks respondents to provide their typical, average responses to conflict across many different settings and situations.

Basically, the second TKI asks respondents to provide their "average" or their typical approach to conflict across all those other situations, which necessarily includes conflicts with their family members, friends, neighbors, other organizations, and so forth. Naturally, there will always be some personal preferences at play when an individual chooses to use one conflict mode or another, based on psychological type or style.

In sharp contrast to the outside perspective, when participants focus on their conflict-handling behavior inside their group, team, or organization, there are various systems and processes in an organization that tend to encourage or require members to use certain conflict modes more than others, in contrast to what modes these members typically use across all the other settings in their life.

Incidentally, I expect that the culture of the organization as well as the specific cultural variations within any work group can significantly influence the choice of conflict modes, especially when there are cultural norms along the lines of do not disagree with your boss, do not make waves, do not rock the boat, keep your new ideas to yourself, do not share information with other groups, and so on.

In a similar vein, through various experiences with their organization's reward systems, members might also have learned that it is best not to use the more assertive modes, since that behavior could hurt their chances for promotion if obedience and loyalty are rewarded more favorably than candor and integrity.

In the same organization, the leaders might also be inclined to publicly announce their decisions to members in a rather assertive and authoritative manner, which might compel members to silently accommodate their boss's views. Moreover, group members might simply avoid challenging their managers during any conversation or group meeting.

So what did I learn by having participants take two TKIs, each with modified instructions for the inside and the outside perspective?

Figure 4.1 shows one way of answering that question: Here we see a symbolic organization chart, with the senior executives at the very top of the hierarchy, the next level of managers right below them, followed by the next level of managers or non-supervisory personnel, and so forth. Naturally, large organizations have many more levels, divisions, and groups, but this simplified organization chart is sufficient for our purposes.

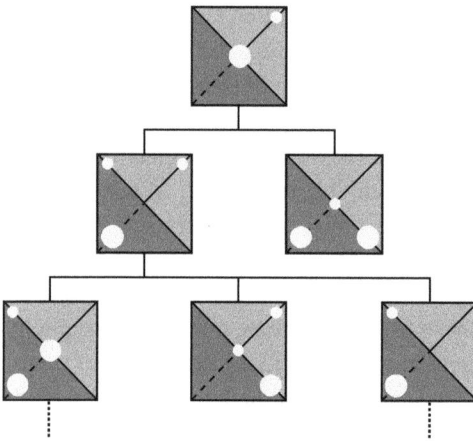

Figure 4.1: An Organization's Inside TKI Results.

Figure 4.1 shows the symbolic organization chart from the inside perspective, which is based on member responses to their first TKI for inside your group, inside your department, or inside your organization.

As you can see, I have found it especially useful to replace each box on the organization chart, which represents a division, department, or workgroup, with the TKI Conflict Model, which then conveniently highlights the particular conflict modes that are being used most often, as shown by the large circles where a conflict mode is positioned on the TKI Conflict Model. At the same time, each box on the chart also highlights the conflict modes that are being used least often, as shown by the small circles on the TKI Conflict Model. For the sake of simplicity and convenience, the con-flict modes that are used moderately are not explicitly designated by any symbol on the TKI Conflict Model. Instead, focusing primarily on those conflict modes that each group or department is possibly using too much or too little tends to provide the most concise information in a visually clear-cut manner.

On this organizational chart, notice that the executives on top of the hierarchy are primarily using the compromising mode, which is moderately assertive, while the next two levels are primarily using the avoiding and accommodating modes, which are the most unassertive modes. What is displayed on this chart is, in fact, a typical result, revealing the overuse of avoiding and accommodating as we move farther down the organization's hierarchy. In fact, it is not unusual to find that the executives at the top of the hierarchy use lots of competing, compromising, and collaborating to address their conflicts inside the organization, while the employees toward the bottom of the hierarchy use lots of avoiding and accommodating to comply with the bosses and managers above them.

On Figure 4.2, the TKI results displayed on each box on the organization chart derives from the outside perspective, meaning that these results were based on members' responses to their second TKI, with the modified instructions to assess their conflict-handling behavior outside their group or organization. As you can see, the more assertive modes are frequently being used outside the organization, and, most striking, this same pattern of conflict-handling behavior emerges up and down the management hierarchy and this pattern is also the same as we look across the various departments and groups at the same level in the organization. Said different,

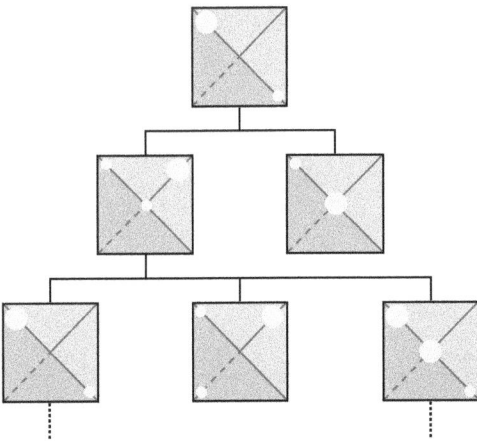

Figure 4.2: An Organization's Outside TKI Results.

every box on the organization chart shows that members are assertive when they approach a conflict situation outside the work setting, as revealed by the frequently used modes of competing, collaborating, and compromising across this entire organization chart.

Now take a quick back-and-forth look between the inside and outside perspective, as vividly portrayed by the two organization charts shown in Figure 4.3. Sometimes, the inside and outside charts are similar for an organization. But most of the time, the two charts are different, which typically reveals that the avoiding and accommodating modes are being used more frequently inside the organization as you move from the senior executive level at the top of the chart, down the hierarchy, to the front-line employees at the bottom of the chart.

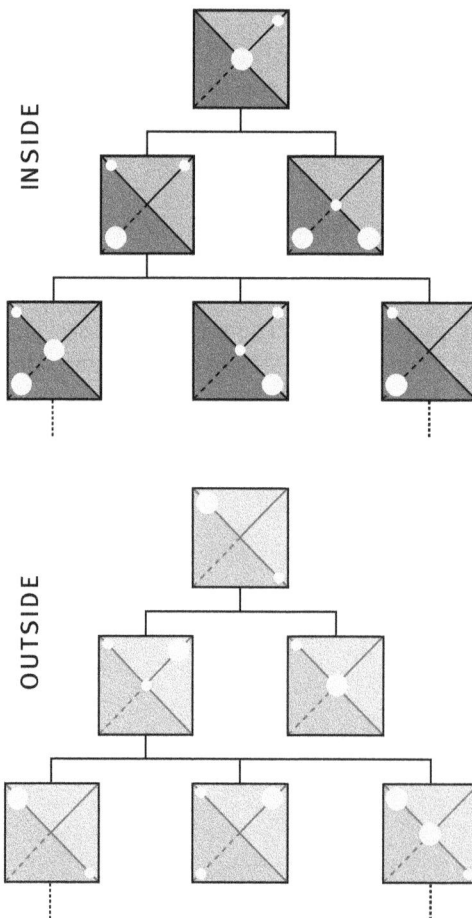

Figure 4.3: Comparing the Inside and Outside TKI Results.

However, I must now confess: Although I have already itemized the probable causes of any large discrepancies between the inside and outside perspectives, such as the organization's culture, the group's culture, the reward system, and the leader's behavior (which are collectively referred to as the organization's systems and processes), technically speaking, my list of probable causes for the differences in the inside and outside perspectives is only a guess, even if it is a good guess based on my knowledge of organizational behavior, since those two TKI assessments are only measuring conflict-handling behavior inside and outside the group. Let me be crystal clear: The TKI only measures conflict-handling behavior and nothing else. The TKI does not measure anything having to do with the systems and processes in an organization, and what impact each of those systems and processes is having on conflict-handling behavior.

More specifically, even if the culture, reward system, and leadership behavior are the principle causes for any observable differences between the inside and outside charts, we still do not know the relative influence of an organization's different systems and processes. Are all these aspects of the organization playing an equal role in shifting members' conflict-handling behavior, or is the culture the chief culprit? Or is it the reward system that compels members to use some modes more than others? Are members more likely to use avoiding and accommodating at the lower levels in the organization due to very assertive, authoritative bosses and leaders?

What is the bottom line here? I cannot emphasize this critical point enough: The TKI only measures conflict-handling behavior in interpersonal settings. It does not measure anything about systems and processes. As a result, to go beyond mere guesses as to why people are approaching conflict differently whether they are inside or outside their organization, we must find a way to measure the impact of systems and processes directly and explicitly and, of course, accurately.

The Complex Hologram: An Organization's Systems and Processes

Before I introduce my Organizational Conflict Instrument and how it explicitly measures the systems and processes in organizations that could be negatively affecting how conflicts are being addressed and resolved, I will first be more specific about what I mean by an organization's systems and processes and why these systems and processes have such a powerful impact on how members approach their workplace conflicts, which might be very different from how members approach conflicts in all the other settings in their life.

In Figure 4.4, I present the "Big Picture" of all aspects of life in an organization, also called, The Complex Hologram, which presents the major topics of organizational behavior that have been studied for ages. I developed the first version of this model back in the late 1970s and then published it in my 1984 book: *Beyond the Quick Fix*.

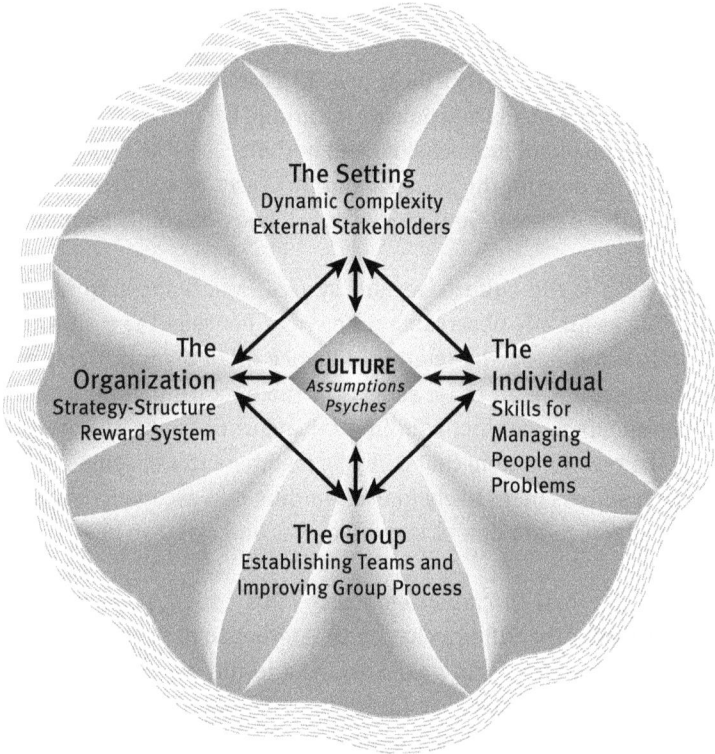

Figure 4.4: The Complex Hologram – Seeing the Big Picture.

Very briefly, on the right side of the Complex Hologram, we can represent all the individuals that are members of the organization, particularly taking note of their individual styles and skills for addressing problems and conflicts. These individuals are officially surrounded by, and thus guided by, the organization's culture, strategy, structure, reward systems, and the immediate work group, which includes, in most cases, a boss or manager. Of course, other organizations and institutions, labeled as "The Setting" on the top of the Complex Hologram, surround the organization itself and make up its external environment. These "External Stakeholders" also affect the kinds of problems and conflicts members face daily.

Overall, the various nodes in the Complex Hologram represent the organization's informal and formal systems (culture, strategy, structure, rewards, groups, and individual skills and styles for managing people and problems). Meanwhile, all the double arrows that are in between these various system nodes represent all the business, management, and learning processes that flow throughout the organization, which include all the tasks, decisions, and actions, which, in essence, include all work-related activities that take place over time, which is exactly what defines any kind of process.

I now present the key principle that derives from the Complex Hologram and thus underscores my inspiration for developing the Organizational Conflict Instrument: Because this key principle is so relevant to life in organizations, I highlight it in bold: **About 80% (or more) of what goes on in an organization is determined by its systems and processes, while only 20% (or less) is determined by member desires or preferences.**

Based on my 2021 book, *Creating a Quantum Organization*, Figure 4.5 provides an even more elaborate model that captures how a completely integrated program of eight tracks can identify and resolve the potential problems and conflicts that are highlighted in the Complex Hologram, which, as we saw before, represents all the systems, processes, and individuals in an organization, including its External Setting, which can dramatically affect which particular conflict modes members choose and use inside their organization.

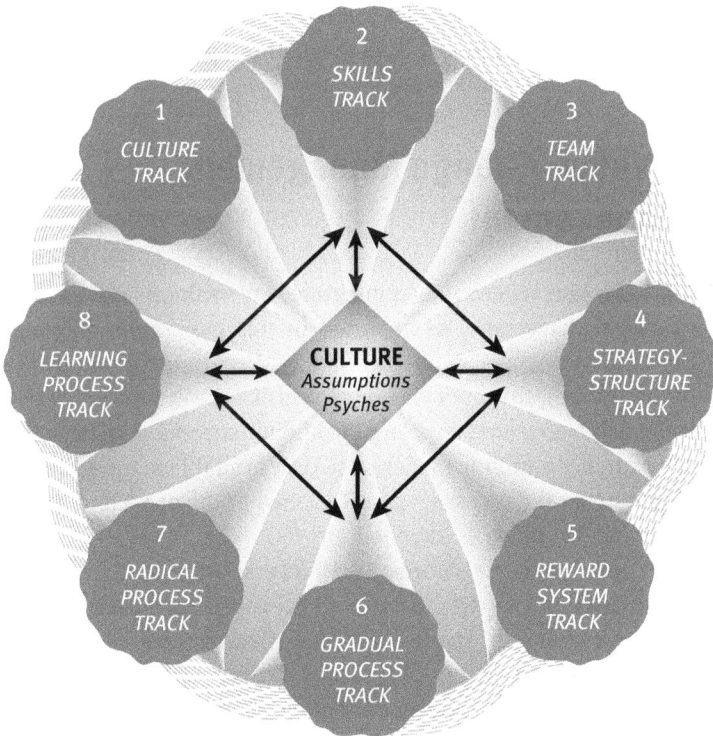

Figure 4.5: The Eight Tracks and the Complex Hologram.

The first three tracks in the sequence of eight tracks represent the quantum infrastructure, also called the informal organization, which considers how well the culture, skills, and teams support long-term organizational success. The next two tracks address the formal systems, which are usually written down on paper or are available in electronic files: Where are we headed (which is termed strategy)? How can we organize all our resources to get there (which is termed structure)? And what do we receive for helping (which is termed rewards)? The last three tracks then enable members to improve the quality and speed of their key processes (decisions and actions that take place over time), as guided by their quantum infrastructure and their formal systems.

What is the principle behind this elaborate sequence of quantum transformation? Each track establishes the foundation for achieving the full potential of each subsequent track. Alternatively, implementing a track out of sequence will make it exceedingly difficult to achieve what each track can provide for the organization and its members. For example, trying to renew the strategy-structure of the organization when the culture discourages members from expressing their true beliefs and feelings in the presence of bosses or managers will undermine any discussion of strategy-structure and will therefore prevent any new strategy-structure document on paper from guiding member behavior on the job. The same logic applies to any other out-of-sequence applications of one or more tracks to quantum transformation.

The Quantum Wheel: Change Management and Conflict Management

Figure 4.6 presents the Quantum Wheel, which integrates my work on both conflict management and change management. As captured in this panoramic diagram, while the HUB of "The Quantum Wheel" is conflict management (represented by the Thomas-Kilmann Conflict Model), the outer ring or spokes of "The Quantum Wheel" are the eight tracks for achieving long-term organizational success and personal meaning. But for all five conflict-handling modes to be fully available to the membership, the organization's systems and processes must first create "the right conditions" for effectively using each conflict mode as intended.

What are the right conditions? The systems and processes that surround each individual must actively allow and support the use of all five conflict-handling modes, so organizational members can choose and use the most effective mode, depending on the key attributes of the situation.

If the surrounding systems and processes only allow the members to use the accommodating mode or the avoiding mode, because members do not feel safe in asserting themselves in the workplace, they will not be able to improve their systems and processes. At the same time, the members will not be able to effectively address

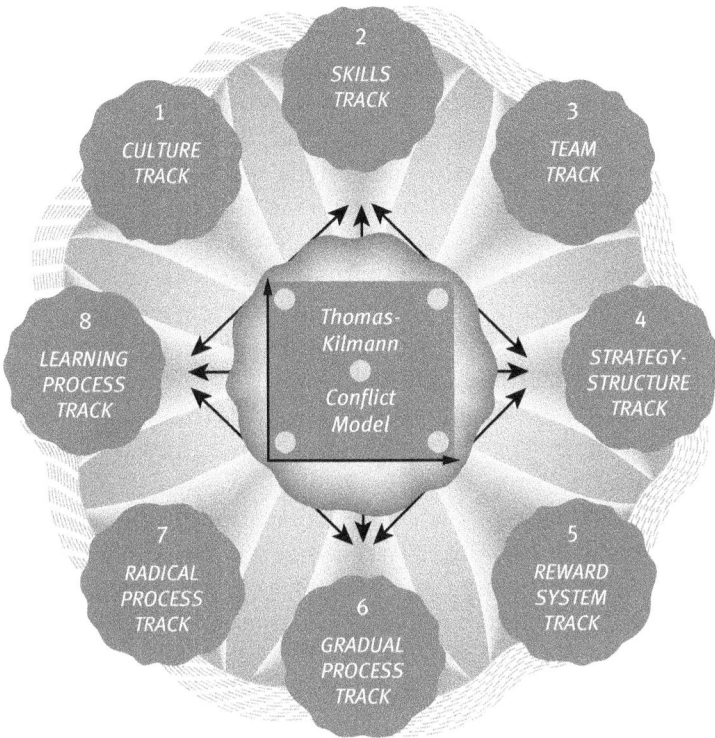

Figure 4.6: The Quantum Wheel.

and resolve all their other business and technical problems if they do not feel comfortable or safe in asserting their knowledge, wisdom, and experience in front of others in the organization.

It is so important that you appreciate this key point: It takes supportive and fully aligned systems and processes for members to not only use all five conflict modes, depending on the key attributes of the situation, but also to use the appropriate conflict modes for successfully addressing all the organization's business, technical, and management problems. Basically, for the organization to succeed both short term and long term, its systems and processes must actively support effective conflict management for its most important problems and conflicts.

When Is It Best to Use Each Conflict Assessment Option?

Given the several choices that are now available for assessing conflict-handling behavior, it is not surprising that I am often asked to help people decide when it is best to use each available assessment tool. Specifically, I am often asked two basic questions. The first type of question is simply this: When is it best to use one TKI per person with those standard TKI instructions? When is it best to use one TKI with modified instructions for inside your group? The second type of question is along these lines: When is it best to use two TKIs per person, each with the modified instructions for inside and outside your group? When is it best to use the Kilmann Organizational Conflict Instrument instead of either one or two TKIs per person?

Regarding the first type of question, having each participant take one TKI with those standard TKI instructions is still the best choice when teaching students or conducting training programs when the respondents are either not employed or come from different organizations. The use of that one standard TKI per person helps respondents learn more about their conflict-handling behavior across all their interpersonal encounters, since there is no immediate interest in learning about their behavior in any specific work or family setting.

However, when the participants all come from the same intact group or intact organization and the focus of the training is on conflict-handling behavior in that particular team or organizational setting, that's the time to modify the standard TKI instructions to a focus on "inside your group" in order to make the assessment more accurate for that specific group or organization, and thus not to dilute the results by members possibly thinking about other situations as they respond to the TKI, which they might be prone to do if they are given the TKI's standard instructions.

Regarding the second type of question that I'm often asked, in those cases when the consultant or trainer wants to know the overall, general, effect of an organization's systems and processes on members' conflict-handling behavior, it's then a good idea to consider asking members to take two TKIs per person, so it becomes possible to discover if members are using different conflict modes inside versus outside their group or organization.

However, as I have stressed earlier, although the two TKIs provide a general impression, an educated guess, about whether or not the organization's systems and processes, as a whole, are having a negative influence on members' conflict-handling behavior, asking members to take two TKIs per person with modified instructions cannot possibly provide any specific information about which particular systems and processes are negatively affecting members and which particular systems and processes are, in fact, positively inspiring members to do their very best.

As a result, when consultants, trainer, and facilitators want to know which particular and specific systems conflicts are negatively affecting members' performance and satisfaction, it is only by having members take the Kilmann Organizational Conflict Instrument that it is possible to obtain accurate information about which specific systems and processes might be undermining the available talent, knowledge, experience, and passion in the organization.

The KOCI Instrument for Assessing Organizational Conflict

Now that I have provided a detailed summary of my efforts to measure conflict-handling behavior in organizations, including my work on change management and quantum transformation, you will be able to fully appreciate what the Kilmann Organizational Conflict Instrument (KOCI) can do for organizations and their members.

First, I will summarize the two parts of the instrument and I will then show the kind of diagnostic information that this instrument reveals, which can then inspire the organization to implement some version of the eight tracks in order to resolve any identified systems conflicts that can get in the way of long-term organizational success and personal meaning.

For Part 1 of the KOCI instrument, you are asked to respond to twenty-seven systems conflicts that derive explicitly from the Complex Hologram. By the way, I purposely constructed separate items for strategy and structure since each of these two formal systems is so important as a guide to member behavior. Later, however, these two formal systems are combined into one strategy-structure category, since structure is always needed to implement strategy, which conveniently corresponds to the strategy-structure track.

More specifically, for Part 1 of the Organizational Conflict Instrument, you are asked to indicate how often you are negatively affected by each of the "systems conflicts" on the instrument by selecting your response on a five-point scale: (1) when you are never affected negatively by that systems conflict; (2) when you are rarely affected negatively by that systems conflict; (3) when you are occasionally affected negatively; (4) when you are frequently affected negatively; and (5) when you are always being negatively affected by that systems conflict.

So you can get a sense what is meant by a systems conflict, here is an item from Part 1 of the instrument concerning the structure of the organization: "I have neither the necessary authority nor the sufficient resources to achieve my assigned goals and objectives, yet I am held accountable for the results." Here is a systems conflict regarding teams in the organization: "During meetings, some members are more reserved than others, but no one makes a special effort to ask those quieter members to express their opinions or ideas."

Here are the instructions for Part 2 of the online KOCI instrument: For each of the nine systems conflicts (treating strategy and structure separately for the time being), you're asked to indicate your relative use of the five conflict-handling modes, by arranging five statements from 1 to 5, where the statement you would drag into the #1 position is the conflict mode you used most often in approaching or trying to resolve that particular kind of systems conflict. Then, you would drag the statement representing your next used approach to that systems conflict into the #2 position, and so forth, eventually dragging your least used conflict mode into the #5 position.

Although this instrument is measuring the same five classic conflict modes as the TKI, the Organizational Conflict Instrument wants you to think of those specific systems conflicts and how you tend to approach them, which is quite different than simply responding to the TKI according to how you approach interpersonal conflict inside your organization.

In case you are wondering, I word the conflict modes on Part 2 of KOCI instrument very differently from the way in which the TKI's 30 items are worded. In particular, the avoiding mode is always worded by this same description for each of the nine systems conflicts: "Sometimes, it's simply not worth the extra time and effort it would take to discuss and examine this particular aspect of the organization, since we're unlikely to find a good solution."

Similarly, the collaborating mode is always worded by this same description for each of the nine systems conflicts "I always ask my boss or team members to take the necessary time to thoroughly discuss this particular aspect of the organization, so we can develop a creative solution." The three other conflict modes, completing, compromising, and accommodating, are also worded in terms of addressing systems conflicts in organizations, not interpersonal conflict in general (which is the prime focus of the TKI assessment).

Regarding how the systems conflicts are worded on Part 2 of the KOCI instrument, I can provide an example. Here is the systems conflict between the organization's reward system and its individual members: "How are you likely to respond when you experience the negative aspects of your organization's rewards regarding the design and functioning of the performance appraisal system?" For this item, you would arrange those five statements into positions 1 through 5 to reflect your relative tendencies to use those conflict modes to approach your reward systems conflicts. You would then do the same for the remaining items in Part 2 of the Organizational Conflict Instrument.

Interpreting an Individual's KOCI Results: Before and After the Eight Tracks

Let us now interpret the actual results for an individual: As seen in Figure 7.1, the raw scores for the systems conflicts are placed in the outer ring of the Quantum Wheel, including which ones are H, M, and L, as based on the established ranges for High, Medium, and Low, which are provided in the instrument's interpretive materials.

As you can see on Figure 4.7, there are three systems conflicts that scored in the high range, which suggests that this respondent to the instrument is frequently being hampered by negative experiences with the culture of her organization or group, the way in which her team's meetings are being conducted, and the lack of clarity and alignment in strategy-structure. These three high scores suggest some serious barriers to long-term organizational success.

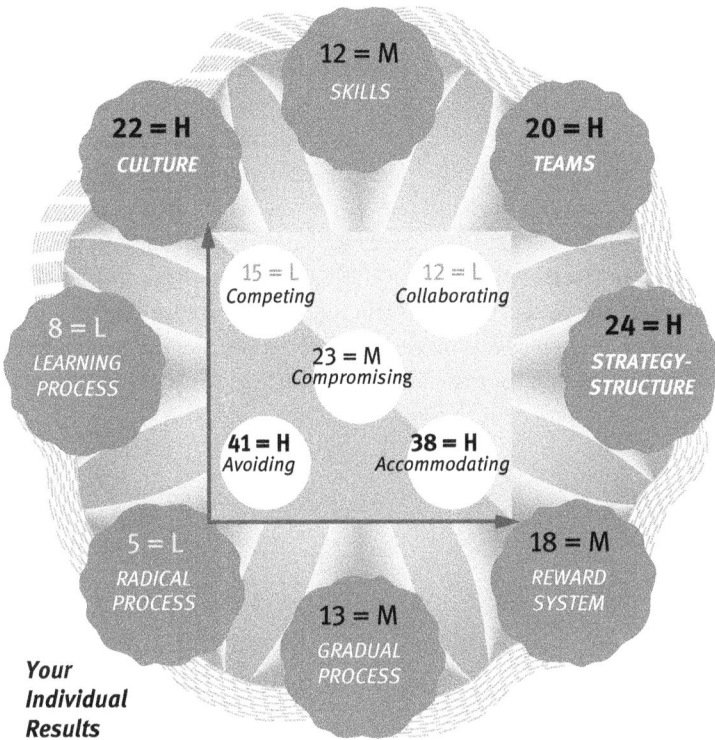

Figure 4.7: KOCI Results for an Individual (First Time).

Three other conflicts are medium in their impact, since they are occasionally interfering with the person's performance and satisfaction: skills, the reward system, and the processes that flow within her group. Yet two systems conflicts are low in their impact, shown by the grayed letter L: radical process and learning process improvement. But not until those earlier organizational conflicts are resolved might the last two process tracks become more challenging.

In the HUB of that same Quantum Wheel, you can see the person's results on the TKI Conflict Model, which shows that avoiding and accommodating are in the HIGH range. As a result, this person is almost always being negatively affected by cultural norms and team dynamics that seem to pressure members to remain quiet, not to express different points of view, and not to disagree with the boss (that is, to avoid such conflicts); or, alternatively, to defer to the experience of other members or managers, which means to accommodate others when considering how to improve the formal systems in the organization.

Indeed, the assertive modes of competing and collaborating are in the low range, which confirms that this person is not bringing all her talent, wisdom, ideas, and experience into the workplace. However, once the eight tracks are underway, members will be given the chance to learn more about how and when to use the five conflict modes, and especially how to change the informal systems regarding their culture, skills, and teams, so all five modes are always available to all members and will be used successfully, as needed.

As shown on Figure 4.8, let us now interpret the results for the same individual after she took the Organizational Conflict Instrument a second time, about nine months later. This time, only the H, M, and L are displayed, which makes it visually easy to immediately focus on the key systems conflicts: These results suggest that the integrated program of eight tracks has been proceeding since the culture, skills, and teams are no longer frequently distracting this member, although more skill development might still be needed. Progress is also occurring for strategy-structure and the reward system, which sets the stage for resolving the conflicts in the last three process tracks of quantum transformation.

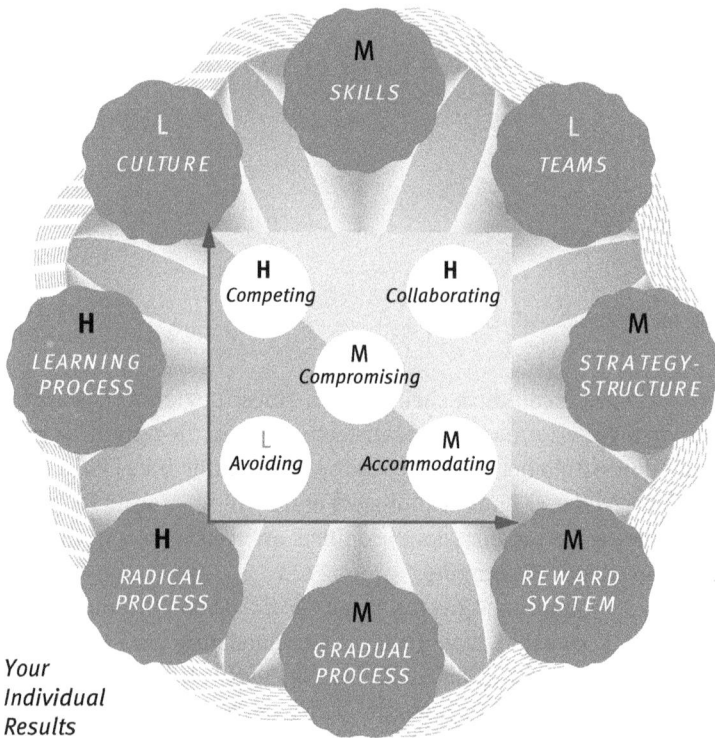

Figure 4.8: KOCI Results for an Individual (Second Time).

In the hub of this Quantum Wheel, you can also review the nine-month follow-up results on the TKI Conflict Model: The assertive modes are now high while avoiding is low, so the pendulum has obviously swung from unassertive (from the prior graph) to highly assertive (using lots of competing and collaborating behavior). Usually, before the results display a balanced TKI profile (which is revealed by the presence of mostly medium scores on the five conflict modes), members go from the extreme use of a few modes to the extreme use of the other modes!

Conclusion

As a reminder, the first key principle that derives from the Complex Hologram: About 80% of what takes place in an organization is determined by its systems and processes, while 20% is determined by member desires or preferences. Now, I will add the second key principle to keep in mind, which follows directly from the first principle: Choose the conflict-handling mode that best matches the key attributes of the situation.

Here is the third key principle to always remember: In the short term, the organization's systems and processes are fixed, so the use of one or more conflict modes might be significantly constrained by the nature and quality of the key attributes of the situation, which are determined by the organization's systems and processes. But in the long term, those systems, and processes (which determine "the situation" for conflict resolution) can be transformed, which then changes the eight key attributes of any conflict situation to support the use of all five modes, as needed.

This third key principle reminds us that the collaborating mode, which is essential for resolving systems conflicts in a manner that satisfies the needs and concerns of all internal and external stakeholders, can only work successfully when the key attributes of the situation support using this mode, as in the case of stimulating (but not overwhelming) stress, high levels of trust among members, sufficient time to address the topic, and so forth. But if the current systems and processes do not support the collaborating mode (and, in fact, primarily support using the avoiding or compromising mode), then members, in the short term, will not be able to use the collaborating mode to resolve their systems conflicts nor will they be able to collaborate successfully on any of their other business, management, and technical problems.

Eventually, however, the organization can transform its systems and processes to support the use of the collaborating mode (as well as all the other conflict modes) to resolve not only any lingering organizational conflicts, but also to resolve any of their other complex conflicts and challenges.

References

Kilmann, R. H. Beyond the Quick Fix: Managing Five Tracks to Organizational Success (Washington DC: Beard Books, 1984).

Kilmann, R. H. Kilmann Organizational Conflict Instrument (Newport Coast, CA: Kilmann Diagnostics, 2020).

Kilmann, R. H. Creating a Quantum Organization: The Whys & Hows of Implementing Eight Tracks for Long-Term Success (Newport Coast, CA: Kilmann Diagnostics, 2021).

Thomas, K. W., and R. H. Kilmann. 1974. The Thomas-Kilmann Conflict Mode Instrument (Sunnyvale, CA: The Myers-Briggs Company, 1974).

Ekaterina Denkova, Costanza Alessio, Jordan Barry, Anthony
P. Zanesco, Scott L. Rogers, Katsiaryna Matusevich, Amishi P. Jha

Chapter 5
Mindfulness Training in Organizational Settings: An Empirical Look at the Research

Abstract: The workplace is commonly conceptualized as a high-stress and high-demand environment. Work-related stressors may have deleterious effects on employees' cognitive functioning, well-being, and work productivity. One promising approach to mitigate such effects is mindfulness training (MT). Yet, there is a paucity of applied research on best practices for MT implementation in organizational settings. We present a proof-of-concept study that examined the efficacy of a contextualized MT program delivered by trained trainers who were embedded within an organization (i.e., Human Resources professionals). We propose that engaging in MT contextualized and delivered in this manner may benefit the very same domains reported to be negatively impacted by work-related stress and demands. Our proposal aligns with a leading organizational stress theory, the Job Demands-Resources (JD-R) theory and suggests that when offered by employers and embedded within organizational settings, MT may serve as a powerful organizational-level job resource targeting the strengthening of employees' personal resources.

Keywords: mindfulness, cognitive functioning, well-being, stress, JD-R theory

The overarching purpose of this chapter is to provide empirical evidence on how to address challenges emerging from high demands and time pressure in organizational settings through innovative and scalable delivery of mindfulness training (MT). First, based on a leading organizational stress theory, we briefly describe the impact of job demands and stress on employees and the urgent need for comprehensive and practical solutions to build job and personal resources. Second, we introduce MT and review its potential as a fruitful solution to build those resources. Then, we present an empirical example of an applied study examining the impact of a short-form MT program on employees when delivered by professionals embedded in the organization who are highly familiar with the workplace context (i.e., Human Resources (HR) professionals). The chapter concludes with a discussion of how these emerging findings have the potential to inform organizational stress theories while providing practical solutions for organizational challenges.

https://doi.org/10.1515/9783110746365-005

Challenges in Organizational Settings: Job Demands and Resources

Over the past decade, the workplace has come to be increasingly categorized by organizational researchers as a high-stress, high-demand environment (e.g., Harvey et al., 2017; Johnson et al., 2020; Reb et al., 2020). Frequently referred to as VUCA (volatile, uncertain, complex, and ambiguous) – an acronym coined in U.S. military education (Barber, 1992) and later embraced in the business vernacular, today's organizational environment is rife with job demands typified by excessive workload, time pressure, and interpersonal conflicts, requiring employees to continuously expend resources to meet demands (Bakker & de Vries, 2021; Crivelli et al., 2019; Schaufeli, 2017).

A leading organizational stress theory, the Job Demands-Resources (JD-R) theory (Bakker & Demerouti, 2018), points out that job demands, namely those aspects of work that cost energy and require sustained cognitive and emotional effort, consistently predict job stress and burnout. Work-related stress and job burnout are major occupational risk factors due to their strong association with deleterious outcomes in cognitive functioning, emotional well- being, as well as job satisfaction and efficacy (Bakker et al., 2014). There is mounting evidence that employees experiencing burnout have cognitive performance challenges related to attentional difficulties (Van Der Linden et al., 2005), feel emotionally exhausted, and report a reduced sense of self-efficacy and job accomplishment (Maslach et al., 2001). Further, burned-out employees may also negatively affect their coworkers by causing personal conflicts at work (Maslach et al., 2001). Indeed, "when people's resources are outstretched or exhausted, they enter a defensive mode to preserve the self which is often defensive, aggressive, and may become irrational" (Hobfoll et al., 2018; p. 104).

To counteract such damaging personal and social contagion effects, evidence-based approaches are needed to bolster cognitive functions, emotional well-being, job efficacy, and satisfaction. As proposed by the JD-R theory, job and personal resources are needed to foster employee well-being, work efficacy, and engagement (Bakker et al., 2014). Job resources (e.g., training opportunities, social support) and personal resources (e.g., self-efficacy, self-development) initiate a motivational process that reduces the negative impact of job demands and is associated with improved emotional well-being (Bakker & Demerouti, 2017, 2018; Crawford et al., 2010; Demerouti et al., 2001). Employees with higher job and personal resources are better equipped to adapt to workplace demands in a more effective way (Hobfoll et al., 2018). One promising approach to enhancing job and personal resources in organizational settings is through mindfulness training (Ahlvik et al., 2018; Good et al., 2016; Roche et al., 2020). We argue that when offered by employers and embedded within organizational settings, mindfulness training (MT) serves as an organizational-level job resource enhancer, targeting the strengthening of personal resources.

Mindfulness Training: A Promising Solution for Challenges in Organizational Settings

Mindfulness is defined as "a mental mode characterized by attention to present-moment experience without judgment, elaboration, or emotional reactivity" (Jha et al., 2010, p. 54). MT programs typically include a combination of didactic content, trainer-led discussions on how to cultivate present-centered attention, and experiential engagement in core mindfulness practices, such as focused attention and open monitoring (Lutz et al., 2015). The initial 'first-generation' MT programs, such as Mindfulness-Based Stress Reduction (MBSR; Kabat-Zinn, 1990) and Mindfulness-Based Cognitive Therapy (MBCT, Segal et al., 2002), were introduced as interventions targeting symptom management and reduction across a variety of clinical populations (Abbott et al., 2014; Lauche et al., 2013). Growing evidence has demonstrated that, indeed, MBSR and MBCT, can alleviate psychological and physical symptoms in various clinical conditions, such as depression (Goldberg et al., 2019; Kuyken et al., 2016), psychosis (Khoury et al., 2013), cancer (Cramer et al., 2012), and vascular disease (e.g., Abbott et al., 2014). Importantly, MBSR and MBCT have been shown to be beneficial for healthy, non-clinical individuals by improving emotional well-being and reducing self-reported stress, depression, and anxiety (Khoury et al., 2015; Querstret et al., 2020). This promising evidence has led to an increased interest in the broader dissemination of MT programs in the professional domains of health care, business, military, and others, as a tool to enhance cognitive functions, improve emotional well-being and increase efficacy and engagement in the workplace (Good et al., 2016).

From a cognitive training perspective, it has been suggested that engaging in MT practice strengthens core cognitive functions, such as attention (Jha et al., 2020). Strengthening attention has been proposed to be a gateway to achieving a variety of MT-related benefits in the workplace (Good et al., 2016). As stated by Roche et al. (2020), "Through higher-quality attention, mindfulness helps us think, feel and act better" (p. 3) and "individuals who attend, think, feel and act in a mindful way also feel and function better at work" (p. 4). With this premise in mind, MT seems to be entering the mainstream as a viable tool to bolster personal resources to promote improvements in three main domains: cognitive (e.g., attending and thinking better), emotional (e.g., feeling better), and workplace (e.g., being more efficient and engaged).

While there is promising evidence for workplace MT (Bartlett et al., 2019; Denkova et al., 2020a; Heckenberg et al., 2018; Vonderin et al., 2020), there is a paucity of applied research on best practices for MT implementation in organizations that take into consideration organizational challenges (Roche et al., 2020; Rupprecht et al., 2018). Chief among these are time requirements, program contextualization, and trainers' knowledge of the particular workplace context. Indeed, the two most well-studied and implemented programs (MBSR and MBCT) emphasize stress and clinical symptom reduction and require about 26 hours of in-class training with an instructor and 45 minutes of daily out-of-class practice by participants over an 8- week interval (Marx, 2019; Crane et al., 2010; Segal et al., 2018). These time requirements are often prohibitively burdensome to offer in time-pressured organizations, warranting examination of shorter duration programs that are also amenable to contextualization for non-clinical settings (Creswell, 2017). Recent studies suggest that MT delivery by trainers well-versed in the organizational norms and culture may be an expeditious route by which to achieve workplace contextualization (Jha et al., 2020; Denkova et al., 2021). Indeed, delivery of training via trainers familiar with the specific context, culture, and challenges employees and teams face every day at work holds promise for increasing program receptivity and accessibility.

Below, we describe a recent MT study in a workplace that asks: Can a short-form contextualized MT program delivered by context-familiar trainers benefit employees' ability to pay attention, feel better, and feel more efficient and productive at work?

Empirical Example: Mindfulness Training Study in an Organizational Setting

Synopsis: Two HR professionals, who previously participated in an MT training practicum to learn how to deliver a short-form MT program, offered the MT program to employees in their organization. Employees who volunteered to participate in the MT program (referred to as the MT group) were compared to employees who did not participate in the training and served as a no-training control group (NTC group) on metrics that examined three domains: cognitive, emotional, and workplace. Two key questions were explored: (i) Does MT delivered by trained in-house HR professionals benefit cognitive, emotional, and workplace outcomes in employees? (ii) If so, are the benefits in each of these domains related to each other?

Participants: Participants were employees in a construction management company in South Florida. Fifty employees volunteered to participate in a short-form MT program at work (MT group; 30 females; mean ± SD age: 37.62 ± 10.67 years). Another group of 45 employees served as a no-training control group (NTC group; 37 females; mean ± SD age: 40.51 ± 11.85 years). All participants provided informed consent in accordance with the Institutional Review Board of the University of Miami.

Mindfulness Training Program: The MT program delivered in the present study is the Mindfulness-Based Attention Training (MBAT,[1] Jha et al., 2020). MBAT is a struc-

---

1 Amishi P. Jha and Scott L. Rogers are co-authors and copyright holders of the Mindfulness- Based Attention Training (MBAT) Program. This project was supported by funding provided by the Lennar Foundation to APJ.

tured and manualized 8-hour program amenable to contextualization for various military (Jha et al., 2020; Zanesco et al., 2019) and high-demand civilian settings (Denkova et al., 2020a; Denkova et al., 2021). MBAT focuses on bolstering cognitive functioning, resilience, and emotional well-being by familiarizing trainees with mindfulness-related concepts and practices that can be integrated into their personal and professional lives. The program includes four central themes (i.e., concentration, body awareness, receptivity, and connection) and their corresponding mindfulness exercises (i.e., focused attention, body scan, open monitoring, and connection). In the present study, MBAT was delivered in-person by HR professionals at work over 4 consecutive weeks with two, 1-hour, sessions per week. In addition, participants were assigned 15 minutes of daily practice to be completed outside of the class sessions.

Data Collection & Metrics: Participants completed two testing sessions (T1 and T2) separated by a 4-week interval over which the MT group received the MBAT program, and the NTC group did not. Testing was completed online via Inquisit Web (Millisecond Software, LLC), an online platform that allows remote data collection for research purposes. Each testing session included metrics related to the cognitive (i.e., attention), emotional (i.e., feel well) and workplace (i.e., being efficient in work engagement) domains.

Cognitive Domain: Attentional performance was measured using the Sustained-Attention-to-Response Task (SART; Robertson et al., 1997). In the SART, single digits (0 through 9) are presented on the computer screen one at a time for 250 msec each, with 900 msec between digit presentation. Participants are instructed to press the spacebar for all digits ('go' trials), except for the number 3 ('no-go' trials), which occurred on only 5% of the trials. SART performance is indexed by A', a signal detection measure, which considers performance on 'no-go' and 'go' trials. A' commonly ranges from 0.5 (chance performance, i.e., responding randomly) to 1 (perfect performance, i.e., always withholding responses to the number 3 and always responding to all other numbers).

Daily cognitive failures were assessed using the Cognitive Failure Questionnaire (CFQ; Broadbent et al, 1982) which asks participants how frequently they experience everyday attentional lapses with questions such as "Do you fail to hear people speaking to you when you are doing something else?" Higher CFQ scores indicate more frequent cognitive failures in daily life.

Emotional Domain: Positive and negative affective states were assessed using the 10-item Positive and Negative Affect Schedule (PANAS; Watson et al., 1988) in which participants rate the extent to which they felt positive (e.g., inspired, determined) or negative (e.g., afraid, upset) emotions over the past month. Scores are calculated separately for positive affect (PA) and negative affect (NA) with higher score indicating higher PA and NA, respectively.

Perceived stress was assessed using the 10-item Perceived Stress Scale (PSS; Cohen etal., 1983), which asks participants to rate the frequency of their stress in the last month by answering questions such as "In the last month, how often have you felt nervous and stressed?" Higher PSS scores indicate frequent experience of stress in everyday life. Anxiety and depression levels were assessed using the 4-item Patient Health Questionnaire (PHQ4; Kroenke et al., 2009), which asks participants how frequently they were "feeling nervous, anxious or on edge" in the last two weeks. Higher PHQ4 score indicates frequent experiences of anxiety and depression symptoms.

Workplace Domain: Self-efficacy was assessed using the 6-item subscale of the General Self-Efficacy Scale (GSE6; Schwarzer & Jerusalem, 1995) by asking participants to rate how true statements were to them, such as "Thanks to my resourcefulness, I know how to handle unforeseen situations." Higher GSE6 score indicates greater perceived sense of self-efficacy.

Work Enjoyment was assessed using the 4-item "Work Enjoyment" sub-scale of the Work-Related Flow Inventory (WOLF; Bakker, 2008), which asked participants to rate how often they felt a certain way in the workplace, such as "My work gives me a good feeling". Higher scores indicated greater experience of work enjoyment.

Results

Question 1: Does MT delivered by HR professionals benefit cognitive, emotional, and workplace outcomes?

We used linear mixed models to compare groups (MT vs. NTC) over time (T1 vs. T2) separately for each outcome of interest. To maximize the sample size, an intent-to-treat approach was applied, in which all participants regardless of their dropout/ withdrawal status and irrespective of whether the individual completed all testing and training sessions (descriptive statistics for each outcome are included in Supplemental Table 1. All supplemental materials are available at https://osf.io/nvx5c/ files/). The group by time interactions, which represents the group-wise differences in the amount of change in a particular metric from T1 to T2, are reported for each metric below (complete results are reported in Supplemental Table 2).

For attentional performance (SART A'), the results revealed a significant group by time interaction, $F (1, 47.05) = 5.66$, $p = .021$, reflecting a greater positive increase over time in A' in MT relative to NTC (see Figure 5.1A). No significant group by time interaction was observed for CFQ, $F (1, 57.62) = 2.32$, $p = .133$.

For PANAS, the results revealed a significant group by time interaction for PA, $F (1, 56.23) = 8.93$, $p = .004$, reflecting a greater increase over time in positive affect for MT relative to NTC (see Figure 5.1B). No significant interaction was observed for NA, $F (1, 56.53) = 3.05$, $p = .086$. For PSS, the results revealed a significant group by time interaction, $F (1, 53.72) = 6.97$, $p = .011$, reflecting a greater decrease over time in perceived stress for MT relative to NTC. For PHQ4, the results revealed a significant group by time interaction, $F(1, 68.41) = 7.35, p = .008$, reflecting a greater decrease over time in anxiety and depression for MT relative to NTC (see Figure 5.1B).

For GSE6, results revealed a significant group by time interaction, $F(1, 57.17) = 5.65, p = .021$, reflecting in a greater increase over time in self-efficacy for MT relative to NTC (see Figure 5.1C). No significant group by time interaction was observed for WOLF, $F(1, 52.94) = 0.33, p = .567$

The relationships between emotional well-being and workplace (self- efficacy) benefits are shown in D for positive affect (top) and anxiety and depression (bottom). The bar graphs are based on estimated mean difference and standard errors. Together, these results suggest that MT delivered by trained HR professionals had salutary effects for each of the domains examined. Specifically, MT-related increases were observed in sustained attention, positive affect, and self-efficacy, and MT-related reductions were found for perceived stress, anxiety, and depression.

Question 2: Do benefits in the three domains relate to each other?

We performed a series of Pearson's correlations between the change over time scores (score at T2 minus score at T1) for the subset of outcomes demonstrating MT-related improvements in the MT group, per above (see Supplemental Table 3 for full correlation matrix).

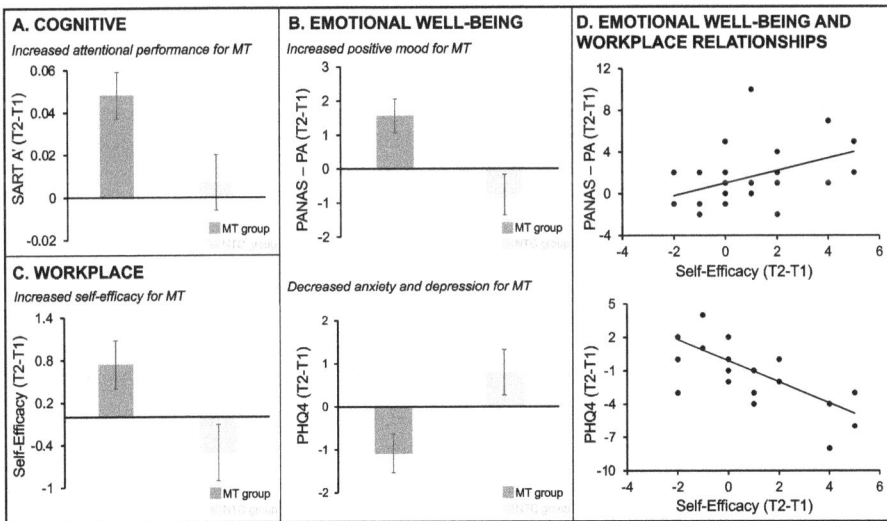

Figure 5.1: MT-related benefits in the (A) cognitive, (B) emotional well-being, and (C) workplace outcomes.

Change over time scores in positive affect were significantly positively correlated with change over time scores in self efficacy (r = 0.433, p = .022), such that across all MT participants, those with greater increases in positive affect also demonstrated greater improvements in self efficacy (see Figure 5.1D, top). In addition, a significant negative correlation was observed between change over time scores in anxiety and depression and self-efficacy (r = $-$ 0.685; p < .001), such that participants wither greater reductions in anxiety and depression demonstrated greater improvements self-efficacy (see Figure 5.1D, bottom). Furthermore, we observed that decreases in perceived stress were associated with increases in work enjoyment (r = $-$ 0.449, p = .017). These results suggest that benefits on the emotional outcomes were related to benefits in workplace outcomes.

Conclusion

The present findings suggest that engaging in a short-form MT program that is contextualized and delivered by trained trainers who are embedded in the organization may benefit the very same domains reported to be negatively impacted by work-related demands and stress. These findings are consistent with the view, inspired by the JD-R theory, that job-related resources, in the form of workplace implementation of an MT program, bolster personal resources, which has salutary effects on employees across three key domains: cognitive, emotional well-being, and workplace. Importantly, these results also suggest that MT delivery by context familiar trainers is a viable approach to improving the accessibility and scalability to MT, as a method by which to build job and personal resources. As such, organizational stress theories such as the JD-R theory, should consider incorporating MT as a viable resource builder in the workplace.

We note that we did not see direct MT-related benefits to work enjoyment. Yet, the correlational results revealed that decreases in perceived stress were associated with increases in work enjoyment. This finding suggests that work enjoyment may be sensitive to individual differences in stress and therefore highlights the need to consider individual variability in outcomes of interest (Tang & Braver, 2020).

While these results provide promising initial evidence for the benefits of MT delivered by HR professionals in an organization, we acknowledge that this is a preliminary study with a relatively small sample size, limited number of outcomes for each of the domains that was examined, and non-random group assignment. Future studies should correct for these short- comings and expand the research scope to examine MT's putative benefits for a broader range of workplace outcomes, from interpersonal interactions and team dynamics to productivity and job performance, leadership, and management.

References

Abbott, R. A., Whear, R., Rodgers, L. R., Betherl, A., Coon, J. T., Kuyken, W. Stein, K., & Dickens, C. (2014). Effectiveness of Mindfulness-Based Stress Reduction and Mindfulness Based Cognitive Therapy in vascular disease. *Journal of Psychosomatic Research*, *76*(5), 341–351. https://doi.org/10.1016/j.jpsychores.2014.02.012

Ahlvik, C., Liddy, C. J., Reina, C., Good, J. D., & Reb, J. M. (2018). Overworked and under- resourced: A mindfulness intervention for middle manager well-being. *Academy of Management Proceedings*, *1*, 14938. https://doi.org/10.5465/AMBPP.2018.14938abstract

Bakker, A. B., (2008). The Work-Related Flow Inventory: Construction and initial validation of the WOLF. *Journal of Vocational Behavior*, *72*, 400–414. https://doi.org/10.1016/j.jvb.2007.11.007

Bakker, A. B., & Demerouti, E. (2017). Job Demands–Resources theory: Taking stock and looking forward. *Journal of Occupational Health Psychology*, *22*(3), 273–285. https://doi.org/10.1037/ocp0000056

Bakker, A. B., & Demerouti, E. (2018). Multiple levels in Job Demands-Resources theory: Implications for employee well-being and performance. In E. Diener, S. Oishi, & L. Tay (Eds.), *Handbook of wellbeing*. Salt Lake City, UT: DEF Publishers. DOI:nobascholar.com

Bakker, A. B., Demerouti, E., & Sanz Vergel, A. I. (2014). Burnout and work engagement: The JD-R approach. *Annual Review of Organizational Psychology and Organizational Behavior*, *1*(1). https://doi.org/10.1146/annurev-orgpsych-031413-091235

Bakker, A. B., & de Vries, J. D. (2021). Job Demands-Resources theory and self-regulation: new explanations and remedies for job burnout. *Anxiety, Stress & Coping: An International Journal*, *34*(1), 1–21. https://doi.org/10.1080/10615806.2020.1797695

Barber, A. E., Dunham, R. B., & Formisano, R. A. (1992). The impact of flexible benefits on employee satisfaction: A field study. *Personnel Psychology*, *45*(1), 55–74. https://doi.org/10.1111/j.1744-6570.1992.tb00844.x

Barlett, L., Martin, A., Neil, A. L., Memish, K., Otahal, P., Kilpatrick, M., & Sanderson, K. (2019). A systematic review and meta-analysis of workplace mindfulness training randomized controlled trials. *Journal Occupational Health Psychology*, *24*(1), 108–126. https://doi.org/10.1037/ocp0000146

Broadbent, D. E., Cooper, P. F., FitzGerald, P., & Parkes, K. R. (1982). The Cognitive Failures Questionnaire (CFQ) and its correlates. *British Journal of Clinical Psychology*, *21*(1), 1–16. https://doi.org/10.1111/j.2044-8260.1982.tb01421.x

Cohen, S., Kamarck, T., & Mermelstein, R. (1983). A global measure of perceived stress. *Journal of Health and Social Behavior*, *24*(4), 385–396. https://doi.org/10.2307/2136404

Cramer, H., Lauche, R., Paul, A., & Dobos, G. (2012). Mindfulness-based Stress Reduction for breast cancer – A systematic review and meta-analysis. *Current Oncology*, *19*(5), 343–352. https://doi.org/10.3747/co.19.1016

Crane, R. S., Kuyken, W., Hastings, R. P., Rothwell, N., & Williams, M. G. (2010). Training teachers to deliver mindfulness-based interventions: Learning from the UK Experience. *Mindfulness*, *1*, 74–86. https://doi.org/10.1007/s12671-010-0010-9

Crawford, E. R., LePine, J. A., & Rich, B. L. (2010). Linking job demands and resources to employee engagement and burnout: A theoretical extension and meta-analytic test. *Journal of Applied Psychology*, *95*(5), 834–848. https://doi.org/10.1037/a0019364

Creswell, J. D. (2017). Mindfulness interventions. *Annual Review of Psychology*, *68*, 491–516. https://doi.org/10.1146/annurev-psych-042716-051139

Crivelli, D., Fronda, G., Venturella, I., & Balconi, M. (2019). Stress and neurocognitive efficiency in managerial contexts: A study on technology-mediated mindfulness practice. *International*

Journal of Workplace Health Management, 12(2), 42–56. https://doi.org/10.1108/IJWHM-07-2018-0095

Demerouti, E., Bakker, A. B., Nachreiner, F., & Schaufeli, W. B. (2001). The Job Demands-Resources model of burnout. *Journal of Applied Psychology, 86*(3), 499–512. https://doi.org/10.1037/0021-9010.86.3.499

Denkova, E., Barry, J., Slavin, L., Zanesco, A. P., Rogers, S. L., & Jha, A. P. (2021).Investigating the impact of peer-trainer delivered mindfulness training on cognitive abilities and psychological health. *Mindfulness 12*, 2645–2661. https://doi.org/10.1007/s12671-021-01713-6

Denkova, E., Zanesco, A. P., Morrison, A. B., Rooks, J., Rogers, S. L., & Jha, A. P. (2020a). Strengthening attention with mindfulness training in workplace settings. In D.J. Siegel and M.S. Solomon, *Mind, Consciousness, and Well-Being* (pp. 1–22). Norton Professional Books.

Denkova, E., Zanesco, A. P., Rogers, S. L., & Jha, A. P. (2020b). Is resilience trainable? An initial study comparing mindfulness and relaxation training firefighters. *Psychiatry Research, 285*, 112794. https://doi.org/10.1016/j.psychres.2020.112794

Goldberg, S. B., Tucker, R. P., Greene, P. A., Davidson, R. J., Kearney, D. J., & Simpson, T. L. (2019). Mindfulness-Based Cognitive Therapy for the treatment of current depressive symptoms: A meta-analysis. *Cognitive Behaviour Therapy, 48*(6), 445–462. https://doi.org/10.1080/16506073.2018.1556330

Good, D. J., Lyddy, C. J., Glomb, T. M., Bono, J. E., Duffy, M. K., Baer, R. A., Brewer, J. A., & Lazar, S. W. (2016). Contemplating mindfulness at work: An integrative review. *Journal of Management, 42*(1), 114–142. https://doi.org/10.1177/0149206315617003

Harvey, S. B., Modini, M., Joyce, S., Milligan-Saville, J., Tan, L., Mykletun, A., Bryant, R. A., Christensen, H., Mitchell, P. B. (2017). Can work make you mentally ill? A systematic meta-review of work-related risk factors for common mental health problems. *Occupational and Environmental Medicine, 74*(4), 301. http://dx.doi.org.ezproxy.barry.edu/10.1136/oemed-2016-104015

Heckenberg, R. A., Pennie, E., Kent, S., & Wright, B. J. (2018). Do workplace-based mindfulness meditation programs improve physiological indices of stress? A systematic review and meta-analysis. *Journal of Psychosomatic Research, 114*, 62–71. https://doi.org/10.1016/j.jpsychores.2018.09.010

Hobfoll, S. E., Halbesleben, J., Neveu, J., & Westman, M. (2018). Conservation of resources in the organizational context: The reality of resources and their consequences. *Annual Review of Organizational Psychology and Organizational Behavior, 5*, 103–128. https://doi.org/10.1146/annurev-orgpsych032117-104640

Jha, A. P., Stanley, E. A., Kiyonaga, A., Wong, L., & Gelfand., L. (2010). Examining the protective effects of mindfulness training on working memory and affective experience. *Emotion, 10*(1), 54–64. https://doi.org/10.1037/a0018438

Jha, A. P., Zanesco, A. P., Denkova, E., Morrison, A. B., Ramos, N., Chichester, K., Gaddy, J., & Rogers, S. (2020). Bolstering cognitive resilience via train-the-trainer delivery of mindfulness training in applied high-demand settings. *Mindfulness, 11*, 683–697. https://doi.org/10.1007/s12671-019-01284-7

Johnson, K. R., Park, S., & Chaudhuri, S. (2020). Mindfulness training in the workplace: Exploring its score and outcomes. *European Journal of Training and Development, 44*(4/5), 341–354. https://doi.org/10.1108/EJTD-09-2019-0156

Kabat-Zinn, J. (1990). *Full catastrophe living: Using the wisdom of your body and mind to face stress, pain, and illness.* New York, NY: Delacorte.

Khoury, B., Lecomte, T., Fortin, G., Masse, M., Therien, P., Bouchard, V., Chapleau, M. A., Paquin, K., & Hofmann, S. G. (2013). Mindfulness-based therapy: A comprehensive meta-analysis. *Clinical Psychological Review, 6*, 763–771. https://doi.org/10.1016/j.cpr.2013.05.005

Khoury, B., Sharma, M., Rush, S. E., & Fournier, C. (2015). Mindfulness-Based Stress Reduction for healthy individuals: A meta-analysis. *Journal of Psychosomatic Research*, *78*(6), 519–528. https://doi.org/10.1016/j.jpsychores.2015.03.009

Kroenke, K., Spitzer, R.L., Williams, J. B., & Löwe, B. (2009). An ultra-brief screening scale for anxiety and depression: The PHQ-4. *Psychosomatics*, *50*(6), 613–21. https://doi.org/10.1176/appi.psy.50.6.613

Kuyken, W., Warren, F. C., Taylor, R. S., Whalley, B., Crane, C., Bondolfi, G., Hayes, R., Huijbers, M., Ma, H., Schweizer, S., Segal, Z., Speckens, A., Teasdale, J. D., van Heeringen, K., Williams, M., Byford, S., Byng, R., & Dalgleish, T. (2016). Efficacy of Mindfulness-Based Cognitive Therapy in prevention of depressive relapse: An individual patient data meta-analysis from randomized trials. *JAMA Psychiatry*, *73*(5), 565–574. https://doi.org/10.1001/jamapsychiatry.2016.0076

Lauche, R., Cramer, H., Dobos, G., Langhorst, J., & Schmidt, S. (2013). A systematic review and meta-analysis of Mindfulness-Based Stress Reduction for the fibromyalgia syndrome. *Journal of Psychosomatic Research*, *75*(6), 500–510. https://doi.org/10.1016/j.jpsychores.2013.10.010

Lutz, A., Jha, A. P., Dunne, J. D., & Saron, C. (2015). Investigating the phenomenological matrix of mindfulness-related practices from a neurocognitive perspective. *American Psychologist*, *70*(7), 632–658. https://doi.org/10.1037/a0039585

Marx, R. (2019). Navigating dilemmas in training people to deliver non-eight week adapted mindfulness-based interventions. *Mindfulness*, *10*, 1217–1221. https://doi.org/10.1007/s12671-019-01110-0

Maslach, C., Schaufeli, W. B., & Leiter, M. P. (2001). Job burnout. *Annual Review of Psychology*, *52*, 397–422. https://doi.org/10.1146/annurev.psych.52.1.397

Querstret, D., Morison, L., Dickinson, S., Cropley, M., & John, M. (2020). Mindfulness-Based Stress Reduction and Mindfulness-Based Cognitive Therapy for psychological health and well-being in nonclinical samples: A systematic review and meta-analysis. *International Journal of Stress Management*, *27*(4), 394–411. https://doi.org/10.1037/str0000165

Reb, J., Allen, T., & Vogus, T. J. (2020). Mindfulness arrives at work: Deepening our understanding of mindfulness in organizations. *Organizational Behavior and Human Decision Processes*, *159*, 1–7. https://doi.org/10.1016/j.obhdp.2020.04.001

Robertson, I. H., Manly, T., Andrade, J., Baddeley, B. T., & Yiend, J. (1997). Oops!': performance correlates of everyday attentional failures in traumatic brain injured and normal subjects. *Neuropsychologia*, *35*(6), 747–758.https://doi.org/10.1016/s0028-3932(97)00015-8

Roche, M., Good, D., Lyddy, C., Tuckey, M. R., Grazier, M., Leroy, H., & Hülsheger, U. (2020).A Swiss army knife? How science challenges our understanding of mindfulness in the workplace. *Organizational Dynamics*, *49*(4), 1–9. https://doi.org/10.1016/j.orgdyn.2020.100766

Rupprecht, S., Koole, W., Chaskalson, M., & Tamdjidi, C. (2018). Running too far ahead? Towards a broader understanding of mindfulness in organizations. *Current Opinion in Psychology*, *28*, 32–36. https://doi.org/10.1016/j.copsyc.2018.10.007

Schaufeli, W. B. (2017). Burnout: A short socio-cultural history. In S. Neckel, A. K. Schaffner, & G. Wagner (Eds.), *Burnout, fatigue, exhaustion: An interdisciplinary perspective on a modern affliction* (pp. 105–127). Palgrave Macmillan.https://doi.org/10.1007/978-3-319-52887-8_5

Schwarzer, R., & Jerusalem, M. (1995). Generalized Self-Efficacy scale. In J. Weinman, S. Wright, & M. Johnston, *Measures in health psychology: A user's portfolio. Causal and control beliefs* (pp. 35–37). Windsor, UK: NFER-NELSON.

Segal, Z. V., Teasdale, J. D., Williams, J. M., & Gemar, M. C. (2002), The Mindfulness-Based Cognitive Therapy Adherence Scale: Inter-rater reliability, adherence to protocol and treatment distinctiveness. *Clinical Psychology & Psychotherapy*, *9*, 131–138. https://doi.org/10.1002/cpp.320

Segal, Z. V., Williams, M., & Teasdale, J. (2018). *Mindfulness-Based Cognitive Therapy for depression* (2nd ed.). New York, NY, US: The Guilford Press.

Tang, R., & Brave, T. S. (2020). Towards an individual differences perspective in mindfulness training research: Theoretical and empirical considerations. *Frontiers in Psychology*, *11*, 818. https://doi.org/10.3389/fpsyg.2020.00818

Van Der Linden, D., Keijsers, G. P. J., Eling, P., & Van Schaijk, R. (2005). Work stress and attentional difficulties: An initial study on burnout and cognitive failures. *Work & Stress*, *19*(1), 23–36. https://doi.org/10.1080/02678370500065275

Vonderlin, R., Biermann, M., Bohus, M., & Lyssenko, L. (2020). Mindfulness-based programs in the workplace: A meta-analysis of randomized controlled trials. *Mindfulness*, *11*(7), 1579–1598. https://doi.org/10.1007/s12671-020-01328-3

Walumbwa, F., Avolio, B., Gardner, W., Wernsing, T., Peterson, S. (2008). Authentic leadership: Development and validation of a theory-based measure. *Management Department Faculty Publications*, *24*. https://doi.org/10.1177/0149206307308913

Watson, D., Clark, L. A., & Tellegen, A. (1988). Development and validation of brief measures of positive and negative affect: The PANAS scales. *Journal of Personality and Social Psychology*, *54*(6), 1063–1070. https://doi.org/10.1037/0022-3514.54.6.1063

Zanesco, A. P., Denkova, E., Rogers, S. L., MacNulty, W. K., Jha, A. P. (2019). Mindfulness training as cognitive training in high-demand cohorts: An initial study in elite military servicemembers. *Progress in Brain Research*, *244*, 323–354. https://doi.org/10.1016/bs.pbr.2018.10.001

Section 2: **Organizational Conflict Management**

Creighlynn D. Thoele

Chapter 6
Understanding Culture to Resolve Conflict: An Introduction of the ADVANCE Through Conflict™ Model

Abstract: Conflict is a normal human interaction, and while it may initially feel uncomfortable and incite feelings of anxiety and frustration, it can also provide an opportunity for personal growth and revelation. Conflicts arise for a number of reasons, but the majority of conflicts can arguably be attributed to differences in perspectives, rooted in different cultural influences. Therefore, it reasons that conflict resolution should begin with understanding our cultural differences and unique perspectives. The BEYOND Culture Wheel™ (the Wheel) is designed to help explain the various elements, relationships, and complexities associated with the concept of culture. Comprised of three distinct yet interdependent sections, the Wheel describes how different aspects of culture interact with one another and how culture influences individual perspectives. Different perspectives are associated with differences in the established values, morals, ethics, assumptions, and beliefs of those cultures in which individuals associate. These cultural attributes are fundamental to a group's identity and directly associated with who we are as individuals within the group – our personal and social identities – so it is not surprising that differences in these components can result in conflict. Unfortunately, conflict due to differences in perspective tends to induce strong emotional, psychological, and/or physical responses which, if not addressed, can amplify a conflict.

The ADVANCE Through Conflict™ Model is a tool designed to help individuals embrace differences in perspective and offers individuals a positive, engaging approach to conflict resolution. It is also effective within any type of culture and can be implemented informally or within an established setting for conflict resolution. Using the ADVANCE Through Conflict™ Model framework, individuals can gain new knowledge and insight; explore differences in experiences and culture; and work through conflict toward a collaborative solution that ends in understanding rather than animosity and aggression. The model enables people to represent who they are as individuals, their interests, and their perspectives in a responsible yet autonomous manner while acknowledging and respecting those whose perspectives differ from their own. Thus, the process of conflict resolution becomes an act of individual awareness and development as well as an achievement of collective cooperation, compassion, and empowerment.

Keywords: Culture, Group Identity, Conflict Resolution, BEYOND Culture Wheel, Narrative Engagement, Collaboration, ADVANCE Through Conflict Model

https://doi.org/10.1515/9783110746365-006

What is culture? We hear that term used around us nearly every day at the workplace, in school, by government officials, on the news and social media platforms and it is likely that we have used the term ourselves from time to time. It is arguably one of the most important, yet controversial terms discussed in our society today. So, what does culture mean? That can be a difficult question to answer. One of the reasons that the notion of *culture* generates contention within our communities is the ambiguity which surrounds the definition of the term. Even in the academic community the definition of culture varies between, and within, the various disciplines. According to renowned Welsh author and culture academic Raymond Williams,

> Culture is one of the two or three most complicated words in the English language. This is so partly because of its intricate historical development, in several European languages, but mainly because it has now come to be used for important concepts in several distinct intellectual disciplines and in several distinct and incompatible systems of thought (1983, p. 87).

The countless definitions of culture create challenges when attempting to identify cultural conflicts within a community and the subsequent resolutions to those identified conflicts. Therefore, before we can discuss cultural conflict resolution we must first establish a definition for the term *culture* wherein all concepts, theories, and frameworks discussed within this chapter fall within the parameters of our definition.

Defining Culture: An Historical Overview

The etymology of *culture* can be traced back as far as the 1700s (Kroeber & Kluckhohn, 1952) with the word and its variations initially originating from the Latin word *colere*, meaning to till or cultivate the ground (Baldwin, Faulkner, & Hecht, 2006); however, the contemporary version of the term culture has been traced to the German word *cultur/kultur*, meaning agricultural development (Williams, 1983). According to Williams (1983), the German etymological path yielded three broad categories of the term's usage throughout its history:

1. The independent and abstract noun which describes a general process of intellectual, spiritual, and aesthetic development (p. 90)
2. The independent noun, whether used generally or specifically, which indicates a particular way of life, whether of a people, a period, a group, or humanity in general (p. 90)
3. The independent and abstract noun which describes the works and practices of intellectual and especially artistic activity (p. 90)

It was through these three distinct categories of usage that came the proliferation of definitions of the term *culture*. In 1952, Kroeber and Kluckhohn attempted to collect and analyze the various definitions of culture to synthesize one accepted definition of the term. After collecting over 150 definitions, Kroeber and Kluckhohn (1952) divided the definitions into the following six groups based on the focus of each definition:

1. Descriptive – emphasis on enumeration of content (p. 43)
2. Historical – emphasis on social heritage or tradition (p. 47)
3. Normative – emphasis on rule or way (p. 50); emphasis on ideals/values and behaviors (p. 52)
4. Psychological – emphasis on adjustment and as a problem-solving device (p. 55); emphasis on learning (p. 58); emphasis on habit (p. 60); purely psychological (p. 60)
5. Structural – emphasis on the pattern or organization of culture (p. 61)
6. Genetic – emphasis on culture as a product or artifact (p. 64); emphasis on ideas (p. 66); emphasis on symbols (p. 69)

After analyzing the collected definitions and taking into consideration the unique types of definitions, Kroeber and Kluckhohn (1952) synthesized a single definition for the term *culture*:

> Culture consists of patterns, explicit and implicit, of and for behavior acquired and transmitted by symbols, constituting the distinctive achievements of human groups, including their embodiments in artifacts; the essential core of culture consists of traditional (i.e., historically derived and selected) ideas and especially their attached values; culture systems may, on the one hand, be considered as products of action, on the other as conditioning elements of further action.
>
> (p. 181)

Though Kroeber and Kluckhohn's definition was well revered in the academic community, many researchers believed it was derived heavily from an anthropological perspective and did not fully represent the perspectives of those in other academic disciplines (Baldwin et. al, 2006). In addition, the attempt to synthesize one definition from multitudinous definitions that span across various academic disciples created an enumerative definition, resulting in a divergence of opinions even among researchers within the same discipline.

Within two decades of Kroeber and Kluckhohn's published work, their synthesized definition of culture had been determined inadequate as the academic and philosophical perspectives of the world had changed (Baldwin et.al, 2006). By the 1970s, the introduction of interpretivism along with the prominent work of Clifford Geertz (1973) had researchers questioning the structural and functional definitions of culture. Denzin and Lincoln (1998) provided a quality summary of Geertz's (1973) work, *The Interpretation of Culture*, stating that "Geertz argued that the old functional, positivistic, behavioral, totalizing approaches to the human disciplines were giving way to a more pluralistic, interpretive, open-ended perspective. This new perspective took cultural representations and their meanings as its point of departure" (p. 18). Largely through Geertz's work, many in the academic community began to change their view, and definition, of culture "from a view of elements to a view of the process by which those elements are continually created and recreated" (Baldwin et. al, 2006, p. 16).

It was also in the 1970s that, arguably, one of the most influential theories in modern day social science was introduced: social identity theory (Tajfel, 1974; 1981; Tajfel & Turner, 1986). The basic premise of social identity theory is that an individual's self-concept is comprised of two components, personal identity, and social identity (Tajfel, 1981). Tajfel (1981) described personal identity as attributes specific to the individual, such as self-evaluations and personality, and social identity as "that part of an individual's self-concept which derives from his knowledge of his membership in a social group (or groups) together with the value and emotional significance attached to that membership" (p. 255). According to Tafjel (1981), an individual's personal and social identities are interdependent and equal contributors to one's self-concept.

The notion that group membership is integral to an individual's social identity and overall general self-concept sparked the development of additional theories and perspectives, to include the intergroup perspective. An intergroup perspective focuses on group membership and certain group processes, such as:
- how people identify with groups
- how others identify people as members of groups
- how groups define themselves and are defined by others
- how groups separate themselves from other groups
- how groups compare themselves with other groups (Hecht, Jackson, & Pitts, 2005)

This perspective shifted society's view of culture once again. Rather than interpreting culture only within the parameters of fixed categories, such as by geography and biology, many researchers were approaching culture through the lens of group membership and how individuals identify with social groups.

The mid-20th century introduced postmodernism to the Western world and continued to bring about new theories and perspectives, many having further implications on the definition of culture. Debates surrounding the topic of culture and its definition continued into the 21st century and still remain today. Some researchers believe the concept of culture to be too vague or too complex while others believe it to be too rigid or too abstract. However, what appears to be constant is that the definition of culture and the very notion of the term itself will continue to change with time, influenced by new perspectives, philosophies, historical events, societal shifts, and other external forces. I believe Skelton and Allen (1999) state it best when they described the concept of culture as "dynamically changing over time and space – the product of ongoing human interaction. This means that we accept the term as ambiguous and suggestive rather than as analytically precise. It reflects or encapsulates the muddles of life" (p. 4).

Understanding Culture

The concept of culture can be ambiguous and certainly complex; however, it is important that we do not shy away from the term since culture is an integral part of who we are as individuals, as groups and communities, and as a society. I approach culture through a broad interpretation of the term with the intent to capture the structural and functional nuances of culture, identified in Kroeber and Kluckhohn's (1952) traditional definition, while providing space for the consideration of the interpretive and intergroup perspectives. Therefore, I define culture as a group's identity expressed through the group's way of life. A group can be defined as two or more people connected and/or classed together by similar histories, experiences, beliefs, purpose, goals, or physical location. A group has boundaries. The individuals in the group know they are part of the group. They also have a sense of who is in the group and who is not in the group. Not every group cultivates a unique culture, but every culture is comprised of a unique group. Once a group is formed, it normally (there are exceptions to everything) takes several years for the group to begin to cultivate a unique culture since culture is developed and shaped through a group's past shared experiences and life events. There must be feelings of connectedness and belonging to the group to develop a collective mindset which is necessary for a group to begin to form its own identity. Often described as collective identity, group identity refers to the distinct ideas, interests, values, and beliefs of a collectivity that become those of its individual members through a strong sense of group belonging. In essence, group identity is a group's collective sense of self. A group can have an identity without having a unique culture, but every culture has a group identity. Once a group's identity is formed, that identity begins to inform the group members' way of life such that the group's way of life becomes unique. This unique way of life based on the group's identity is what I describe as the group's culture.

Dimensions of Culture: The BEYOND Culture Wheel™

As we see from its etymology, culture is a very complex term. Yes, that one word – culture – describes the way of life of a group of people or a specific community, but it also represents how (and why) different "pieces and parts" of human thoughts, feelings, and behaviors were crafted together to create the mosaic of acceptable practices for that community. Culture shapes how we think, feel, and behave. It effects how we see and treat other people, how we celebrate and honor traditions, how we lead and how we like to be led, how we structure our organizations and manage our employees, and even how we write our policies and govern. It is integrated into every aspect of our lives.

I developed the BEYOND Culture Wheel™ (the Wheel) to help better understand the complexities of culture. The Wheel is illustrated in Figure 6.1 and is comprised of three parts: the **Hub**, the **Spokes**, and the **Tire**. Each section of the Wheel is distinct yet dependent upon the other sections.

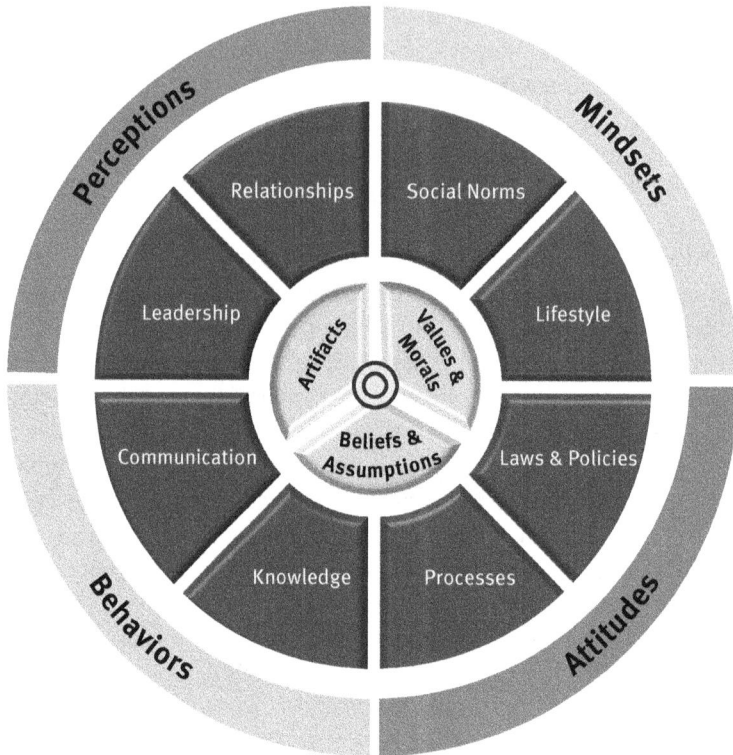

Figure 6.1: BEYOND Culture Wheel™.

The Wheel is also designed to work as a cipher wheel to assist in the assessment of different types of culture which we will explore in the next section.

The Hub

Let us start with the most inner part of the Wheel, the Hub. The components of the Hub, as illustrated in Figure 6.2, are based on the ideas of psychologist Edgar Schein. Though Schein's (1992) work is normally associated with organizational culture, it can be applied to any type of culture as Schein viewed an organization as a type of group and approached the concept of culture from a broad functional perspective. According to Schein, there are three levels of culture: artifacts, espoused values, and basic assumptions. Normally illustrated as a pyramid, Schein's three-level model of culture is typically used as the foundation for organizational culture analysis by the academic community as it encompasses the tangible-intangible spectrum of cultural manifestation (Breslin, 2000).

Figure 6.2: The Hub.

The top of Schein's (1992) pyramid represents artifacts. According to Schein, artifacts are typically visible or conscious to the group, such as symbols, stories, ceremonies, and climate, and are normally expressions of the two lower levels of culture. Though the Hub is not designed as a triangle, I agree with Schein's concept of an artifact. Many people think of the traditional definition of an artifact which is something representative of the past. In the Hub, an artifact is something representative of a culture. I define the term artifact as a tangible, visible, verbal, and/or audible element associated with and/or representative of a defined community. An artifact is normally something an individual can see, touch, taste, hear, smell, or sense. Symbols, ceremonies, traditions, stories, heroes, languages, clothing, music, food, art, literary works ... these items are all considered artifacts since they differ between various cultures. Every culture has different artifacts that are associated with the collective group and are typically tied to past events, experiences, or emotions of the group. Independence Day is an example of an artifact within the American culture. This holiday or tradition is tied to an event in American history and is part of our national culture. Artifacts can also be manifestations of the other two components of the Hub, expressing the values, morals, beliefs, and assumptions of a group's culture. A great example of this are the sacred texts within different religious cultures.

The middle of Schein's (1992) pyramid is espoused values. Espoused values are values established by a group or organization that provide guidelines for acceptable behavior for its members. Since the BEYOND Culture Wheel™ was designed to explain all types of culture (including organizational culture), the Hub consists of values (encompassing both espoused and enacted values) as well as a group's collective morals and ethics. I define a value as a fundamental belief that motivates and guides an individual to behave in one way or another; a moral as a deeply ingrained principle of what an individual believes to be right and wrong regarding human behavior; and ethics as the compilation of moral principles and acceptable standards of behavior based on those moral principles for a group.

Values, such as trust, integrity, commitment, efficiency, and openness to name a few, can be conscious or subconscious to the group, and typically guide how individuals within the group act, how the group acts as a collective entity, how the group views risk, and how the group handles the uncertainty associated with difficult or uncontrollable events. Morals and ethics can also be conscious or subconscious. Different groups have different sets of collective values, morals, and ethics; however, it can be difficult to determine what these are because one cannot physically see, touch, hear, smell, taste, or sense a value, moral, or ethic principle. What are visible, though, are a group's behaviors which represent the group's collective values, morals, and ethics.

The bottom section of Schein's (1992) culture model is basic underlying assumptions. Schein described these assumptions as deeply embedded beliefs of a group that are typically subconscious and manifested through artifacts, attitudes, and behaviors. I agree with Schein regarding underlying assumptions, yet in addition to assumptions I also include "beliefs" in the Hub in an effort to represent various types of culture. I define assumption as an idea formed that is believed to be true or accepted as truth based on past outcomes and experiences, and belief as an acceptance or certainty that a statement is true or that something exists regardless of proven evidence. Many times, our automatic responses to certain events, situations, or circumstances are based on our underlying assumptions and beliefs. Assumptions can be superficial or deeply rooted in a group's collective mindset depending on the number of past outcomes and/or experiences that supported the assumption. Though difficult, an underlying assumption can be shifted over time through outcomes and experiences that repeatedly contradict the assumption. With beliefs, this may not be the case. Beliefs are typically melded with a group's morals and ethical principles and are usually unwavering since they are embedded within the fabric of a group's identity.

The Hub is designed in a "pie" shape to illustrate that though each component is unique there is an interdependent relationship between the three elements. The Hub is also centered in the Wheel to show that together the components establish the fundamental core of a group's culture while indicating that each of its components can distinctly influence the dimensions of the Spokes as well as the aspects of the Tire.

The Spokes

The middle section of the Wheel is comprised of the Spokes. The Spokes represent eight dimensions of a group that play an integral role in fostering the group's culture. The placement of each dimension within the Spokes section of the Wheel is intentional as it helps to illustrate additional cultural nuances of a group (refer to Figure 6.3). The top hemisphere is designed to show cultural dimensions that are human-oriented while the bottom hemisphere indicates structure-oriented dimensions. The left hemisphere represents cultural dimensions that are individual-based whereas the right hemisphere represents those dimensions that are more collective-based in nature. The top left quadrant delineates personal interactions while the top right quadrant illustrates group interactions. Lastly, the bottom left quadrant indicates dimensions representative of learning interactions whereas those dimensions in the bottom right quadrant are characterized as system interactions.

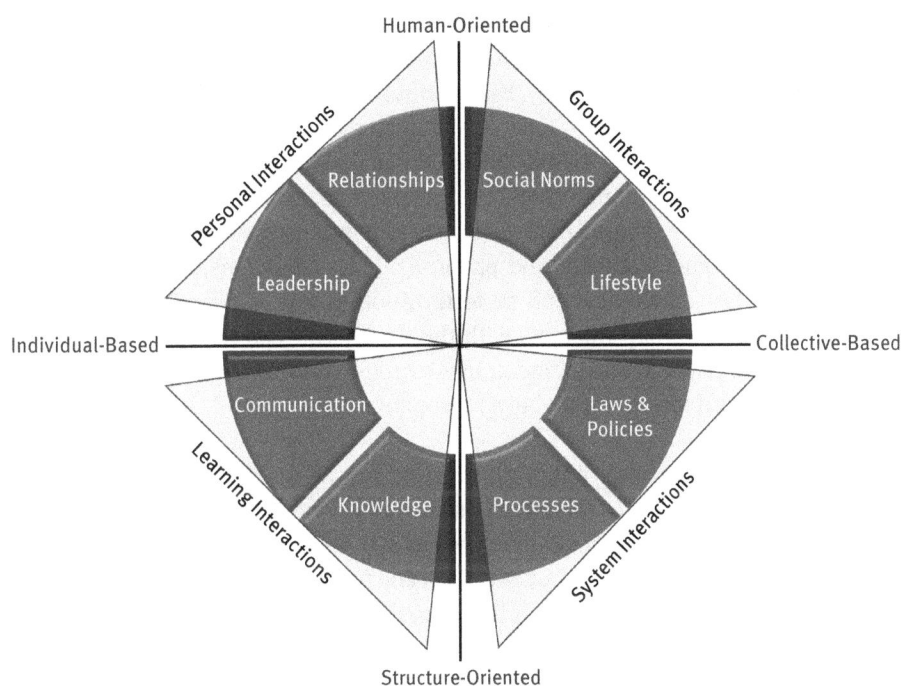

Figure 6.3: The Spokes.

"Leadership" is a cultural dimension located in the top left quadrant of the Spokes section of the Wheel. Thus, it is considered a human-oriented, individual-based dimension that is representative of a personal interaction within a group's culture. I define leadership as a process of social influence implemented by an individual, whether consciously or subconsciously, to motivate and increase the efforts of those within a defined community toward the achievement of established and/or subconscious goals. Within the context of culture, the leadership dimension addresses the acceptable practices of how one leads (as well as how one follows) within the group. The dimension of "relationships" is also located in the top left quadrant of the Spokes and, therefore is also perceived as a human-oriented, individual-based dimension that is representative of a personal interaction within a group's culture. Relationships, defined singularly as a way in which two or more individuals regard each other and behave toward one another, are how individuals connect with others within and outside the group. Different cultures have different acceptable standards and practices with regard to how individuals foster and maintain relationships with ingroup and outgroup members.

The cultural dimension of "social norms" is located in the top right quadrant of the Spokes section of the Wheel. Though human-oriented, this dimension is considered collective-based and representative of a group interaction within a culture. Social norms can be described as the unwritten rules of beliefs, attitudes, and behaviors that are considered acceptable in a particular social group and tend to govern the behavior of that specific community. Essentially, social norms regulate how members act within the group. "Lifestyle", located in the top right quadrant, is also considered a human-oriented, collective-based dimension and representative of a group interaction within a culture. Though similar to social norms, lifestyle describes how individuals live within the group. I define lifestyle as a group's overall manner of living, to include sets of circumstances and patterns of social relations, habits, activities, behaviors, interests, attitudes, and so forth. Another way to describe the lifestyle dimension is how a group interacts with the world. This can include how a group interacts with its physical environment; how a group acquires, distributes, and maintains its wealth and resources; and even what types of goods and services the group prefers to consume.

The "laws and policies" cultural dimension is located in the bottom right quadrant of the Spokes. Thus, it is considered a structure-oriented, collective-based dimension that is representative of a system interaction within a group's culture. Laws are defined as formal sets of standards, principles, and procedures that compel or prohibit behaviors within a group whereas policies are defined as systems of principles that guide behaviors, actions, and decisions to achieve desired outcomes within a group. Broadly speaking, laws and policies are intended to provide structure and stability to a group. The bottom right quadrant also includes "processes" as a structure-oriented, collective-based dimension representative of a system interaction within a culture. Processes, defined singularly as a series or set of actions, activities, behaviors, and/or psychological approaches that interact to achieve a specific result, are intended to help a group accomplish its goals and objectives.

"Knowledge" is located in the bottom left quadrant of the Wheel's Spokes section. Though still considered structure-oriented, knowledge is an individual-based dimension that is representative of a learning interaction within a group's culture. I define knowledge as the facts, information, and skills acquired by a person through experience and/or education, as well as the theoretical and/or practical understanding of a topic. The knowledge dimension captures how individuals learn within a group and includes various types of knowledge, to include explicit, implicit, tacit, embedded, priori, intuitive, and rational, to name a few. "Communication" is also located in the bottom left quadrant, and considered a structure-oriented, individual-based dimension that is representative of a learning interaction within a culture. Communication can be defined as a process of exchanging information, transferring knowledge, and/or developing meaning among entities or groups through the use of mutually understood language, behavior, signs, sounds, symbols, and/or other semiotic conventions. Essentially, communication can be described as how individuals give or exchange thoughts, feelings, information, and ideas within a group.

As discussed earlier, the Hub creates the core foundation of a group's culture by cultivating a unique group identity. The Hub also directly influences the eight dimensions of the Spokes which are designed to capture the various elements of living as a community, thereby supporting the description of culture as a group's identity expressed through the group's way of life. At this point, you may be questioning why there is a third section to the Wheel if culture can be described through the components of the Hub and the dimensions of the Spokes. And it would be a valid question. The third section of the Wheel does not specifically represent elements of culture. However, it is of profound significance as it represents the one concept that is tightly intertwined with culture: the concept of climate.

The Tire

The outer section of the Wheel is called the Tire and represents the "climate" of a group. Though it is common to use the terms "culture" and "climate" interchangeably, they are two distinct constructs. Typically, the concept of climate is addressed when discussing organizations and, therefore, is normally defined within that context. However, climate is relevant to all types of culture. I define the overall concept of climate as the shared perceptions, mindsets, attitudes, and behaviors of a group's members which represent how the group subconsciously experiences, characterizes, and/or understands its culture. Arguably, a group's climate is the manifestation of its culture. Many researchers even contend that for some group cultures the climate is so distinct that it can be felt when in the presence of the group. I agree as I have experienced this phenomenon when visiting different types of groups with unique cultures.

Contrary to culture, climate is relatively easy to change since the aspects of climate are based on the group's collective state of mind rather than embedded within the fabric of a group's identity. The Wheel is an analogy for the relationship between culture and climate. The Hub and Spokes of a Wheel provide the structural foundation necessary for the Wheel to operate. The components within these two sections are strong and relatively immobile as they provide structural integrity for the Wheel. Though possible, it is difficult to change the components of the Hub and Spokes without greatly affecting the overall effectiveness of the Wheel. The Tire is different. The Tire is made

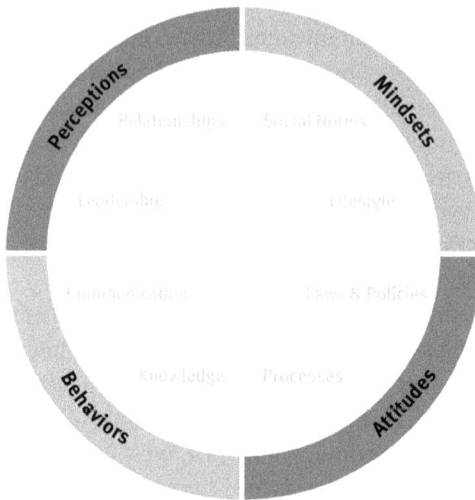

Figure 6.4: The Tire.

of a durable material but is designed to be easily changed and replaced as it is exposed to the elements of the environment. The shape and material of the Tire are dependent on the collective shape of the Hub and Spokes. The Tire protects the components of the Hub and Spokes; thus if the Tire is not maintained it can negatively affect the Hub and Spokes over time.

There are four aspects of the Tire section of the Wheel (refer to Figure 6.4). The first aspect is "perception." I define perception as a way of organizing, identifying, regarding, interpreting, understanding, and/or becoming aware of information received through the senses. Essentially, perception is the conscious awareness and understanding of one's surroundings. It is how we interpret the world, people, situations, and even ourselves. An individual's "mindset" normally represents his or her perceptions. As the second aspect of the Tire, a mindset can be described as a person's usual mental state, attitude, and disposition that shapes how he or she thinks and makes sense of the world, resulting in predetermined responses to and interpretations of situations. A mindset is a habitual way of thinking and seeing the world, people, situations, and themselves. The third aspect of the Tire is "attitude." An attitude is the way an individual views or feels about another person, place, thing, idea, or situation. An attitude can also refer to an evaluation of or a set of emotions toward a person, place, thing, idea, or situation. Attitudes are how an individual feels about the world based on his or her mindset and are typically manifested through behaviors. Behavior is the fourth aspect of the Tire and defined as an action or mannerism of an individual in response to a particular situation or stimulus. Behaviors are how we act toward the world, people, situations, and ourselves.

A great example of how the above aspects of the Tire (group climate) are manifestations of the components of the Hub and Spokes (group culture) is the atmosphere in American schools and businesses on Monday mornings (Gruenert, 2008). Typically, students and employees alike dread Monday mornings which brings decreased levels of morale and engagement to the start of this day every week. Many times, this mindset and attitude toward Monday mornings shifts behavior to a point where individuals call in sick to work or school to avoid this day. These thoughts, feelings, and behaviors toward Monday mornings are aspects of group climate. But why are Mondays perceived as miserable days of the week and other days, such as Fridays, considered to be fun? The answer is culture, and in this case, American culture. In the United States, we place higher levels of value on different days of the week. Based on this belief, group social norms dictate how we should act on different days, to include Monday mornings (i.e., if you have ever shown up to work happy on a Monday morning, you may have gotten looks of disapproval from most of your coworkers as your attitude and behavior were not aligned with the group's accepted norms). This is not the case in other national cultures. According to Gruenert, "it is the culture that dictates how members of the group are supposed to feel. The culture tells us that we're supposed to feel miserable on Mondays" (2008, p. 58). In the United States, the climate in schools and businesses on Mondays continues to be negative week after week, month after month, year after year, because Americans continue to teach this preference in days of the week to each new generation, thus reinforcing cultural norms regarding Monday mornings. This negative perception of Mondays will not change until the American culture changes, and when people of the United States change their beliefs (a Hub component) about different values being placed on different days of the week which will then influence the group social norms (a Spokes dimension) surrounding the different days. Once a culture shift takes place, then the American people's perception, mindset, attitude, and behavior (aspects of the Tire) toward Monday mornings will change.

The Hub, Spokes, and Tire are interdependent sections of the BEYOND Culture Wheel™ and are designed to help explain the various elements, relationships, and complexities associated with the culture construct. Table 6.1 is provided as a quick reference that outlines the concepts illustrated within the Wheel. Understanding how different aspects of culture interact with one another and how climate is associated with culture will be of great benefit when attempting to resolve conflict resulting from cultural differences between two parties. Having an awareness of the different types of culture will also be beneficial during conflict resolution which is why it is our next topic of discussion.

Types of Culture

Now that we have a better understanding of the various elements of culture, let us take a brief look at the different types of culture. There are two broad types of culture: geographic-based and association-based. Cultures by geographic region tend to nestle within one another while association-based cultures tend to cross-section geographic

Table 6.1: Elements of the BEYOND Culture Wheel™.

The *Hub*	Artifacts	Our tangible, visible, verbal, and audible representations of the group
	Values and Morals	Our principles that guide and motivate the actions of the group
	Beliefs and Assumptions	Our perceived collective truths about the group and the world
The *Spokes*	Leadership	How we lead and follow within the group
	Relationships	How we connect with others within the group
	Social Norms	How we act within the group
	Lifestyle	How we live within the group
	Laws and Policies	How we structure and manage the group
	Processes	How we accomplish goals and objectives within the group
	Knowledge	How we learn within the group
	Communication	How we exchange feelings and information within the group
The *Tire*	Perceptions	How we interpret the world, people, situations, and ourselves
	Mindsets	How we think about the world, people, situations, and ourselves
	Attitudes	How we feel about the world, people, situations, and ourselves
	Behaviors	How we act toward the world, people, situations, and ourselves

locations as illustrated in Figure 6.5. A geographic-based culture is just as it sounds – a culture cultivated by a group of individuals living within a specific geographic location. This location can be as small as a neighborhood or as large as a country or even a continent, but a geographic-based culture always has some sort of physical boundary that distinguishes a specific group from other groups. Association-based cultures are different. With association-based cultures, group boundaries are not identified by geographic location but by association or sense of belonging – we look the same, we sound the same, we believe the same, we live the same, we identify the same, and so forth. Though not physical in nature, these types of boundaries also distinguish different groups.

Typically, an individual identifies with at least two geographic-based cultures and two association-based cultures. Here is an example:

Cameron lives in the United States and identifies as an American (national culture). Cameron grew up in the "Deep South" (regional culture), specifically in the State of Louisiana (subregional culture). For 40 years, Cameron has lived in the City of Shreveport (city culture) and

Types of Culture

Race
Ethnicity
Age/Generation
Gender Identity
Religion
Urban/Rural
Sexual Identity/Orientation
Political Affiliation
Socio-Economic
Profession
Team
Family
And more ...

National

Regional / Sub-Regional

City/Town

Neighborhood

Individual Perspective

Group

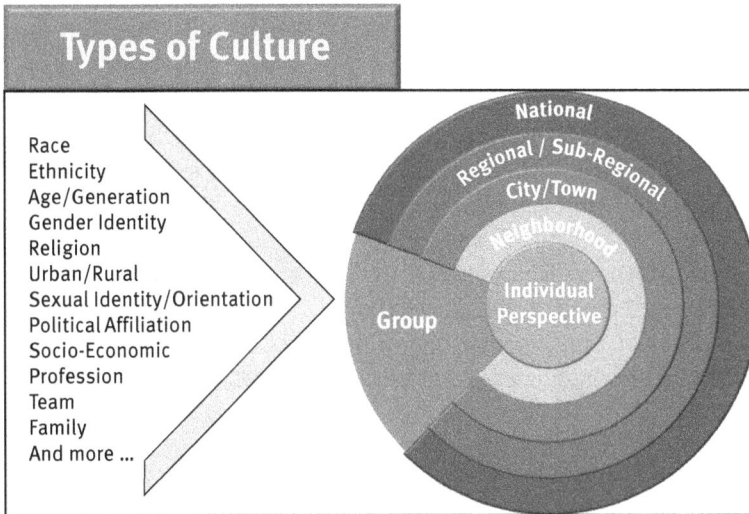

Figure 6.5: The various types of culture.

calls "The Cooper Road" (neighborhood culture) his home. Cameron identifies as an African American male. He is a proud member of the Southern Baptist Church and a prominent physician with strong family ties and traditions (five distinct association-based cultures).

In our example, Cameron is a member of five distinct geographic-based groups which each have a unique geographic-based culture. Additionally, Cameron identifies with five distinct association-based groups which each have a unique culture. Similar to how an individual can be a member of multiple associations, an individual can also be a member of multiple groups having distinct cultures.

Culture and Conflict

It is evident throughout history and even in our current society that conflict can be rooted in cultural differences. But why? First, we must understand that human beings are complex social creatures – so much so that we can (and normally do) alter our thoughts, feelings, behaviors, and even our way of life to align with our most current group affiliation as well as with the specific culture to which we most currently identify. For example, I have lived in Shreveport, Louisiana, for the last six years and have assimilated into the city, state, and regional cultures; thus, the unique identities of these three geographic locations can be seen through my daily way of life (yes – I do say y'all, drink sweet tea, and speak with a bit of a southern accent). I did not grow up in the South, though. I grew up in New England, specifically in a small rural town in the State of Vermont.

An interesting phenomenon occurs each time I return to my hometown in Vermont. I almost immediately revert back to my "old" way of life with my northern accent and all. Why does this happen? It ties back to the notion of social identity. Since I had once identified with the geographic-based groups within this region, my sense of social identification with these groups is subconsciously expressed through my thoughts, feelings, attitudes, and behaviors when I return to this region; hence, I quickly reassimilate with the Vermont and New England cultures. This is an important concept to understand as it shows how the groups and cultures with which we have identified in the past continue to impact our lives.

We must also understand that our past cultural influences, coupled with our current geographic-based and association-based cultural influences, shape our perspective. I define perspective as a particular way an individual thinks about something, which is typically informed by how one judges something as good, bad, important, irrelevant, and so forth in comparison with other things, and which is strongly influenced by one's beliefs and/or past experiences. Every person has a unique perspective since every individual has unique cultural influences (refer back to Figure 6.5). Even members of the same immediate family have different perspectives as their association-based cultures may be different, they may be influenced differently by various elements of a shared culture, and/or they most likely have different past group affiliations and cultural associations.

While differences in perspective can generate a multitude of positive outcomes, differences in perspective can also create conflict. Conflict can be defined as a disagreement or clash between two or more individuals, resulting from a difference in thought process, understanding, interest, or perspective. Thus, one reason why cultural differences can result in conflict is due to differences in perspectives shaped by diverse past and present cultural influences.

The ADVANCE Model for Conflict Resolution

I developed the ADVANCE Through Conflict™ Model (ADVANCE Model) after personally experiencing conflict due to cultural differences. Arguably, the majority of true conflicts are likely rooted in cultural differences with many of those conflicts attributed to differences in perspective regarding Hub components. Our Hub components are directly associated with who we are as individuals – our personal and social identities – so it is unsurprising that differences in these components can result in conflict. Conflict due to differences in perspective regarding Hub components can also induce strong emotional, psychological, and/or physical responses which, if not addressed, can amplify a conflict to a point in which violence is introduced. The ADVANCE Model (illustrated in Figure 6.6) is designed as a tool to help individuals work through their conflict toward a collaborative solution that ends in understanding and empowerment rather than animosity and/or aggression.

A – Acknowledge

The base step in the ADVANCE Model is Acknowledge. It is critical that this is the first step in the model as the completion of this step determines whether or not two individuals are ready to engage in conflict resolution. The Acknowledge step is comprised of three separate acknowledgements and is designed as a type of decision path (shown in Figure 6.7). The first acknowledgement is to recognize that there is indeed a conflict that needs resolution. At this point, some of you may be questioning why I would need to include this type of acknowledgement in the model while others of you are nodding your heads in agreement of the need for this step based on past experiences. There are times when one party perceives a conflict exists while the other party does not. Additionally, there are times when one party not only perceives a conflict exists but will escalate the conflict to a physical altercation before the other party realizes there is a conflict.

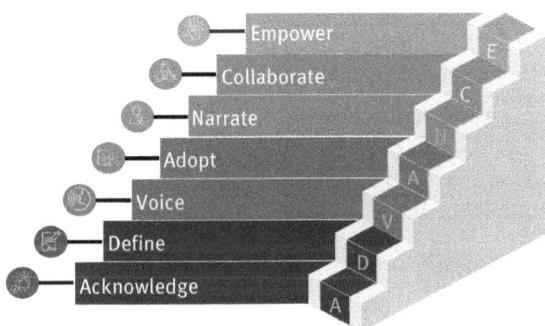

Figure 6.6: ADVANCE Through Conflict™ Model.

Conflict cannot be resolved if one of the parties involved is unaware of its existence. Therefore, both parties must recognize and accept that there is a conflict for there to be conflict resolution. This is one of the decision points in the Acknowledge step of the ADVANCE Model. If one party does not acknowledge the conflict then the two parties should stop to address this issue or both parties should walk away. If both parties recognize that there is a conflict then they proceed to the next acknowledgement.

The second decision point in the Acknowledge Decision Path is to acknowledge emotions. Emotions can be quite powerful and, even for those of us that perceive ourselves to be emotionally and psychologically stable and well-grounded, certain emotions can significantly influence our attitudes and behaviors and even bias our decision-making processes. Therefore, it is important for both parties to identify their current emotions prior to engaging in conflict resolution in order to mitigate negative emotional influence on the process. If either party identifies an emotion of rage, fear, apathy, contempt, or grief in themselves or perceives one of these emotions in the other party then the two parties should stop to address the emotion or both parties should walk away. If an emotion of anger, frustration, anxiety, annoyance, or hurt is identified in oneself or perceived in the other party then both parties should acknowledge this emotion and then cautiously proceed to the next acknowledgement (these five emotions will be addressed in one of the later steps of the model). It is important to note that there are many other emotions not listed here that may be identified during the Acknowledge step of the ADVANCE Model which will require the use of good judgment by one or both parties to determine how an identified emotion may impact the conflict resolution process.

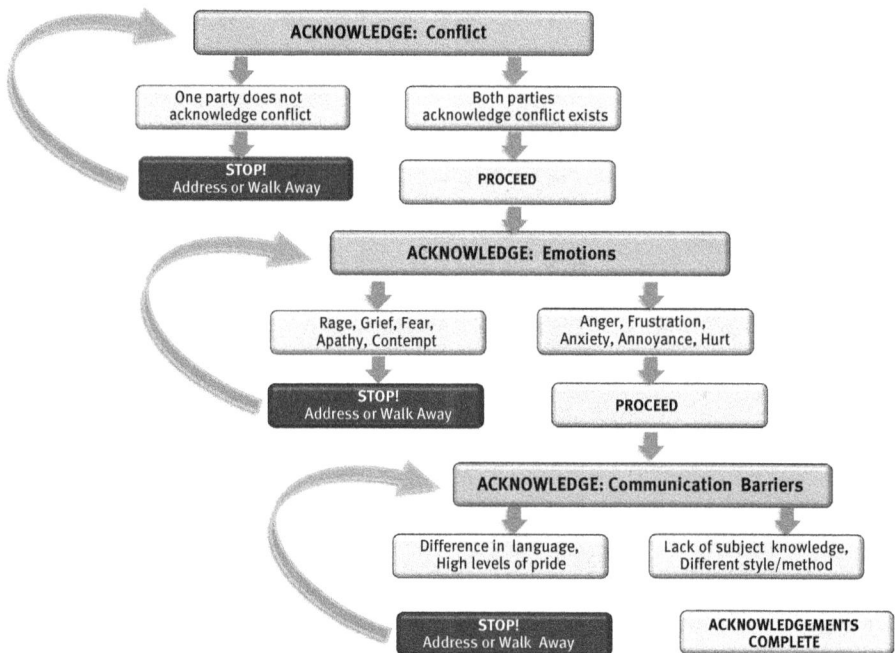

Figure 6.7: Acknowledge Decision Path of the ADVANCE Through Conflict™ Model.

Acknowledging communication barriers is the third decision point of the Acknowledge step. I define communication barrier as a tangible or intangible hindrance that prevents an individual from receiving, transferring, and/or understanding the ideas, feelings, knowledge, and/or information attempting to be conveyed. There are various types of communication barriers, ranging along a spectrum from actual physical barriers (i.e., attempting to listen to someone speak through a mask, and most of us can likely relate to this type of communication barrier) to psychological barriers (i.e., emotions as well as mental limitations), with each type of barrier influencing effective communication in its own way. Some communication barriers will significantly inhibit effective communication. The most obvious of these types of barriers is a difference in the spoken language of the two parties. If this is the case, the two parties should stop to address the language difference or both parties should walk away.

A less obvious barrier that can substantially impede effective communication is pride. Pride is often considered a self-conscious emotion derived from social awareness and can be perceived as positive or negative based on situational context (Azar, 2006). Unhealthy pride (i.e., hubristic or egotistical pride) can prohibit effective communication and collaboration; thus, if high levels of unhealthy pride are perceived in one or both parties the two parties should stop to address this issue or both parties should walk away. If communication barriers such as a difference in preferred communication method/style or a lack of subject knowledge are identified then both parties should acknowledge these barriers and then cautiously proceed to the next step in the ADVANCE Model. It is also important to note here that there are a variety of communication barriers that may be identified during the Acknowledge step of the ADVANCE Model. If a communication barrier is identified that is not listed in the Acknowledge Decision Path, one or both parties should use good judgment to determine how the barrier may impact the conflict resolution process.

D – Define

The second step in the ADVANCE Model is Define. There are two aspects of this step – defining the conflict and defining the desired end-state. I like to use a road trip analogy to explain this step. Before a road trip can begin, one must know two points: the starting point and the destination. The definition of the conflict is the starting point in the conflict resolution process. This aspect of the Define step is essential as there are many times when the two parties involved in a conflict define the conflict differently or, within the context of our analogy, are attempting to take a road trip together but are at different starting points. (i.e., Have you ever been in a heated argument with a loved one over his or her lack of compassion and understanding for how hard you work every day to find out an hour into the fight that your loved one thinks the conflict is about the dirty dishes left in the sink?) Clearly defining the conflict at its onset mitigates any initial confusion between the two parties and helps set the framework for the conflict resolution process.

One simple approach to defining the conflict is to use the Five Ws: Who, What, When, Where, and Why (and sometimes How, if applicable). This approach begins by each party answering the following five questions about the conflict:

- WHO is involved in the conflict?
- WHAT is the subject or situation of the conflict?
- WHEN did the conflict begin?
- WHERE did the conflict begin?
- WHY is the subject or situation causing conflict?

Though these questions can be answered verbally, I find it more effective when both parties write down their Five Ws since it is makes it easier to identify differences in the answers. Figure 6.8 provides an example.

In Figure 6.8, it is evident that the wife and husband have different definitions of the conflict. Since it is normally necessary for both parties to have a mutual understanding of the conflict prior to its effective resolution, the couple in our example will need to discuss the differences between their perspectives and come to a consensus on the definition of the conflict prior to moving to the next step in the conflict resolution process. Within the context of our analogy, both wife and husband need to meet each other at the agreed upon starting point location if they plan to take a road trip together. It is important to note that defining the conflict is intended to clarify the elements and parameters of the conflict, not resolve the conflict; however, defining the conflict can help alleviate misunderstandings and/or misperceptions between the two parties, leading to more effective communication practices and positive outcomes.

The second point that must be known within our road trip analogy is the destination. Without a destination, travelers would aimlessly drive in random directions, never knowing when they have reached a desired end to their trip. The definition of the desired end-state is the destination in the conflict resolution process. This second aspect of the Define step helps both parties clearly state and mutually agree upon a desired end-state prior to moving to the next step in the conflict resolution model. Similar to defining the conflict, there are times when the two parties involved in a conflict have different desired end-states or do not have an established end-state. Without a defined desired end-state the parties will not know when they have effectively resolved the conflict.

In the ADVANCE Model, a mutually agreed upon desired end-state could range from a specific objective to an over-arching goal to simply a general understanding and acceptance of each party's perspective. The end-state is dependent on the individuals as well as the various cultural differences contributing to the conflict (i.e., conflict relating to organizational cultural differences may have a specific objective as the desired end-state while conflict relating to religious cultural differences may only have a desired end-state of general understanding and acceptance of each party's perspective). Regardless of the type and specificity, it is important that the defined

The Five Ws of the Conflict

	Wife's Perspective	Husband's Perspective
WHO is involved in the conflict	*Spouse*	Spouse
WHAT is the subject or situation of the conflict	*He doesn't help with the housework*	Dirty dishes in the sink
WHEN did the conflict begin	*When I started my new job*	6pm today
WHERE did the conflict begin	*The most recent argument started in the kitchen*	In the kitchen
WHY is the subject or situation causing conflict	*It shows he has a lack of compassion and understanding for how hard I work*	I forgot to clean the dishes

Figure 6.8: Defining the Conflict.

desired end-state is written down and that both parties agree to it prior to beginning the conflict resolution process.

V – Voice

The third step in the ADVANCE Model is Voice. Though this step can be completed rather quickly, it is critical to the conflict resolution process as it addresses individual choice. Individuals may not want to participate in the conflict resolution process for a variety of reasons, such as issues identified during the Acknowledge step of the ADVANCE Model (i.e., heightened emotions or significant communication barriers), time constraints that would negatively impact the effectiveness of the process, or the perception that there is no resolution as the conflict is attributed to differences in deeply rooted cultural beliefs. Regardless the reason, it is important to acknowledge that not everyone desires to resolve conflict. It is also important to note that the conflict resolution process does not work unless both parties want to resolve the conflict. Therefore, each party should voice his or her choice to resolve the conflict prior to moving to the next step.

A – Adopt

Adopt is the fourth step in the ADVANCE Model. During the Adopt step, both parties establish and adopt the guidelines for the conflict resolution process. The guidelines are established by setting the ground rules, outlining the parameters, and identifying the non-negotiables. The ground rules are defined as a set of expected attitudes and behaviors agreed upon by a specific group or, in our case, two or more individuals. These ground rules articulate the code of conduct for both parties and help maintain good order and discipline. For the purpose of the ADVANCE Model, outlining the parameters refers to setting limitations on the upcoming conversation, including time constraints and what topics will not be discussed during the resolution process. Outlining conversation parameters help both parties stay focused on the topics related to the current conflict and can ease a party back on course if he or she has deviated from the relevant topics.

In an earlier section, I described how cultural beliefs can often be embedded within the fabric of an individual's identity. These beliefs are normally unwavering and not open for discussion. I call these types of beliefs non-negotiables. It is important to identify non-negotiables prior to engaging in conflict resolution as attempts to negotiate these beliefs will likely halt the resolution process. After the guidelines have been established, both parties should adopt the guidelines (verbally or in writing) and move to the next step in the ADVANCE Model.

N – Narrate

The fifth step in the ADVANCE Model is Narrate. The Narrate step is unique as it is designed to address the negative emotions identified during the Acknowledge step of the model (i.e., anger, frustration, anxiety, hurt, or annoyance), and then temper those emotions by evoking empathy and compassion in both parties (resolving a conflict is less difficult when both parties can moderate their own emotions while feeling empathy and compassion for the other). This occurs through a process I call narrative engagement. I like to describe narrative engagement as a mutual exchange between two parties wherein each party gives his or her full physical, mental, and emotional attention to the other party who is communicating a personal story, perspective, or idea. During a narrative engagement, there is the narrator who is the individual conducting the storytelling and the audience who is the individual listening to the story. Let us begin with the narrator role.

The role of the narrator is to communicate the story of the conflict from his or her own perspective, ensuring to include the cultural influences, values, and beliefs that inform this perspective. The DESCRIBE-ME approach is designed to help narrators effectively convey their perspectives of the conflict to their audiences. This approach is outlined in Figure 6.9. The first phase of the approach is to detail the emotions. These are the emotions that the narrator identified during the Acknowledge step. To detail an emotion means to not only describe the emotion but also provide the "why" behind the emotion. The narrator should try to answer the question, "Why am I having this emotion over this conflict?" There are times when a narrator will not be able to answer this question at the beginning of the narrative engagement. This is normal. If this occurs, the narrator should acknowledge that he or she does not know why the conflict is causing a certain emotion and then move on to the next section as the why behind the emotions will be readdressed during a later phase of the approach.

Detail	• your emotions
Engage	• your audience
Set	• the stage
Create	• your characters
Recount	• the conflict
Investigate	• your perspective
Build	• the backstory
Explore	• the "cliffhangers"
Make	• a connection
Examine	• your findings

Figure 6.9: The DESCRIBE-ME approach to perspective storytelling.

In the DESCRIBE-ME approach, the narrator should use I-statements to describe his or her emotions. I like how GoodTherapy® (2018) describes the term, first by defining an I-statement as "a style of communication that focuses on the feelings or beliefs of the speaker rather than thoughts and characteristics that the speaker attributes to the listener" (para. 1), and then by expounding on the definition, stating that:

> "I" statements enable speakers to be assertive without making accusations, which can often make listeners feel defensive. An "I" statement can help a person become aware of problematic behavior and generally forces the speaker to take responsibility for his or her own thoughts and feelings rather than attributing them – sometimes falsely or unfairly – to someone else (para. 2).

As stated earlier, the initial emotions the narrator feels will likely be negative in nature, so it is important that the narrator conveys his or her emotions in an open yet constructive manner. It may be beneficial to establish the use of I-statements as a ground rule during the Adopt step to help foster positive communication between both parties for the entire conflict resolution process. This would also provide the opportunity to identify and address any cultural sensitivities toward using I-statements early in the process as various cultures do have different views on individuals openly expressing emotions and vulnerability.

Once the narrator has detailed his or her emotions, it is time to engage the audience. This step is necessary since the narrator is trying to evoke empathy and compassion within the audience which normally requires the audience to be engaged in the story. Typically, an audience is engaged by the way a story is told (i.e., imagine an action-packed story being read in a whisper or a sci-fi thriller being told in a monotone – now imagine how the audience reacts as they listen to those stories). Therefore, how a narrator tells his or her story will impact the level of connection the audience has to the story and, ultimately, to the characters in the story.

Engagement begins with eye contact. This may be difficult for the narrator at first since certain emotions, feelings, and personality traits can hinder an individual's ability to maintain eye contact. Even just the thought of being in a conflict with someone can inadvertently make us look away. However, eye contact is important when trying to engage an audience. Body language is also important as the majority of communication between two individuals is nonverbal. Narrators should, at a minimum, keep their arms uncrossed and use small hand or arm gestures to help clarify their thoughts and/or words when telling their stories. Several other key components to a good story are the volume, tone, and inflection of the narrator's voice. This can be difficult to do without prior practice, but I have found that telling my story in my mind first helps me plan out the voice I want to use to convey my perspective aloud. Illustrations or other visual aids can also help to engage an audience and should be used when possible, especially if the conflict resolution process is taking place in a structured or formalized environment.

As with all great stories, the narrator begins the story by setting the stage. Setting the stage means explaining the surroundings, atmosphere, and/or events that were taking place prior to the conflict. Once the stage is set, the narrator must create the characters. The narrator introduces himself or herself as the leading role, speaking in first person, but all other characters are introduced in third person, including the audience. This helps the audience listen to the story from the narrator's point of view rather than attaching to one's own character in the story. It is also common for the narrator's story to have additional characters other than the audience; however, the narrator should fully describe these characters and their relevance to the story as the audience may not know or understand the level of importance these characters play within the narrator's storyline.

After all of the characters have been introduced to the story, the narrator recounts the conflict by describing the event or experience that caused the conflict between the narrator and the audience. It is critical that the narrator recounts the audience's role in the conflict in third person and continues to use I-statements during this section of the approach. The narrator does not speculate the thoughts or feelings of the audience during the conflict. The audience will address this when it is his or her turn to take on the narrator role. Normally, recounting the conflict is relatively quick since the narrator is simply describing the event or experience that caused the conflict. Explaining why the event or experience created a conflict, though, usually takes longer as this is the main event of the story plot. I call this section of the story investigating the perspective.

The narrator investigates the perspective by seeking the underlying reasons why the specific event or experience caused the conflict. An understanding of the BEYOND Culture Wheel™ (Wheel) may be helpful during this step. By recalling the different elements of the culture wheel within the context of the various cultures in which he or she identifies, the narrator can determine the cultural influences playing a role in the conflict. I find it easier to analyze my perspective when I start with aspects of the

Tire and work inward toward the Hub. Figure 6.10 provides an example of a conflict to help clarify this step.

Example of a Conflict

An employee and his supervisor are in a conflict regarding tele-working. The employee has been tele-working two days a week for the past year and the supervisor just decreased the employee's tele-working days to one day a week. The employee is very angry with his supervisor and is considering quitting his job over his supervisor's decision.

Narrator = Employee; **Audience** = Supervisor

➤ The narrator describes his emotions as anger, frustration, and confusion
➤ The narrator engages with the audience
➤ The narrator sets the stage at his place of employment, a healthcare organization. The narrator states that a company policy letter dictating that each office should maximize tele-working has been in place for nearly two years, and that the narrator has been tele-working two days a week for over a year.
➤ The narrator creates the characters – the narrator is a senior program analyst for the healthcare organization but also states that he is a licensed nurse and a decorated retired U.S. Army officer of 20 years; the audience is the narrator's supervisor.
➤ The narrator recounts the conflict as the narrator had just received a glowing annual performance evaluation from his supervisor and was then told that his tele-working days will decrease to one day per week without explanation for the decision.
➤ Investigate the perspective:

Narrator: I'm angry and also really confused by the decision to take away one of my tele-working days, especially after my performance evaluation shows that tele-working doesn't affect my performance but, if anything, helps it. I think my mindset on this topic is influenced by my time in the Army. In the Army, policies and procedures are strictly adhered to unless they are deemed unlawful. This is such an important part of the Army culture that following policies and procedures has become part of my guiding principles, part of my morals. So not following the company's policy letter on maximizing tele-working seems wrong to me and makes me uncomfortable. I also think my time in the Army influences my mindset on relationships. In the Army, a high-ranking, experienced employee is treated more as a colleague by his supervisor than simply a subordinate and is part of collaborative discussions because the supervisor values, trusts, and respects his employee's years of experience and hard work. From this perspective, the change to my tele-working days without discussion or explanation would indicate that I'm not viewed as an experienced, hard-working employee or valued, trusted, and respected by my supervisor.

Figure 6.10: Example of the "Investigate the Perspective" step.

In Figure 6.10, the narrator determines that his identification with the U.S. Army's organizational culture is a major source of influence on his perspective of the conflict. Using the Wheel as a reference, the employee identifies his mindset as the aspect of the Tire currently being impacted by the conflict (shown in Figure 6.11). Moving inward on the Wheel, the employee recognizes that cultural influences from two of the dimensions of the Spokes (laws & policies and relationships) are informing his perspective of the situation, and that these cultural influences are connected to specific values & morals located within the Hub.

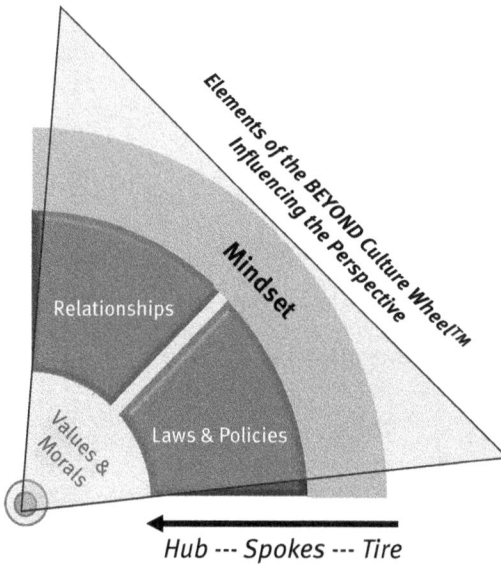

Figure 6.11: Example of elements of the Wheel influencing the perspective.

Investigating the perspective can be a difficult step in the DESCRIBE-ME approach for several reasons. First, learning how to recognize cultural influences on one's perspective is a skill that takes time and practice to master – self-reflection is difficult for many people. Second, identifying certain influences on our perspectives can evoke new positive and/or negative emotions that may need to be addressed prior to moving forward with the storyline. Finally, taking ownership for one's perception, mindset, attitude, and/or behavior can be difficult. Thus, it may be necessary to repeatedly remind both parties that this part of the story focuses solely on the narrator and how his or her perspective of the situation was derived. A narrator should avoid assigning blame to the audience and/or other characters.

Once the narrator has investigated the perspective, it is time to build the backstory. Building the backstory is the character development for the leading character, the narrator. This is the point in the story where the narrator provides additional details about his or her perspective or describes other information relevant to the conflict that the audience may not have known. The audience may begin to empathize and feel compassion for the narrator during the backstory since this part of the story shows the "human side" of the conflict. If our example of the employee and supervisor had continued to the backstory section of the story, the narrator would have described how hard he worked to attain his military rank and how difficult it was to leave the Army. The narrator would have also explained that his reluctance in starting a new career in the civilian sector was his concern that a civilian company would not value his time and experience in the Army, and that this concern resurfaced when his tele-working days decreased without discussion or explanation.

There are times during the backstory when the narrator or the audience identifies a cliffhanger. A cliffhanger can be described as an emotion, feeling, or statement with no identified association to a current conflict. As my son so eloquently says, "nobody likes a cliffhanger without a follow-on season", so it is important that the narrator explore the cliffhangers prior to moving onto the next step in the approach. It is during the cliffhanger section that the narrator would explore any emotions in which he or she could not explain during the first phase of the approach. In our example, a cliffhanger would be if the narrator had made a statement about work-life balance without providing additional information or without discussing it within the context of the conflict.

Throughout the story, the narrator seeks to make a connection with the audience. This is an important aspect of the approach as the intent of the Narrate step is to not only bridge gaps in understanding between the two parties but also to evoke empathy and compassion for one another. Empathy and compassion enhance the conflict resolution process by mitigating negative emotions and helping to promote opportunities for cooperation and collaboration. The narrator can make a connection with the audience simply by being open, honest, and genuine throughout the story.

The last phase of the DESCRIBE-ME approach is to examine the findings. During the story, the narrator may have gained new or better insight into his or her own perspective of the conflict. I call this insight the findings from the story. The narrator should identify and examine these findings as it depicts self-awareness and personal growth, two attributes that can help build a stronger connection between the narrator and the audience. I like to conclude the narrative with a short summary of the story's main points and by asking the audience if any section of the storyline needs further clarification.

The listener of the story is called *the audience* as the title is intended to psychologically depict a setting of a play, movie, or other similar event in the listener's mind. The role of the audience is to engage in immersive listening. I define immersive listening as a state of listening in which an individual listens with the full intent of becoming deeply absorbed and emotionally connected with the story and its characters. I equate this type of listening to an individual watching his or her favorite television show, reading his or her favorite novel, or listening to his or her favorite song. During a narrative engagement, the audience listens to the narrator's story as if it is the audience's favorite story and the narrator is the audience's favorite character. Immersive listening is different than active listening. There is no restating or paraphrasing what the narrator says – it is simply about listening to the story.

During the storytelling, the audience should attempt to limit questions as the intent is to be immersed in the narrative. The audience should only ask questions that help clarify the story or make statements that show empathy and/or compassion for the narrator. I find the following tips helpful when engaged in immersive listening:

- Ask open-ended questions
- Ask questions that bring out the narrator's personality
- Ask the narrator to describe settings, characters, events, etc. in detail to create mental illustrations
- Incite positive emotions in the narrator through words of understanding and encouragement
- Provoke feelings of nostalgia within the audience and/or narrator, whenever possible
- Search the story for an "unforgettable moment"

It is important for the audience to remember that the story is told from the narrator's perspective and may sound very different than what the audience expects to hear. It should also be noted that it may be difficult for the audience to hear a story in which they are involved from someone else's perspective.

Once each party has functioned as both narrator and the audience, both parties should individually map out the conflict – from the other party's perspective. I like to think of this step as giving each party the opportunity to view the conflict through the other's eyes (or, as the well-known idiom says, a chance to put oneself in another's shoes). This step is important to the conflict resolution process as it reinforces emotional bonds between the two parties and helps shift the parties' mindsets, thereby creating an atmosphere more conducive to collaboration.

Conflict mapping can be done verbally, but I find it more effective when each party maps out the conflict on a piece of paper. Each party uses the information received when functioning in *the audience* role to illustrate the conflict from the other party's perspective, asking questions to help clarify any aspect of the conflict that may still be causing confusion. The intent is to portray a thorough, accurate map of the conflict from the other party's perspective; thus, the map is complete when the other party agrees that it is an accurate reflection of the conflict from his or her point of view. Once the conflict has been mapped from both perspectives, the parties should move to the next step in the resolution process.

C – Collaborate

The Collaborate step is the sixth step in the ADVANCE Model. During the Narrate step of the model, the two parties should have mitigated their negative emotions and evoked a certain level of empathy and compassion for each other. Empathy and compassion help pave the way toward successful collaboration. The term collaboration can be defined as two or more individuals working jointly with one another to accomplish a shared goal or objective. In this instance, the goal or objective is the desired end-state that was agreed upon during the Define step. It is critical to note that during the Collaborate step the two parties should engage in collaboration, not compromise, as collaboration leads to the final step of the model. Figure 6.12 illustrates the difference between the two terms.

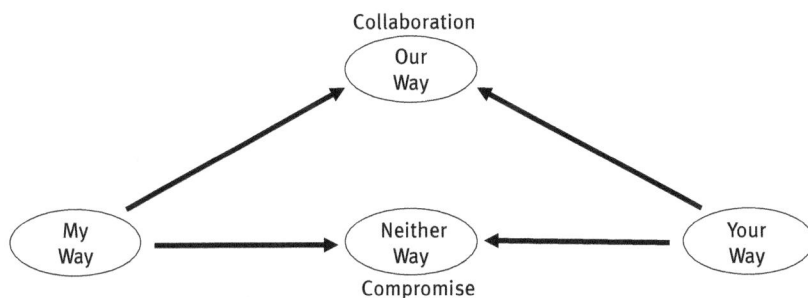

Figure 6.12: The difference between collaboration and compromise.

The Collaborate step begins with a joint review and analysis of the conflict maps completed during the Narrate step. The intent is not to combine the maps as this would degrade the integrity of each perspective, but to seek and identify similarities between the two maps. These similarities, along with the defined conflict that was agreed upon during the Define step, are then used as the foundational elements for the conflict resolution framework while the defined desired end-state is its pinnacle.

During the Collaborate step, both parties employ brainstorming and other problem-solving techniques to develop a solution to resolve the conflict. Within the context of our road trip analogy, this solution is the agreed upon plan that advances both parties from the starting point (the defined conflict) to the destination (the desired end-state). The intended solution to the conflict should be designed jointly by both parties through effective communication, cooperation, and collaboration. An effective solution is one in which the solution accomplishes the desired end-state of the conflict resolution process while being viewed as a "win-win" by both parties.

Collaboratively developing solutions to a conflict can be challenging, especially if one party has a more dominant personality than the other. Voicing one's concerns and acknowledging the concerns of others are both essential to effective conflict resolution. Identifying gaps within the conflict resolution framework or within the intended solution is also important as these gaps can lead to future conflict if not adequately addressed during the resolution process. Additionally, conflict resolution will not occur if the intended solution compromises a party's personal values or attempts to alter a party's deeply rooted beliefs. While the parties do not have to agree with each other's cultural beliefs, they do have to acknowledge and respect the differences in perspective for the conflict resolution process to be effective.

E – Empower

The last step in the ADVANCE Model is Empower. This step is relatively quick if the previous six steps were completed successfully as the conflict resolution process outlined in the ADVANCE Model is designed to empower both parties. I define the term empowered as the feeling of inner authority, or of being more in control of one's life while feeling more confident and capable to make decisions for oneself. Empowerment is key to successfully resolving conflict since it enables both parties to represent who they are as individuals, their interests, and their perspectives in a responsible yet autonomous manner. Individuals are also more likely to be engaged in the collaboration process when they feel empowered, resulting in more successful solutions to the identified conflicts.

The ADVANCE Through Conflict™ Model is effective within any type of culture and can be implemented informally or within an established setting for conflict resolution. It is also important to note that while we have specifically been addressing conflict due to cultural differences, the ADVANCE Through Conflict™ Model is designed as a tool to resolve any type of conflict, regardless the reason behind the conflict.

Conclusion

Though the concept of culture can be ambiguous and contentious at times, it is arguably one of the most important terms within the English vernacular as it describes who we are as individuals, as groups, as communities, and as a society. Cultural influences are woven into the fabric of our social identities and shape our unique perspectives. It is through our differences in perspectives that we generate the most positive outcomes in life, but it is also through these differences in perspectives that we create conflict with one another. Conflict resolution begins with understanding our cultural differences and unique perspectives while working together and empowering one another to find successful solutions.

References

Azar, B. (2006, March). The faces of pride. *American Psychological Association, 37*(3), 24.
Baldwin, J.R., Faulkner, S. L, & Hecht, M. L. (2006). A moving target: The illusive definition of culture. In J. R. Baldwin, S. L, Faulkner, M. L. Hecht, & S. L. Lindsley (Eds.), *Redefining culture: Perspectives across disciplines* (pp. 3–26). Mahwah, NJ: Lawrence Erlbaum Associates.
Breslin, C. B. (2000). *Organizational culture and the military*. Carlisle Barracks, PA: U.S. Army War College.

Denzin, N. K., & Lincoln, Y. S. (1998). Introduction: Entering the field of qualitative research. In N. K. Denzin & Y. S. Lincoln (Eds.), *Strategies of qualitative inquiry* (pp. 1–34). Thousand Oaks, CA: Sage Publications.

Geertz, C. (1973). *The interpretation of cultures*. New York City, NY: Basic Books.

GoodTherapy. (2018, February 14). *"I" message*. Retrieved from GoodTherapy website: https://www.goodtherapy.org/blog/psychpedia/i-message

Gruenert, S. (2008, March/April). School culture, school climate: They are not the same thing. *Principal*, 56–59. Retrieved from www.naesp.org.

Hecht, M. L., Jackson, R. J., II, & Pitts, M. J. (2005). Culture. In J. Harwood & H. Giles (Eds.), *Intergroup communication: Multiple perspectives* (pp.21–42). New York City, NY: Peter Lang.

Kroeber, A. L., & Kluckhohn, C. (1952). *Culture: A critical view of concepts and definitions*. Cambridge, MA: Harvard University Press.

Schein, E. (1992). *Organizational culture and leadership* (2nd ed.). San Francisco, CA: Jossey-Bass.

Skelton, T. & Allen, T. (1999). Culture and global change: An introduction. In T. Skelton & T. Allen (Eds.), *Culture and global change* (pp. 1–10). New York City, NY: Routledge.

Tajfel, H. (1974, April). Social identity and intergroup behaviour. *Social Science Information, 13*(2), 65–93.

Tajfel, H. (1981). *Human groups and social categories: Studies in social psychology*. Cambridge, MA: Cambridge University Press.

Tajfel, H., & Turner, J. C. (1986). The social identity theory of intergroup behavior. In S. Worchel, & W. Austin (Eds.), *Psychology of intergroup relations* (2nd ed., pp. 7–24). Chicago, IL: Nelson-Hall Publishers.

Williams, R. (1983). *Keywords: A vocabulary of culture and society (revised edition)*. London, Great Britain: Fontana Paperbacks.

Neil H. Katz, Michael A. Wahlgren

Chapter 7
Utilization of Frames and Reframing for Organizational Leadership and Conflict Management Effectiveness

Abstract: Framing is a common practice used to interpret situations and guide responses through mental mapping. Frames serve as anchor points that help clarify issues and identify solutions. Oftentimes we are limited in our scope of understanding and hampered by personal biases to fully open our perspectives to other viewpoints. Frames can go underutilized because people are unable to visualize and access multiple perspectives. In that case, reframing the issue from a limited frame to multi-frames will augment one's ability to analyze complex situations and uncover opportunities. Join Professor Rossin, a semi-fictional character who has accepted a new leadership challenge, as he utilizes an approach to framing and reframing that opens his aperture of understanding the issues and challenges at his new job. Developed by researchers Bolman and Deal, this framework for utilizing multiple perspectives provides four anchors for a more holistic and sophisticated understanding of challenges and opportunities leaders face daily. Through Professor Rossin's story, readers will learn the "what" "why" and "how" of framing and reframing and the importance of looking beyond a single or limited perspective.

Keywords: frames, reframing, reflective practice, organizational conflict, leadership, structural frame, human resource frame, political frame, symbolic frame

Professor Rossin had enjoyed a successful and meaningful three-decade-long career in academia and organizational consulting. However, he was eager to apply some new leadership and conflict management material that he was exposed to at the Cape Cod Institute in Massachusetts – A Four Frame/Reframing Model developed by Lee Bolman and Terrance Deal promoting the benefits of utilizing structural, human resource, political and symbolic lens thinking and action. Professor Rossin realized that, until now, he had been in a unique position of leading 2–6 person task-oriented work teams, a situation in which he was able to select the people who worked under him. On these occasions, he chose his teaching, training, and research assistants, and clear lines of authority were established. Almost all the inter-dependent task work had gone well, and positive relationships were maintained and enhanced. In this favorable setting, exercising effective leadership was relatively easy.

Now, Professor Rossin decided to take on a new challenge. He accepted an offer to move to a new University as their first externally hired department chair. There he would have to provide leadership to a group of 13 faculty, many of whom he didn't

https://doi.org/10.1515/9783110746365-007

know and who were used to one of their own colleagues serving in that position – a situation which often meant they could or could not follow their hand-picked in-house leadership without serious consequences. In addition, he knew there had been some recent conflicts among different stakeholders – administration, faculty, staff, and students – which led to several resignations, firings, and lawsuits. Nevertheless, Professor Rossin accepted the position with excitement about the opportunity to apply the framing/reframing material to leadership and conflict challenges. He hoped, with guarded confidence, that if he demonstrated competency in the Bolman and Deal approach, he would be successful.

The Function of Frames and the Need for Multiple Frames and Reframing

The concept of frames refers to a cognitive and behavioral disposition that we often rely on to make sense of people and situations. Frames function as a mental map to help us understand where we are and what we need to do to navigate through the world on a day-to-day basis to get from where we are to where we want to be. Research findings support the view that most people have a natural inclination or predisposition to rely on one or two primary frames that function as "automatic responders" to guide what we pay attention to, the interpretation of our experience, and our behavior (Katz, 2020). Furthermore, these preferred frames serve as windows and lenses, which are windows to help us look outward and notice certain things, and lenses to bring the outside world of people and situations into greater focus and clarity.

However, they both help us and limit us. Frames are reliable anchors and assets that allow us to utilize our strengths to experience success much of the time. Nevertheless, they also constrain us by limiting our ability to utilize situational reflection to take a holistic view of a circumstance from multiple perspectives. The art and science then of reframing is the ability to access and utilize our heretofore underutilized frames and engage the appropriate frame at the appropriate time when encountering complex challenges. By viewing situations, events, and people through multiple perspectives, leaders augment their ability to analyze complex challenges to understand more thoroughly what is going on and to consider different options can enhance strategy and actions.

In addition to understanding and using both frames and reframing effectively, Professor Rossin also needed to appreciate the necessity of mastering "principled flexibility" and matching. As Bolman and Deal discovered in their voluminous research, "great leaders rely on multiple lenses, possess the skill to use each, enjoy the wisdom to match frames to situations, and have created a leadership story that assembles what they see into a powerful and coherent script that is right for the times and circumstances" (Bolman & Deal, 2015).

Essential Elements of the Four Frames

Within the two months of his acceptance of the offer and the commencement of his role as department chair, Professor Rossin spent some time reviewing the essential characteristics of each of the Bolman and Deal four frames.

Structural Frame

Structural leaders see their primary task as addressing confusion and chaos by clarifying goals, roles, and expectations. The main activities of a structural leader are to establish, maintain, and reaffirm procedures and policies, focus on tasks, facts, and logic (as opposed to personalities and emotions), and design and implement a structure that fits the circumstances and aligns with the environment. The leader ensures the structure is clear to everyone and appropriate for what needs to be accomplished so that people perform optimally and are successful through achieving goals. Meetings are formal occasions to transmit facts and information, conduct objective analysis, and make rational decisions. The metaphor for understanding the structural frame is the "well-oiled machine" or "factory", with the leader serving as the architect or analyst.

Human Resources Frame

The Human Resources leader addresses anxiety and uncertainty by primarily focusing on human needs, desires and building positive relationships. The leader's main task is to keep people involved and communication open so participants can share information and feelings. By being responsive to the needs of individuals and supportive of their goals, leaders can count on their subordinates' dedication and loyalty. Leaders demonstrate their responsiveness by communicating warmth and concern, listening, and respecting the aspirations of others, and giving people the resources, autonomy, and opportunity to succeed in their jobs. Decision-making is an open, empowering, consensus-based process to ensure understanding and commitment. The metaphor for understanding the human resource frame is the "extended family", with the leader serving as a caring parent, facilitator, or servant.

Political Frame

The Political leader addresses conflicts and feelings of disempowerment by creating forums where issues can be negotiated, and alliances redrawn. An effective leader is an advocate for their group and an astute negotiator who makes sure they fight for resources for those they represent. They understand politics and are comfortable with conflict, realizing that conflict is inevitable and rooted in gathering and distributing scarce resources. The main agenda of the political leader is to manage resources and conflicts as productively as possible by creating a power base and exercising influence carefully, particularly with key players. Recognizing that individuals and groups will not get everything they want and that there will always be enduring differences in values, beliefs, information, perceptions, and interests, the leader creates arenas where stakeholders can jockey for influence, negotiate their differences, and come up with reasonable compromises and trade-offs. The political leader understands that the meetings and decision-making forums are mainly an opportunity to air grievances, to exercise or gain power, and to win concessions. The metaphor for this frame is the "jungle", with the leader posing as the advocate or negotiator that assists the parties with survival resources and strategies.

Symbolic Frame

The Symbolic leader deals with the formidable barriers of loss of direction and hope and clinging to the past by providing vision, meaning, and inspiration. Symbolic leaders believe their most important job is to give people hope and something they can believe in. They realize that events have multiple meanings, so what is important about events is not what happened but what it means to people. The focus of symbolic leaders is on creating meaning, belief, and faith, and they do this by using metaphors, ceremonies, rituals, myths, stories, and artifacts. Meetings and conflict resolution procedures are used to develop shared values and experiences and to maintain an image of co-cooperativeness, responsibility, and accountability. At the same time, participants act out in various roles to contribute to a compelling and meaningful story. Indeed, the metaphor for this frame is the "theater" or "temple", whereby the leader serves as playwright, poet, or prophet.

Limitation of Frame Under-Utilization

Let us now return to the story of Professor Rossin. As part of his preparation for leadership of the department faculty, Professor Rossin completed several assessments to determine his preferred disposition or readiness frame that he relied heavily on, and which frames he was under-utilizing or neglecting. Upon reflection, he understood he had habitually relied almost exclusively on the human resource (HR) frame to get what he needed to achieve for both task and relationship goals. Indeed, his success with interpersonal relationships provided evidence that his utilization of the HR frame was a determining factor in his career accomplishments to date and in navigating through challenges in his life in general. However, he knew this new assignment as Department Chair would rely on his ability to access additional frames and alternate frames when needed. He committed to expanding his knowledge and actions in his habitually underutilized frames in accepting the new position. He also noted research findings that traditionally, managers and supervisors tend to rely on logic and structure and good communication and rapport-building skills to control situations and gain the trust and cooperation of stakeholders. This observation suggested that the political and symbolic frames are often the most underutilized frames and, therefore, might lend the most benefit by their use.

Although Professor Rossin had only a few weeks to think about his "game plan" on utilizing the Four Frame approach in working with his faculty, he was determined to begin activities in each of the frames during the first few months of his chairmanship. Structurally, he would gain knowledge of the college and University's organizational chart, understand the "chain of command" and its importance, and begin to find out about the rules, policies, and procedures that he and others were expected to follow. In addition, he would review the job description of each of the faculty and staff and commit to familiarizing himself with their performance reviews when time allowed.

In harnessing his instincts within the Human Resource Frame, he would arrange one-on-one meetings with each faculty member to get to know them as people, colleagues, and supervisees and assure them of his interest in their well-being and success. Furthermore, there would be discussions on how each of them assessed their career within the Department and University and how they were doing in meeting their aspirations on making a meaningful contribution and their overall work satisfaction. The meetings would conclude with some dialogue on what they expected and needed from a chair and ideas on how Professor Rossin could help them achieve their individual and departmental goals.

In thinking about the Political Frame, Professor Rossin was determined to get to know the various stakeholders within the College and the University and begin building networks and alliances with those he needed to get things done. Recognizing that "who gets what" in the distribution of resources is critical to success, he prioritized establishing credibility and positive relationships with key resource holders as one of the most important elements of his role. He knew that advocacy and astute negotiation skills would be important factors in his success in this highly competitive environment in which there would likely be winners and losers in terms of resource distribution.

Professor Rossin was most excited about exercising his knowledge about the potential power of the symbolic frame in his new role. He understood that recognizing and leveraging the positive elements of organizational culture would be critical for success while also understanding the challenge of altering some of the more destructive elements of the culture. Most importantly, he knew the symbolic frame would often be one of "high reward; high risk." At best, utilization of his passion and commitment, as well as his articulation of a compelling vision and mission, could act as strong positive motivators for his colleagues. He also reminded himself that symbolic features, applied frivolously, could backfire in terms of enhancing the credibility of his leadership.

One promise he made to himself was to utilize his experience from the University he had served under for the three previous decades to benefit his new College. Symbols of the pre-eminence of his former school were readily apparent, from the placards proudly displayed in the halls proclaiming the school was rated "#1 in rankings of U.S. News and World Report", (for 20+ consecutive years) to the impressive and massive bookcases in the lobby filled with publications from the faculty; or in students purchasing hats, T-shirts and sweatshirts proclaiming their attachment and pride in the school; or in demonstrated loyalty of alumni through donations directly to the school (as opposed to donations to the University); or in statues and paintings/photographs of recognizable and inspiring leaders in citizenship and public affairs who had been affiliated with the school. The vision he hoped to impart in his new role would inspire his new colleagues to replicate this obvious pride in being a member of their own department, college, and university.

Application of Framing through Reflective Questioning

In preparation to utilize the multi-frame approach in his leadership role, Professor Rossin created a chart of questions he sought to answer based on the individual frames (see Figure 7.1). This chart was an exercise he picked up along his leadership enhancement journey and he felt that it would help him focus on each frame using a systematic approach. He also committed himself to periodically revisit this chart to update, modify, or add additional questions.

Lessons Learned and Traps to Avoid

Over time, Professor Rossin was effective in using framing and reframing in his role as chair. He achieved some notable successes in influencing faculty to follow guidelines for class protocols and committee participation, improving teamwork performance, gathering and distributing resources, and establishing a culture conducive to high-quality graduate-level education while enhancing the department's reputation both within and outside of the University. However, he did learn some important lessons while experiencing various challenges and setbacks along the way:

Structure	How might I function as a designer, architect, or analyst to provide focus, clarity, and a conducive environment to accomplish organizational goals? What does the current organization chart look like? How important is it to follow the "chain of command?" Are roles clarified and understood for staff and faculty within the organization? Do employees understand how their work will be evaluated and what they are expected to accomplish? How are decisions made? Are they based on rational thinking and objective facts? Is the process efficient/effective? Are rules, regulations, duties, and expectations of employees clearly communicated and understood?
Human Resources	How do I function as the head of the extended family to provide support and caring, and operationalize the belief that people are the heart of the organization? What is the overall morale of the department and individuals? What are each of the employees' strengths and weaknesses? How can I leverage their strengths and/or mitigate their weaknesses? What are my subordinates' needs and how am I meeting them? What challenges are preventing me from demonstrating "caring" and meeting their needs? What are my subordinates' goals and aspirations? How am I meeting them? Can I better align their goals with the department/college/university goals? What motivates the employees? How can I find additional ways to recognize/reward them? How do I empower them to succeed and build a strong sense of camaraderie at the school?
Political	How do I function as the savvy politician to navigate successfully in competitive waters in which some will come out winners and some losers? How am I going to make sure I can successfully acquire adequate resources for my group? How am I going to handle the distribution of resources and the impact of those decisions? What conflicts exist at this point? What is contributing to those conflicts? How should I respond to those conflicts? How have I established my base of authority and power?
Symbolic	How do I function as the playwright or poet or sage to provide inspiration and sense of purpose and meaning? What is the culture of the organization? Is the organizational culture aligned with the values of the organization? Is there a strong connection between the "espoused values" and the "values in use?" Are the employees finding a compelling purpose and meaning in what they do? What types of ceremonies/ rituals/ habits are established to bring esprit de corps to the workforce? How do I inspire them with something to believe in? Is there a compelling mission and vision that provide an "anchor" and "sign-posts" for employees?

Figure 7.1: Summary of the Four Frames (Bolman & Deal, 2015).

In higher education, there are mixed, somewhat contradictory cultures, and each brings unique characteristics germane to leadership. Faculty are used to autonomy and collegiality and loosely defined expectations and supervision. Administrators and staff work much more under a bureaucratic, formalized structure of policies and procedures, defined regulations, adherence to the chain of command, and accountability guidelines at least partially objective and understandable. As a long-standing faculty member who was new to administration, Professor Rossin quickly realized that he needed to pay more attention to the Structural Frame to understand the day-to-day experience of administrators and staff. Furthermore, he needed to become more sensitive to the probability that his minimization of the importance of the Structural Frame was shared by many of his faculty colleagues, and how that might contribute to the formidable challenges of anyone serving as chair of a faculty group.

With the Human Resource Frame, he also experienced some challenges, especially around boundary definition. He had always enjoyed friendships with his colleagues, and his "people skills" were his acknowledged strengths and ones he most relied on. However, now he was the supervisor for faculty as well as their faculty colleague. He needed to hold them accountable to specific standards and procedures while inspiring them to achieve personal and departmental goals. Managing these dual roles and boundary issues was more difficult than he initially thought and necessitated that he withholds his natural inclination to rely heavily on the Human Resource frame.

Regarding the Political Frame, the chair enjoyed building networks and alliances among influential stakeholders and negotiating for his department's resources. With effort, he was able to distribute resources based on merit, although it went against his strong desire to get along with everyone and operate in the Human Resource frame. He also learned that working in the political arena called for a more sophisticated analysis on whom he could trust to "have his back", and who, when trusted, might attempt to gain power at his expense. Furthermore, Professor Rossin successfully worked with conflict constructively by engaging in conflict coaching sessions, conducting supervisory mediation sessions, or facilitating discussions among disputing parties, whether staff, faculty, or students.

While utilizing the symbolic frame to inspire students and faculty, the chair also learned some important lessons regarding paying more attention to the importance of understanding unique aspects of organizational cultures, especially the composition, aspirations, and talents of the student body and faculty of his new University which was much different from the school he had left. Although he could attempt to strive to replicate some of the ways in which pride and loyalty had been gained and expressed in his old school, new strategies and goals would need to be developed to match both the strengths and limitations of the new school, which had a different mission and vision and served a significantly different population.

Practical Application of the Frames

In his role as chair of a medium-sized department, he had multiple opportunities to use the reframing approach in his dealings with faculty, administrators, and students. He often led with the Human Resource frame to establish rapport with individual students, yet sometimes needed to shift to the Structural frame to remind them of requirements and regulations on qualifying exams and dissertations and taking required courses in sequence. With faculty, after first attempting to get voluntary participation and compliance with meeting expectations of departmental faculty for committee work and other duties, Professor Rossin realized that he would need to shift his frame approach depending on the situation and audience.

Sometimes he would have to take the more direct approach compatible with the Structural frame by bringing out the faculty manual, or pivot to the Political frame to remind them of consequences of negative performance reviews, or switch to the Symbolic frame utilizing stories and rituals to reinforce the shared commitment to enhancing the department's reputation within the College and University. With administrators, Professor Rossin quickly realized the limitations of depending on the Human Resource frame. He shifted to heavy use of the Political frame, especially interest-based negotiation, and advocacy strategies while lining up support from alliances he had built by networking with influential stakeholders.

The chair also frequently relied on his knowledge and skills of the Four Frame approach in acting as a third-party facilitator or mediator, all responsibilities accompanying his supervisor role. Utilizing the frames as one of his many "tools in his leadership toolbox", he needed to apply multiple frames to establish rapport and encourage movement toward constructive dialogue and options for possible settlement. One of his surprises was how impactful the symbolic frame could be to induce positive movement among the parties, particularly the use of metaphors and stories to elicit a desired outcome. He accessed popular culture and historic references through the symbolic frame, such as the scene from the Gettysburg battle site in the movie "Remember the Titans", or the story of then-President Jimmy Carter bringing the leaders of Egypt and Israel to Gettysburg in 1976 during the Camp David Accords Negotiation. In both instances, the visits to the bloody battlefield were to remind the parties of potentially disastrous consequences of non-cooperation and provide a potent catalyst to the necessity of positive movement to work together.

Conclusion

As Professor Rossin continued along his leadership journey, he progressively realized the beneficial power of frames and reframing each year while appreciating the challenges in using them effectively, particularly in instances of workplace conflict. The shifting required in utilizing multiple frames and reframing was especially difficult for him since he had relied heavily on operating under one frame which worked most of the time in representing himself but had limitations in leading diverse individuals who sometimes were involved in workplace conflict. He was continually reminded of the need for awareness of the dangers of over-utilization of preferred frames and under-utilization of less familiar frames in applying the frame/reframing approaches to self-examination and situational appropriateness. However, although the art and science of using multiple frames and reframing needed constant attention, practice, and improvement, he acquired even more recognition of its potency to serve as an effective diagnostic tool to make sense of what is going on, allowing for sophisticated judgment and engagement in multi-faceted and effective action.

In the months and years that followed, he would gain a particular appreciation for the ability of the Framing/Reframing model to help him in dealing constructively with complex conflict situations, realizing the full meaning of Bolman and Deal's claim that:

> When the world seems hopelessly confusing and nothing is working, reframing is a powerful tool for gaining clarity, regaining balance, generating new options, and finding strategies and actions that work.
> (Bolman & Deal, 2017, p. 23)[1]

References

Bolman, L.G. and Deal, T.E. (2015), "Think or sink – leading in a VUCA world". *Leader to Leader, Vol. 2015 No. 76*, pp. 35–40.

Bolman, L. G., & Deal, T. E. (2017). *Reframing Organizations: Artistry, Choice, and Leadership* (Sixth edition.). Jossey-Bass, a Wiley brand, Hoboken, New Jersey.

Katz, N. H. (2020) "Reaching Beyond 'The Tools of the Trade': Anchors and Signposts to Enhance Mediator Effectiveness." *Cardozo Law School of Yeshiva University Journal of Conflict Resolution. Vol. 22, No. 1.*

---

1 The popular and influential book "Reframing Organizations: Artistry, Choice and Leadership" by Lee G. Bolman and Terrance E. Deal has been in print since 1991. It is currently in its seventh edition (2021, Jossey-Bass).

Kenneth Cloke, Joan S. Goldsmith

Chapter 8
10 Separations in Conflict Resolution

Abstract: People in conflict lose perspective, and with it, the ability to separate what matters from what gets in the way. When this happens, conflicts become confusing and more difficult to resolve. If we can separate the core elements of conflict and distinguish, for example, positions from interests, people from problems, commonalities from differences, future from past, emotions from negotiations, and ourselves from others, it becomes far easier to get unstuck and shift from destructive outcomes to constructive ones. This chapter offers ten ways leaders can create such separations, with sample questions to help them do so.

Keywords: separations, interests, positions, zero-sum, commonalities, structure

When we are in conflict, we tend to lump the issues that upset us into a mass of indistinguishable complaints that become intertwined and difficult to understand, negotiate, fix, or resolve on their own. As strange as it may seem, creating separations between discrete elements of conflict can produce significant shifts, allowing us to approach them more constructively.

The goal of separating these aspects or elements of conflict is not, however, to *keep* them separate, but to clarify what lies hidden beneath and between them, thereby laying the groundwork for their subsequent recombination, and the emergence of a higher order synthesis. Doing so can reveal previously ignored exits from impasse and suggest transformational possibilities.

What follows are just ten out of a countless number of imaginable separations. What is important is for mediators to explore these dichotomies with the parties, by asking questions, facilitating dialogues, and searching for the deeper concerns that mean the most to them.

Separate Positions from Interests

In every conflict, parties take positions and insist on what they want. Yet when we analyze these positions, we discover that they are based on an unspoken perception that their conflicts are fundamentally competitive, win/lose, zero sum games; that

Note: [Portions of this chapter are based on our book, *Resolving Conflicts at Work: Ten Strategies For Everyone On The Job* 2010 (3rd Edition)].

https://doi.org/10.1515/9783110746365-008

there will not be enough to go around; that they do not have the power to get what they want without fighting for it, and that they need to compete and win in order not to lose what is important to them.

Yet beneath their positions lie a set of *interests*, which invite and give rise to cooperative, win/win, *non*-zero sum games, which are based on the assumption that there are deeper reasons why they have held fast to their positions; that there can actually be enough to go around; and that both sides' interests can be satisfied without anyone losing.

It then becomes possible to shift the problem solving process, so that instead of both sides debating increasingly polarized positions, negotiating adversarially for what is exclusively beneficial to them and demanding unilateral victories, they are invited to listen empathetically, engage in honest dialogue, and bargain collaboratively in an effort to satisfy both sides' interests.

We can begin separating positions from interests by posing or answering the following questions, among others:

- What do you want?
- Why is that important to you?
- If you could have any solution, what would you want?
- Why do you care so deeply about this?
- What fears, worries, or concerns do you have about this?
- What would be wrong with . . .?
- Why not do it this way . . .?
- What would you do if you were in charge?
- Why not just accept their [or my] proposal?
- What would your proposal be if the other side were willing to satisfy your interests?
- If you were to accept their proposal, what would you want in exchange?
- What could they do to make their proposal more acceptable to you?
- What would it take for you to give up your proposal?

Separate People from Problems

As Roger Fisher and William Ury explained in their classic text, *Getting to Yes*, when we separate the *person* with whom we are in conflict from the *problem* their behaviors or actions are creating, it becomes possible for us to be "soft on the person" and simultaneously "hard on the problem," allowing us to focus our attention on issues that can actually be resolved without triggering defensive or aggressive responses.

When we do so, we are able to see that our opponents – no matter how painful or despicable their behaviors – have redeeming human qualities we should be able to recognize, appreciate, and enlist in solving our common problems. If we can't, we may begin behaving toward them as they have behaved toward us, demeaning our-selves and making it more difficult to find solutions.

There are three steps we can take in labeling the problem as an "it," rather than as a "you." The first is to separate the person from the problem; the second is to be soft on the person; and the third is to be hard on the problem, in collaboration or alliance with the other person. We can begin, for example, by asking the following questions:

- Could you describe the problem as an "it," rather than as a "you"?
- What are three positive qualities your opponent possesses?
- How might you acknowledge and reinforce these qualities in your communica-tions and relationship with each other?
- What specifically is your opponent *doing* that is bothering you?
- How do you usually respond when your opponent engages in this behavior?
- What do you want or expect from your opponent? Why do you expect that? Is your expectation realistic? If not, what might you do instead?
- Has your response been successful in changing your opponent's behavior? Why not? How could it be more successful?
- Are you in some indirect way rewarding behaviors you do not like?
- What could you do differently to respond more skillfully to your opponent's behaviors?

Separate Problems from Solutions

When we are in conflict, we can become so focused on our disagreements, or what the other side did, or on bolstering our positions, or on seeking quick solutions, that we lose perspective, fail to see the problem from multiple perspectives, and end up ignoring the deeper and more important issues.

As a result, we can end up solving the wrong problem, or our solution can get rejected because the other side was not invited to participate in defining the problem, or we did not take their interests into account. We may then become locked in moun-tainous disputes over molehills, and unable to communicate or find constructive solutions without replicating the very conditions that created the conflict in the first place.

Research on problem solving reveals that the effectiveness of solutions increases by nearly 85 percent once the real problem has been identified. When we spend time together identifying, discussing, and analyzing the problem, resolution often emerges effortlessly. We can begin do so by posing the following questions:

- What exactly is the problem? What is the conflict about? Why is it about that?
- When did the conflict first begin? Why then?
- Who does it impact or involve? Why them?
- What kind of conflict is it? Why that kind?

- What aspects of the conflict have so far been overlooked? Why those?
- How has your understanding of the problem or conflict changed or evolved over time?
- What specific actions or inactions do you think helped cause or aggravate the conflict?
- What does your opponent think caused the conflict? What do your colleagues think?
- Can you break the conflict down into separate parts? What are they?
- How would you prioritize these parts?
- What might you or others have done to prevent the problem from occurring, or made it easier to handle?

Separate Commonalities from Differences

When we are in conflict, we pay great attention to our differences and tend to disregard our similarities, so that it becomes difficult to remember what we have in common. Cultivating awareness of shared interests allows us to recognize that we all care about similar issues. Indeed, by definition, conflicts always take place between people who care deeply and oppositely about the same issues. The following questions can help define a *context* of commonalities within which differences can be surfaced, discussed, and appreciated without canceling or overwhelming what we share:

- What are three things you think you may have in common with your opponent?
- If you were reluctant, resistant, or unable to identify three, what was it in *you* that made it difficult to do so?
- How much do you actually know about your opponent?
- What is one thing you do not know but would like to find out?
- What questions could you ask to learn more about your opponent?
- What are some things you assume about your opponent without trying to discover whether they are true or not?
- How have these assumptions influenced your choices? How have they impacted your responses and reactions?
- What are three values, beliefs, goals, or principles you think you might have in common?
- What are three possible solutions to your conflict that you think you both might be willing to accept?

Identifying what we have in common with our opponent can be transformational – not only because we begin to see them differently, but because doing so makes *us* less reactive and adversarial, and more positive and powerful in solving problems. It encourages us to surrender the idea that our conflicts can be solely defined in terms of "good" and "evil," or solved with "either/or" approaches, and invites us to focus instead on our commonalities, and search for "both/and" options.

Separate the Future from the Past

In every conflict, the past weighs heavily both on the present and on the future. This is especially true in couples, families, and organizations with cultures of blaming and conflict avoidance; and where disputes are routinely suppressed, denied, settled partially, and resolved incompletely. In these organizations, conflicts are permitted to fester and multiply; or they are isolated, shunned, compromised, and sidelined. Most often, they are passed on to others through gossip and rumors, and are nursed or hoarded, often for generations.

We can disagree forever about what happened in the past, or who did what to whom, or who did it first, or who is most at fault. We each have our own stories to tell based on what we have perceived and filtered through our physical responses, emotions, biases, preconceptions, and needs. We each sincerely believe our own stories to be true, because if they weren't, we might see ourselves as wrong, or bad, or at fault, or unentitled to get our needs met and interests satisfied.

By starting with what we want for the future, rather than ascribing blame for what happened in the past, we may begin to see that ultimately, none of our efforts to fix fault, or shame and blame others for what happened, or punish them for what is now over, really matters, and that the only healthy and intelligent thing to do is to let it go and work together to create a future that is different from the past. In doing so, it may be helpful to ask the following questions:

– What issues regarding the past are you stuck on and unable to agree?
– Are your disagreements about the past about who is to blame?
– Is it likely that you will *ever* succeed in resolving these issues?
– Is it likely that the other person will ever agree with you?
– If not, what would it take for you to give up your efforts to convince your opponents that they are wrong, and you are right?
– What would the consequences be for both of you if you could instead agree on what you want for the present or the future?
– What might you have to give up? What might you gain?
– What are your goals for the present? For the future?
– Why not focus on those instead of on the past?

Separate Emotions from Negotiations

We generally think of emotions as irrational, uncontrollable, dangerous, and useless in problem solving. Yet we are all emotional beings, every conflict has an emotional component, and suppressing our emotions does not make them disappear, but simply encourages them to submerge and reappear elsewhere, preoccupying our conscious and unconscious attention, and creating an appearance of irrationality. These unaddressed and unresolved emotions distract us, and make it more difficult to focus attention on finding logical or strategic solutions to our problems.

At the other extreme, when we dump our emotions onto others, we risk escalating our conflicts and becoming unable to identify or focus on practical priorities. We may fail to perceive openings for dialogue and opportunities for resolution and find it difficult to remember what is actually important. As a result, we may behave destructively and be unable to negotiate mutually acceptable solutions.

Emotions, however, are positive and constructive, as well as negative and destructive, and they are not so much irrational as *non*-rational. Emotions can help us recognize what people care most deeply about, and can be highly useful, if we can discover how to turn them in the direction of problem solving. The following questions can help us identify the emotional issues in conflict, support people in expressing their feelings constructively, and assist them in negotiating without feeling trapped in counter-productive emotional exchanges, or being drawn into pointless "tit-for-tat" accusations:

- What emotions have you experienced in your conflict?
- What do you need to say or do in order to let go of them?
- Have you tried communicating your emotions to your opponent? If so, what was their response? If not, why not?
- How might you express your emotions more constructively or skillfully, and not generate responses you do not like?
- Do you know what your opponent is feeling emotionally? What are they? What have you done to find out? Has that been successful? What might you do instead?
- What level of permission have you given to your opponent to express emotions to you?
- What would it take for you to give greater permission?
- What could you do to encourage your opponent to communicate his or her emotions, let them go, and negotiate more logically?
- What might you lose by doing so? Would it be possible for you to initiate an emotionally honest conversation with your opponent and not lose anything in the process? How?
- Have your emotions gotten in the way of your ability to negotiate logically? Have your opponent's emotions gotten in the way?
- How have either of your emotions blocked the ability to have a constructive conversation?
- What could you do to complete them, and get them out of the way?

Separate Process from Content

In nearly every conflict, we become so focused on content and what we want, that we pay far less attention to process and how we go about getting it. Yet it is often the process, rather than the content, that leads to impasse, and changing the means we use to achieve our ends *automatically* leads to a different end.

Conflicts that only concern content – for example, over the accuracy of information, or data, facts, chronology, precise recollections, and matters of substance – are significantly different from those that concern process – for example, over *how* we are working together, talking to each other, negotiating agreements, building relationships, and developing respect and trust for one another. Both are important, but where people differ on content, process can provide a common ground for reaching agreements. The following questions can help to separate process issues from content:

- What role has process played in your conflict?
- How could the process you are using to communicate or make decisions be improved?
- How might changing the process impact the content of your communications or decisions?
- How might it improve your relationship?
- Do the process conflicts you have been experiencing reveal any underlying content issues? How? What are they? How might they be addressed?
- What process rules do you think might be agreeable to your opponent? Which may not? Why?
- What could you suggest as an alternative if your opponent does not agree?
- What values do you believe should underlie and inform your processes? What values would your opponent suggest?
- How might you develop process rules together with your opponent that express your shared values?

Separate Options from Choices

Before agreeing on solutions to our conflicts, it is useful to expand the range of potential alternatives and not assume the options are fixed. By playing with ideas, brainstorming alternatives, and considering all the possibilities, we can increase our chances of finding a better method for resolving disputes and revealing options that satisfy both side's interests.

Options are creative possibilities, and the most effective way of generating them is to give your imagination full sway. Creativity automatically arises when we search together for new ways of solving problems, rather than arguing over whose solution is best. This means *not* evaluating or rejecting anyone's suggestions until all ideas have been expressed; encouraging wild, funny, and creative ideas; piggybacking on each other's suggestions and improving earlier proposals; and going for broke – asking for everything we want. The following questions may help identify creative solutions:

- What creative options can you think of for resolving your conflict that have not been fully considered or creatively re-imagined? (List everything you can think of without considering whether they are realistic or acceptable to your opponent.)
- What would you prioritize as the top three options?
- What are three silly, outrageous, completely ridiculous, or impossible options? How might they be reframed to apply to your problem?
- How is the problem like some object you see in front of you? What options can you derive from this list?
- What words would you use to describe the problem? What are the opposites of these words, and might they lead you to solutions?
- What ideas might your opponent or experts or outsiders suggest for resolving your dispute that you haven't fully considered?
- Close your eyes and imagine coming up with the perfect solution. What was it?
- How might you search for solutions together?

Separate Criteria from Selection

An alternative approach is to focus instead on identifying criteria for a successful outcome *before* coming up with a solution, which may make it easier to determine whether it will be effective. Criteria can consist of the elements in what we imagine as a perfect solution; or what would satisfy everyone's interests; or what may be required to achieve common goals or conform to shared values; or what would provide the greatest benefit to others. Some criteria in resolving conflicts may include:

- Equality in treatment, or outcomes
- Agreed-upon ethical standards, values, or principles, such as fairness
- Jointly seeking the advice of experts or professionals
- Ranking or weighting different priorities according to some agreed-upon system
- The least costly alternative
- The least time-consuming alternative
- Bartering or exchanging one thing for another
- What the likely legal outcome would be
- Tradition or precedent
- What it would cost to buy or replace the item
- An algorithm or mathematical formula
- Chance (for example, a coin toss)
- Whoever has the greatest emotional commitment or investment in the outcome

- Letting each side take turns picking a solution based only on subjective preferences
- The likely effect on third parties, such as customers, society, co-workers, or children
- The likely impact on shared values, such as communication or teamwork
- The likely future consequences, for example, on a strategic plan, vision, or mission

The following questions may help in identifying criteria that can lead to better solutions:

- What criteria could you use to select the best option for resolving your issues?
- What would make any solution seem fair?
- What outcomes would allow you to achieve what you both want?
- How have other people solved the problem?
- What expert opinion might be useful?
- What would happen if you litigated the issue? Why?
- What ethical or value considerations might influence your choice?
- Why do you think a particular criterion would *not* work? Do those reasons suggest a way of modifying it so it might work?
- What outcomes would make you both feel you had won?
- What outcomes would achieve the best results in your future communications and relationship? Why?
- What would provide the greatest benefit to your family members, neighbors, colleagues, customers, and the public?
- What insights have you gained from your conflict experiences so far? How might they be used to improve the outcome?

Separate Yourself from Others

Adversarial emotional exchanges often paradoxically end up blurring the lines that separate us from our opponents, causing us to lose sight of who we really are, what is rightfully and appropriately ours, and what rightfully and appropriately belongs to our opponents, or to both of us. We can easily lose track of what we know is right and become confused by what our hostile emotions of the moment tempt us to do or say.

Here are some questions that can help create clearer separations between you and your opponent. They need to be authentic and natural, and if they seem staged or artificial, others may feel manipulated, insulted, or betrayed. They should be phrased to demonstrate willingness to accept responsibility for our part in keeping the conflict going:

- What did I do that upset you? How could I fix that in a way that would feel satisfying to you? What is one thing I could do differently to improve our communication and relationship?
- Here is what I understand you are asking for: [specific statement]. Is that correct?
- Now, would you like to know one thing I think you could do differently to improve our communication and relationship?
- What do you believe I'm asking for? Would you like to know if you're right?
- Here's what I think you are asking for . . . . Here's what I hear that you want that I agree with . . .
- Here's where I think we may disagree. [Insert specific statements for each]. Do you agree?
- Instead of using the word 'you,' would it be possible to make the same statement using the word 'I'?
- What do you see as the main differences between us?
- What do you see as our main similarities?
- What role would you like me to play in this conversation?
- I hear that you feel I am being [insert specific statement, such as "controlling"]. Would you like to know what I'm really worried about or afraid of?
- Here is what I am prepared to do in response to your requests. Is there something more you would like me to do?
- What are you prepared to do in response to my requests? Would you like to know what more I would like you to do?
- Thank you for your ideas. I appreciate your concerns and hearing your point of view. Would it be okay if I think about what you said and let you know my response tomorrow?

Conclusion

Every conflict *already* contains the seeds of its own resolution, and we are able to find these seeds faster and more effectively by initially separating what matters from what gets in the way, then searching for solutions to both. The secret is to center ourselves in what *really* matters, to learn how to unlock what gets in the way, and to discover the hidden opportunities that lie hidden in the places where they meet, which are also the places where we get stuck.

We can do so only by eliciting and listening to the profound, poignant, and vulnerable moments in our conflict conversations, deciphering their cryptic subconscious signals, and unveiling their deepest and most important meanings. When we succeed, there is nothing left to separate, and the divisions between us begin to heal.

Robin Cooper, Terry Morrow Nelson

Chapter 9
Collaborative Practices in Organizations: Managing Conflict and Leading Constructive Change

Abstract: As our society becomes more diverse and issues become increasingly complex, organizations are challenged to transcend boundaries and inspire team members to understand and navigate diverse practices, perspectives, and interests. Conflict is inevitable in organizations, and collaboration is one pathway for managing conflict and engaging stakeholders in jointly resolving a problem or producing a desired outcome. Collaborators have high concern for both personal goals and relationships. Because collaboration requires a commitment to finding mutually agreeable solutions, this also communicates mutual respect, which can strengthen relationships and support team-building. In addition, collaboration fosters creative idea generation, with the potential to bring about unanticipated positive outcomes. Multiple forms of power can be leveraged to create positive results for the organization and its stakeholders, and this chapter discusses five forms of power as well as the importance of engaging informal and formal leaders to utilize their unique power to tackle complex issues and create sustainable outcomes together. An example of how collaboration has been used to promote positive health outcomes by promoting collaboration between multiple stakeholders is discussed.

Keywords: collaboration, collaborative practices, organizational conflict, workplace conflict, stakeholder engagement, power, leadership

It is easy for people to agree in theory that collaboration in the workplace is desirable. It is not always as easy to explain what collaboration consists of and how to go about practicing collaboration in the midst of deadlines, demands, and diverse stakeholders. In this chapter we explore those issues, looking at the following questions:

1. What does collaboration mean within the organizational context?
2. How does one identify and engage with internal and external stakeholders?
3. How do effective collaborative practices reduce organizational conflict?
4. How can collaborative leadership practices promote engagement and positive change?

In addition to addressing these questions conceptually, we share an example from our professional context to illustrate challenges, successes, and lessons learned.

https://doi.org/10.1515/9783110746365-009

What Do We Mean by Collaborative Practices?

Collaboration in an organizational context is generally thought of as the act of working together to produce something or jointly resolve a problem. In the field of conflict resolution, collaboration is identified as one of the five major approaches to managing conflict, also referred to as conflict styles – the others being avoidance, accommodation, compromise, and competition (Wilmot & Hocker, 2001). According to the two-dimensional model of conflict (Katz & Lawyer, 1992), collaborators fall high on the scales of concern for personal goals and concern for relationships. As Katz and Lawyer explain,

> The collaborator's approach to conflict is to manage it by maintaining interpersonal relationships and ensuring that both parties to the conflict achieve their personal goals. This attitude toward conflict is one in which the collaborator acts not only on behalf of his or her self-interest but on behalf of the opposing party's interests as well. Upon recognizing that a conflict exists, the collaborator utilizes appropriate conflict management methods to manage the conflict. This is a *win/win* posture, in which both the collaborator's stance toward conflict management and that of the other party are *win*. (p. 95)

While this passage is referring specifically to managing conflict, the concept applies to problem-solving in the organizational context, whereby those involved in addressing a concern or problem in the workplace need to work together. The collaborator approaches that effort from the perspective of cooperation and constructive engagement. Collaborators focus on a team effort and finding mutually agreeable solutions. Wilmot and Hocker (2001) observe, "Collaboration differs from compromise because in compromise, the parties look for an easy intermediate position that partially satisfies them both, whereas in collaboration, the parties work creatively to find new solutions that will maximize goals for them both" (p. 161).

When we refer to constructive engagement, and collaborative practices, what specifically are we referring to? Collaboration is manifested in several different ways in an organizational context. This would include inviting the participation of multiple people in the problem-solving process (see section on stakeholders below), hearing all perspectives, and being open to many ideas. Collaboration also involves broad communication, sharing information openly and making sure communication is flowing in all directions, not just top down. Collaborative practices also include joint decision-making, whereby the decisions and solutions developed are agreed upon through a collective process.

As with each of the approaches people may take to addressing conflicts or problems, there are advantages and disadvantages to collaboration. Clearly, one advantage of collaboration is that all parties have an opportunity to be involved in the solution to a shared problem. Because collaboration requires a commitment to finding mutually agreeable solutions, this also communicates mutual respect, which can strengthen relationships and support team-building. In addition, it fosters creative idea generation, with the potential to bring about unanticipated positive outcomes. At the same time, collaboration does require a lot of time and energy! There is also the risk of individuals in positions of power using what could be called *pseudo-collaboration* as a way to manipulate procedures and outcomes, making a show of being collaborative, but really using their power to influence outcomes in a manner that preserves their power (Wilmot & Hocker).

Based on these advantages and disadvantages, the best times to use collaboration in an organizational context may be when there is the time and opportunity to engage in a thoughtful, creative process that includes the input of all involved. When team building or relationship maintenance are important, collaborative practices are an excellent choice because those who engage in collaboration find their relationship strengthened as a result of this constructive, respectful engagement. At times of urgency, or in situations where a unilateral decision is needed from an organization's leader, collaboration would not be the best approach; in these situations, it is best to be clear about the fact that the decision will not be made collectively.

Who is Included in Collaborative Practice?

One of the first steps in developing a collaborative process is the identification of participants, which calls for conducting a stakeholder analysis. A stakeholder is someone who is involved in or impacted by a process. This can include both internal and external stakeholders – that is, people within or outside of the organization who can influence or may be affected by a process or decision. Justice and Jamieson (1999) highlighted four questions that can guide the identification of stakeholders, which leads to the selection of participants. They asked:
1. Who has power to block decisions/actions?
2. Who cares about these decisions/actions?
3. Who can/will support the work of the group?
4. Who has special skills or interests relevant to the group?

Bringing together the people identified in the answers to these questions increases the likelihood that the collaborative process will be based on good information, have the required resources, and that any decisions will be implemented and have a strong chance of being effective.

Power is an important element of collaboration. For some, the word "power" can conjure up thoughts of "power over" someone or something. Another perspective on power is "power to" or influence. French and Raven (1959) have identified five common types of power. Each type is characterized by unique qualities of social influence.
1) *Reward Power* is based on the perception that an individual can offer perceived benefits or remove elements that are perceived to be negative. It includes both the

value of the specific reward and the probability that the individual can ultimately provide the reward.

2) *Referent Power* is based on one's identification with another individual. Strong relational ties between individuals, for example, increase their influence upon one another. An individual who is loved or respected by others within a group will likely have more leverage than someone who is disliked or unknown.

3) *Legitimate Power* is rooted in one's perception that the individual meets a certain cultural standard that denotes influence. This type of power could be rooted in one's formal position within an organization or community, gender, or age, for example.

4) *Expert Power* is held by individuals who are perceived to have knowledge, experience or expertise that is valuable within a specific context.

5) *Coercive Power* stems from one's ability to create punishments. It is also dependent on whether the punishment is a perceived threat and the individual's ability to follow through on the punishment.

Individuals reflecting multiple types of power within an organization can make valuable contributions to collaborative efforts.

Once the relevant stakeholders have been identified, there are several aspects of engaging with participants that contribute to a smoother process and stronger outcomes. These include making sure there is a setting for collaborative work that supports discussion and any physical activity that may be required; monitoring and managing the group dynamics, paying attention to the relations between group members; and selecting procedures that will support the group's goals and be perceived as fair. These have been referred to as environmental, relational, and procedural aspects of group facilitation (Isenhart & Spangle, 2000), and they apply to collaborative practices more broadly.

How Do Collaborative Practices Relate to Conflict in Organizations?

Workplace conflict results in multiple negative outcomes within organizations. Dana (2003) demonstrated the various costs associated with workplace conflict, including not only the expense of lost employees, but also the costs of wasted time, lower decision quality, and even sabotage or theft of supplies and equipment among those who remain. He noted that research shows 65% of performance problems in the workplace are tied to relationship problems between employees. As noted earlier, collaboration offers positive results related to both outcomes and relationships in the workplace. Having said that, it would be a mistake to assume that collaboration automatically means there will not be conflict! With a collaborative process, we are engaging more participants with varying perspectives, so conflict is inevitable. However, when participants feel the process has been fair and transparent, there is a higher likelihood of acceptance and support of a decision, even if it was not someone's desired outcome.

At times when conflict does arrive during collaborative efforts, the tools of organizational conflict resolution can be effectively applied. These include listening sessions, identification of the interests and needs that lie behind positions, conflict coaching with individuals, as well as mediation between individuals in conflict, or facilitation of group conflict resolution or problem-solving sessions.

How Can Collaborative Leadership Practices Promote Engagement?

As organizations seek to provide inclusive workplace environments, efforts to be inclusive carry over into collaborative practice. At each step of the process: identifying stakeholders, communicating and sharing information, brainstorming, decision making, implementing and evaluating activities, to be truly inclusive it is important not only to have a diversity of participants involved but also to invite the active participation and differing perspectives of those bringing diverse experience to the effort. Organizations are challenged to transcend boundaries and inspire team members to understand and navigate diverse practices, perspectives, and interests. Inclusive collaborative practice recognizes that time is needed to allow for all perspectives to be heard, and time is needed to be sure the reasoning behind those perspectives is shared and understood before proceeding.

Effective leadership is necessary to promote effective collaboration. The Center for Creative Leadership (CCL) describes boundary-spanning leadership as "leadership that bridges boundaries between groups in service of a larger organizational vision, mission, or goal" (Ernst & Yip, 2009, p. 1). CCL researchers have identified five boundaries that impede the effectiveness of organizations and systems:

1. *Vertical boundaries*: hierarchical lines within organizations.
2. *Horizontal boundaries*: the lines that divide organizations, disciplines, departments, and product lines.
3. *Stakeholder boundaries*: the varying perspectives, goals, needs, and roles of clients, partners, vendors, regulators, and others who are connected to the organization.
4. *Demographic boundaries:* differences that emerge from individuals' identity including generational, gender, religious, education, cultural, physical ability, skills, and training.
5. *Geographic boundaries*: the influence of different regions, cultures, and physical locations. (Yip, Ernst, & Campbell, 2009)

These boundaries can lead to divisive conflict, competition for resources, and diminished outcomes as individuals compete with one another and navigate fractured relationships. At the same time, boundaries can also create opportunities for new ways of thinking. The most effective leaders find ways to overcome boundaries such as peer-to-peer competition and personality differences, organizational power dynamics, group norms and cultures, ideologies, and regions to prevent silos and promote innovation.

One aspect of overcoming boundaries is to involve both formal and informal leaders. Vera & Crossman (2004) and Berson et al (2006), suggest that leadership practices involve both formal and informal leaders situated in multiple levels throughout the organization that engage in various degrees of shared leadership. The idea that some people are always leaders and others are always followers is a static perspective that is more valuable for an organizational chart than for understanding the reality of organizational leadership. "Leaders" and "Followers", according to Pearce (2004), are identified better by their levels of influence within the system as opposed to their official positions within the organization. In a dynamic open system, like that of today's organizations, an individual can oscillate between being a leader and a follower depending on her expertise in the given situation, social capital within a given network, and passion for a certain issue or project.

Learning Together to Adapt Together

The process of sharing individual perspectives, referred to by Van Meter & Stevens (2000) as collaborative elaboration, leads to an environment where learners are constructing understanding together that would be impossible on their own (Greeno et al., 1996). Kukla (2000) asserts that reality is constructed by our individual activities, and people collectively co-create an understanding of the world. In essence, knowledge is a product of humans and is developed through a process of social and cultural construction (McMahon, 1997; Prawat & Flooden, 1994).

According to Hanah (2009), in order to flourish in the knowledge economy, organizations must develop effective learning practices. In our dynamic, global system, organizations are open systems and must be able to constantly adapt to the opportunities and threats of their external environment (Burke, 2002). Leaders can employ a reductionist strategy with the goal of controlling learning using a top-down approach, or they can focus on adaptability. Research shows that that the latter approach tends to promote increased organizational effectiveness (Marion & Uhl-Bien, 2001).

Hamel (2000) argues that learning and adaption occur best when coalitions of activists, rooted in social networks at multiple levels of the organization (or system), serve as catalysts that promote learning through social interaction. These individuals are termed knowledge catalysts. In addition to employing knowledge catalysts, organizations will do well to establish conditions that promote engagement of knowledge catalysts within social networks in a way that promotes organizational or system learning (Hanah, 2009). Here, the top leaders are responsible for creating the conditions that maximize the emergence of knowledge creation and diffusion but limit their involvement in the actual creative process of how it is integrated into the organization or system. Kozlowski and Klein (2000) point out that "a phenomenon is emergent when it originates in the cognition, affect, behaviors, or other characteristics of individuals, is amplified by their interactions, and manifests as a higher-level collective phenomenon" (p. 55).

Positive organizational scholarship is a growing field of scholars and practitioners who are interested in promoting organizational and community development and change using an opportunity-centered approach rather than a problem-centered approach. Rather than focusing on diagnosing the problems within the system, the appreciative or opportunity-centered approach searches for areas of strength and health within the organization or community and corresponding opportunities for expansion and further growth. Additionally, data collection in the problem-centric approach tends to create a sense of fear, anxiety and skepticism which generally leads to less buy-in and motivation from community members receiving the feedback, thereby making the solutions less sustainable (Fredrickson, 2003). Collaborative, opportunity-focused approaches lead to healthier work environments as well as better outcomes.

Collaborative Practices in Action

In this section, we offer an example of collaborative practice within a large private university's health professions program: the Interprofessional Diabetes Education and Awareness (IDEA) Initiative. The National Diabetes Prevention Program recommends a collaborative approach and points to the importance of partnerships between health care professionals, academia, employers, community-based organizations, insurers, federal agencies, and other stakeholders. As diabetes-related health care costs rise along with the rapid increase in the number of adults and children with diabetes, it is important that the capacity of the entire system be fully leveraged. The objectives of the IDEA initiative were and continue to be:

– To increase the awareness of diabetes, knowledge about diabetes, and create behavior change to promote the prevention and management of diabetes among residents of Broward County, Florida.
– To build a model for community partnerships between academia, corporations, non-profits, government, and civic society that impacts the prevention and management of diabetes.
– To prepare emerging health care professionals to develop and serve on collaborative interprofessional teams, a skill increasingly needed in our health care system.

The IDEA Initiative involves 85–100 students and faculty each year from 15 different health care professions across multiple regional campuses in collaboration with over 20 community partners to address the diabetes epidemic in their community.

Those involved with the initiative have encountered the five boundaries discussed earlier that have the potential to impede the effectiveness of organizations and systems, and so project leaders have been intentional about transcending these boundaries. The students and faculty involved do not receive any payment for their efforts, so the program leaders rely on other strategies for promoting commitment and collaboration. As discussed earlier, considering the best type of power or influence to employ is key. In this initiative, two of the most effective forms of power are referent power and reward power. The initiative leader is intentional about building relationships with the faculty and student team leaders and promoting a sense of team among the participants throughout the year, especially at the very beginning.

During the IDEA Kick-off, teams do a Strengths Finder assessment, share their results with one another, and discuss the collective strengths of their team. They also create a team name and logo. The goal of this activity is to help participants transcend their professional identity as a physician assistant, pharmacist, or dentist, for example, and create a new team identity that they collectively own. These relational ties and sense of team promote a sense of commitment to their team members in addition to their commitment to the initiative's mission.

Reward power is also intentionally employed. At the kick-off event, participants learn about why the work they will do throughout the year is so important. They learn about the mission, the impact, and the challenges. Throughout the year, leaders continue to talk about why the work we are doing is so important and share stories of impact and change. The goal is to make it personally meaningful and intrinsically rewarding. At the end of the year, team faculty and students receive a letter of recognition that they add to their portfolio. Team leaders also are included in the grants that the leader has been awarded, which is an added benefit to their faculty promotion efforts.

Clear roles and responsibilities are an important part of collaboration. In this initiative, the IDEA Director leads the overall initiative, the Research Director focuses on research and grants, and the Community Collaboration Director works with community partners to set up workshop topics, dates, times, and locations while ensuring that partners' interests and needs are met. Partners are identified initially either through personal phone call invitations from the Community Collaborations Director or by word of mouth from other community partners. In an effort to promote a sense of belonging within the initiative and thank partners for their collaborative efforts, every partner receives an IDEA t-shirt and other gift such as a water bottle with the IDEA logo. The research team is in the process of developing an action research project to engage community partners in shaping the initiative processes and outcomes.

The success of the initiative depends largely upon the faculty team leaders that volunteer their time – some have remained with the program since its inception 10 years ago. The faculty team leaders and student team leaders meet regularly to make decisions about the direction of the program, solve challenges, develop solutions, and share wins. The positional leaders and team members oscillate between roles as leaders and followers depending on their area of expertise, and all members have ownership in the outcomes and success of the initiative.

Multiple presentations and publications have been completed on the initiative. At the end of each year, faculty and student focus groups are held in an effort to promote continuous learning and program development. Faculty report that they continue to stay involved because they believe in the mission, enjoy the camaraderie of the faculty team, and feel a sense of pride in the work the team is doing. Students also report that the new interprofessional relationships they build are valuable, and they enjoy the opportunity to interact with workshops participants and contribute to our mission of diabetes prevention and management in our community.

Conclusion

In conclusion, we have learned that when conducted according to best practices, collaboration is generative and inclusive and generally promotes higher morale. Stakeholder engagement is key to success, and this includes individuals not only who may impact or be impacted by the outcomes of the process, but also individuals reflecting various types of power within the organization. Collaborative efforts will be most successful if all stakeholders understand why the work is important and have a role in crafting the desired outcomes as well as the strategies for achieving those goals. Relational ties are foundational to success in collaborative efforts, so team-building is important. In addition, crafting an optimal environment for dynamic collaboration to occur is important.

It is also important to understand what impedes collaboration and times when using alternatives to collaboration is the wisest choice. In cases of urgency or emergency, the time required for a genuinely collaborative process is not available, and so other decision-making processes are more appropriate. When collaboration is the stated approach, it is important that the process genuinely be inclusive of various perspectives and ideas, rather than being collaboration in name only. When employed authentically, positive change will follow.

References

Berson, Y., Nemanich, L.A., Waldman, D.A., Galvin, B.M., and Keller, R.T. (2006). Leadership and organizational learning: A multi-levels perspective. *The Leadership Quarterly*. 17, 577–594.
Burke, W.W. (2002). *Organizational Change: theory and practice*. Thousand Oaks, CA: Sage.

Dana, D. (2003). *Managing differences: How to build better relationships at work and home.* Prairie Village, KS: MTI Publications.

Ernst, C. & Yip, J. (2009) Boundary spanning leadership: Tactics for bridging social boundaries in organization. In T. Pittinsky (Ed.) *Crossing the divide: Intergroup leadership in a world of difference* (pp. 89–99). Boston, MA; Harvard Business Press.

Fredrickson, B. L. (2003). The value of positive emotions. *American Scientist*, 91, 330–335.

French, J. R. P., Jr., & Raven, B. (1959). The bases of social power. In D. Cartwright (Ed.), *Studies in social power* (pp. 150–167). Ann Arbor, MI: Institute for Social Research.

Greeno, J. G., Collins, A. M., & Resnick, L. B. (1996). Cognition and learning. In D. Berliner and R. Calfee (Eds.), *Handbook of Educational Psychology* (pp. 15–41). New York, NY: MacMillian.

Hamel, G., Leading the revolution. Harvard Business School Press, Boston, 2000.

Hanah, S.T. (2009). Leadership and Organizational Learning: A multi-level approach to building and leading learning organizations. *The Leadership Quarterly*. 20(1), p 34–48

Isenhart, M. W. & Spangle, M. (2000). *Collaborative approaches to resolving conflict.* Thousand Oaks, CA: Sage.

Justice, T. & Jamieson, D. W. (1999). *The facilitator's handbook.* New York, NY: AMA Publications.

Katz, N. H. and Lawyer, J. W. (1992). *Communication and Conflict Resolution*. Dubuque, IA: Kendall/ Hunt Publishing.

Kozlowski, S.W.J. & Klein, K.J. (2000) A Multilevel Approach to Theory and Research in Organizations: Contextual, Temporal, and Emergent Processes. In: Klein K.J. and Kozlowski, S.W.J., Eds., Multilevel Theory, Research, and Methods in Organizations: Foundations, Extensions, and New Directions, Jossey-Bass, San Francisco, 3–90.

Kukla, A. (2000). *Social Constructivism and the Philosophy of Science.* New York, NY: Routledge.

Marion, R. and Uhl-Bien, M. (2001). Leadership in complex organizations. *Leadership Quarterly*. 12(4), 389–218.

McMahon, M. (1997, December). Social Constructivism and the World Wide Web: A Paradigm for Learning. Paper presented at the ASCILITE conference. Perth, Australia.

Pearce, C.L. (2004). The future of leadership: combining vertical and shared leadership to transform knowledge work. *Academy of Management Executive*. 18, 47–57.

Prawat, R. S., & Floden, R. E. (1994). Philosophical Perspectives on Constructivist Views of Learning. *Educational Psychologist*, 29(1),37–48.

Van Meter, P. and Stevens, R.J. (2000), The role of theory in the study of peer collaboration. *Journal of Experimental Education*, 69, 113–117.

Vera, D. and Crossan, M. (2004). Strategic leadership and organizational learning. *Academy of Management Review*. 20(2),222–240.

Wilmot, W. W. and Hocker, J. L. (2001). *Interpersonal conflict* (6th ed.). New York, NY: McGraw-Hill.

Yip, J., Ernst, C., and Campbell, M. (2009). *Boundary spanning leadership: Mission Critical perspectives from the executive suite.* Greensboro, NC: Center for Creative Leadership Organizational Leadership White Paper.

Brian Polkinghorn, Brittany Foutz

Chapter 10
Shifting the Focus from Stand-Alone Dispute Systems Design Elements to Creating Self-Correcting and Fluid Organizations

Abstract: Modern Dispute Systems Designs literature typically places an emphasis on precision analysis of conflict sources, especially those deeply embedded in structural and systemic elements of organizations and institutions. Subsequent processes and programs are then "designed" to address the system manifestations and symptoms arising from disputes and conflicts. What is not given as much scholarly thought is the context within which an organization resides. Just as an organism exists, thrives, and dies in a given environment, so too do organizations. The more hostile the environment, the more armor the organization needs, along with a requisite shift from mere tactical risk management methods to more defensive strategic risk management practices. More importantly, what is further missing from the design literature is a focus on the effective use of ADR processes and programs as the basis upon which organizations learn to self-correct and remain fluid and vibrant. Incorporating creative problem solving into daily decision making allows for a variety of process paths to expand to provide more inclusive input, and other value driven actions that allow the organization to shift out of the mechanical process analogy, which dominates our current thinking, into a more biological process analogy where self-corrections are built into system maturation. This shift to an evolutionary focus opens many new forms of intervention that allow organizations to "experiment with their structure and function" as a means to evolve, in a fast and fluid manner, to meet current and emerging needs, as well as survive, even thrive, and hopefully remain relevant.

Keywords: soft systems, open systems, external control, contextual environments, self-correcting organizations, fast thinking

Since the dawn of time, humans have been innovating, experimenting with, and building tools, methods, processes, and systems to regulate and manage disputes. Evidence of this is found on a massive scale. Stories have been passed down through countless generations depicting specific instances of disputing where valuable social survival lessons continue to be woven into *evolving* social fabrics. Myths, legends, symbols, traditions, norms, rules, laws, and other devices serve the collective purpose of holding groups, organizations, and societies together. By default, this means they must regulate a variety of forms and types of conflict. Conflict is embedded in all our societies. It is not all that unusual for many groups to chart their origin history to include conflict episodes being peppered throughout. Some historical accounts

https://doi.org/10.1515/9783110746365-010

involve armed conflict, such as the Israelites engaging in many skirmishes with rivals across millennia. Other instances are precisely recorded, such as on June 28, 1389, at the battle at the Field of Blackbirds. This is the location and event that, for the Serbian people, shaped their modern nationalist and spiritual identity. Under the gallant leadership of Prince Lazar Hrebeljanovic, Serbian forces fought the invading Ottoman forces under Sultan Murad I. The Serbians, choosing death over submission, were annihilated but a national identity was born.

Conflict also shapes deeply held belief systems and such is the case with all three of the great monotheistic faiths, Judaism, Christianity, and Islam. They share many common beliefs, one of which is that all humanity is descended from Adam. And what is one of the first things Adam and Eve do in the Garden of Eden? They disobeyed God and thus we inherited "the fall." It did not just impact Adam and Eve but their descendants which currently account for nearly six of every ten people in the world.[1] This story clearly implies, as humans we make mistakes and from those disputes arise.

One of the first known written environmental resource conflicts is recorded in the Book of Genesis where Abraham asks for and receives permission to dig a well (in Beersheba) from King Abimelech. Some of the King's subjects seized the well and Abraham brought the issue to the King where it was settled. It was not just a story of a struggle over a valuable and limited natural resource, but of two parties taking an oath and setting a pattern to resolve disputes. By engaging twice on the same issue, the parties were, in effect, constructing one of the first recorded dispute resolution systems. Likewise, in ancient Babylon, King Hammurabi developed one of the earliest known legal aids to dispense advice and judgments on what everyday people might do to settle their disputes. Known as the Code of Hammurabi it provided repercussions or penalties, sometimes quite harsh, for misconduct in civil and criminal cases. That is, depending on the status of the offender. If they are a slave, palace employee or average citizen the repercussions differ. Given this distinction, the impact of the role of the offender, within this system, provides for different penalties. Here we see a system that embeds unequal application based on systemic roles.

During the period of Pax Romana, an even more complex system of dispute settlement was developed to regulate Roman citizen to citizen conduct disputes as well between citizen and non-citizen, slave, foreigner and so on. Rules of trade between various parts of the empire, conquered territories, and kingdoms, were codified and

---

1 Life Science estimates the world's population in July 2020 to be roughly 7.80 billion (https://www.livescience.com/global-population.html). Compiling numbers on adherents of each of the three monotheistic faith, places their combined numbers at roughly 4.51 billion humans. That accounts for 58% of humanity. Whether or not individuals believe the Adam and Eve story is inconsequential. Using this idea as a starting point on human interaction impacts most institutions structures and functions. Societal rules, regulations, laws, and dictates are affected and that can, and often does, impact the rules of conflict engagement.

disseminated. Likewise, over many historical periods, Pax Sinica or Chinese Peace, saw a flourishing of civilizations throughout many parts of Asia. Here too we see how systems evolved to address a plethora of issues.

Hundreds of years before Europeans set foot on the American continent, the Haudenosaunee lived in what is now Central and Western New York. They created the "Great Law of Peace" which is democratic and more evenly applied. This became the platform upon which the Six Nations built the Iroquois Confederacy. Common elements of the law appear to have influenced the drafters of the US Constitution.

These as just a few of countless examples of humans developing systems to manage disputes. One might reasonably argue that one of the oldest professions is that of dispute systems designer and yet it is relatively a new and, somewhat unsophisticated, lacking in elements that create flexibility and self-learning mechanisms for the organization or institution.

Modern Dispute Systems Design

Dispute Systems Design (DSD) is an awkward term, but it has been around for decades, and we are stuck with it. The Program on Negotiation at Harvard Law School provides a generic definition and description. Here we learn that it is a process of "identifying, designing, employing, and evaluating an effective means of resolving conflict within an organization. To be truly effective, dispute systems design must be thoroughly thought out and carefully constructed."

The question we need to ask is, are we importing a system to manage disputes into an already existing operating system or are we changing that system to incorporate means by which to prevent or manage disputes that may arise from system sources? That may sound odd but some of classic works in the field such as Ury, Brett and Goldberg (1988) and Costantino and Merchant (1996) are ambiguous on this topic.

DSD is applicable in any human group setting be it a scout troop or ground control operations at NASA. In each instance, systems come into play, and how the organization is constructed and the environment it inhabits are major factors on how and why disputes arise. Stroh (2015) applies systems thinking and problems solving goal orienting behaviors that are working on social change efforts while Lipsky's et al. (2003) comprehensive study focuses on workplace conflict management systems design where they intentionally bring in external features into the design equation. More recent work by Blomberg et. al. (2020) merges DSD into cases were disputes have a legal basis of action. The list of great work is slowly developing into a solid canon of literature. The good news, there are always new thinkers out there putting a twist on things and in this case, it is wise to bring in practitioner/scholars who can combine models with real world applications to shed more light on how DSD can evolve into much more than a management program or set of processes.

Things do not always go as planned though. I assisted a federal government agency that just wanted to build a program office and a set of processes and procedures to use in addressing issues and concerns. It was a classic "plug and play" approach and, as a result, the design effort missed opportunities to reinforce the values of the organization. The office languished and eventually merged under a human resources service sending messages to employees that their issues and concerns were not that of upper management. It suffered from a lack of a whole system thinking approach.

Then again, when the entire operating system is the focus for the organization, interesting things can happen. We have assisted organizations to reimagine, rethink and rebuild their organizations based on organizational values, mission, and goals. When we put our skills to good use as designers, we become a co-architect and remodeler of structure, function, and flow. We can be helpful in designing mechanisms that serve to recreate, recast, reaffirm, reinvent, and realize an organizations mission, vision, and goals. Managing disputes is therefore a manifestation of the organization's values and, as we will show later on, some organization's infuse conflict as a problem-solving growth opportunity to both reinforce and insulate a healthy and successful mission.

Designing a system therefore requires a wholistic systems approach where we examine not only flaws and sources of tension but also to highlight the healthy, successful parts of the organization. Locating those healthy parts of the system and attaching new prevention elements reinforces the backbone of an organization. Do not be fooled though; this is not "status quo" maintenance. This approach prepares the organization for all types of changes and not just from internal sources. It makes it more likely that the organization will be able to weather external storms and "bend like a reed" in times of turbulence, whereas other, more rigid organizational structures, take the full brunt of it and oftentimes address issues with maladaptive responses.

What we propose here is to shift the focus to *challenging some of the basic systems thinking* that dominates most of the design discussion and pay attention to the *lack of attention to the context within which organizations reside as sources of conflict* requiring other tools and methods of engagement. Most importantly, we make the case for incorporating other analytical tools that are designed to project the organization into a healthy future. In other words, many DSD programs today are built to address issues that arise right now. They are built to stabilize the status quo which, in bureaucratic theory, is usually a good thing. However, these systems can also be passive and reactive to allow conflict developments and merely serve as another part of a fire wall to allowing in healthy change. We can do better. By adopting another systems model approach and incorporating tools used in futures research we can design systems that are able to adapt swiftly to environmental changes; to be proactive and engaging even when the weakest of signals of conflict are barely detectable. We can adopt some of the forecasting models and terrain mapping of both military and private sector analysts to go a step further and design and imbed self-learning into systems. Before we explore that topic though, we will briefly review some of the system frameworks used by designers to address disputes in organizations.

Systems Thinking

To visualize an organization's system, it makes sense to start off by focusing on its mission. What do you do? How do you get it done? This leads into and an examination of the structure and function and how they align to meet the organization's goals. This is an internal closed system approach and a good starting point for any design effort. By nature, it possesses stabilizing mechanisms designed to maintain the system although it can make the organization rigid to change. This is clearly not the only focus for organizations, or at least those that interact with the outside world where clients, patrons, consumers, volunteers, citizen groups, competitors, governments, and other entities impact the organization's ability to achieve its goals. This is an external open systems approach. By nature, it has to me nimble and fast to make course adjustments, and hopefully before something bad happens. These two approaches are not sufficient by themselves to address all sources of disputes. They co-exist and provide the designer and clients with more data to build a system that is both practical and responsive.

Closed Systems

Some groups do not need an elaborate dispute system to function. A wide range of indigenous restorative practices, such as community circles, simply need a space big enough to accommodate however large a group shows up. This kind of process is embedded in a social system that is designed to focus on the humanity of victims and offenders. It is a self-correcting system that ensures social group survival. It attends to a victim's needs and reintegrates the offender back into the group. In a small religious order, you may see an informal system that carries over from the common values and beliefs of the group. A Benedictine order follows the rule of St. Benedict in prayers, thoughts, words, and actions. The beliefs and values are the foundation of the group's existence and following them as guides on how we relate and reinforces – in a closed loop – the system. Whereas, in other groups, the dispute system originates from outside entities such as those seen between labor and management and here different values, approaches to conflict and conduct toward others also show some predictable behaviors.

In closed systems we work with a limited universe of actors, typically one structure, several associated functions and a range of issues that are amenable to a limited number of procedures and processes. That makes for a better chance at predicting events arising. All one needs to do is fit the issues to the right process and, if everything works as planned, the issues in dispute are effectively managed and resolved – until they are not.

Open Systems

No organization is immune from external forces so what happens when the proverbial sand starts to shift? Is the organization fast enough to strategically maneuver to a more stable position? Open systems incorporate external actors and forces and place the organization's structural and functional pieces into the larger theater of operations. Organizations usually have competitors. Public sector agencies and departments, often thought of as immune from competition, have internal government actors such as legislators who impact the funding of the agency. They can have private sector vendors and partners who undertake some or most of their activities. The private sector environment is even more complicated and to survive in it, organizations invest huge sums of money to project future markets, build early warning systems to steer away from impending conflicts and otherwise strive to survive. As such, much of the innovative advances in design are found in the private sector where you only eat what you kill or go the way of the dinosaur. It therefore behooves the private sector organization to focus not just on internal conflict but to embed its thinking in open systems in anticipation of conflict arising from the outside.

Soft Systems

There are other ways to think about system that can help the designer. "Hard" Systems thinking is a useful analytical framework that examines operational aspects of organizations. It does well in explaining mechanical or biological systems, but often comes up short when applied to process systems involving (unreliable) human activity. In response to this dilemma a different approach to problem solving and the management of change needed to be developed. This is how Soft Systems Methodology (SSM) came to pass. It counters these types of traditional systems analysis shortcomings (Checkland, 2000). SSM addresses a high level of complex problems by using a cyclical (self-learning) approach that focuses on human activity within a system to explore issues, perceptions, and the readiness of actors (and systems) to change. Soft systems atomize complex problems into component parts and then conducts a classic problem-solving process but with a focus on people with in systems. What is it about the system that is not functioning as intended? What other systems could address the issue? How do we measure changes in system functions and how do we take action are some of the core questions that guide the steps in the SSM diagnostic process? In other words, soft systems methodology takes the best part of closed and open systems concepts and merges into a focus on people within a system to manage change.

Contextual Environments, External Control, and Internal Conflict

Another framework that is often acknowledged, but not by name nor usually incorporated into the DSD framework, is external control, especially as it impacts the context within which organizations exist. What happens when external forces become burdensome to the organization? How does it effectively respond to these challenges instead of addressing them with a slow moving maladaptive and poorly conceived reaction? What are the unintended consequences to the dispute system already in place?

A case in point involves giant Amazon and how they have chosen to confront external control elements impacting their operations. To address eternal constraints, Amazon routinely reviews and modifies policies regulating their dispute system. When they make changes, it is reasonable to expect there will be a ripple effect in the industry as competitors follow suit and adopt a similar approach. At the turn of the century many companies began to shift some of their sales function to online platforms. This new method of consumer interaction required adjustments in robust face-to-face dispute resolution systems that offered several, sometimes costly, means to address grievances. However, when external forces come to play on the dispute system in ways the designers never intended, the system must adjust. Policies need to change, and the options need to shift to means and processes that are more effective and efficient for the company. In 2020 Amazon found itself deluged with a backlog of 75,000 consumer arbitration cases. The culprits, they claim, are law firms who dominate the consumer grievance industry space, who have misused the arbitration procedure set up by Amazon. In response, Amazon strategically shifted and changed it policies by throwing out arbitration in favor of litigation. Now, if you are an individual consumer, the less formal, less expensive, and less time-consuming alternative is no longer available. If you have a problem with Amazon, then sue them but make sure it is filed in the district court in Seattle Washington. Given the forces that impact the private sector, not even to mention government relations, this is not at all surprising. It impacts customers and therefore has a measurable effect on Amazons goals.

External Control and Organizational Responses

Emery and Trist (1965) are some of the earliest researchers on external control and organizational responses. Their theoretical framework lays out four different environmental textures ranging from placid to turbulent. The vortical environment, developed by Baburoglu (1988), is added to demonstrate a theoretical instance where environmental forces become so strong systems begin to collapse. Although extremely rare, some say never seen, it could occur under extreme institutional and systemic distress where multiple functions begin to collapse simultaneously.

TEXTURE	TACTICAL	STRATEGIC	OPERATIONS	CONFLICT RESOLUTION REQUIRED?	RESPONSE TO ENVIRONMENT
TYPE I "PLACID"	ADEQUATE	NO	NO	NO	CONTROL
TYPE II "CLUSTERS"	NECESSARY	SUFFICIENT	NO	NO	MANAGE
TYPE III "DISTURBED"	YES	YES	NECESSARY	POSSIBLY AND PROCESSES	ALLIANCES
TYPE IV "TURBULENT"	INADEQUATE	INADEQUATE	POSSIBLE ADEQUATE	ADR PROCESSES NECESSARY	ADAPT TO ETERNAL FORCES
TYPE V "VORTEX"	INADEQUATE	INADEQUATE	NOT LIKELY TO BE ADEQUATE	CRISIS MANAGEMENT	MALADAPTIVE

Figure 10.1: Modified Emery and Trist Causal Textures Combining ADR logic and processes.

Approaches to conflict management are embedded in the various cells in Figure 10.1 and are intended to demonstrate an organization's orientation toward conflict by use of various mechanisms (minor tactics, more encompassing and organized strategies, complex operational thinking, involving partners in the environment, all the way to the development of advanced internal and external conflict resolution programs, processes, and procedures (Polkinghorn 1994). The place where dispute systems design theoretically gets the least attention is in upper left-hand corner of the table, namely, where the placid environment exists. There is little need for a plan to deal with (external) conflict forces and sources as the organizations exist in an environment with little or no competition. This might be found in small specialty markets or organizations that are not driven so much by realizing every increasing profit but by other goals such as might be seen with artisans and craftsmen. Conflict arising in the environment is minimal and adjustments usually appear to be slight course corrections which, in theory, reduces at least one source of conflict within the organization. Slowly moving in a diagonal manner to the bottom right corner of the table we find the organization getting into more and more trouble. The organization needs to shift its orientation toward such things as cooperative competition, clustering with other organizations to create a somewhat controllable environment via herding to survive the larger competition. But at some point, the organization's responses become less and less effective. Indeed, for Emery and Trist, this is the point where poor leadership, lack of a preparation i.e., developed set of strategies (operations), leads to maladaptive responses and the turbulence from the outside environment creates havoc on the inside.

Environments change and organizations adjust

Using an open systems approach and framing it within an environment of causal textures creates a framework that leverages both an internal and external approach when developing a dispute resolution system. The following examples come from the Bosserman Center for Conflict Resolution at Salisbury University's research on system design and provide insights on some rather crafty and creative ideas to consider when designing or modifying systems.

Transportation Security Administration Integrated Conflict Management System

The establishment of the Transportation Security Administration (TSA) came as a direct response to the 9–11 attacks. The sense of urgency in creating TSA compressed the startup operations as several existing Federal Department and Agency units merged, and not necessarily smoothly, into a new agency. TSA proceeded to hire roughly 55,000 employees in a matter of months. These employees shared little in regard to organizational culture as they came from a wide variety of backgrounds. Some had a sense of the command and control mindset that would invariably be part of TSA operations. Retired military, former police and transferred air marshals had some knowledge of this command and control environment and the expectations demanded of employees. However, other transportation security officers came from the airline industry, which is customer service oriented, and many other occupations so the mix was a cocktail for conflict. The TSA did not have its own culture, operating procedures, policies, or a clear means of resolving disputes and they needed to develop it quickly and focus it directly on its mission of protecting the traveling public and the protection of commercial aircraft.

A plan was launched to get the agency functionally operational without the benefit of routine start up procedures. Luckily, embedded in the launch was a well-conceived dispute system design project aptly named the Integrated Conflict

Management System (ICMS). It is a flexible, soft system driven (self-learning) program that integrates the best of closed and open systems functions. ICMS also rested on a phased in approach or maturity model that mandated some methods and procedures be functionally integrated by a certain time. However, the maturity model deliberately left open room for unique site-specific methods and processes to address conflict in all of its 440 airport facilities.

Our extensive research of the ICMS development and maturity model all showed a self-learning system was making modifications on the ground in real time. In 18 selected facilities we visited we documented 22 different methods and procedures being used, on site, to address TSA employee issues and concerns as well as issues that arise between Transportation Security Officers (TSO), the flying public, other airport employees, vendors, and just about anyone else in their theater of operations (Polkinghorn et al, 2011). It is worth noting that Transportation Security Officers (TSO) have a "duty to engage" anyone acting in a suspicious manner or otherwise, through detection methods, raising attention or concerns. Engaging, in and of itself, is both an internal workplace and external contextual conflict scenario all wrapped into one. This should reinforce that there is not a sharply defined line between closed and open systems boundaries.

TSA built ICMS to be both an inward workplace (traditional closed system approach) and an external engagement (open systems) means of managing disputes. It also, unknowingly, adopted the basic methodological approach found in soft systems most notably in allowing each site to develop some of its own means of addressing issues. Interestingly, many of the creative program ideas were developed not in large airport facilities (Category X as they are called) such as Denver, Chicago, or Los Angeles, but in smaller airports such as Milwaukee where the Federal Security Director (FSD), the top TSA person on site, was a huge champion of ICMS.

This research also provided a chance to see what "shifting sands" can have on a dispute system. When Barrack Obama was running for President he pledged to get more federal workers into unions and specifically set his sights on TSA. In 2011, TSOs were allowed to move forward with collective bargaining and when the union came into TSA the ICMS system abruptly changed. The range of methods of addressing disputes was culled of those that did not fit the union rules or the union management-context. The irony is rich. Unions stand a good chance of taking root in organizations with lousy management, poor means of addressing issues or a callous culture that sees workers as expendable. TSO, who are now union members, developed these creative means to address dispute issues but the union, how came in to help, required their elimination or modification under the current union management agreements. Finally, in regard to external control theory and differing casual textures, TSA clearly began in a turbulent environment, where both internal and external ADR was necessary. It theoretically fits exactly where it should be in the modified Emery and Trist model. As the environment changes and union representation made its impact felt, the TSA still hovers more in the lower right-hand corner but ten years later, in 2021, the

Biden administration extended union rights to most TSA workers. It will be interesting to see how that shift in the external forces impacts the type and number of disputes.

Woodrow Wilson Bridge – Merging Project Planning and Internalized Dispute Resolution Systems

One of the most effective tools used in the construction industry is called "partnering." It is essentially an enhanced project planning method that integrates several self-learning DSD elements into the process. On the preventative end, partnering builds in both project monitoring as well as detection of "weak conflict signals" using an array of human factor early warning devices (soft systems.) Project planning is also enhanced by the incorporation of on-site conflict management steps, often referred to in the industry as the "resolution ladder", to address issues in a timely low cost and efficient manner. Partnering also embeds facilitated problem solving meetings (a.k.a. partnering sessions) and, notably, it does not introduce situ rights-based processes. Legal means of dispute settlement arise post construction and luckily, partnering has done an excellent job of reducing post project litigation (Polkinghorn, SHA 2005). In short, partnering incorporates into the project planning model a means of monitoring external control threats, soft systems-based problem-solving procedures in an open system framework.

We took part in the building of the Woodrow Wilson Bridge, also known as the "national bridge." It is part of the Washington D.C. beltway system and connects suburban Maryland and Virginia on the I-95 corridor. Lasting nine years and coming in at a cost of $2.54 billion, it was the largest bridge construction project of its time and proceeded to set thirty-eight world records in the construction industry. Most important, the project came in on time and with less than 1 percent inflation of the budget. This is an incredible outcome, and in the construction industry, it is legendary. As a part of our work, we monitored the construction partnering process performance measures, and intervened, when necessary, mostly in preventive or early crisis conditions, to keep parts of the project moving. On the research side we tracked 354 project management variables over 30 plus ongoing independent projects on site, which was quite the task, but the project managers followed their dispute systems processes knowing that one stoppage of work would throw the entire project into chaos. (Anderson and Polkinghorn 2011a; Anderson and Polkinghorn 2011b). The biggest takeaway from this case, for the designer, is to develop a simple and easy to follow set of steps for contractors, managers, and the owner to address issues as fast as possible. One flow chart with less than four steps is all it takes to manage routine or show stopping issues.

Casual Factors and Systems Design Comparing Public and Private ADR Programs

In an ongoing study we are examining 431 ADR program in the US federal government along with all the ADR programs found in Fortune 500 companies. This study clearly demonstrates the need to deliberately construct dispute systems to meet specific issues with an emphasis on demarcating where they arise either inside the workplace or from the external environment. There are distinctions between public and private organizations and how they manage disputes. The preliminary results tend to suggest that the processes being used are subject to the context (public and private) along with the nature of the dispute, as well as if they are a result of internal or external focus.

We developed a categorization system to demarcate internal workplace disputes form external disputes and the results are shown in Figure 10.2.

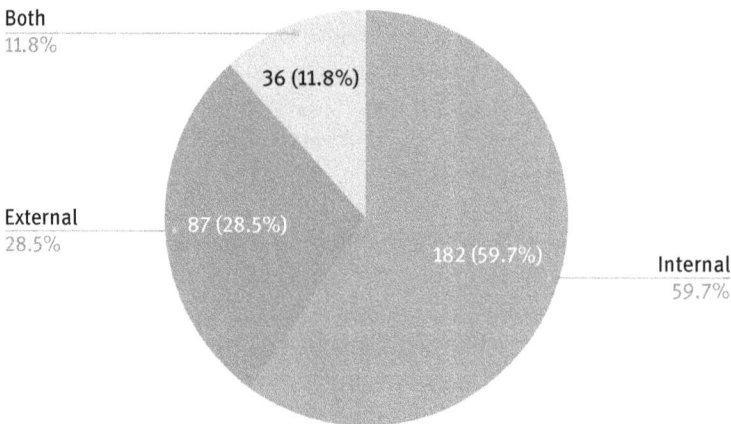

Figure 10.2: Federal Programs with an internal, external, or both orientation.

Roughly 60% of programs focus on internal dispute, 30% on external and 10% on both. The external are dominated by regulatory, executive agencies, which have to deal with constituents or those entities that have a say in how things are done at a particular agency. Splitting the federal departments and agencies into two groups – internal and external ADR program foci – shows different types and rates of ADR processes being used that indirectly supports the modified Emery and Trist model. See Figures 10.3 and 10.4 for details.

Switching to the private sector we examined all Fortune 500 companies (on the 2020 list) for ADR programs and processes. The top performing companies have more robust programs while the companies at the bottom tend to employ mandated procedures and processes. See Figures 10.5 and 10.6 for more details. Two findings are

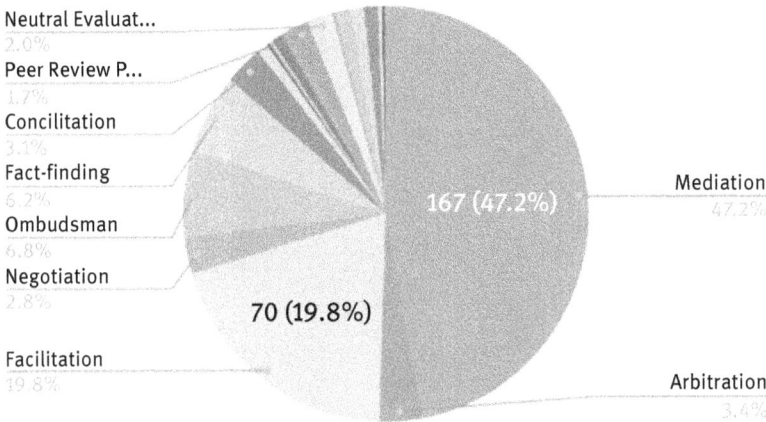

Figure 10.3: Processes offered by internally oriented program.

Processes offered by externally oriented programs

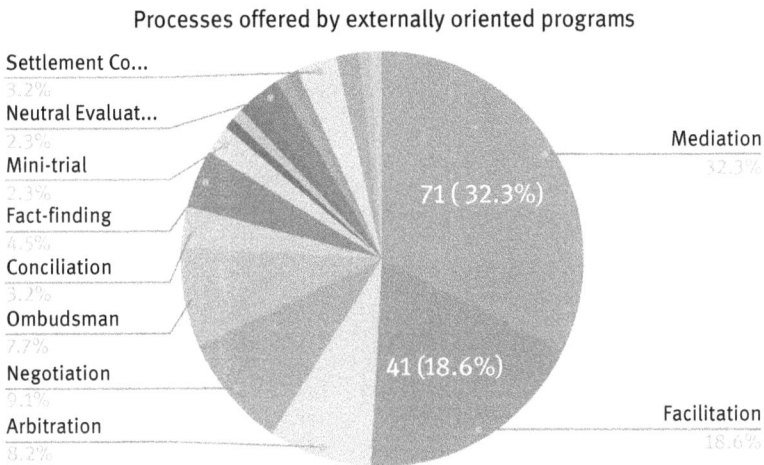

Figure 10.4: ADR Processes Used by Federal entities with external parties.

noteworthy. Private sector companies (both publicly held and privately owned) use more ADR processes and usually have more developed and robust dispute systems in terms of mature program offices providing more ADR options for managing cases then government counterparts. This too falls in line with the modified Emery and Trist model. In other words, in behooves the designer of dispute systems to pay close attention to context and to also acknowledge that successful organizations are the source of creative dispute systems that, as far as we can tell, are driven by and supportive of the organizations, values, mission and goals.

What service is offered in the first 250 Fortune 500 Companies?

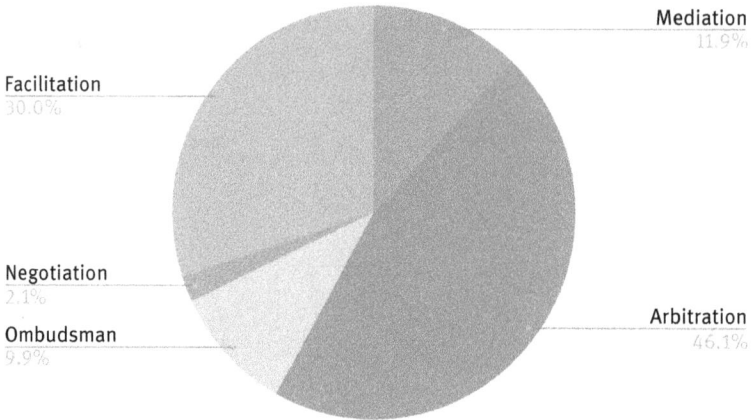

Figure 10.5: Top 250 on the 2020 Fortune List (ADR Processes Used).

What service is offered in the last 250 out of Fortune 500 Companies?

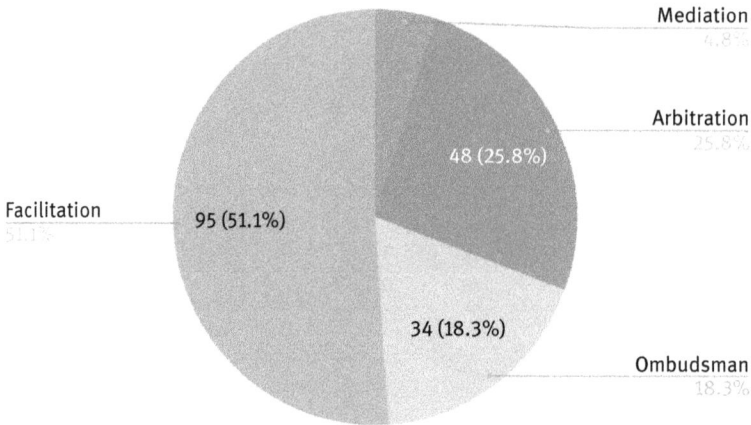

Figure 10.6: Bottom 250 of the 2020 Fortune 500 Companies (ADR Processes Used).

Creating Robust Dispute Resolution Systems

Thinking of disputes in a static short-term manner, which drives the use of plug and play programs, ignores the positive impact disputes may have on the organization's overall system and thus its future. Futurology is not often associated with dispute systems, but this arena of research does, in fact, have a lot to offer. By incorporating some of the tools used from this field of inquiry we can more fully incorporate dispute systems design into self-learning soft systems approaches to help guide organizations over the next set of horizons. Futurology focuses organizations attention on being nimble, as is more often seen in the private sector and why the public sector lags behind. It challenges us to get past Ogburn's (1957) "Cultural Lag as Theory" conundrum (think of placid environments in the Emery and Trist model) by anticipating conflict and strategically positioning the entire organization in a position that is less exposed to negative consequences but more open to receiving change. It is not aversion; it is practical thinking.

Conclusion

Futurologists use tools that project the organization into thinking about what conflict can do in terms of its possible, probable, and preferable future existence. Some probable outcomes are not good. Some preferable outcomes are sub optimal and the preferable future avoids those conditions. Incorporating more methods and tools such as scenario building, Delphi studies, appreciative inquiry, various types of trend analyses, risk assessments, backcasting, forecasting, horizon scanning, causal layer analysis (inspired by Emery and Trist) and other methodologies, organizations can map out various routes to a variety of points along the horizon and prepare scenarios in the event any of them develops. Generating options is, as we know, a part of the dispute resolution business so this should be something familiar to all of us.

References

Anderson, L. & Polkinghorn, B. (2011a). Managing Conflict in Construction Megaprojects: Leadership and Third Party Principles. Reprint for May 2011 *Special Online Issue of Conflict Resolution Quarterly*. http://onlinelibrary.wiley.com/journal/10.1002/(ISSN)1541-1508.

Anderson, L. & Polkinghorn. B. (2011b) Efficacy of Partnering on the Woodrow Wilson Bridge Project: Empirical Evidence of Collaborative Problem-Solving Benefits. American Society of Civil Engineers *Journal of Legal Affairs and Dispute Resolution in Engineering and Construction*, Volume 3, Number 1, pp.17–27.

Baburoglu, O., (1988). The Vortical Environment: The Fifth in Emery-Trist Levels of Organizational Environments. *Human Relations*, Vol. 41, pp.81–210.

Blomberg-Amsler, L., Martinez, J. K., & Smith, S.E. (2020). *Dispute Systems Design: Preventing, Managing and Resolving Conflict*. Stanford: Stanford University Press.

Checkland, P. (2000). Soft Systems Methodology: A Thirty Year Retrospective. *Systems Research and Behavioral Science*, (17), S11–S58.

Costantino, C. A. & Sickles-Merchant, C. (1996) *Designing Conflict Management Systems: A Guide to Creating Productive and Healthy Organizations*. San Francisco: Jossey-Bass.

Emery, F.E. and Trist, E.L. The Causal Texture of Organizational Environments. *Human Relations*, 1965, Vol. 18 No. 1, 21–32.

Lipsky, D. B., Seeber, R.L., & Fincher, R. (2003). *Emerging Systems for Managing Workplace Conflict: Lessons from American Corporations for Managers and Dispute Resolution Professionals*. San Francisco: Jossey-Bass.

Ogburn, W. F. (1957). Cultural Lag as Theory. Sociology and Social Research, (41), January-February, pp, 167–174.

Polkinghorn, B. (1994). The Impact of Regulatory Negotiations on EPA as an Institution. (Dissertation – Maxwell School of Citizenship and Public Affairs, Syracuse University).

Polkinghorn, B. (2005). An Evaluation of the Construction Partnering Program for the State Highway Administration of Maryland State Highway Administration of Maryland.

Polkinghorn, B., McDermott, P. & Obar, R. (2011) Evaluation of Integrated Conflict management System (ICMS) as the Transportations Security Administration (Contract No. HSTS-03-08-3-MWP011).

Stroh, D. (2015). *Systems Thinking for Social Change. A practical Guide to Solving Complex Problems. Avoiding Unintended Consequences, and Achieving lasting Results*. White River Junction Vermont: Chelsea Green.

Ury, W., Jeanne M. Brett. J. M., & Goldberg, B. (1988). *Getting Disputes Resolved: Designing Systems to Cut the Costs of Conflict*. San Francisco: Jossey-Bass.

Kuryakin C. Rucker

Chapter 11
Stereotypes, Bias and Microaggressions in Organizational Conflict Management (OCM)

Abstract: All organizations experience conflict. The right type of conflict can lead to high levels of organizational performance through the sharing and challenging of ideas among team members. The wrong type of conflict can lead to poor decision making within the organization and foster mistrust, hostility, apathy, and cynicism among team members. Stereotypes, biases and microaggressions create division among employees, produce and reinforce inequities within organizations, and drive destructive conflict. Stereotypes are trait or behavioral associations that are attributed to a social group that alter the perception of members of that group. Biases are the outgrowth of stereotypes and can be either explicit or implicit, positive, or negative, as well as interpersonal or structural. Biases lead individuals and organizations to favor one social group over another. Microaggressions are the sometimes-unintentional behaviors that are the result of stereotyping and bias that serve to assault, insult, or invalidate the experiences of, members of marginalized groups. Organizations must focus on both interpersonal and organizational interventions that reduce or eliminate stereotyping, biases and microaggressions. Education and training, reorientation of organizational culture driven by organizational leaders, and interpersonal interventions are all effective tools for reducing destructive conflict in organizations.

Keywords: soft systems, open systems, external control, contextual environments, self-correcting organizations, fast thinking

When one thinks of stereotyping, bias, and discrimination in an organizational context, usually one imagines a bygone era where someone is hurling racial epithets toward a member of a racial or ethnic minority, or purposefully treating someone as inferior. While such treatment was once a facet of organizational life, antidiscrimination laws and changing social dynamics have reduced (but not eliminated) overt expressions of bias and discrimination in the organizational setting. Today's organizations face the challenge of creating inclusive workspaces where all individuals feel respected and valued regardless of their backgrounds, heritages, or physical abilities. Central to creating an inclusive organizational environment is the reduction and eventual elimination of stereotyping and bias in the organization.

https://doi.org/10.1515/9783110746365-011

Stereotypes

Stereotypes are a set of associations that attribute a set of characteristics or traits with a particular group (Lippmann, 1922; Dovidio, Hewstone, Glick & Esses, 2010; Dovidio & Jones, 2019). Lippmann (1922) coined the term to refer to the typical picture that was evoked when thinking about a specific social group. This picture not only contains the traits and characteristics of the members of the social group, but include status or social role characteristics, and expectations about members' behaviors (Oakes & Turner, 1990; Eagly & Diekman, 2005; Pearson, Dovidio & Gaertner, 2009; Dovidio & Jones, 2019). Stereotypes are learned through socialization and serve as a mental shortcut by which one can predict the behavior and traits of someone with whom they are unfamiliar (Hilton & von Hippel, 1996; Dovidio et al., 2010; Dovidio & Jones, 2019).

Stereotypes act to promote discrimination in organizations because they systematically influence perceptions of marginalized group members and color the interpretations of group members' actions or behaviors (Oakes & Turner, 1990; Devine & Elliot, 1995; Hilton & von Hippel, 1996). Stereotypes also influence the judgements made about the interpretations of group members' actions or behaviors (Devine & Elliot, 1995; Bobo, 1999; Dovidio et al., 2010; Dovidio & Jones, 2019). In that way, stereotypes can also form the basis of justification for continued discrimination against, or mistreatment of, members of marginalized communities (Devine & Elliot, 1995; Bobo, 1999; Dovidio et al., 2010). Marginalized groups often are socialized by the dominant group to adopt the stereotypic beliefs about their own group, and to conform their behaviors to those stereotypes (von Baeyer, Sherk & Zanna, 1981; Dovidio et al., 2010). When members of marginalized groups behave in ways that do not conform to the stereotype, those behaviors are seen as a situational deviation, or "the exception that proves the rule", while stereotype-consistent behavior reinforces the stereotype for members of the dominant group (Dovidio et al., 2010). Members of marginalized groups can be sensitive to the stereotypes that exist about their group, and as a result can be very self-conscious about their behavior, especially when they are one of a few members of the group or the only member of the group in the organization (Eagly &Diekman, 2005; Pearson, et al., 2009; Dovidio et al., 2010). This self-consciousness can reduce their ability to think or act effectively and negatively affect performance (Dovidio et al., 2010).

We can see the various ways that stereotypes work in organizations by looking at the various groups represented in the workplace. Individuals from racial or ethnic minorities may be limited in their career prospects because of stereotypes that regard them as lazy, less intelligent, loud, or docile. For example, an Asian American woman may be passed over for a promotion to a leadership position because of the stereotype of Asian women as docile and unable to display the assertiveness that is necessary for leadership. Individuals from marginalized groups may also be perceived as less competent or having received their positions in the organization not through merit, but rather as a way to fulfill an organizational quota. Individuals who belong to the dominant group may benefit from the stereotypic assumption that they are competent, and that they have earned the position they occupy within the organization through merit rather than through social network connections.

Bias

Bias has been described by Scott (2013, p. 27) as "a preference that influences impartial judgment". Bias is also understood to be the tendency to favor one group over another (Greenwald & Krieger, 2006; Friedman, 2017). Biases are the outgrowth of stereotypes that individuals have learned through socialization (Greenwald & Krieger, 2006; Faigman, Kang, Bennett, Carbado & Casey, 2012; Friedman, 2017). Bias can be explicit (conscious), implicit (unconscious), or structural, and favorable or unfavorable (Faigman et al., 2012). In organizations, these preferences and the favor tendencies that result, can lead to discrimination against members of marginalized communities.

Explicit or conscious biases are those that are consciously and openly held and freely expressed to others because no social norm exists to counter them (Clarke, 2018). Therefore, these biases are seen as appropriate both to the individual and organization. Individuals may conceal their conscious biases to manage others' perceptions of them if those biases are seen as socially taboo (Clarke, 2018).

In an organization, explicit biases are expressed as discrimination: actively favoring or promoting one group's interests over others or inhibiting one group's prospects or prevent the group's interests from being considered (Clarke, 2018). Despite the societal taboo and legal proscriptions against overt discrimination in organizations, explicit bias persists (Clarke, 2018). According to the Equal Employment Opportunity Commission (EEOC), in fiscal year 2020, there were almost 67,500 charges of discrimination filed against US employers by employees, which resulted in $106 million in monetary recovery (EEOC, 2021). This number does not include complaints filed with state-based Fair Employment Practices Agencies or monetary recoveries from either state-based agencies or private litigation (EEOC, 2021).

Implicit or unconscious biases are those that an individual is not consciously aware of, and if made aware, may reject as inappropriate (Greenwald & Krieger, 2006; Faigman et al., 2012). An individual's behaviors and judgments may be influenced by their implicit biases and contribute to patterns of discriminatory behavior, despite their conscious intentions (Greenwald & Krieger, 2006; Faigman et al., 2012). Consider the case of a professor in a university's math department, who sees himself as antiracist and feminist. He strives to treat his students equally and he believes that he adheres to the egalitarian views he professes. Despite his conscious rejection of racism and sexism, the professor nonetheless harbors the implicit biases he learned as an adolescent that positively associate mathematical ability with whiteness and maleness. As a result, the professor exhibits microaggressions (discussed below) toward his minority and female students, evaluates the academic work of his minority and female students more critically, and his interactions with his nonwhite and female students are less patient and inviting. If there are other professors in the department that harbor similar implicit biases, the cumulative effect could be to reduce the numbers of minority or female students who pursue math as a major or minor, or who seek to enter graduate study in mathematics, and ultimately reinforce the stereotype that minorities and females are not suited for high level mathematics.

Similarly, the implicit biases of managers and executives in an organization work against employees from marginalized communities. Even if implicit bias does not direct a manager's actions to discriminate *against* any particular group but instead works to *favor* groups with which he identifies, inequitable outcomes still result (Faigman et al., 2012). Discrimination based on implicit bias can be difficult for organizations to address, because managers may be oblivious to the harm they are causing and believe they act in a nondiscriminatory manner (Faigman et al., 2012). They therefore resist efforts to change their behavior (Faigman et al., 2012).

Structural biases exist in policies, processes, and norms of organizations (Green, 2003; Faigman et al., 2012; Reskin, 2012; Wiececk & Hamilton, 2014). Structural biases are often not expressed as explicit preferences in favor of or against a particular group, but rather are framed as neutral policies and processes that nonetheless produce, reproduce, and reinforce inequities experienced by marginalized groups (Green, 2003; Faigman et al., 2012; Wiececk & Hamilton, 2014). Structural biases are often seen as normal, reasonable, and rational by the dominant group, whose power position in the organization is reinforced by such biases (Faigman et al., 2012).

An example of structural bias: a law firm chooses a recruiting strategy of only hiring attorneys who have graduated from ivy league law schools. Because those law schools have smaller populations of members of racial and ethnic minority communities than non-ivy league schools, the resulting pool of attorneys available is less likely to include members of racial and ethnic minorities. Therefore, the law firm is less likely to employ members of racial and ethnic minority communities as attorneys. While the recruiting strategy is neutral on its face and does not explicitly seek to exclude minority attorneys from joining the firm (indeed, the firm may hire some minority attorneys who have graduated from ivy league law schools), the policy reduces the *likelihood* that the firm will hire minority attorneys.

Microaggressions

Microaggressions are the "brief, commonplace, and daily verbal, behavioral and environmental slights and indignities directed toward" people of color, women, LGBTQIA+ and other marginalized individuals (Sue, et al., 2008, p. 329, Sue & Spanierman, 2020). Many, but not all, microaggressions occur automatically and unintentionally (Sue et al., 2008, Sue & Spanierman, 2020). Microaggressions can be either interpersonal or structural/environmental. Three forms of interpersonal microaggressions have been identified: microassault, micro-insult and micro-invalidation (Costantino & Sue, 2007; Sue, et al., 2007; Sue, et al., 2008; Holder, Jackson & Ponterotto, 2015). Microassault is an intentional, overt act of bias or discrimination such as the use of racial, ethnic, gender, or sexual identity-based slurs, or other purposefully discriminatory behavior (Sue et al., 2007). Micro-insult is a verbal or nonverbal communication that demeans one's heritage or identity (Costantino & Sue, 2007; Sue, et al., 2007). Microinvalidation is a communication that negates or nullifies the thoughts, feelings, or experienced reality of a marginalized person (Costantino & Sue, 2007; Sue, et al., 2007).

Microassaults and microinsults convey hidden messages to, and reinforce the "otherness" of, the target (Sue & Spanierman, 2020). For example, when one raises their voice when speaking with a vision impaired individual, the message that is sent is that a person with a disability is impaired in all aspects of bodily function (Sue & Spanierman, 2020). Similarly, when one remarks to a member of a racial or ethnic minority that the person is "articulate" the message is delivered that there was an expectation for that person to use broken or vernacular English, and not to have the ability to speak well. Other hidden messages conveyed by microaggressions include intellectual inferiority, physical, cultural, sexual, or social abnormality, untrustworthiness, or sameness (Sue & Spanierman, 2020). These hidden messages undermine the target's ability to integrate into the organization fully or effectively because they erect a barrier between the target and the perpetrator.

Microinvalidations also send hidden messages to the individual who is the target: your experience was not what you experienced, your feelings about your experience are unjustified and invalid, and you are simply too sensitive or seeking attention (Costantino & Sue, 2007; Sue, et al., 2007; Sue & Spanierman, 2020). Microinvalidations are often defensive expressions that occur after a target of some overt or subtle discrimination confronts the perpetrator or describes their experience to another. Remarks like, "I'm colorblind", or, "that wasn't my intention, so you shouldn't be upset" work to deny the target the legitimacy of their experience and of the feelings that result from it. Further, microinvalidations seek to distance the perpetrator not only from the specific complained-of conduct, but also from the recognition of the privilege and power that the perpetrator may enjoy (Sue & Spanierman, 2020). In short, microinvalidations act to preserve the self-concept of the perpetrator as a good person.

Structural and environmental microaggressions are those that are not direct interpersonal interactions but are a part of the general atmosphere or culture of a workplace (Sue & Spanierman, 2020). These microaggressions can create an oppressive work environment where team members feel isolated, tokenized, or like second class citizens of the organization (Sue & Spanierman, 2020; Rucker, 2021). Structural and environmental microaggressions often lead to loss of productivity and higher turnover for the organization (Rucker, 2021).

Microaggressions have negative psychological impacts on targets (Costantino & Sue, 2007; Sue, et al., 2007; Sue & Spanierman, 2020). Individuals who have experienced microaggressions have reported feelings of invisibility, isolation, powerlessness, and anger, among others (Sue & Spanierman, 2020). Individuals may feel pressure to conform their identity to a standard that runs counter to who they really are (Sue & Spanierman, 2020). For example, a lesbian employee may feel pressure to dress and act in a feminine way in the workplace that does not reflect how she dresses and acts outside of it. Or an African American employee may "code switch" (change the tone and inflection of their voices and alter their word choices) to avoid being accused of using "Ebonics" (also known as African American Vernacular English, or AAVE) in the office because of the negative connotation ascribed to AAVE by his white coworkers. This forced compliance can eventually lead to employees feeling that they are living without integrity or as their genuine selves at work (Sue & Spanierman, 2020). The repeated experience of microaggressions causes individuals to feel unwelcome in their organizations, which leads to loss of productivity and, eventually, a desire to leave the organization (Rucker, 2021).

Individuals experiencing microaggressions utilize coping mechanisms to help them function in the organization. The primary mechanisms used are avoidance and confrontation, which are analogous to the "fight or flight" response induced by physical danger (Sue & Spanierman, 2020; Rucker, 2021). Avoidance behaviors include silence, "laughing off" the offending statement, leaving the interaction, etc. (Sue & Spanierman, 2020). Individuals use avoidance for several reasons: fatigue after experiencing repeated microaggressions, belief that additional microaggressions might result from confronting the perpetrator, belief that confrontation will be fruitless, belief that the organization will do nothing, or worse, side with the perpetrator, and others (Sue & Spanierman, 2020; Rucker, 2021). Targets of microaggressions, while avoiding direct confrontation with the perpetrator, may nonetheless confide in peers or trusted friends or family as a coping mechanism (Sue & Spanierman, 2020; Rucker, 2021). Ultimately, many targets of microaggressions leave their organizations as a way to end the microaggressions while avoiding confrontation with the perpetrators (Rucker 2021). The avoidance/confrontation coping mechanisms of targets of microaggressions may be correlated to the coping mechanisms of targets of workplace bullying (Rucker, 2021).

How Stereotypes, Bias, and Microaggressions Increase Unproductive Conflict

All organizations experience conflict (Amason, Hochwarter, Thompson & Harrison, 1995; Amason & Schweiger, 1997; deWit, Greer & Jehn, 2012). In fact, conflict is a useful tool that can enhance team productivity (Amason et al., 1995; Amason & Schweiger, 1997). Any time individuals from different backgrounds, educations, areas of expertise, *et cetera*, come together to solve organizational problems, there is potential for conflict simply because the members of the team may have divergent ideas of how to address the organizational problem (Amason et al., 1995; deWit, Greer & Jehn,

2012). Work teams that are able to use communication to resolve the conflicts that inevitably arise and move forward on one accord tend to produce better results for the organization (Amason et al., 1995; deWit, Greer & Jehn, 2012).

This type of conflict, called cognitive or constructive (C-type) conflict is the fuel that drives successful organizations (Amason et al., 1995; Amason & Schweiger, 1997; deWit, Greer & Jehn, 2012). Teams that can remain focused on the substantive issues and how those issues can be resolved for the benefits of the organization tend to produce high-quality decisions that are more accepted by all members of the team (Amason et al., 1995). Research has shown that decisions that are a product of C-type conflict are also more easily implemented by the organization (Amason et al., 1995; Amason & Schweiger, 1997; deWit, Greer & Jehn, 2012).

Affective, or A-type conflict is the opposite of C-type conflict (Amason et al., 1995; Amason & Schweiger, 1997; deWit, Greer & Jehn, 2012). A-type conflict is harmful to team decision making (Amason et al., 1995; Amason & Schweiger, 1997; deWit, Greer & Jehn, 2012). A-type hostility engenders mistrust, hostility, apathy, and cynicism among team members (Amason et al., 1995; Amason & Schweiger, 1997). Where C-type conflict is focused on the substantive issues facing the organization and the team's genuine difference of opinion as the best way to solve problems, A-type conflict is centered around personal animus or resentments between or among team members (Amason et al., 1995; Amason & Schweiger, 1997; deWit, Greer & Jehn, 2012). Teams that engage in A-type conflict not only produce lower-quality decisions, but they also have less buy-in from team members, which makes implementation more difficult (Amason et al., 1995; Amason & Schweiger, 1997; deWit, Greer & Jehn, 2012). Team members also tend to disassociate themselves from the decisions made by the team in these situations (Amason et al., 1995).

Stereotypes and biases feed A-type conflict because they rest on assumptions about team members and their abilities and expectations about their behavior that may not be accurate. When these biases are intentional or explicit, there may be direct confrontation between team members that disrupts team cohesion (Hewstone, Rubin & Willis, 2002; Tekleab, Quigley & Tesluk, 2009). Conversely, explicit biases can trigger avoidance in the marginalized team member, causing them to withdraw from interaction with the biased team member or from the team altogether (Major & Townsend, 2010; Clarke, 2018).

Bias increases A-type conflict in organizations because it creates ingroups and outgroups (Hewstone et al., 2002; Yzerbyt & Demoulin, 2010). Factions may develop as team members that belong to the in-group prioritize views and ideas from other members of the ingroup rather than those that come from team members from the out-group (Hewstone et al., 2002; Yzerbyt & Demoulin, 2010). Members of the ingroup may also see the other members of the ingroup as more competent than members of the outgroup (Hewstone et al., 2002; Yzerbyt & Demoulin, 2010). Moreover, ingroup team members may begin to go beyond simply prioritizing ingroup views and opinions to derogating the outgroup team members and their ideas and opinions (Hewstone et al., 2002; Yzerbyt & Demoulin, 2010). When this happens, team members from the outgroup may react by withdrawing and disassociating from the team and its decisions, by withholding their ideas from the team, or by confronting team members from the ingroup, which can create an "us versus them" dynamic that is destructive to team decision making (Hewstone et al., 2002; Yzerbyt & Demoulin, 2010).

Similarly, stereotyping and bias may increase A-type conflict between managers and subordinates in the context of performance evaluation. A non-marginalized manager evaluating the performance of a subordinate from a marginalized community may begin with a lower baseline expectation of performance for that subordinate (Castilla, 2008; Castilla, 2016). Because that manager starts with a lower expectation of the subordinate's performance, the subordinate's mistakes are amplified (thus confirming the stereotype or bias) and the successes are diminished (taken as an anomaly, and not indicative of the subordinate's true performance) (Castilla, 2008; Castilla, 2016).

Microaggressions produce A-type conflict in organizations in several ways. First, interpersonal microaggressions interfere with the ability of team members to form trust relationships (Rucker, 2021). When an individual either intentionally or unintentionally targets a team member with a microaggression, the recipient begins to look at that person with suspicion (minimally) or as a threat (Sue & Spanierman, 2020; Rucker, 2021). The recipient may begin to avoid interactions with that individual as a way to protect themselves from receiving further microaggressions from them (Sue & Spanierman, 2020; Rucker, 2021). Conversely, the recipient may confront the individual, which may provoke a defensive response and cause both parties to disengage from interaction (Sue & Spanierman, 2020; Rucker, 2021). Additionally, recipients of microaggressions experience loss of motivation that negatively impacts productivity (Sue & Spanierman, 2020; Rucker, 2021).

Structural or environmental microaggressions can negatively impact the long-term prospects of the team because team members that experience these microaggressions may intentionally reduce their efforts on behalf of the organization (Sue & Spanierman, 2020; Rucker, 2021). These team members may also begin looking for other opportunities outside of the organization, where they believe the environment is more welcoming (Sue & Spanierman, 2020; Rucker, 2021). Either way, team performance and decision making suffers.

Reducing Stereotyping, Bias, and Microaggressions in Organizations

Many organizations have sought to reduce or eliminate stereotyping and bias because of the harmful effects on team cohesion and decision making. Some organizations are driven by a desire to reduce legal liability from discrimination lawsuits, others see the elimination of stereotyping and bias as a moral imperative (Pearson et al., 2009). Whatever the motivation, reducing stereotyping and bias in an organization is complex because these issues are both interpersonal and structural (Greenwald & Kreiger, 2006; Pearson, et al., 2009; Faigman et al., 2012). The solutions must be, therefore, a combination of both individualized and organizational interventions.

Individuals can reduce their explicit biases and stereotyping by self-regulation, especially when the organization creates an environment where the expression of or actions based on those explicit stereotypes and biases are considered unacceptable (Clarke, 2018). Individuals can, in the short-term, suppress their explicit stereotypes and biases in response to organizational pressure to behave in egalitarian ways, however, there is the possibility of backlash (Dovidio & Gaertner, 2009; Montieth, Arthur & Flynn, 2010). Backlash occurs when an individual becomes angry over the pressure to adopt egalitarian behavior because it runs counter to their preference to utilize stereotyping and bias in their everyday thinking and can result in the individual reaching a point where they lash out in biased behavior (Montieth et al., 2010).

Reducing implicit biases and stereotypes may prove more difficult, especially because such stereotypes and biases often run counter to the conscious beliefs of the individual. As with explicit biases and stereotypes, self-regulation can be effective in reducing implicit biases and stereotypes in the short-term, however, for long-term reduction, organizational interventions may provide better outcomes (Hewstone et al., 2002). To be effective, organizational interventions cannot be grass roots phenomena; the leadership of the organization must commit to a cultural shift that over time that makes individuals (including the leaders themselves) aware of their biases and the consequences of those biases.

Organizations can begin this process by providing opportunities for team members to hear from members of marginalized communities both without and within the organization (Hewstone et al., 2002; Devine, Forscher, Austin & Cox, 2012). This contextualizes stereotyping and bias and can make these abstract concepts real for the team members (Devine et al., 2012). Organizations can also provide opportunities for increased positive formal and informal contact between individuals belonging to marginalized and non-marginalized communities, which can reduce implicit bias (Smith, Brief & Colella, 2010). Seeing marginalized individuals in non-stereotypic roles in the organization may also lead to stereotyping and bias reduction (Smith et al., 2010).

Reducing microaggressions in organizations similarly requires leader commitment and the education of team members (Sue & Spanierman, 2020; Rucker, 2021). Individuals who experience microaggressions are often silent because of fear of negative repercussions or not knowing how to respond appropriately (Sue & Spanierman, 2020; Rucker, 2021). Additionally, team members who witness microaggressions may make matters worse by trivializing the experience (Sue & Spanierman, 2020). Organizations can help both the targets of microaggressions, and bystanders respond to interpersonal and structural/environmental microaggressions by educating the members of the team about what Sue and Spanierman (2020, p. 258) call "micro-in-terventions". Micro-interventions are strategies and tactics that can be utilized to support the target and validate their experiential reality (Sue, Alsaidi, Awad, Glaeser, Calle & Mendez, 2019; Sue & Spanierman, 2020). Strategic micro-interventions include making the hidden message of the microaggression explicit, disarming the microaggression, educating the offender, and seeking external intervention (Sue et al., 2017; Sue & Spanierman, 2020).

Conclusion

Stereotyping, bias and microaggressions promote dysfunction in the organizational setting. Stereotypes are a device that attributes assumptions (often false) about the characteristics or behaviors of a group to individuals from that group. Bias is the outgrowth of stereotyping, and often manifests as favoritism toward one group and prejudice against another group. Microaggressions are the operationalization of stereotyping and prejudice: interpersonal and structural/environmental slight and indignities that work to demean, invalidate, isolate, and delegitimize individuals from marginalized communities.

When stereotyping, bias and microaggressions are present in organizations, they increase destructive conflict by dividing team members into ingroups and outgroups and increasing interpersonal strife among team members. Team cohesion can be disrupted when members of marginalized communities are subjected to microaggressions that cause them to feel isolated and like second-class citizens in the organization. Stereotyping, bias and microaggressions also drive avoidance responses from members of marginalized communities that can impact organizational decision making and decision implementation.

Organizations can reduce stereotyping, bias and microaggressions by being intentional about creating inclusive environments. Organizational leadership must be invested in changing the organizational culture. By educating team members about stereotyping and bias, exposing team members to individuals from other groups in non-stereotypical roles, and promoting increased formal and informal contact between team members from different backgrounds, organizations can set the table for individualized change. Individuals can utilize strategic micro-interventions to reduce the impact of microaggressions and provide support to the targets of interpersonal and structural/environmental microaggressions.

References

Amason, A. C., Thompson, K. R., Hochwarter, W. A., & Harrison, A. W. (1995). Conflict: An important dimension in successful management teams. *Organizational Dynamics*, *24*(2), 20–35.

Amason, A. C., & Schweiger, D. M. (1997). The effects of conflict on strategic decision making effectiveness and organizational. In C.K.W. De Dreu and E. Van de Vliert (Eds.), *Using conflict in organizations* (p. 101–115). Thousand Oaks, CA: Sage Publications, Inc.

Amodio, D.M. & Devine, P.G. (2006). Stereotyping and evaluation in implicit race bias: Evidence for independent constructs and unique effects on behavior. *Journal of Personality and Social Psychology*, *91*(4), 652–661.

Bobo, L. (1999). Prejudice as a group position: Microfoundations of a sociological approach to racism and race relations. *Journal of Social Issues*, *55*(3), 445–472.

Castilla, E. J. (2008). Gender, race, and meritocracy in organizational careers. *American Journal of Sociology*, *113*(6), 1479–1526.

Castilla, E. J. (2016). Achieving meritocracy in the workplace. *MIT Sloan Management Review*, *57*(4), 35.

Clarke, J.A. (2018). Explicit bias. *Northwestern University Law Review*, *113*, 505–586.

Costantino, M. G., & Sue, D. W. (2007). Perceptions of racial microaggressions among black supervisees in cross-racial dyads. *Journal of Counseling Psychology*, *54*(2), 142.

Devine, P.G. & Elliot, A.J. (1995). Are racial stereotypes *really* fading? The Princeton Trilogy revisited. *Personality and Social Psychology Bulletin*, *21*(11), 1139–1150.

Devine, P.G., Forscher, P.S., Austin, A.J. & Cox, W.T. (2012). Long-term reduction in implicit race bias: A prejudice habit-breaking intervention. *Journal of Experimental Social Psychology. Nov; 48*(6):1267–1278.

deWit, F.R.C., Greer, L.L. & Jehn, K.A. (2012). The paradox of intragroup conflict: A meta-analysis. *Journal of Applied Psychology*, *97*(2), 360–390.

DiBrito, S. R., Lopez, C. M., Jones, C., & Mathur, A. (2019). Reducing implicit bias: Association of Women Surgeons #HeForShe task force best practice recommendations. *Journal of the American College of Surgeons*, *228*(3), 303–309.

Dovidio, J. F., Hewstone, M., Glick, P., & Esses, V. M. (2010). Prejudice, Stereotyping and Discrimination: Theoretical and Empirical Overview. *The SAGE Handbook of Prejudice, Stereotyping and Discrimination*, 1.

Dovidio, J. F., & Jones, J. M. (2019). Prejudice, stereotyping, and discrimination. *Advanced Social Psychology: The State of the Science*, 2.

Eagly, A.H. & Diekman, A.B. (2005). What is the problem? Prejudice as an attitude-in-context. In J.F. Dovidio, P. Glick & L.A. Rudman (Eds), *On the Nature of Prejudice: Fifty Years After Allport* (p.19–35). Malden, MA: Blackwell.

Emerson, K.T.U. & Murphy, M.C. (2014). Identity threat at work: How social identity threat and situational cues contribute to racial and ethnic disparities in the workplace. *Cultural and Ethnic Minority Psychology*, *20*(4), 508–520.

Equal Employment Opportunity Commission (2021). *EEOC Litigation Statistics, FY 1997 through FY 2020*. Retrieved from www.EEOC.gov./statistics/eeoc-litigation-statistics-fy-1997-through-fy-2020.

Faigman, D.L., Kang, J., Bennett, M.W., Carbado, D.W., Casey, P., Dasgupta, N., Godsil, R.D., Greenwarld, A.G., Levinson, J.D. & Mnookin, J. (2012). Implicit bias in the courtroom. *UCLA Law Review*, *59*, 1124–1186.

Friedman, S.H. (2017). Culture, bias, and understanding: We can do better. *Journal of the American Academy of Psychiatry and the Law*, *45*(2), 36–39.

Gendler, T. S. (2011). On the epistemic costs of implicit bias. *Philosophical Studies*, *156*(1), 33.

Green, T.K. (2003). Discrimination in workplace dynamics: Toward a structural account of disparate treatment theory. *Harvard Civil Rights-Civil Liberties Law Review*, *38*, 91–157.

Greenwald, A.G. & Krieger, L.H. (2006). Implicit bias: Scientific foundations. *California Law Review*, *94*(4), 945–967.

Hewstone, M., Rubin, M. & Willis, H. (2002). Intergroup Bias. *Annual Review of Psychology*, *53*, 575–604.

Hilton, J.L. & von Hippel, W. (1996). Stereotypes. *Annual Review of Psychology*, *47*, 237–271.

Holder, A.M.B., Jackson, M.A., & Ponterotto, J.G. (2015). Racial microaggression experiences and coping strategies of black women in corporate leadership. *Qualitative Psychology*, *2*(2), 164–180.

Kennedy, K. A. & Pronin, E. (2008). When disagreement gets ugly: Perceptions of bias and the escalation of conflict. *Personality and Social Psychology Bulletin*, *34*(6), 833–848.

Lippmann, W. (1922). *Public Opinion*. New York: Harcourt, Brace.

Major, B. & Townsend, S.S.M. (2010). Coping with bias. *The SAGE Handbook of Prejudice, Stereotyping and Discrimination*, 410. Thousand Oaks, CA: Sage Publications.

Montieth, M.J., Arthur, S.A. & Flynn, S.M. (2010). Self-regulation and bias. *The SAGE Handbook of Prejudice, Stereotyping and Discrimination*, 493. Thousand Oaks, CA: Sage Publications.

Oakes, P.J. & Turner, J.C. (1990). Is limited information processing the cause of social stereotyping? In W. Stroebe, & M. Hewstone (Eds). *European Review of Social Psychology* (Vol. 1, p. 111–125). Chichester, UK: Wiley.

Pearson, A.R., Dovidio, J.F. & Gaertner, S.L. (2009). The nature of contemporary prejudice: Insights from aversive racism. *Social and Personality Psychology Compass*, *3*(3), 314–338.

Reskin, B.F. (2012). The race discrimination system. *Annual Review of Sociology*, *38*, 17–35.

Rucker, K.C. (2021). *An Interpretive Phenomenological Study of the Lived Experiences of African American Attorneys with Workplace Racial Microaggressions and the Effect on Motivation* (Doctoral dissertation, Sullivan University).

Scott, C.L. (2013). Believing doesn't make it so: Forensic education and the search for truth. *Journal of the American Academy of Psychiatry and the Law 41*(1), 18–32.

Smith, A. N., Brief, A. P., & Colella, A. (2010). Bias in organizations. *The SAGE Handbook of Prejudice, Stereotyping and Discrimination*, 441. Thousand Oaks, CA: Sage Publications.

Sue, D. W., Alsaidi, S., Awad, M. N., Glaeser, E., Calle, C. Z. & Mendez, N. (2019). Disarming racial microaggressions: Microintervention strategies for targets, White allies, and bystanders. *American Psychologist*, *74*(1), 128.

Sue, D. W., Capodilupo, C. M., Torino, G. C., Bucceri, J. M., Holder, A., Nadal, K. L., & Esquilin, M. (2007). Racial microaggressions in everyday life: implications for clinical practice. *American psychologist*, *62*(4), 271–286.

Sue, D. W., Capodilupo, C. M., & Holder, A. (2008). Racial microaggressions in the life experience of Black Americans. *Professional Psychology: Research and Practice*, *39*(3), 329–336.

Sue, D.W. & Spanierman, L.B. (2020). *Microaggressions in Everyday Life* (2d ed.). Hoboken, N.J.: John Wiley & Sons, Inc.

Tekleab, A.G., Quigley, N.R. & Tesluk, P.E. (2009). A longitudinal study of team conflict, conflict management, cohesion, and team effectiveness. *Group & Organizational Management*, *34*(2), 170–205.

Von Baeyer, C.L., Sherk, D.L. & Zanna, M.P. (1981). Impression management in the job interview: When the female applicant meets the male (chauvinist) interviewer. *Personality and Social Psychology Bulletin*, *7*, 45–51.

Wiececk, W.M. & Hamilton, J.L. (2014). Beyond the Civil Rights Act of 1964: Confronting structural racism in the workplace. *Louisiana Law Review*, *74*(4), 1095–1160.

Yzerbyt, V., & Demoulin, S. (2010). Intergroup relations. *Wiley Handbook of Social Psychology*, 1024. Hoboken, NJ: John Wiley & Sons, Inc.

Zetland, D. (2011). Intra-organizational conflict: Origin and cost. *The Economics of Peace and Security Journal*, *6*(1), 12–21.

Section 3: **Intercultural, International, and Ethic Conflict Management**

Charity Butcher, Maia Carter Hallward

Chapter 12
Managing Workplace Conflicts:
Considerations of Ethnicity and Religion

Abstract: This chapter explores actions that individuals and organizations can take to proactively reduce not only individual-level ethnic and religious conflict in the workplace, but also those conflicts resulting from systemic and/or institutional operating procedures that consciously or unconsciously benefit certain groups and exclude others. Discussing strategies such as openly recognizing all religious and ethnic holidays, developing inclusive mission and vision statements, training employees in horizontal and vertical conflict management strategies, and conducting facilitated identity exercises can help encourage a welcoming and inclusive workplace environment.

Keywords: ethnic diversity, religious diversity, institutional racism, inclusivity, self-reflective practice, organizational culture

Workplaces often have significant diversity, including people from different gender, racial, ethnic, cultural, and religious backgrounds. Diversity, when recognized, valued, and engaged with constructively, can be a great strength by providing multiple angles on complex issues and varying perspectives for problem-solving. However, when ignored or used – consciously or unintentionally – as grounds for discrimination, such differences have the potential to lead to latent or overt conflict. While ethnicity and religion are sometimes linked or conflated with culture, Avruch (2003, p. 8) notes that "ethnic groups are defined by the boundaries between them; culture is used to constitute and maintain the boundaries." Culture – and this can include workplace culture – provides the "lenses through which the causes of conflict are refracted" (Avruch, 2003, p. 20) even when culture itself is not necessarily a direct cause. Further, we are more likely to attribute "cultural" explanations to those who are different than us, and less likely to recognize how culture – and with it ethnicity and religion – affects our own actions.

This chapter focuses on managing ethnic and religious workplace conflicts. It is important to note, however, that such conflicts are not simply the result of individual attitudes, behaviors, and characteristics, but also are influenced by structural and institutional factors. Many potential conflicts are avoidable if employers and employees are sensitive to cultural issues within the workplace and strive to accommodate individuals from a variety of backgrounds; however, recognizing one's own privilege and adjusting expectations accordingly can also potentially lead to conflict, as those who have benefited from the system may react negatively to what they see as an attack on their position or identity rather than a quest for equality of treatment. Conflicts

https://doi.org/10.1515/9783110746365-012

around ethnicity and religion vary in their intensity as well as how difficult they are to confront. Some examples of conflicts around ethnicity and religion that might be easier to address include the availability of breaks and space for religious and cultural practices, such as prayer, the storage of and preparation of foods in the workplace, training regarding different communication patterns in terms of degree of directness, and orientation to individual versus collective accomplishment. More difficult to address are the conflicts that arise from structural or institutional factors as these may be invisible to those in the dominant culture and/or those that benefit from those cultural/institutional norms. These might include expectations regarding working hours, how promotions and job assignments are determined, and the extent to which offsite socializing and/or networking events involving alcohol or activities that are only accessible to a subset of the organization influence career trajectories and office relationships.

While some sources of workplace conflict can be readily addressed through raising individual-level awareness and changing department level policies, others require more challenging structural changes to address racism, prejudice, bias, and microaggressions that take place within the workplace and create a toxic work environment for employees. These types of issues may run deeper and will be more difficult to tackle. However, it is essential that employers create and enforce an environment that is safe for all employees and ideally fosters a sense of community that seeks understanding and acceptance of difference – not only in terms of "outward" culture (language, dress, food, etc.), but also in terms of the less obvious ways ethnic and racial differences influence attitudes, behaviors, and assumptions of what is "right" and "normal."

Importance of Ethnic and Religious Diversity in the Workplace

Ethnic and Religious diversity is an important component of the workplace and can bring great benefits in terms of critical thinking, novel viewpoints on problems, creativity, and ability to reach out to global audiences. However, traditional U.S. workplaces are not always open to ethnic and religious subcultures that do not operate in concert with the implicit Protestant dominated workplace culture (Cromwell, 1997, p. 165). In addition to the psychological, health-related, and social costs of ethnic and racial conflict in the workplace (Low et al., 2007, p. 2292), there are material costs to organizations in terms of discrimination lawsuits, worker's compensation, and high turnover rates of employees, as well as indirect costs including those due to lost productivity and quality defects resulting from low morale (Fox & Stallworth, 2005, p. 227).

Research indicates that ethnic and racial minorities may feel institutionally and socially isolated in the workplace (Smith & Calasanti, 2005; Bergbom & Vartia, 2021), particularly when the burden is placed on them – rather than the institution – to promote diversity (Osseo-Asare et al., 2018). While bullying, micro aggressions, and verbally abusive treatment are some of the causes of ethnic and racial workplace conflict, sometimes conflict can arise from activities seen as more benign, such as workplace humor. What may be humorous in one cultural context may not be humorous to other ethnic or cultural groups, not only because of the topic of the joke itself, but also because of different beliefs regarding what humor is and how it manifests itself (Holmes and De Bres, 2013). Similarly, there are cultural differences regarding expectations of how authority figures should behave as well as how individuals and groups in an organization engage in – or avoid – confrontation and conflict (Loh, Restubo and Zagenczyk, 2010; Leung, 1987; Leung et al., 1992).

Practical Steps for Managing Ethnic and Religious-Based Workplace Conflicts

One of the most important steps organizations can take to address ethnic and religious-based workplace conflicts is to gain an understanding of how different groups approach and express conflict. When doing field work in Israel/Palestine, one of the authors heard some of the workplace challenges faced by members of a joint Israeli-Palestinian organization as a result of cultural differences. One of the organizational leaders noted that if in a staff meeting they were reviewing the cover design for their latest publication and an Israeli staff person said "this is horrible, I've never seen anything as awful as it, the color is all wrong …" in a heightened voice, they probably meant "it's fine" whereas if a Palestinian staff person stated "well, it will do" they probably meant "this is a disaster." The ability to read between the lines in terms of body language, tone of voice, what is (un)said, and other signals is critical for identifying and addressing potential conflicts before they emerge. While tools such as Geert Hoftede's (2003) cultural tendencies for various countries around the world are imperfect measures – and do not account for variation within cultures nor the diversity of ethnicities and religions within countries – they can be a useful starting point for thinking about how different individuals and groups in the workplace might approach various topics such as hierarchy/equality, individualism/teamwork, direct/face-saving communication, etc. It is critical, however, to remember the internal variation of ethnicities and religions. One helpful trick before projecting an assumption onto another ethnicity or religion is to self-reflect: would I say this about my own ethnic or religious group? Am I projecting the actions of an individual onto a group? Am I making assumptions about the universality of my own ethnic or religious views onto others?

Fox and Stallworth (2005, p. 453) recommend interventions including seminars, mandatory training for managers, grievance procedures, zero tolerance for abuse, open door policies at the top, and well-trained HR specialists for some of the more difficult workplace conflicts related to ethnicity and religion. However, such policies themselves may reflect cultural biases related to trust of such offices and require institutional policies to be free of systemic bias themselves. There are increasing numbers of resources and trainings that deal with building an anti-racist mindset and unlearning unconscious biases. However, instituting such trainings and introducing such concepts needs to be considered carefully since many who have benefitted from the implicit cultural norms influenced by white Protestant (cis-male) culture may feel attacked or threatened by shifts to new modes of operation. It is critical to focus on institutional, structural, and cultural dimension of racism and bias so as not to insinuate personal attacks or moral judgement. Conflict from those resisting change from the status quo requires as much preparation as conflict stemming from those who are harmed by the status quo. Book discussion groups on books written by racial and ethnic minorities – such as *So You Want to Talk about Race* by Ijeoma Oluo or *Stamped from the Beginning* by Ibrahim Xendi are two examples in the nonfiction realm, while *Homecoming* by Yaa Gyasi and *Slay* by Brittney Morris could be used in the fictional realm.

The first step for any company, business, or employer in managing workplace conflicts is to prevent them from occurring in the first place. Of course, this is much easier said than done. However, there are steps that employers can take to reduce the likelihood of ethnic and religious conflicts arising in the first place. First and foremost, public company policies, such as mission, vision, and diversity statements, should clearly promote the ideas and norms of religious and ethnic (as well as racial and gender) inclusivity. If your company does not have a formal written mission, vision, and diversity statement, you need to create them. The vision and mission of a company is the first thing potential employees and clients will see and sets the tone for what type of company you are. An inclusive mission and vision can help attract more diversity in both employees and clients. It also signals to all employees the types of norms that you promote. When crafting such statements, it is critical that the group is as diverse as possible, since otherwise the statements may perpetuate cultural blind spots due to the positionality of the drafters. For example, just as the research suggests that in order to broaden the diversity of employees at an institution one needs to have diverse hiring committees, one needs a diverse committee to capture the multiplicity of perspectives on institutional mission and vision and how various framings of these statements may affect various organizational constituencies.

In addition to your vision and mission statements, your company should "walk the walk" and not just "talk the talk." That means that there should be clear policies and norms in place that promote and enforce the ideas in your mission and vision. Once such policy should be a conflict resolution process or processes that are clearly outlined. Managers and employees should have a clear understanding of how workplace conflicts will be managed – and this process should be inclusive of different conflict management styles and approaches. It would be useful to create a menu of conflict management strategies and policies for managers and employees, with options and strategies for conflict management that are both vertical and horizontal (i.e., employee to employee versus involving management). Ideally, these conflict management approaches and policies would be created through a workshop that includes all stakeholders and actors. Having more than one possible approach and allowing employees to choose their strategy when dealing with conflicts, can help provide a stronger environment for managing workplace conflicts. Having such strategies being publicly available to all actors also allows individuals to manage their own conflicts with one another without necessarily always having to engage those higher up in the hierarchy. At the same time, all employees should feel supported by management should they be unable to manage conflicts and need greater institutional support.

There are also simple tasks that your company can do to address issues that could lead to potential conflicts related to ethnicity and religion. First, learn to correctly pronounce all employee names and insist that employees learn each other's names. Names often have cultural, ethnic, and/or religious significance for people. Learning to correctly pronounce the names of your colleagues can help create a more inclusive workplace environment and demonstrate your commitment to diversity and inclusion. Also, encourage all members of the workplace to speak up for each other when they notice a mispronunciation, an injustice, or some other action that, intentional or not, could be perceived as a religious or ethnic slight. For example, if you notice that white males have dominated the conversation at a staff meeting while others have patiently waited their turn to speak, make a suggestion that others have been waiting, suggest to the facilitator that they call on those other people, or correct a name mispronunciation so that the individual does not always have to do so themselves. Such actions can also be done in private after a meeting, in person or via email.

You should also review your office space with considerations of how shared spaces may be viewed by different groups of people and cultures and assess whether spaces for cultural activities, such as prayer, are available. Ask your employees what types of space they need to conduct their work and for their breaks, including for meals. Cultural practices around food preparation and storage are often easy to accommodate and can help create a safer and more inclusive workplace environment. Similarly, recognition and acknowledgement of holidays of all employees – rather than those in the dominant ethno-religious group helps promote a sense of inclusion and value for all.

Workplace Identity Exercise

Issues related to ethnicity and religion are ultimately related to identity. Having employees and employers think purposively about the impact of identity and the salience of identity within the workplace can help create an open and supportive atmosphere and address issues before they become conflictual. To this end, we present an identity exercise, based on one created by Asal and Griffith (2017), that can be conducted at the workplace, either in a regularly scheduled meeting or in one specifically focused on the workplace environment and potential conflicts. Ideally, an external facilitator from outside your workplace would lead this session. While it is ideal for managers and those in authority positions to participate alongside other employees, there is also a risk to this approach. If institutional problems exist within the workplace, having managers present for this type of exercise may prevent employees from feeling comfortable participating. On the other hand, if there are a few workplace "bullies" present, employees may feel more comfortable sharing openly if there are authority figures present. Consider the dynamics of your workplace carefully when conducting these activities and consult with others from various backgrounds and perspectives before deciding on a format if you are unsure.

Given the sensitive nature of identities, it is important that no one be forced to share anything personal during this exercise. You want to create an environment where everyone feels comfortable sharing their experiences and ideas, and this cannot be done if people feel compelled to participate. It might be useful for managers or others in authority positions (if they are participating in the exercise) to commit to fully participating and sharing their own answers, which may help break the ice in the group and make others feel safer sharing their own thoughts. But no employee, regardless of rank, should feel compelled to provide any personal information if they do not want to. At the outset of the exercise, be sure everyone understands that they can keep any information private that they do not wish to share.

With that caveat in mind, the first step of the exercise is to have participants write down five key self-identifiers that they will hopefully share with others. We suggest the following prompt:

- Write down five key self-identifiers that are a key part of your identity and that shape how you work and/or how you self-identify in the workplace. Consider identities that make you part of a larger community or social group.

Once everyone has written down five identities, ask everyone to cross one off. Once they have done this, have them cross another off. Then, ask them to cross out a third identity. Finally, have them cross one more identity off the list. Now, everyone will have a list of five identities, with four crossed out. Some people may find this a difficult exercise. Cutting the first identity may be easy, but the task becomes increasingly difficult as they must choose additional identities to drop. Be understanding of this difficulty but encourage them to cross out the identities, nonetheless. Giving a moment or two for individuals to self-reflect and consider each decision can be helpful; do not rush through the process.

Next, ask the group the following:

- If you are willing to share, tell us some of the broader categories that the identities you first identified (your five identities) fall under.

The categories of identities that people identify will usually be things like ethnicity, nationality, religion, gender, race, age, familial roles, demographic references (Southerner, Californian, etc.), professional qualifications and such. Once participants have identified various broad categories of identities, ask them the following:

– If you are willing to share, tell us the category of the final identity you chose to keep.
– Again, if you are willing to share, tell us why you chose to keep this last identity. Why is it important to you? How does it impact your presence in our workplace community?

These general questions begin to allow you to see how different identities may be important for different groups of people. However, since you are especially interested in how these identities might impact workplace dynamics, and how managers and those in positions of authority might best accommodate difference within the workplace, it is important to take the conversation further and deeper. Next, we suggest discussing the following (making sure to reemphasize that no one is required to provide answers to these discussion questions):

– How much did your current context (at this company/organization with these colleagues and in this specific geographical area) shape the identities you put down on your list and the ones you crossed off?
– What patterns do you observe about the types of categories highlighted by the group? Are there noticeable similarities and differences among certain subsets of your workforce? If so, what might that mean in terms of ensuring employee morale, inclusion, and support?
– Do you feel supported in openly embracing these identities in your workplace? Have you ever experienced situations at work where you felt that you were ostracized or left out by those in a different identity group? Have you felt like you needed to downplay or suppress one or more of your identities?
– Which of your identities are more recognized and/or accepted within your workplace? What policies, practices, or other actions might make you feel more supported and accepted in all of your various identities?

The second question above allows employees to think broadly about these differences and offer suggestions for improving the workplace without necessarily discussing their own situation. Some of these questions are more personal, and thus some employees may be particularly reluctant to offer feedback. Those leading the session should take cues from the participants before proceeding with these questions. Facilitators may also encourage employees to write and reflect individually, giving space for silence and space for all to make their own set of notes which they can then choose to share publicly with the group, privately with others at a later point, or to keep to themselves. This can also prevent those who are most confident speaking in the group from dominating the airspace and give room for those who may feel less comfortable to share.

Conclusion

Individuals rarely want to think of themselves as racist or biased against other ethnic or religious groups, yet we do not always see the ways in which we and/or our environments contribute systematically to the exclusion of certain groups and/or unintentionally create a workplace influenced by the norms of a dominant religion, culture, or ethnicity. Being aware of and intentionally engaging with this possibility can make a workplace more inviting to diverse individuals and groups and can create a more positive and productive working environment for all. While there are no quick fixes to institutional biases or to correcting systems of privilege in society, workplace leaders can and should strive to prevent and ameliorate conflicts stemming from ethnicity and religion to the best of their abilities. Engaging in transparent and self-reflective practices, such as the identity exercise presented here, is one approach to building a more positive working environment for all.

References

Asal, V., & Griffith, L. (2017). A terrible beauty is born: Teaching about identity salience and conflict. *Dynamics of Asymmetric Conflict*, 10(1): 3–13. DOI: 10.1080/17467586.2017.1300291

Avruch, K. (2003). Integrating ideas of culture, ethnicity, and multiculturalism into conflict resolution and ADR practice. Tuzla, Turkey: Sabancı Üniversitesi.

Bergbom, B., & Vartia, M. (2021). Ethnicity and workplace bullying. In P. D'Cruz, E. Noronha, C. Caponecchia, J. Escartín, D. Salin, & M. R. Tuckey (Eds.)., *Dignity and inclusion at Work* (pp. 393–432). Singapore: Singer Singapore.

Cromwell, J. B. (1997). Cultural discrimination: The reasonable accommodation of religion in the workplace. *Employee Responsibilities and Rights Journal*, 10(2),155–172.

Fox, S., & Stallworth, L. E. (2005). Racial/ethnic bullying: Exploring links between bullying and racism in the US workplace. *Journal of Vocational Behavior*, 66(3),438–456.

Hofstede, G. (2003). *Culture's Consequences: Comparing Values, Behaviors, Institutions, and Organizations Across Nations*. (2nd edition). Thousands Oaks, California: Sage Publications.

Holmes, J., & De Bres, J. (2013). Ethnicity and humour in the workplace. In J. P. Gee & M. Handford (Eds.), *The Routledge handbook of discourse analysis (pp. 520–534)*. London: Routledge.

Leung, K. *(1987)*. Some determinants of reactions to procedural models for conflict resolution: A cross-cultural study. *Journal of Personality and Social Psychology, 53, 898–908.*

Leung, K., Au, Y., Fernandez-Dols, J. M., & Iwawaki, S. *(1992)*. Preference for methods of conflict processing in two collectivist cultures. *International Journal of Psychology, 27(2),195–209.*

Loh, J., Restubog, S. L. D, & Zagenczyk, T. J. (2010). Consequences of workplace bullying on employee identification and satisfaction among Australians and Singaporeans. *Journal of Cross-Cultural Psychology*, 41(2),236–252.

Low, K. S. D., Radhakrishnan, P., Schneider, K. T., & Rounds, J. (2007). The experiences of bystanders of workplace ethnic harassment. *Journal of Applied Social Psychology*, 37(10),2261–2297.

Osseo-Asare, A., Balasuriya, L., Huot, S. J., Keene, D, Berg, D., Nunez-Smith, M., Genao, I, Latimore, D., & Boatright, D. (2018). Minority resident physicians' views on the role of race/ethnicity in their training experiences in the workplace. *JAMA Network Open*, *1(5)*, e182723–e182723. doi:10.1001/jamanetworkopen.2018.2723.

Smith, J. W., & Calasanti, T. (2005). The influences of gender, race, and ethnicity on workplace experiences of institutional and social isolation: An exploratory study of university faculty. *Sociological Spectrum*, 25(3),307–334.

Yashwant Pathak
Chapter 13
Hindu Philosophy and the Resolution of the Roots of Conflict: Adi Shankaracharya's 'Nirvana Shatakam'

Abstract: Nirvana Shatakam are the six verses written by Adi Shankarcharya (12th Century) from Bharat (India). He was a great saint and had written many books and devotional resources is his short 32 years of life. These six verses discuss the eternal questions for humanity: Who I am? Why I am here? Where I will go after death? And how understanding oneself can help us to resolve the conflicts in our life?

This chapter covers various aspects of understanding oneself based on these six verses and how the concepts in these verses can bring peace at three levels.

Keywords: eternal questions to humanity, understanding oneself, who i am not, peace at three levels

For ages and in many cultures, humanity has had some common eternal questions, which every philosophy in the world has tried to answer. The first question is basic to our existence:

Ko Aham? (Sanskrit) Who am I?

The second question that humanity has asked is:

Where will I go after the death?

The answer to this question is based on one's understanding of these two questions:

- Who I am, and
- What am I doing here?

Confusion about one's self-understanding or misunderstanding leads to Conflicts at various levels in life.

Roots of Conflicts According to Hindu Philosophy

The majority of conflicts happening around us can be categorized under the following headings:

1. Conflicts due to ego – misunderstanding and misinterpretation of oneself
2. Conflicts due to fear of death
3. Conflict due to Shadripus (six enemies)' The shadripus have been listed as

https://doi.org/10.1515/9783110746365-013

1. Lust (Sanskrit: *Kama*)
2. Greed (Sanskrit: *Lobha*)
3. Anger (Sanskrit: *Krodha*)
4. Pride (Sanskrit: *Mada*)
5. Attachment (Sanskrit: *Moha*)
6. Covetousness (Sanskrit: *Matsarya*)

Hindu philosophy tries to explore various aspects of understanding the human being through well-known scriptures. Mundoka Upanishad tries to explain how the Jivatman (the apparent self) becomes one with the Parmatman (The real self or Brahman). If one can give up the Jivatman, one should realize one's real nature as none other than the supreme Brahman. This realization is what is known as liberation. Even if we proceed a step in this direction, we can easily get over the conflicts in life at various levels.

Once a person dies, what is lost? As per the Hindu philosophy everyone is divine, "Vayam Amrutsasya Putraha" (We are the children of the Divine). Once the divine is lost to the body, the body is useless. That is why the Hindus cremate the bodies. What is lost is the spirit, which gives the body the life, the life spirit, also known as Soul or Atman. The Atman is considered part of the Paramatman, the greater sprit, or ultimate God. As every creation of God carries a part of the Parmatman, it is considered to be divine.

Adi Shankaracharya was a great saint, who lived for only 32 years. However, he contributed significantly to the world of Hindu philosophy by writing many books and commentaries on Veda, Vedanta, Geetha and many Great Scriptures. Some of his great works are Vivek Chudamani, Bhashya on many Upanishads, Geetha Bhasya, Brahma sutras, Nirvana Shatakam and many more.

Nirvana Shatakam

Adi Shankara (first Shankaracharya) summarized the entirety of Advaita Vedanta (non-dualistic philosophy) in six stanzas. When a young boy of eight, while wandering in the Himalayas, seeking to find his guru, he encountered a sage who asked him, "Who are you?" The boy answered with six verses, which are known as "Nirvana Shatakam" or "Atma Shatakam: six verses to understand oneself". "Nirvana" is complete equanimity, peace, tranquility, freedom, and joy.

"Atma" (Soul) is the True Self. The sage the boy was talking to was Swami Govindapada Acharya, who was, indeed, the teacher he was looking for. These verses can be of tremendous value to progress in contemplation practices that lead to Self-Realization and understand the true self and therefore the root causes of all the human conflicts.

From a conflict resolution point of view these six verses are great guidelines for human beings. The instruction emphatically conveyed by the six verses of Nirvana Shatkam is that identification of oneself with the body, mind, and senses is the root cause of all sorrow and conflicts. If we can learn to disassociate ourselves from this root cause of conflict, then there will always be peace within ourselves and around the world. This knowledge is beyond any religions or philosophies. It is applicable to total humanity irrespective of their backgrounds, races, nationalities, and religious inclinations.

Who and what I am not? (First verse)

The first verse goes:

मनोबुद्ध्यहंकार चत्तिानिनिाहं न च श्रोत्रजहिव्े न च घ्राणनेत्रे ।
न च व्योम भूमर्नि तेजो न वायुः चदिानन्दरूपः शविोऽहम् शविोऽहम् ।। 1 ।।)

I am not mind, nor intellect, nor ego, nor the reflections of inner self. I am not the five senses. I am beyond that. I am not the ether, nor the earth, nor the fire, nor the wind (i.e., the five elements). I am indeed, that eternal knowing and bliss, Shiva, love, and pure consciousness.

First Verse of Adi Shankaracharya

In the first verse Adi Shankaracharya talks about who and what I am not. The verse intends to disown everything proposed in normal science and discussion which is considered to be part of human being. It tries to take you through a passage that is something beyond the perceptions of human beings experienced by five senses or beyond five basic elements which are believed by many to be source and content of the creation. If you read between the lines, it says why I should not be fighting; if I am not either of human perceptions or of the five elements, then I am something beyond them. I am beyond mind, ego, and intellect; whatever I perceive by five senses, I am beyond that. If this is true, then there can be no reasons to get involved in any conflicts and put oneself into such conflicting scenarios.

As explained in Atma Bodha (knowledge of oneself), our existence is perceived through Sharira (in Sanskrit) or the gross body or the body is what is visible to us. The subtle body runs the gross body in different ways from inside, and the causal body causes the existence of the gross and casual bodies. The casual body remains dormant. These are Micro level bodies. At the Macro level, the five great elements cause the existence of all the three micro bodies in each of us.

In the first verse of Nirvana Shatakam, Adi Sankaracharya is negating that part of the causal body which feels as the 'I,' the perceiver. He is thus also negating the sense organs (indriyaas) which act as the medium of transactions between this perceiver and the external world.

Therefore, the 'I' of oneself becomes free of emotions, desires, transactions, dilemmas, and decisions to make. I am not also any of the five great elements. When 'I' am the only one, without any others, then I am the all-pervading bliss. Where is the question of the 'I' feeling, as different from you and others?

Liberate yourself from what you are not and be what you are. Once I can get over my ego associated with my emotions, desires, transactions, dilemmas, and decisions, then how can I be involved in the conflicts which occur stemming from my ownership of these things. If I do not own my decision or emotions, whatever I do should not be attached to myself or my ego. If one can reach this state of mind, then neither is there a place for any sort of conflict in life nor there is a need for conflict resolution.

Second Verse of Adi Shankaracharya

The second verse of the Adi Shankaracharya asks the question: Who and what I am not?

न च प्राणसंज्ञो न वै पंचवायुः न वा सप्तधातुःन वा पञ्चकोशः।
न वाक्पाणिपादौ न चोपस्थपायु, चिदानन्दरूपःशिवोऽहम् शिवोऽहम् ।। 2 ।।)

> Neither can I be termed as energy (Praana), nor five types of breath (Vaayu), nor the seven material essences (Dhaatu), nor the five coverings (Panca Kosha). Neither am I the five instruments of elimination, procreation, motion, grasping, or speaking. I am indeed, that eternal knowing and bliss, Shiva, love, and pure consciousness.

I am not the Praana, the energy of life in the body. I am not any of the Pancha Vayus (the five gases), namely, the Praana, Apaana, Vyaana, Udaana and Samaana vayus. I am not any of the Seven Dhathus (elements that make the body parts), namely, the marrow, bones, brain, meat, blood, skin, and the muscles. I am not any of the five Pancha Kosas, (sheaths of the body), namely, Annamaya Kosa, Praanamaya Kosa, Manomaya Kosa, Vijnanamaya Kosa and Anandamaya Kosa. I am not any of the Karmendriyaas (the organs of action), namely, the tongue, hands, legs, reproductive organs, and excretory organs. I am the all-pervading, universal consciousness and eternal bliss. I am the Siva; I am the Siva.

Praana: The Energy of Life. Praana is the essential life energy in creation including us as human beings, and it also represents one of the five Vayus or gases circulating in the body. Once we are dead the prana is lost. On death of the gross body, the prana life energy merges back into the five great elements of the Universe. In most meditations watching breath (not necessarily controlling breath) is important. You can clearly feel the prana energy going out and coming in along with breath. Let us also understand that prana energy comes in and goes out along with Praana Vayu but is different from Praana vayu. Praana Vayu is the vehicle on which prana energy rides. Does it not make it clear that Praana energy is not the Self? So, affirm and assert that it is not the 'I.' 'I' am not that Praana life energy.

Pancha Vayus: The Five Gases. There are five vayus described in scriptures. Praana Vayu resides in the nostrils and also in the ears, eyes, and mouth. It is responsible for inhalation and exhalation from the nostrils to the lungs and the regulation of circulation. As we can easily discern, Praana Vayu is external to us, though it ensures the passage of prana energy into us. Apaana Vayu circulates in excretory organs and regulates their functions. Samaana Vayu resides in and around the navel, inside the stomach and assists in digestion and distribution of digested food and water to all parts of the body depending on their needs. Udaana Vayu moves throughout the body with an upward trend or bias and has some functions at the death.

Vyaana Vayu regulates prana and apaana and is the cause of actions requiring strength.

All Vayus assist the gross body in many functions. The gross body dies and the functions of all these vayus stop that day. They merge back into the great universal element of Vayu. Therefore, affirm and assert that the self is not the Pancha Vayus.

'I' am not the Pancha Vayus.

Dhathus: The Seven Elements that Make the Body Parts. The seven dhatus are the essential elements of the body – the marrow, bones, brain, meat, blood, skin, and the muscles (majja, asthi, medha, pala, raktha,Charma, thvak). These also die and degenerate. They cannot be the self. Affirm and assert that 'I' am not the self. 'I' am not the Saptha Dhathus.

Panch Pancha Kosas: The Five Sheaths of the Body. My body has five sheaths, covering it. Annamaya Kosa is born of and grows out of food. The only tangible part of the body, it is subject to birth, growth, degeneration, disease, and death. It comes from the earth. On death, it goes back to the earth.

When you are sufficiently relaxed – you exist only in your mental world. Your physical world no more exists for you. Do you sense your body? No. Not all. If you are sufficiently relaxed, you cannot feel your legs or hands or any other part without moving it, unless, of course, there is some pain in it, and any pain again pertains to the mind. The Saptha Dhathus earlier mentioned are all part of Annamaya Kosa. A healthy body is not YOU! Even if a part has been removed from your body, you cannot feel it. If, in your relaxed state, even when the mind functions, if the Annamaya Kosa cannot be felt how it can be YOU?! You are not Annamaya Kosa. Affirm that you are not it. Assert that you are not it. 'I' am not this Annamaya Kosa.

Praanamaya Kosa is the sheath consisting of the five vital airs. As the body dies, the airs merge back into the great universal element of air. 'I' am not this Praanamaya Kosa.

Manomaya Kosa is made up of mind and the five organs of perception, namely, sight, smell, hearing, taste, and touch. It is the seat of all feelings, emotions, and perceptions. It vacillates between indecisions. Here, organs of perception refer to very subtle organs which are part of causal body. They do not refer to the physical ear, eyes etc., which are called Golakams, and which are part of Annamaya Kosa or Gross Body. Mind is Avidya itself, but it can be the cause of both attachments and liberation. 'I' am not this Manomaya Kosa.

Vijnaanamaya Kosa is the sheath of the intellect, Buddhi, ego and their vritthis. Compared to Gross body, Manomaya Kosa is more likely to experience the reflection of Atma in itself by its proximity with Buddhi and Chidhabhasa. Vijnanamaya Kosa, consisting of Buddhi and ego is the very seat of Chidaabhasa where the reflection of the consciousness takes place. Vijnaanamaya Kosa experiences the reflection of the consciousness but is not itself the consciousness. It also takes birth, grows, degenerates, and dies. 'I' am not the Vijnanamaya kosa.

Anandamaya Kosa is the subtlest sheath. It is the sheath of bliss. It is born of Thamoguna. It has qualities of affection, joy, and experiences of happiness. It gives joy to those who turn their attention inward. It is the Kaarana Sareera or causal body and is the seat of primal ignorance or Avidya. It is active during deep sleep when other organs are asleep. It is also subject to births and deaths. 'I' am not this Aanandamaya Kosa.

These five sheaths constitute the Sareera Thrayam. Understand I am not any of the Panch Kosas which constitute the Sareera Thrayam.

The Emotional Mind

It is not your emotional mind that influences your interactions with other human beings, animals, and even inanimate things like money and your house. It is the main cause of all attachments. If you look at everything around with a detached mind and thought process, you will never get involved in any conflicts nor will you need conflict resolution. At the same time, it is the same emotional mind which can free us from all these attachments when it is used along with the Buddhi and when re-directed to a spiritual goal. It is an instrument for the goal of self. It is not the self. Assert and affirm this.

Third Verse of Adi Shankaracharya

न मे द्वेषरागौ न मे लोभमोहौ, मदो नैव मे नैव मात्सर्यभावः।
न धर्मो न चार्थो न कामो न मोक्ष; चिदानन्दरूपःशिवोऽहम् शिवोऽहम् ।। 3 ।।)

The third verse of the Adi Shankaracharya says, "I am beyond them." I have no hatred or dislike, nor affiliation or liking, nor greed, nor delusion, nor pride or haughtiness, nor feelings of envy or jealousy. I have no duty (dharma), nor any money, nor any desire (refer: kama), nor even liberation (refer: moksha). I am indeed, that eternal knowing and bliss, Shiva, love, and pure consciousness.

We are now negating our vritthis, the actions and functions we indulge in, in this verse. We are now negating dualities like likes and dislikes as not our qualities and not pertaining to us. All dualities are not mentioned in the verse, but the mention of one duality and one each from two other dualities implies the inclusion of all dualities, e.g., happiness and unhappiness, love and hate, greed and generosity, delusion and clarity, friendship, and enmity. All dualities stand negated, by implication, though not mentioned explicitly. 'I' do not indulge in or abide by any of the dualities. I am beyond them. I am Sthitha Prajna. I am one with equanimity in all circumstances. This is the knowledge and firm understanding to be generated through Nidhidhyasanam (meditation) on this verse.

Sankara goes on to say that the four Purusharthas, the great goals of human life, extolled in the Vedas, are also not needed for him. If Sankara claims that 'I' do not need Dharma, Artha, and Kaama, it can sound logical for a Sthitha Prajna who has transcended all dualities. However, how can even Adi Sankara claim that 'I' do not need Moksha, the most desirable and exalted goal of life. The aim for human existence is nothing other than Moksha. The one who has attained Atma Jnanam, is already in a state of Nitya Muktha and Jeevan Muktha, the already liberated one even while alive and one who is already freed from future births. This is moksha, the ultimate.

Fourth Verse of Adi Shankaracharya

न पुण्यं न पापं न सौख्यं न दुखं, न मन्त्रो न तीर्थो न वेदा न यज्ञ ।
अहं भोजनं नैव भोज्यं न भोक्ता, चिदानन्दरूपःशिवोऽहम् शिवोऽहम् ।। 4 ।।)

The fourth verse of the Adi Shankaracharya discusses the unseen fruits of karma. I have neither virtue (punya), nor vice (paapa). I do not commit sins or good deeds, nor have happiness or sorrow, pain, or pleasure. I do not need mantras, holy places, scriptures, rituals, or sacrifices (yajna). I am none of the triad of the observer or one who experiences the process of observing or experiencing, or any object being observed or experienced. I am indeed, that eternal knowing and bliss, Shiva, love, and pure consciousness.

Punyam is the result of good deeds. Paapam is the result of bad deeds. Punyam and Paapam, can be perceived in relative terms. The Unseen fruits of the karma (Adrista Phalam) are the fruits that are given to us later than the deed at some time unknown to us. The direct results of our deeds are known to us immediately. For instance, if we commit a theft, the drista phalam is the stolen money that we get. We may be happy with it, but the unseen fruits as punishment for the theft will visit us later, in some form and time, when we least expect it. Why this postponement? Why not this also be given simultaneously with the deed? Well, you also have a store of good deeds and bad deeds from the past and these deeds are waiting in queue for giving you their respective fruits.

You cannot escape any of them, but you get them in the queue. Just when the Unseen fruits of a certain past deed may mature is decided not by you but by the controller of the law of Karma!! He is the Karma Fruit donor (Phala Dhatha). If he so wills, your theft today may give you both seen fruits (Drista Phalam) and unseen fruits (Adrista Phalam) today itself by being found out, beaten up and hauled into jail. On the other hand, you may enjoy the stolen booty and wait for Adrista Phalam to come sometime later. When it comes to you, you cannot link it up with your past deeds. This disjunction between the timing of bad deeds (and good deeds) and their Adrista Phalam deludes most individuals into perpetrating more and more heinous acts, thinking that they are getting away with all of their heinous acts!! No, they are going to pay for all of their acts at the most unlikely time and in the most unlikely ways.

Alternatively, good people may seem to be suffering for their good deeds, but that is not what is happening. Good people especially are quickly finishing their past Prarabdha karma, taking their difficulties, their Adrista Phalam of past deeds, in their stride. The Karma Phala Dhatha is especially kind to them in this respect if we understand it right. Good deeds accumulate our store of Punyam, and bad deeds accumulate our store of Paapam. Their effect comes to us in the future in the same birth or in a future birth.

Good deeds (Punyam) and bad deeds (Paapam) both lead us to rebirth (Punar Janma) – repeated future births – either directly after death or after spending some time in the heavens or the hell. Punyam and Paapam cannot lead to Moksha, the ultimate liberation. What comes along with you after your death is not your accumulated wealth, name, fame, or relations. Rather, it is your unspent store of Punyam and Paapam. Therefore, we can decide what we want to take!!

Punyam and Paapam have absolutely no effect on an Atma Jnani, like Sankara, who has been liberated already from Avidya. In considering many such Atma Jnanis (like Sankara), we find them departing from their bodies very early in life. It is because they only need to finish their already-matured Prarabdha Karma Phalam. Their past store of Sanchitha Karma is burned out by their Atma Jnanam and there is no more Aagami Karma for them. However, the already matured Prarabdha Karma Phalam has to be finished. Once this is done, they have no more need for bodily life. This is why Sankara says: 'I' have neither Punyam nor Paaapam.

Likewise, the Atma Jnani (one who knows himself truly) remains untouched by pleasures and sorrows. He is the highest Aananda, or joy, himself. He has no need for any other pleasures (or sorrows). These have no effect on him. No dualities can touch the Atma Jnani. So, Sankara affirms: 'I' have neither pleasures nor sorrows. Manthram (chanting / Prayer) is needed to please the celestial powers or to attain earthly goals or some heavenly pleasures along with Theertham (Sacred waters all over the world), which can bestow our desires or cleanse our sins. Atma Jnani has no such needs at all, and Sankara says: 'I' need neither Manthram nor Theertham.

Atma Jnani is changeless and all pervading. All change that happens in one who eats, the eatable and the seeming process of eating, is Maya or Avidya. All these relate at the micro level to Annamaya Kosa and at macro level to the great element of earth. Earth becomes Annamaya Kosa (Gross body) this moment and becomes earth again the next moment, in an incessant, unending process even if we cannot see it clearly or realize it with our gross eyes and gross thinking. It is the earth everywhere and all the time in the process. Not YOU at all!!

In reality, there is neither an eater, nor an eating process nor an eatable. All are one and the same Mithya. This is the ultimate reality in which the Atma Jnani is. Readers may kindly read the three stories on Maya in an earlier post to further attain clarity on Maya.

Atma, the self, is action-less, transaction-less, and change-less. It is the witness of all. It is all pervading but not itself the Pancha Bhoothas or their variants at the micro level. What undergoes changes is Mithya or Maya. The Jeeva, who is not Atma Jnani, is perennially facing Maya and its effects.

As Atma Jnani, Sankara affirms I am the all-pervading, universal consciousness and eternal bliss. I am the Siva; I am the Siva.

Fifth Verse of Adi Shankaracharya

न मे मृत्युशंका न मे जातिभेद; पिता नैव मे नैव माता न जन्मः।
न बन्धुर्न मित्रं गुरूर्नैव शिष्य; चिदानन्दरूपःशिवोऽहम् शिवोऽहम् ।। 5 ।।)

The firth verse of the Adi Shankaracharya explains being birth and deathless. I do not fear death, as I do not have death. I have no separation from my true self, no doubt about my existence, nor have I discrimination on the basis of birth. I have no father or mother, nor did I have a birth. I am not the relative, nor the friend, nor the guru, nor the disciple. I am indeed, that eternal knowing and bliss, Shiva, love, and pure consciousness.

For an all pervading, eternal, 'birth and deathless,' all-knowing consciousness principle, the only one entity existing without a second, what death can be there and what foreboding or fear of death can be there? For the one who is all pervading and who is without any second entity, where from any caste (or religious, or racial, or national, or any other) can distinctions come? Sankara had affirmed this in Maneesha Panchakam too.

For one who is birth-less and death-less, from where can a father, mother, or birth come? When there is **no second entity** at all from where can any friends, relations, Gurus, or Disciples come?

Therefore, Sankara asserts and affirms *I am the all-pervading, universal conscious-ness and eternal bliss. I am the Siva; I am the Siva.*

Sixth Verse of Adi Shankaracharya

अहं निर्विकिल्पो निराकार रूपो, वभित्वाच सर्वत्र सर्वेन्द्रयियाणाम् ।
न चासङ्गतं नैव मुक्तर्नि मेय; चिदानन्दरूपःशिवोऽहम् शिवोऽहम् ।। 6 ।।)

The sixth verse of the Adi Shankaracharya proclaims that I am all pervasive as I am the divine. I am without any attributes, and without any form. I have neither attachment to the world, nor to liberation. I have no wishes for anything because I am everything, everywhere, every time, always in equilibrium. I am indeed, that eternal knowing and bliss, Shiva, love, and pure consciousness.

> **I am** the divisionless whole (Nir-vikalpa).
> **I am** the formless form (Niraakara roopa).
> **I am** the controller and ruler, pervading everywhere, all the time, on all the sense organs and therefore beyond them.
> **I am** ever the same everywhere in equilibrium without the need for either liberation or attachments.
> **I am** the all-pervading, universal consciousness and eternal bliss. I am the Siva; I am the Siva.

Sankara very clearly affirms and asserts that he is division-less, changeless, all pervading, ever in equilibrium, and is ever the eternal bliss and universal consciousness. The last verse tells the true nature of "Me" and once one realizes the true nature of oneself, the dark clouds of misunderstanding vanish, and the person can go beyond any conflicts in his life. Everything can be crystal clear for him/her and over the period of time the person gets detached from the ego, worries, fear of the death and the Shadripus (the six enemies mentioned at the beginning of the article). A person can look at everything happening around him/her in a detached mind as if it may be happening to his body, to his intellect or mind, but the soul is much above all these things. Such type of mindset once developed, the person is above any types of the conflicts and is always in the state of ultimate Anand or eternal peace and happiness.

Hence, Adi Shankaracharya has given excellent guidance for the resolution of the worldly conflicts and one can learn to look at conflicts from a very different perspective and very positive perspective. Once we understand clearly who we are, why we are here, and our ultimate goals of life, we will be better able to steer our way through any kinds of conflicts in life and reach the peace.

That is why the last verse says:

ॐ शान्तिः

The first Shanti will free us from physical burdens. It filters negative thoughts related to our etheric body like disabilities, diseases, and illnesses.

The second Shanti cleanses our mind and soul. We can shed negative thoughts like jealousy, hatred, anger, worries from our mind. This takes us a step closer to our higher soul.

The third Shanti is meant to protect us from accidents and natural calamities. Let there be peace to one and all and let us have a conflict-less life and respect each other as what Atman I carry is exactly the same Atman you carry, and every creation carries. All of us are the part of the Parmataman, hence there is no place for a conflict at the individual level, or organizational level.

The mantra can give us peace and free us from stress, particularly when we are feeling depressed, frustrated, angry and any other negative emotions. This will create a field of calmness around us and help us to meditate properly.

References

Prashant (2010, June 3). *Gunche*. http://gunche.blogspot.com/2010/06/atma-shatakam-chidanand-roopah-shivoham.html

Shankaracharya, A. (2022, February 27). *Atma Shatakam*. http://en.wikipedia.org/wiki/Atma_Shatakam

Shankaracharya, A. (n.d.). *Atma-Shatakam / Nirvana Shatakam the Song of the Self*. http://www.swamij.com/shankara-atma-shatakam.htm

Shankaracharya, A. (March 2022). *Green Message: The Evergreen Messages of Spirituality, Sanskrit and Nature*. http://www.greenmesg.org/mantras_slokas/advaita-nirvana_shatakam.php

Shankaracharya, A. (2022, May 10). Nirvana Shatakam. http://www.slideshare.net/SridharIriventi/nirvana-shatakam

Shankaracharya, A. (2010, November 24). *Nirvana Shatakam*. http://wisespiritualideas.blogspot.com/2010/11/nirvana-shatkam-post-1-of-adi-sankara.html

Shankara Bhagawat Pada, A. (.n.d.). *Nirvana shatakam*. http://www.hindupedia.com/en/Nirvana_shatakam

Shankara Bhagawat Pada, A. (.n.d.). *Nirvana Shatakam Stotra Lyrics – Shiva Devotional Prayer Lyrics*. http://www.hindudevotionalblog.com/2008/12/nirvana-shatakam-stotra-lyrics-by-adi.html

The Speaking Tree (n.d.). http://www.speakingtree.in/spiritual-blogs/seekers/god-and-i/and-he-was-enlightenednirvana-shatakamatma-shatakam

Alisa V. Moldavanova, Frederic S. Pearson

Chapter 14
Political Conflicts in the Workplace: What are Their Effects, and Can They be Avoided?

Abstract: As society becomes more polarized, political conflicts spill over into a variety of social institutions, including families, organized groups, social movements, and workplaces. This chapter examines the subject of political conflict in the workplace, a key social milieu in which most adult individuals actively engage during their productive years. We review the effects of politically-driven workplace conflicts on organizational climate and individual performance, as well as structural, cultural, and leadership factors associated with workplace political conflict escalation and de-escalation. We argue that while political conflicts that mimic broader societal trends are unavoidable, the workplace setting nevertheless presents a fertile ground for establishing boundaries as well as productive political debate and exchange, further strengthening mutual understanding among groups and individuals and leading to a more tolerant society overall. However, for a workplace to promote civilized political exchanges, it needs to have structures and processes in place that support such exchanges. Analysis presented in this chapter suggests several take-away points in terms of future research on the subject, as well as practical recommendations on how such conflicts can be handled productively and constructively.

Keywords: political conflict, polarization, social exchange, political socialization theory, social capital, workplace

Recently we have seen many societies becoming more polarized and divided along ideological and political lines, and these divides are exacerbated by increasingly important globalization processes, human and other forms of capital migration, more porous borders, and more dynamic informational spaces that result from social media. On the one hand these transmission links allow the creation of epistemic communities that aid in addressing such problems as climate change and global health pandemics. However, we have also seen many unintended effects of such technology-based advances, such as a faster spread of global terrorism networks and a higher propensity of people to lock themselves in exclusionary groups or "echo chambers", thus perpetuating rather than opening their views to more diverse perspectives.

Such tendencies often lead to increased inter-personal and inter-group conflicts, whether "virtually" or in person, including those that rest on ideological and political grounds. While such conflicts are increasingly likely to occur in local settings and in such micro- or macro-scale institutions as families and communities, some also spill over to more institutionalized social settings, such as the workplace (Feldman, 2020;

https://doi.org/10.1515/9783110746365-014

Johnson & Roberto, 2018; Noguchi, 2020; O'Leary, 2019). The uniqueness of the work-place, as compared to other types of social institutions, however, stems from its likely heterogeneity, including race, gender, generational, as well as ideological and polit-ical forms of diversity (Geurkink, Akkerman, & Sluiter, 2020; Mutz & Mondak, 2006). Arguably, no other social institution brings all these diverse identities under the same "roof" and to the same extent, creating a unique setting for exchanging diverse views and positions. Indeed, this can be a good thing in broadening workers' perspectives and mutual understanding through close encounters and shared experiences, but it can also lead to dysfunctionality and polarization.

Academic interest in the subject of workplace political conflict and its effects on a productive political dialogue is on the rise. However, scholarship produced on this subject to date remains scarce. While political conflict that mimics broader societal trends is unavoidable in a workplace setting, that setting nevertheless presents fertile ground for productive political debate and exchange. Therefore, organizational struc-tures and cultures that support and embrace open, reasonable, and respectful politi-cal dialogue and discourse play instrumental roles in furthering mutual understand-ing among the groups and individuals found in a workplace, leading to a more open and tolerant society overall.

We begin with an overview of the current research on the subject of political con-flicts in organizations, focusing on relevant theoretical perspectives and research findings that highlight the dynamic interplay among three organizational layers – structure, culture, and leadership. Our analysis, informed by previous studies, shows that for a workplace to serve as fertile ground for civilized political exchanges, it needs to have structures and processes in place that support such exchanges. The chapter wraps up with practical recommendations on how workplace political con-flicts can be handled and moderated productively and constructively, and with take-away points and potential questions for future research.

Background and Significance of the Problem

In the U.S. as well as other countries there has been ample and mounting evidence of political polarization as well as its spillover effects into the workplace which often serve as both an outlet and breeding ground for toxic polarization, resentment, and even threat perception.

During the 2020 US presidential campaign, for example, more than 25 percent of voters were convinced that one presidential candidate or the other was likely to engage in cheating in order to win the election, and 64 percent were convinced of foreign interference in the elections process (Feldman, 2020). The divide along the liberal-conservative spectrum has also intensified, as more individuals in this decade identify as strongly conservative or strongly liberal, as compared to the previous decade (Johnson & Roberto, 2018).

Moreover, one in six Americans has reported being harassed online over a political opinion (Feldman, 2020); many individuals experience the same effects when they choose to disclose their political views directly to their co-workers (Yudhistira & Sushandoyo, 2020). The quality of political discourse by both elites and non-elites has diminished and become more intense and bitter, while levels of civic education and political awareness among the general population have declined (Wright, 2018). Increasing political polarization and the dismissal of alternative political views, therefore, are exacerbated by the lack of general political knowledge and civic awareness, and the subsequent lack of critical thinking and open-mindedness that would otherwise allow political opponents to better understand alternative positions.

Corporate politicization, or an increasing tendency of private employers to embrace corporate political stances, is yet another recent trend, and it contradicts the previously common avoidance of unnecessary alienation of certain customer groups by taking open corporate political stances (Johnson & Roberto, 2018; Wright, 2018). These days, some executives tend to embrace strong political positions either as part of their corporate social responsibility or because of the expectation of potentially more effective and lucrative business interests (Wright, 2018). Therefore, political stance-taking may potentially damage or enhance the company bottom line, and, of course, some businesses choose to make their political affiliations known in pursuit of the public good – such as on questions of environmental or social justice.

These types of beneficial but also polarizing social trends spill over into workplaces (Johnson & Roberto, 2018; Noguchi, 2020). According to a recent survey by the Society for Human Resource Management, 42 percent of U.S. workers have experienced political disagreement at work and over 50 percent reported that such disagreements have become more common in the past four years (Noguchi, 2020). Furthermore, an increasing use of political labeling along the liberal/conservative divide makes it more difficult for people to compromise or put their divisions aside in order to focus on work-related tasks (Johnson & Roberto, 2018). These trends have led to diminished trust, slower work pace, and growing perceptions of discrimination, especially as directed towards political or racial minorities in the workplace.

From a legal standpoint, political expression in a workplace setting, and sometimes online in social media, is linked to the freedom of speech provisions that may affect employee job security and tenure. When it comes to protection from potential repercussions and ensuring job security, employees working in the private sector generally are less protected than those working in the public sector, as private sector employment is at-will and employees can be more easily dismissed at the discretion of their employer, even in those areas where private sector unions are still relatively powerful.

In fact, private sector employees as well as job applicants are not legally protected from employment discrimination on the grounds of political belief and expression, with rare exceptions, such as, for example, protections embedded in the California

Labor Code (Wright, 2018) which, while protecting employees and prospective employees from political discrimination, does not specify the boundaries of what is defined as "politics" and "political", leaving it to the discretion of the courts. Therefore, at a time of increasing socio- political polarization, ideological considerations that enter the workplace make private sector employees particularly vulnerable to arbitrary treatment by their employers with differing political views (Johnson & Roberto, 2018).

At the same time, while public sector employees have more institutional protections, they may have even fewer free-speech rights than private workers (Barrett & Greene, 2017). While the courts have gone back and forth determining the proper amount of free speech that should be given to governmental workers, in its 2006 Garcetti v. Ceballos case, the US Supreme Court held that "speech by a public official is only protected if it is engaged in as a private citizen, not if it is expressed as part of the official's public duties" (Garcetti v. Ceballos). Furthermore, the setting and context matter, and free speech is protected only if it does not interfere with one's job duties and agency mandates.

Common Forms and Negative Effects of Political Conflicts in the Workplace

Academic researchers have established the significance of a workplace setting as a unique context for social interaction that has the potential to foster cross-cutting political dialogue and contribute to a more tolerant and less polarized society overall (Geurkink et al., 2020; Greenberg, 1986; Mutz & Mondak, 2006; Yudhistira & Sushandoyo, 2020). However, there is also a recognition that the quality of political discourse itself as well as organizational culture matter for the quality of outcomes. Most US workers report discussing politics at work, and almost half witness political differences on the job escalate into full-blown arguments. Polls also show that a quarter of both Republicans and Democrats would not want to work with someone who votes for a presidential candidate they do not like (Jacobson, 2021); many disdain bringing up politics on the job.

Commonly recognized effects of unresolved political conflicts and tensions in organizations include diminished individual productivity and overall organizational effectiveness; erosion of 'bridging' types of social capital; and a growing sense of isolation and increasing negative effects on individuals' morale, mental and physical health. Aside from dysfunctional loss of productivity, some 60% of surveyed workers in a Glassdoor poll of 1200 employed adults worried that they could lose their jobs or be passed over for career advancements if their political opinions became known (see Guerkink, Akkerman and Sluiter, 2020; Johnson and Roberto, 2018). Indeed, so called "third rail" issues such as race and gun control are reportedly especially difficult to discuss with others who may disagree in diverse settings such as at work (See Feldman, 2020; and Deans, 2019).

As reduced productivity and potential volatile encounters related to conflict entail worsened quality of work outputs, difficulty getting work done, a more negative view of coworkers, feelings of tension and stress, and increased hostility (Johnson & Roberto, 2018; Noguchi, 2020; Yudhistira & Sushandoyo, 2020; Wright, 2018), in turn, these tendencies increase turnover rates and create unattractive organizational climates (Johnson & Roberto, 2018; Yudhistira & Sushandoyo, 2020). Furthermore, individual productivity has been linked to organizational effectiveness (Berman, 2006; Goodsell, 2014); a more engaged and more productive workforce has been linked to better organizational mission fulfillment (Kelman & Meyers, 2011). In sum, unresolved political disputes and tensions are likely to damage organizational effectiveness.

As workplaces become more politically polarized, as seen for example in the rise of LGBTQ rights and Black Lives Matter movements or the election rhetoric, individuals tend to link their opportunities for promotion and growth to whether their views are aligned with those in positions of power. Workers whose views may not align with those of supervisors or "company policy" may feel voiceless, marginalized, and perceive a lack of career advancement opportunities. Such situations may diminish opportunities for a healthy political debate and open exchange of views that otherwise would seem appropriate and even necessary in such an environment as academia, for example (Johnson and Roberto, 2018; Langbert, Quain and Klein, 2016).

Thus, unproductive political conflicts in a workplace especially tend to diminish one important form of social capital – bridging norms – that constitute a cornerstone of democratic society connecting and facilitating exchange of ideas among groups and individuals (Putnam, 2000). Considering the amount of time that individuals in their productive years spend at work, a workplace setting is particularly important for spreading diverse ideas and facilitating opportunities for dialogue and trust-building among diverse groups (Mutz & Mondak, 2006).

Furthermore, according to political socialization theory, workplace settings mimic the structure and values of society, providing feedback to individuals on the various forms of behavior in which they engage (Geurkink et al., 2020; Greenberg, 1981, 1986; Johnson & Roberto, 2018; Mutz & Mondak, 2006). Therefore, civilized political discourse in a workplace provides a model for similar engagements at a macro societal level. On the other hand, if political conflict escalates and becomes dysfunctional, it exerts detrimental effects on heathy dialogue, exchange of views, and teambuilding, and promotes selective bonding rather than heterogeneity or plurality of ideas. (Wright, 2018).

The effects of political conflicts on individuals' mental and physical health are not insignificant as well, considering that a reported 18 percent of working adults in the U.S. already experience some form of mental health issues, such as depression and anxiety, ringing the alarm and increasing the importance suicide prevention and other types of workplace wellness initiatives (MacDonald-Wilson, Fabian, &

Dong, 2008). Open political conflict, as well as underlying tensions that come with it, increase employees' stress, reduce their sense of job satisfaction and overall wellbeing, and exacerbate any pre-existing health issues (Wright, 2018).

Furthermore, disclosing one's "unfavorable" political views in a workplace, or even outside of the workplace, e.g., online, that then become known to colleagues, can damage trust among co-workers and worsen otherwise positive relationships and support systems, creating a sense exclusion and individual isolation (Yudhistira & Sushandoyo, 2020). By the same token, excessive or repetitive assertion of political views can be perceived by others as harassment and even as threatening (Milligan, 2015).

Organizational Context and Management of Workplace Political Conflicts

Workplace political conflicts unfold in organizations, and their dynamics are therefore mediated by three organizational layers – organizational structure, culture, and leadership. The structural aspect of this issue implies that organizations need to have proper institutional channels in place to ensure that their employees have the ability to voice their diverging views without fear of retribution or repercussion (Geurkink et al., 2020; O'Leary, 2019; Yudhistira & Sushandoyo, 2020). In the absence of such structural forums, there is a possibility that employees with diverging views will express their dissent publicly or divisively, which may cause disruptions in organizational functioning (O'Leary, 2019). In terms of ensuring the presence of healthy workplace political dialogue, existing structures and systems should be used to protect, rather than penalize, those engaging in political debate.

For example, employees' political views *per se* should have no bearing on task assignment, promotion, and career advancement decisions made by their supervisors. However, this type of backlash is not uncommon as supervisors use their formal authority and existing structure to silence those with diverging political views. Equally of concern, though, is properly dealing with disruptive employees who harass or demean others or put the organization in disrepute. To that end, human resource units play critical roles in safeguarding individual employees' rights, including those related to political differences.

Additionally, organizational culture and workplace climate, as well as particular leadership styles and approaches, tend to exert even more powerful effects on organizational tolerance towards diverging political views and appreciation of political debate, as compared to organizational structural elements. Cultural norms and underlying assumptions, in particular, tend to be very stable and difficult to change, while they can both enable and inhibit certain organizational patterns (Schein, 2010), including those related to a political dialogue (Geurkink et al., 2020; Mutz & Mondak, 2006; Yudhistira & Sushandoyo, 2020). Such cultural norms can be a product of many years of organizational socialization and knowledge transferred from one generation of staff to the next (Schein, 2010).

Therefore, there tends to be a certain path dependency in how organizations handle political conflict and disagreement. Organizational cultures that do not appreciate knowledge sharing tend to condemn political views' disclosure and discourage dialogue (Yudhistira & Sushandoyo, 2020). More open organizational cultures tend to be more tolerant and appreciative of the diverging views, which can facilitate productive exchange and mutual learning.

Finally, organizational leaders and those in the supervisory positions set the example and model behaviors that they expect others in the organization to emulate (Geurkink et al., 2020; Mutz & Mondak, 2006). Supervisors who embrace an open-door policy and a more shared leadership style tend also to be more welcoming of diverging views and political debates. On the other hand, more hierarchical leadership styles, especially when supported by hierarchical structure and cultural norms, tend to create exclusionary and less tolerant organizational climates where political dissent is not appreciated (Geurkink et al., 2020; Mutz & Mondak, 2006).

Workplace political issues can originate not just verbally, but also in reactions to any form of expression, such as signs or photos on desks, or certain hostile signals such as "nooses" hanging in view. One employee might want to counter another's bumper sticker with one of their own. These issues can be addressed by HR or management through mediation between the employees or setting overall rules, so that no one feels threatened or unduly isolated. Some people might be unaware of the offensive nature of their displays as perceived by others (Milligan, 2020).

While employers may or may not be able to engage employee participation in useful training sessions, it is important that they set rules and expectations for certain depolarization sessions and exercises, including by serving as a role mode via their own participation, which can produce more workplace political civility and mutual understanding. Among these approaches which have proven effective in various contexts are the following:

- Recognition of implicit bias and stereotyping of all sorts.
- Active, reflective, and positive listening and response techniques (e.g., "I" rather than "you" type statements).
- Expectation of respectful forms of communication and suggestion that there may be more or less propitious times for political debate among coworkers in or outside the workplace.
- Techniques for teambuilding, shared histories, and task-oriented conflict resolution approaches among diverse individuals.

There is a fine line between free and constructive expression and offensive harassment on the job. HR staff need to be observant of relevant laws regarding expression, such as labor organizing rights, but since most private workplaces are legally entitled to regulate their employees' job-related expression particularly in the workplace, rules can be established for example, not to let politics interfere with job tasks or to set and observe guidelines for respectful communication (see Milligan, 2020). Management itself should recognize that its own political rhetoric or opinionating can be objectionable and provocative, especially as related to particular groups such as racial, ethnic, religious, or LGBTQ minorities. A general pattern of "do no harm" to anyone's belief or status should be employed and encouraged.

So-called "Better Arguments" and "Courageous Conversations" projects have been launched in recent years at major American corporations (Jacobson 2021) and have demonstrated that people are willing to undertake difficult but satisfying dialogues if they feel respected and heard (Feldman, 2020). Generally, the format of such remedial sessions is to hear from an initial speaker presenting on topics related to civil discourse and then adjourn to smaller "breakout" sessions with discussion facilitators to exchange views, comments and suggestions and gradually build trust and civility among employees.

As an example of the type of workshops that can promote civility in political discourse, the organization "Braver Angels" includes the following points in its "Depolarizing Within" curriculum which can be amenable to workplace trainings:

Part 1: Recognizing My Inner Polarizer: You can use the following questions to think about your inner polarizer.

Read and circle your responses.
1. How often do I find myself thinking about "those people" on the other political side without much regard for the variation among them? Circle one: Often, Sometimes, Never
2. How often do I find myself assigning mainly self-serving or negatives motives to the other group – and mainly positive motives to my group? Circle one: Often, Sometimes, Never
3. How often do I find myself focusing on the most extreme or outrageous ideas and people on the other side, thereby making it hard to see how a reasonable person could remain in that group? Circle one: Often, Sometimes, Never
4. How often do I find myself comparing the worst people on the other side with the best people on my side? Circle one: Often, Sometimes, Never
5. How often do I feel a "rush" of pleasure with friends when we ridicule those crazies on the other political side? Circle one: Often, Sometimes, Never
6. Which of the following is closest to my overall emotional attitude towards the majority of people who support the other side?

Circle the one closest to where you are now and then the one you aspire to if they are different.
1. Hate. They are enemies out to destroy the country.
2. Disdain. They are ignorant and should know better.
3. Pity. They are well meaning but duped.

4. Basic respect. They make contributions even if they are mostly off base.
5. Respect and appreciation. They make unique and necessary contributions.

Part 2: Strategies to Counteract My Inner Polarizer: Following are ways to offset polarizing thoughts and feelings when you notice them arising in you:

1. Challenge your stereotypes. Stereotypes are how outsiders over-simplify, dismiss, lump together, and disparage the "Other." Based on Braver Angels red/blue workshops where we ask each side to identify the most common stereotypes they run into about their own side, these are the most common stereotypes:

Blues tend to believe that reds are racist, anti-immigrant, uncaring about those in need, homophobic, anti-woman, anti-science, bible thumpers.

Reds tend to believe that blues are arrogant/elitist, favor big government for its own sake, and are fiscally irresponsible, unpatriotic, anti-religious, against free speech if it's not politically correct, and hypersensitive "snowflakes."

Ways to counter stereotypes in your own thinking:
6. Tell yourself that the other side is more varied than the stereotype.
7. Acknowledge that their political views and motivations are no doubt more complicated than the rhetoric you've been hearing.
8. Read and listen to thought leaders on the other side who present complex arguments.
9. Recognize that the life experiences informing their views are likely different from your own.
10. Develop relationships with a variety of people who differ with you politically. Relationships tend to undermine stereotypes.
11. If you want to go all out, you can work to develop an understanding of the history and current strands of thought in the other side.

2. Make depolarizing distinctions
1. Distinguish between positions and people. You can believe that a viewpoint is completely wrong without believing that everyone who holds it is stupid or ill motivated.
2. Distinguish between policies and core values. Policies are means to ends, ways to support or enact values, not the values themselves. People can differ sharply on policies like the role of government and have similar ultimate goals for the country and its people.
3. Distinguish between inconsistency and hypocrisy.

Part 3: How to Talk about the Other Side in a Non-polarizing Way. Avoid the following:
– Using pejorative labels: ("wingnuts", "bible thumpers", "libtards", "snowflakes")
– Using the phrase "they all" or its equivalent "The Democrats/Republicans." These are the classic stereotyping phrases.

 – Painting all supporters of a politician with the same brush you use for the politician.

If you go on a rant about a particular politician, make it clear that you are not putting all supporters into the same box. ("I'm talking about (so and so) right, and not everyone who voted for him/her.")

Part 4: Skills for Depolarizing Conversations with Like-minded People: LAPP – Listen, Acknowledge, Pivot, Perspective (offer).

Listen for the other's values and emotions influencing the stereotyping, ridicule, or contempt – often it's from frustration, fear, worry for the country or groups in the country, or personal experiences of being put down by people on the other side. When there are strong emotions, there's a deeper story there.

Acknowledge what you are hearing and share your own worries and concerns by responding:
1. "I'm sorry you've had to deal with those put downs in your family."
2. "I hear you and I'm with you on your concerns about . . . ."

Pivot by signaling a shift in your part of the conversation.

Perspective: Offer a context for why you are introducing another perspective into the conversation. Be personal and use I-statements.

The authors go on to suggest readings from the perspectives of conservatives and liberals.

(Excerpted from Better Angels, "Depolarizing Within", Standard Online V 1.7.1. Used with permission.)

Best Practices

Organizational leaders, and especially HR staff, also have been advised on best practices for managing political conflict at work, such as fostering a culture of tolerance; treating employees with respect in allowing them to reasonably voice opinions; encouraging employees to walk away from heated encounters; reminding employees of organizational policies, particularly regarding harassment; and stepping in with disciplinary action when necessary (Miron, 2016). Thus, excessive politicking on the job can be discouraged without management appearing censorial; employees can be encouraged to disengage from unwanted conversations and take complaints promptly to HR if necessary (Jacobson, 2021).

Some workplaces seek to promote a politically neutral ("Switzerland type") work environment (CDA, 2020; Noguchi, 2020) by such means as preventing biased news streaming of one side or another on office media devices during the workday; however, preventing newsfeeds completely or barring employees' use of their own devices could be objectionable. Employees should be encouraged to begin conversations by finding common ground on less polarizing issues, such as those related to sports, shopping, or traffic, before engaging in more controversial issues; then revert to the commonalities to defuse the conversations positively (Mizna, 2020).

Positive cultural environments can also be furthered by offering incentives and allocating time and space for civic responsibilities such as joint community volunteering and voting. Expert speakers also can be brought to teach seminars on latest developments in foreign and domestic politics.

The realm of social media is especially tricky for workplaces. Employees at all levels need to be reminded that their media comments and posts can reflect on the organization and that these "should not be inflammatory or personal" (Mizna, 2021) or carry the impression of workplace endorsement. Employees also should be reminded that co-workers might be reading these posts and forming opinions or reactions that reflect positively or negatively on their interpersonal relations, quality and openness of communication, and task collaboration at the workplace (see Yudhistira and Sushandoyo, 2020).

Conclusion

While there is an increasing scholarly interest in the subject of workplace political conflict and its effects on individuals, organizations, and society, scholarship produced on this subject to date remains sparse. Nevertheless, as this review demonstrates, it is important to recognize the importance of the workplace as a valid research setting for the study of political conflicts. Some possible research directions inspired by this review may include researching organizational structural factors associated with productive political dialogue and viewpoint plurality, researching the relationship between a particular leadership style and appreciation for healthy political disagreement in a workplace, and the relationship between organizational cultural norms and appreciation for the diversity of political views.

It is also important to research how individual and group characteristics, such as race, ethnicity, national origin, level of education, and gender, impact individuals' propensity to share and openly discuss their political views in a workplace, as well as what might be the institutional and organizational factors that affect these dynamics and produce constructive rather than destructive outcomes.

References

Barrett, K. & Greene, R. (February 4, 2017). Can Government Employees Criticize Government? *Governing Magazine*. Retrieved from: https://www.governing.com/archive/gov-free-speech-public-employees.html.

Berman, Evan. (2006). *Performance and Productivity in Public and Nonprofit Organizations*. Armonk, NY: M.E. Sharpe.

CDA (2020). Political discussions: Create workplace boundaries to reduce tension. *California Dental Association*, October 30. Retrieved from: www.cda.org/Home/News-and-Events/Newsroom.

Deans, B. (2019). How to Manage Political Conflicts in the Workplace. *Employment Law Handbook*. April 18. Retrieved from: www.employmentlawhandbook.com/?s=Political±views.

Feldman, B. (2020). Do not Let Election Passion Roil Your Workplace. *Harvard Business Review*. Retrieved from: https://hbr.org/2020/10/dont-let-election-passions-roil-your-Workplace.

Garcetti v. Ceballos. (n.d.). *Oyez*. Retrieved from: https://hbr.org/2020/10/dont-let-election-passions-roil-your-workplace https://www.oyez.org/cases/2005/04-473.

Geurkink, B., Akkerman, A., & Sluiter, R. (2020). Political participation and workplace voice: The spillover of suppression by supervisors. *Political Studies*, OnlineFirst doi: 0032321720960969.

Goodsell, C. T. (2014). *The New Case for Bureaucracy*. Washington, DC: CQ Press. Greenberg, E. S. (1981). Industrial democracy and the democratic citizen. *The Journal of Politics*, *43*(4), 964–981.

Greenberg, E. S. (1986). *Workplace Democracy: The Political Effects of Participation*. Ithaca, NY: Cornell University Press.

Jacobson, A. (2021). Defusing Political Conflicts in the Workplace. *Risk Management Magazine*. Retrieved from: http://www.rmmagazine.com/2021/02/01/defusing-political-conflict-in-the-workplace/.

Johnson, A. F., & Roberto, K. J. (2018). Right versus left: How does political ideology affect the workplace?. *Journal of Organizational Behavior*, *39*(8), 1040–1043.

Langbert, M., Quain, A. J., & Klein, D. B. (2016). Faculty voter registration in economics, history, journalism, law, and psychology. *Economic Journal Watch*, *13*(3), 422–451.

Kelman, S. & Myers, J. (2011). Successfully achieving ambitious goals in government: An empirical analysis, *American Review for Public Administration*, *41*(3), 235–262.

MacDonald-Wilson, K. L., Fabian, E. S., & Dong, S. L. (2008). Best practices in developing reasonable accommodations in the workplace: Findings based on the research literature. *The Rehabilitation Professional*, *16*(4), 221–232.

Milligan, S. (2020). How Should HR Handle Political Discussions at Work? *HR Magazine*, Society for Human Resource Management. Retrieved from https://www.shrm.org/hr-today/news/hr-magazine/spring2020/pages/political-talk-in-the-workplace.aspx.

Milligan, S. (2015). Political Debates in the Workplace: Where to Draw the Line. Society for Human Resource Management. from: www.shrm.org/ResourcesAndTools/hr-topics/employee-relations/Pages/office-politics.aspx.

Miron, A. (2016). 5 Ways to Manage Confrontations at Work Due to Politics. Retrieved from: www.eskill.com/blog/confrontations-politics/.

Mizna, D. (2021). Politics at Work: How to Maintain Team Productivity Despite Opposing Views. Guest Post, *15Five*, originally published on *The Next Web*. Retrieved from: www.15five.com/blog/how-politics-impact-workplace-teamwork.

Mutz, D. C., & Mondak, J. J. (2006). The workplace as a context for cross-cutting political discourse. *The Journal of Politics*, *68*(1), 140–155.

Noguchi, Y. (2020). I Can't Work with You! How Political Fights Leave Workplaces Divided. National Public Radio. Retrieved from: https://www.npr.org/2020/01/28/798593323/i-cant-work-with-you-how-political-fights-leave-workplaces-divided.

O'Leary, R. (2019). *The Ethics of Dissent: Managing Guerrilla Government*. Washington, DC: CQ Press.

Putnam, R. D. (2000). *Bowling Alone: The Collapse and Revival of American Community*. New York: Simon and Schuster.

Putnam, R. D., Leonardi, R., & Nanetti, R. Y. (1994). *Making Democracy Work*. Princeton, N.J.: Princeton University Press.

Schein, E. H. (2010). *Organizational Culture and Leadership*. Hoboken, N.J.: John Wiley & Sons.

Yudhistira, D.S., & Sushandoyo, D. (2020), Does political self-disclosure in social media hamper tacit knowledge sharing in the workplace?, *Journal of Information and Knowledge Management Systems*, 50(3),513–530.

Wright, R. G. (2018). Political Discrimination by Private Employers. *University of Cincinnati Law Review*, *87*, 761.

Section 4: **Methods for Managing Organizational Conflicts**

Jack Nasher, Leigh Thompson

Chapter 15
Detecting Deception in Negotiation: From Natural Observation to Strategic Provocation

Abstract: The benefits along with ease of deception make it a common occurrence in negotiations. Whereas the majority of previous research on deception in negotiations has focused on motivational and ethical issues, we focus on cues to deception and how negotiators might detect it when seated at the negotiation table. We examine natural cues to deception in negotiation, via the use of nonverbal expressions and emotion. And we review strategic techniques that negotiators may consciously employ to detect deception. The observational and strategic techniques that we review are designed to be part of a negotiator's repertoire for constructive negotiations with long-term business partners.

Keywords: negotiation, deception, authentic emotion, stress, questioning

In a high stakes negotiation between the internet pioneer AOL (American Online) and a prospective client, AOL negotiators would present their pitch on a PowerPoint deck that included the name of the client's rival – as if AOL had accidentally mixed up what appeared to several pitches for different companies. The AOL rep would then feign embarrassment and apologize. However, the slip was staged and meant to (falsely) signal AOL's alternatives to the prospective client (Klein, 2003).

Negotiation is a mixed-motive situation in which parties have conflicting interests and seek to reach mutual agreement (Thompson, 2020). In business negotiations, self-interest is presumed, and people are not obligated to truthfully reveal their bargaining position, reservation price, alternative options, nor incentives to the counterparty. However, actively misrepresenting factual information is considered to be unethical and can even be illegal (Shell, 1991). Because of the mixed-motive nature of negotiation, parties may be tempted to deceive each other so as to gain advantage. Rationally speaking, negotiators are best advised to reach mutual agreement if they can reach a settlement term that is superior to their other alternatives. Therefore, a key element of negotiation is the value of the negotiator's alternative. To be sure, if negotiators had information about the counterparty's alternative, this would be very valuable information. For this reason, people actively conceal the value and existence of their alternatives and in many cases attempt to signal to the counterparty that their alternatives are better than they actually are.

Detecting deception is challenging because negotiators who are using deception are actively trying to avoid detection and obscuring their intentions. For this reason, many of the behaviors and clues that negotiators use to detect deception are not in

https://doi.org/10.1515/9783110746365-015

fact diagnostic. In this chapter, we begin by examining the types of deception that people may use in negotiation. Then, we examine the "clues" that negotiators use to detect deception in others. We examine clues that involve natural observation and those that involve strategic provocation of the counterparty.

Information in negotiations is typically asymmetric, such that each party is only privy to their own alternatives, valuations, and does not have direct access to the other party's key information (Schweitzer & Croson, 1999). For this reason, it is to a negotiator's advantage to conceal information about one's own position, but also gain as much information about the other party. The benefits along with ease of deception make it a common occurrence in negotiations (Lewicki, 1983; Schweitzer & Croson, 1999; Gaspar & Schweitzer, 2012; Boles, Croson, & Murnighan, 2000; Koning, van Dijk, van Beest, & Steinel, 2010; O'Connor & Carnevale, 1997; Olekalns & Smith, 2009; Aquino, 1998; Aquino & Becker, 2005; Volkema, 2004).

Types of Deception

There are many different types of deception in negotiations. Lewicki and colleagues have created a useful typology for examining ethically-questionable behavior in negotiation, including: making false promises (e.g., making verbal commitments that one has no intention of honoring), attacking their opponent's network (such as posting negative information on social media), inappropriate information gathering (such as paying someone to obtain proprietary financial information), misrepresentation (such as claiming one has a competitive job offer that does not actually exist), and being particularly competitive at the negotiation table, including the use extreme emotion, making threats to walk away, and pretending that time pressure is not a factor. In our chapter, we focus on how negotiators may more accurately detect deception with regard to: the counterparty's reservation price, their BATNA (best alternative to a negotiated agreement), and their intentions to honor the terms of the negotiation. To be sure, just because a negotiator may want to know the counterparty's alternative (just as a supplier may want to know what other competitor may be offering as their best price), does not obligate the counterparty to freely disclose such information. For this reason, failure to disclose information in a transactional negotiation about one's own alternatives, market value is often not considered to be unethical; however, failure to disclose known information about a product or service that could affect its value is considered unethical (e.g. a home seller who fails to disclose information about water damage or termites to a prospective buyer is considered to be behaving unethically).

There are two main types of lies (Gordon & Fleisher, 2011) lying by commission (active lying) or lying by omission (leaving something out). These two types are presumed to be of differing ethical value, leading to different emotions and thus behavior: Lying by omission generally leads to lesser feelings of guilt (Gudjonsson, 2003), leading to less cues. Especially within the negotiation context, omission is perceived as being more acceptable (Lewicki & Robinson, 1998; Lewicki & Stark, 1996; Fulmer, Barry, & Long, 2009; Spranca, Minsk, & Baron, 1991). However, "bluffing" in negotiations, a lie by commission, is also typically expected within a negotiation (Carr, 1968; Michelman, 1983; Anton, 1990; Lewicki & Robinson, 1998; Allhoff, 2003; Koehn, 1997; Varelius, 2006), thus weakening emotional cues to deception. Also, emotional deception, such as faking anger or disappointment, is perceived as being more acceptable than informational deception (Fulmer, Barry, & Long, 2009).

In this chapter, we focus on how negotiators can better detect deception at the negotiation table. We focus on two types of "strategies" that negotiators may use when seated at the bargaining table: strategies of natural observation and proactive, provocative strategies that involve active questioning. The goal of both types of methods is to increase the quality of negotiated agreements and ultimately improve the relationship between negotiators at the bargaining table.

Why it is Difficult to Detect Deception in Negotiation

It is difficult to detect deception in negotiation because the deceiver is actively trying to disguise their attempts to mislead. For this reason, people are only slightly better than chance at detecting lies (Bond & DePaulo, 2006; DePaulo & Bell, 1996; Ekman & O'Sullivan, 1991; Lewis & Saarni, 1993; Ekman, O'Sullivan, Friesen, & Scherer, 1991; Ekman, O'Sullivan, & Frank, 1999). Even experts from the fields of criminology and psychology are about as good as chance (Levine, Kim, & Blair, 2010; Vrij, Edward, Roberts, & Bull, 2000; Vrij & Mann, 2001; Vrij & Mann, 2004). Cognitive overload severely curtails a person's ability to detect deception as the negotiator must simultaneously engage in the act of negotiation. Indeed, observers of a conversation are better at detecting lies than the parties involved (Vrij, 2000; Forrest & Feldman, 2000). Moreover, detectors typically lack accurate feedback about their accuracy as liars rarely disclose their lie immediately (Vrij, Granhag, & Porter, 2010). Moreover, people communicate within a *truth bias*, as experience has taught that constant suspicion destroys relationships and as most people indeed do tell the truth more often than they lie (Levine, Kim, Park, & Hughes, 2006; Park & Levine, 2001; Vrij, 2008; O'Sullivan, Ekman, & Friesen, 1988). Next, we examine the detection of deception via passive observation and also strategic provocation.

Detecting Deception via Natural Observation

By "natural observation" we refer to the passive observation of another person. In this situation, the observer is not trying to intervene, test or provoke the subject of inquiry.

Several research investigations have examined people's ability to observe others and detect whether deception has occurred; the most notable of these research programs being the comprehensive work of Paul Ekman (Ekman, 2001), whose research found its way to popular culture and inspired a TV show, *"Lie to Me"* in which Ekman used his research-based insights to make real-time predictions of whether a given person had lied (Ryan, et al., 2009–2011).

Authentic Emotion

For Ekman (1981; 1993; Ekman & Friesen, 1969; Barry, 1999; Van Dijk, Van Kleef, Steinel, & Van Beest, 2008), emotions are paramount in the deception process, which is why observing signs of emotions to detect deceit. One research finding from the large literature on nonverbal behavior is that liars tend to focus on *content* of communication, and neglect bodily factors, such as facial expressions (Ekman, 2001; Vrij A, 2008). Deception can be detected in fraction of a second in "micro expressions" (Ekman, 2001).[1] Micro expressions are fleeting facial expressions that emerge, but most untrained people fail to detect them. One observation about deception is that liars may express emotion, but this emotion is typically followed by a "fake smile" (Ekman & Frank, 1993; Ekman, Davidson, & Friesen, 1990; Ekman, Friesen, & O'Sullivan, 1988; Ekman, 1981; Ekman & Friesen, 1982). Fake smiles can be identified by the lack of wrinkles at the corners of the eyes (Duchenne de Boulogne, 1876).

The ability to swiftly detect seven universal emotions (fear, guilt, happiness, surprise, anger, contempt, and disgust) is regarded as sufficient (Ekman, 1981; 2001) and feasible (Freshman, 2010). Even one hour of practice in the detection of micro expressions appears to significantly improve the ability to identify them (Warren, Schertler, & Bull, 2009; Freshman, 2010). However, only five seem to suffice: the two typical emotions when being falsely accused surprise and particularly anger; (Ekman, 2001); three emotions prevalent in deception are fear, guilt, and delight (Ekman, 1981; Ekman & Frank, 1993). Improving the recognition of these emotions leads to better lie detecting (Warren, Schertler, & Bull, 2009).

Fear. Liars often experience a range of strong emotions when engaged in deception. One of those emotions is fear. Liars typically fear real or personal consequences of using deception, such as the termination of a deal or reputational damage, etc. (Gudjonsson & Petursson, 1991; Gudjonsson & Bownes, 1992; Sigurdsson & Gudjonsson, 1994; Deslauriers-Varin, Lussier, & St-Yves, 2011). Fear leads to particular nonverbal signs such as a higher blinking rate, the facial (micro) expression of the eyes wide open and the corners of the mouth stretched to the ears; and to verbal signs such as pauses, stuttering, repetitions and a higher voice pitch (Ekman, 2001).

---

1 Warren et al. (2009) argues against the significance of micro expressions.

Guilt. Guilt may be felt when lying, particularly by women (DePaulo, Epstein, & Wyer, 1993; DePaulo & Bell, 1996; Vrij, 2008). The facial (micro) expression of guilt resembles sadness: the eyes lose focus, and the corners of the mouth are hanging down (Ekman, 2001). When guilt is felt, eye contact tends to be avoided. However, because reduced eye contact is (falsely) regarded a well-known clue to deception, liars tend stare in order to appear honest, which is why looking away or unnatural staring are both signs of guilt (Ekman, 1997; Ekman & Friesen, 1972; Kleinke, 1986; Vrij, 2008).

Liars tend to physically distance themselves from the lie, with their body and feet leaning away from the communication point toward a window or an exit (DePaulo, et al., 2003), referred to as the "liar's lean" (Mackey & Miller, 2004). There are verbal indicators of guilt: Liars want to avoid being associated with the lie and hence use much fewer personal pronouns such as "I" or "me" (Vrij, 2008), a phenomenon exploited by Scientific Content Analysis, a veracity test based on a word analysis (Vrij, 2005; Smith, 2001).

Delight. Liars feel happy when lying (Ruedy, Moore, Gino, & Schweitzer, 2013). "Duping delight" (Ekman, 1981; 2001; Bursten, 1972), or "cheater's high" (Gaspar & Schweitzer, 2012) is a feeling of elation with the deception. Delight is displayed by a genuine smile and by intense, enthusiastic movements (Vrij, 2008).

Behavioral Control

Liars tend to control their behavior and appearance so as to disguise deceit. Liars may have a higher incidence of "adaptors", which are nonverbal behaviors that are not illustrating a point, but rather appear to be excessive adjustments, including: straightening clothes, re-arranging hair, cleaning fingernails, caressing the beard, hitting off dust (Geiselman, Elmgren, Green, & Rystad, 2011). Contrary to the common belief that liars fidget (Kraut & Poe, 1980), their nonverbal behavior actually tends to be stiff (Vrij, 2008; Burgoon & Buller, 1994; DePaulo, Kirkendol, Tang, & O'Brien, 1989). Liars control their body language so as to not emit signs of deception: hand and finger movements are thus decreased (DePaulo, et al., 2003; Vrij, 2008; Ekman & Friesen, 1972), head movements are reduced (Fiedler & Walka, 1993). Aside from the 'Fight or flight' response (Cannon, 1929), people tend to react with a 'freeze' to danger, possibly in an unconscious attempt to remain undetected (Gallup, 1977; Schmidt, Richey, & Maner, 2009).

Verbal communication is also "stiff", typically lacking details (Kohnken, 2004; Kohnken, Schimossek, Aschermann, & Hofer, 1995; Steller & Kohnken, 1989; Vrij A, 2008). Interrogation handbooks suggest that liars thus only lie as much as "necessary" (Inbau, Reid, Buckley, & Jayne, 2013). The liar's behavior hence appears deliberate, regarding nonverbal as well as verbal communication (Landstrom, Granhag, & Hartwig, 2005; Landstrom & Granhag, 2008; Vrij, Edward, & Bull, 2001; Vrij, 2008;

Buller & Burgoon, 1996; Burgoon & Buller, 1994; Burgoon, Buller, Guerrero, Afifi, & Feldman, 1996; Burgoon, Buller, White, Afifi, & Buslig, 1999; Krauss, Apple, Morency, Wenzel, & Winton, 1981).

Signs of Stress

Liars may feel stress, as they constantly monitor their communication (DePaulo, et al., 2003; Kassin, 2005; Kassin & Gudjonsson, 2004; Kassin & Norwick, 2004; Vrij, 2008; Caso, Gnisci, Vrij, & Mann, 2005; Gozna & Babooram, 2004; Granhag & Stromwall, 2002; Hartwig, Granhag, Stromwall, & Kronkvist, 2006; Stromwall, Hartwig, & Granhag, 2006; Vrij, Edward, & Bull, 2001; Vrij & Mann, 2006; Vrij, Mann, & Fisher, 2006a; Vrij & Semin, 1996; White & Burgoon, 2001; Colwell, Hiscock-Anisman, Memon, Woods, & Michlik, 2006; Granhag & Stromwall, 2002; Granhag, Stromwall, & Hartwig, 2007; Hartwig, Granhag, & Stromwall, 2007; Stromwall, Granhag, & Landstrom, 2007; Stromwall, Hartwig, & Granhag, 2006) and also monitor the communication partner to check whether their deception is successful (Buller & Burgoon, 1996; Vrij, 2008; Ekman & Frank, 1993; Vrij & Mann, 2001). Because of the stress felt through this cognitive load, liars typically repeat parts of their answers or even the question that was asked (Davis & Hadicks, 1995). Liars typically make longer pauses (DePaulo, et al., 2003; Sporer & Schwandt, 2006; Vrij, 2008) and speak in a higher pitched voice (Goldman-Eisler, 1968; Vrij, 2008; Ekman, 2001).

Authentic emotion, followed by behavior control, and then signs of stress are typical signs of deception. The clues and indicators that are associated with deception are difficult to detect and not those that the typical negotiator focuses upon (as opposed to e.g., eye contact) (Mann, Vrij, & Bull, 2004). Combined with the fact that negotiators are often active participants at the negotiation table, not merely watching a subject, makes deception even more difficult to detect. On the other hand, negotiators have the opportunity to take an active role in the conversation, amplifying those signs to facilitate the process.

Detecting Deception via Strategic Provocation

There is a large literature on interrogation methods that may often involve intimidation and other forms of accusation such as used in criminal investigations (Nasher, 2015). Because negotiation is a mutually voluntary activity and in most cases embedded in long-term relationships or those that have significant reputational consequences, negotiators must balance building trust and goodwill with their desire to detect deception. For this reason, it would be impractical and inadvisable to sit down at the negotiation table, turn on the bright lights, and inquire, "are you lying to me?."

Our review of planful, direct methods is therefore selective, focusing on methods that can be used in long-term business relations with peers, customers, and clients in the corporate world.

Direct Questions

Probably the most straightforward detection strategy is to simply ask direct questions that make it incumbent upon the counterparty to respond transparently (Malhotra & Bazerman, 2007). However, it is not realistic to expect the counterparty to disclose information that would negatively affect their own bargaining position. In one study, some negotiators were coached to ask direct questions about the counterparty's interests, others were coached to share information about their own interests, and yet another group was not given any instructions (Thompson, 1991). Both the "questioners" and the "information providers" reached more mutually profitable outcomes than did the "control group". Moreover, the questioners tended to get accurate responses from the counter-party. For these reasons, it makes sense for negotiators to not simply be passive, but to ask structured questions.

The most straightforward detection strategy is to ask direct questions (Malhotra & Bazerman, 2007). Even though it is not realistic to expect the counterparty to freely disclose information that would negatively affect their own bargaining position, such as direct questions about their batna (best alternative to a negotiated agreement), the direct question provokes more lies in order to facilitate the detection process.[2] In contentious negotiations in which the negotiator may have good reason to believe that the counterparty may falsify information and the product quality cannot be tested, a negotiator may be advised to ask direct questions (Gaspar & Schweitzer, 2012). In one investigation in which people had to knowingly sell a faulty product, 61% revealed crucial information about their (poor) alternative option when they were directly asked about it versus 0% when not asked (Schweitzer & Croson, 1999).

Truthful responders tend to answer without hesitation and remain relaxed (Inbau, Reid, Buckley, & Jayne, 2013). Conversely, deceitful responders weigh options, focus on appearing credible and try to come up with answers free of contradictions, leading to a "cognitive load" (Gilbert, 1991; Walczyk, Roper, Seemann, & Humphrey, 2003; Walczyk, et al., 2005; Vrij A, 2008, p. 40). Because of this cognitive load, liars typically repeat parts of their answers or even the question that was asked (Davis & Hadicks, 1995), make longer pauses (DePaulo, et al., 2003; Sporer & Schwandt, 2006; Vrij, 2008) and raise their pitch (Goldman-Eisler, 1968; Vrij, 2008; Ekman, 2001). A direct

---

2 Under normal circumstances, the negotiator is best served to ask questions about the other party's interests, the quality of the product or service (if it cannot be independently examined) and their position on the negotiation issues.

question thus leads to rather strong signs of deception, facilitating the veracity assessment for the interviewer.

A direct question must not be confused with an accusation, as an accusation can lead to emotions that resemble signs of deception even in the truthful negotiator (Vrij, 2008; Kleinke, 1986; Davis & Hadicks, 1995; Matarazzo, Wiens, Jackson, & Manaugh, 1970). If the conversation has the character of an accusation, a change of behavior is typical, which is also one of the main problems of the classic lie detector approach (Podlesny & Raskin, 1977; Lykken, 1998; Raskin & Honts, 2002). For this reason, direct questions should be posed in a in a friendly and interested way and be followed by silence in order to observe behavior changes.

Binary vs. Open-Ended questions. When asking direct questions, negotiators should avoid binary (yes/no) questions because people tend to answer affirmatively (Kebbell, Hatton, Johnson, & O'Kelly, 2001). Open questions lead to longer answers and provide more opportunity to find deception (Vrij, 2008; Vrij, Mann, & Fisher, 2006b). In a negotiation, an open question would be: "Is there anything else I should know about the car?" Moreover, each question should only address a single issue (Gordon & Fleisher, 2010), because when asking two questions at once, e.g., if they liked the offer and have an alternative offer, deception detection will be almost impossible.

Repeating Questions. Negotiators may not realize when the counterparty is dodging the question, because they have forgotten it (Rogers & Norton, 2011). For this reason, negotiators may want to write their questions and keeping them in sight (Inbau, Reid, Buckley, & Jayne, 2013; Freshman, 2010). It is ideal to start with less serious questions, as liars typically prepare the most serious ones and often fail to consider the less important factors (Gordon & Fleisher, 2010). However, similar questions should be re-phrased to avoid sounding like an interrogation (Walczyk, et al., 2005; Vrij, 2008).

Probing

It is advisable to ask about details and keep digging deeper (Franck, 2009). If more and more direct questions are asked in a non-aggressive way, the liar typically lies bolder and bolder, eventually getting entangled in a net of lies (Stiff & Miller, 1986; Ford, 1996; Ekman, 2001; Vrij, 2008). More lies can either lead to obvious contradictions or to clear signs of deception.

Probing refers to focused scrutiny on a particular subject. There are three types of probing questions (Inbau, Reid, Buckley, & Jayne, 2013):
1. Probing for details ("Please tell us more about your alternative offer")
2. Probing for explanations ("Why did you change your offer?")
3. Probing for feelings or thoughts ("What did you feel when you saw our offer?" or "What did you think when we turned down your offer?")

The assumption is that liars have typically prepared details concerning their lie but rarely prepare details that are not directly involved with it (Inbau, Reid, Buckley, & Jayne, 2013). In purchasing negotiations, for example, when negotiators lie about their company policy that does not allow them to negotiate about differing terms and conditions, one could ask about other details of this very policy: "What do you think about your company's policy", or: "Have there ever been exceptions to this rule?".

Contingent Contract

The contingent contract is a structured strategy in which a negotiator can essentially test the counterparty's stated position. The contingent contract involves three key steps: first, the negotiator acknowledges that the parties have different information (usually about an unknown or future event, such as future real estate prices); second, the negotiator proposes that parties agree to use a particular event, report, or arbiter to resolve the differences of opinion (e.g., a stock price on a given future date); finally, the negotiators agree in writing that their (current) difference of opinion will be resolved by this mutually-agreed upon information. In one situation, a prospective buyer made an offer on a house. The seller responded by claiming that there was another competitive offer on the house and cajoled the buyer to increase their offer. However, the buyer was suspicious because the house had been on the market for over 400 days. The buyer used an "escalation contingency clause" and stated that if the seller could provide proof of the other competitive offer, the buyer would increase their offer by 5%. The seller responded by saying, "You know, I'm anxious to not complicate things and so I will accept your initial offer". The conclusion that the buyer reached was that the seller could not in fact provide evidence of a competitive offer. One feature of the contingent contract approach is that it may allow for a face-saving way for negotiators to challenge counterparties that preserves the relationship.

Multiple Equivalent Simultaneous Offers

Another highly-structured questioning technique that negotiators may fashion to detect deception is the multiple, equivalent, simultaneous offer technique (Leonardelli, Gu, McRuer, Medvec, & Galinksy, 2019). This technique is particularly useful in surfacing the true interests and priorities of the counterparty. In this technique, the negotiator follows three steps: First, the negotiator unbundles the negotiation into several issues, such as price, volume, payment schedule, delivery date, etc. Second, the negotiator prepares at least two multi-dimensional proposals that are of equal value to him or her. For example, in one negotiation, a vice president of commercial sales prepared three different proposals for a (demanding) customer who was threatening to take their business to a competitor. Third, the negotiator asks the receiving party to rank order (not choose) which of the proposals is of most value to him or her. By pivoting the conversation away from accept-reject to hot-warm-cold, the negotiator can reverse-engineer (i.e., deduce) the counterparty's true preferences.

In one negotiation, the counterparty was holding firm and refusing to make concessions, claiming they had a better alternative. The proposing party doubted that was true and so pivoted the conversation away from accept-reject to one of "tell me which of these proposals is the least offensive". By the end of the conversation, the negotiator learned (via deduction) that the counterparty was price-sensitive but was not concerned about where the product would be assembled. Even though the counterparty did not directly share this information, through a careful pattern of testing, the negotiator was able to discern the counterparty's true interests. Because this technique is non-confrontational, it improved the relationship between the parties.

Conclusion

In this chapter, we have examined when and why people are most likely to engage in deception in negotiation. We made the point that people do not feel obligated to reveal information in negotiation that could hurt their own bargaining position and that self-interest is presumed. We examined naturalistic clues that may reveal deceit and we also considered how negotiators can actively stage questions during a negotiation. Cues to deception are the authentic emotion, followed by behavior control, and signs of stress. These cues can be observed without any direct questioning and are therefore well-suited for the negotiation context. As deception is difficult to detect (Mann, Vrij, & Bull, 2004), we also considered methods by which negotiators can proactively intervene during the negotiation itself to facilitate deception detection. Negotiators can use strategic questioning, probing, contingent contracts, and multiple, equivalent simultaneous offers to unearth deception in a non-confrontational fashion, thereby preserving and even strengthening the relationship.

References

Allhoff, F. (2003). Business bluffing reconsidered. *Journal of Business Ethics*, 45(4), 283–289.
Anton, R. J. (1990). Drawing the line: An exploratory test of ethical behavior in negotiations. *International Journal of Conflict Management*, 1(3), 265–280.
Aquino, K. (1998). The effects of ethical climate and the availability of alternatives on the use of deception during negotiation. *International Journal of Conflict Management*, 9, 195–217.

Aquino, K., & Becker, T. E. (2005, August). Lying in negotiations: How individual and situational factors influence the use of neutralization strategies. *Journal of Organizational Behavior*, 26(6), 661–679.

Barry, B. (1999). The tactical use of emotion in negotiation. *Research on Negotiation in Organizations*, 7, 93–121.

Boles, T., Croson, R., & Murnighan, J. (2000). Deception and retribution in repeated ultimatum bargaining. *Organizational Behavior and Human Decision Processes*, 83, 235–259.

Bond, C. F., & DePaulo, B. M. (2006). Accuracy of decption judgments. *Personality and Social Psychology Review*, 10, 214–234.

Buller, D. B., & Burgoon, J. K. (1996). Interpersonal deception theory. *Communication Theory*, 6, 203–242.

Burgoon, J. K., & Buller, D. B. (1994). Interpersonal deception: III. Effects of deceit on perceived communication and nonverbal dynamic. *Journal of Nonverbal Behavior*, 18, 155–184.

Burgoon, J. K., Buller, D. B., Guerrero, L. K., Afifi, W. A., & Feldman, C. M. (1996). Interpersonal deception: XII. Information management dimensions underlysing deceptive and truthful messages. *Communications Monographs*, 63(1), 50–69.

Burgoon, J. K., Buller, D. B., White, C. H., Afifi, W., & Buslig, A. L. (1999). The role of conversaton involvement in deceptive interpersonal interactions. *Personality and Social Psychology Bulletin*, 25, 669–685.

Bursten, B. (1972). The manipulative personality. *Archives of General Psychiatry*, 26, 318–321.

Cannon, W. B. (1929). *Bodily changes in pain, hunger, fear, and rage*. New York, NY: Appleton-Century-Crofts.

Carr, A. Z. (1968, January). Is business bluffing ethical? The ethics of business are not those of society, but rather those of the poker game. *Harvard Business Review*, 46(1), 143–153.

Caso, L., Gnisci, A., Vrij, A., & Mann, S. (2005). Process underlying deception: An empirical analysis of truths and lies when manipulating the stakes. *Journal of Interviewing and Offender Profiling*, 2, 195–202.

Colwell, K., Hiscock-Anisman, C., Memon, A., Woods, D., & Michlik, P. M. (2006). Strategies of impression management among deceivers and truth tellers: How liars attempt to convince. *American Journal of Forensic Psychology*, 24, 31–38.

Davis, M., & Hadicks, D. (1995). Demeanor and credibility. *Semiotica*, 106, 5–54.

DePaulo, B. M., & Bell, K. L. (1996). Truth and investment: Lies are told to those who care. *Journal of Personality and Social Psychology*, 71(4), 703–716.

DePaulo, B. M., Epstein, J. A., & Wyer, M. M. (1993). Sex differences in lying; How women and men deal with the dilemma of deceit. In M. Lewis, & C. Saarni (Eds.), *Lying and deception in everyday life* (pp. 126–147). New York, NY: Guilford Press.

DePaulo, B. M., Kirkendol, S. E., Tang, J., & O'Brien, T. P. (1989, September). The motivational impairment effect in the communication of deception: Replications and extensions. *Journal of Nonverbal Behavior*, 12, 177–202.

DePaulo, B. M., Lindsay, J. J., Malone, B. E., Muhlenbruck, L., Charlton, K., & Cooper, H. (2003). Cues to deception. *Psychological Bulletin*, 129(1), 74–118.

Deslauriers-Varin, N., Lussier, P., & St-Yves, M. (2011). Confessing their crime: Factors influencing the offender's decision to confess to the police. *Justice Quarterly*, 28(1), 113–145.

Duchenne de Boulogne, G. B. (1876). *Mecanisme de la physionomie humaine ou analyse electro-physiologique de l'expression des passions*. Paris: Librairie J.B. Bailliere et fils.

Ekman, P. (1981, June 12). Mistakes when deceiving. *Annals of the New York Academy of Sciences*, 364(1), 269–278.

Ekman, P. (1997). Expression or communication about emotion. In N. Segal, G. E. Weisfel, & C. C. Weisfeld (Eds.), *Uniting psychology and biology: Integrative perspective on human development* (pp. 315–338). Washington, DC: American Psychological Association.

Ekman, P. (2001). *Telling lies: Clues to deceit in the marketplace, politics, and marriage.* New York, NY: W.W. Norton.

Ekman, P., & Frank, M. G. (1993). Lies that fail. In M. Lewis, & C. Saarni (Eds.), *Lying and deception in everyday life* (pp. 184–200). New York, NY: Guilford Press.

Ekman, P., & Friesen, W. V. (1969). The repertoire or nonverbal behavior: Categories, origins, usage and coding. *Semiotica, 1*(1), 49–98.

Ekman, P., & Friesen, W. V. (1972, December). Hand movements. *Journal of Communication, 22*(4), 353–374.

Ekman, P., & Friesen, W. V. (1982, June). Felt, false, and miserable smiles. *Journal of Nonverbal Behavior, 6*, 238–252.

Ekman, P., & O'Sullivan, M. (1991). Who can catch a liar? *American Psychologist, 46*(9), 913–920.

Ekman, P., Davidson, R. J., & Friesen, W. V. (1990). The Duchenne Smile: Emotional expression and brain physiology: II. *Journal of Personality and Social Psychology, 58*(2), 342–353.

Ekman, P., Friesen, W. V., & O'Sullivan, M. (1988). Smiles when lying. *Journal of Personality and Social Psychology, 54*(3), 414–420.

Ekman, P., O'Sullivan, M., & Frank, M. G. (1999). A few can catch a liar. *Psychological Science, 10*(3), 263–266.

Ekman, P., O'Sullivan, M., Friesen, W. V., & Scherer, K. R. (1991). Invited article: Face, voice, and body in detecting deceit. *Journal of Nonverbal Behavior, 15*, 125–135.

Fiedler, K., & Walka, I. (1993, December). Training lie detectors to use nonverbal cues instead of global heuristics. *Human Communication Research, 20*(2), 199–223.

Ford, C. V. (1996). *Lies! Lies!! Lies!!! The Psychology fo Deceit.* Arlington: American Psychiatric Press.

Forrest, J. A., & Feldman, R. S. (2000). Detecting deception and judge's involvement: Lower task involvement leads to better lie detection. *Personality and Social Psychology Bulletin, 26*(1), 118–125.

Franck, A. (2009). Vernehmungsledre und Aussagepsychologie. *Seminar gehalten in der Kanzlei Thumlein und Kollegen in Kempten.* Interrogation theory and statement psychology. Andreas Frank, Public Prosecutor LG Munich. April 24, 2009. https://www-kanzlei--thuemlein-de. translate.goog/Veranstaltungen/Archiv?_x_tr_sl=de&_x_tr_tl=en&_x_tr_hl=en&_x_tr_pto=sc

Freshman, C. (2010). Yes, And: Core concerns, internal mindfulness, and external mindfulness for emotional balance, lie detection, and successful negotiation. *Nevada Law Journal, 10* (2),Article 4.

Fulmer, I. S., Barry, B., & Long, D. A. (2009). Lying and smiling: Informational and emotional deception in negotiation. *Journal of Business Ethics, 88*(4), 691–709.

Gallup, G. G. (1977). Tonic immobility: The role of fear and predation. *Psychological Record, 27*, 41–61.

Gaspar, J., & Schweitzer, M. (2012). The emotion deception model: A review of deception in negotiation and the role of emotion in deception. *Negotiation and Conflict Management Research, 6*(3), 160–179.

Geiselman, E. R., Elmgren, S., Green, C., & Rystad, I. (2011). Training laypersons to detect deception in verbal narratives and exchanges. *American Journal of Forensic Psychology, 32*, 1–22.

Gilbert, D. T. (1991). Now mental systems believe. *American Psychologist, 46*(2), 107–119.

Goldman-Eisler, F. (1968). *Psycholinguistics: Experiments in spontaneous speech.* London: Academic Press.

Gordon, N. J., & Fleisher, W. L. (2010). *Effective interviewing and interrogation techniques.* Burlington, MA: Academic Press.

Gordon, N. J., & Fleisher, W. L. (2011). *Effective interviewing and interrogation techniques* (3rd ed.). New York: Associated Press.

Gozna, L. F., & Babooram, N. (2004). Non-traditional interviews: Deception in a simulated customs baggage search. *14th European Conference of Psychology and Law, Krakow, Poland*, (pp. 7–10).

Granhag, P. A., & Stromwall, L. A. (2002). Repeated interrogations: Verbal and non-verbal cues to deception. *Applied Cognitive Psychology, 16*(3), 243–257.

Granhag, P. A., Stromwall, L. A., & Hartwig, M. (2007, January). The SUE technique: The way to interview to detect deception. *Forensic Update, 88*, 25–29.

Gudjonsson, G. H. (2003). *Wiley series in the psychology of crime, policing and law. The psychology of interrogations and confessions: A handbook*. New York, NY, U.S.: John Wiley and Sons, Ltd.

Gudjonsson, G. H., & Bownes, I. (1992). The reasons why suspects confess during custodial interrogation: Data for Northern Ireland. *Medicine, Science and the Law, 32*, 204–212.

Gudjonsson, G. H., & Petursson, H. (1991). Custodial interrogation: Why do suspects confess and how does it relate to their crime, attitude and personality? *Personality and Individual Differences, 12*(3), 204–306.

Hartwig, M., Granhag, P. A., & Stromwall, L. A. (2007). Guilty and innocent suspects' strategies during police interrogations. *Psychology, Crime and Law, 13*(2), 213–227.

Hartwig, M., Granhag, P. A., Stromwall, L. A., & Kronkvist, O. (2006). Strategic use of evidence during police interviews: When training to detect deception works. *Law and Human Behavior, 30*, 603–619.

Inbau, F. E., Reid, J. E., Buckley, J. P., & Jayne, B. C. (2013). *Essentials and the Reid technique: Criminal interrogation and confessions*. Burlington, MA: Jones Bartlett Learning.

Kassin, S. M. (2005). On the psychology of confession: Does innocence put innocents at risk? *American Psychologist, 52*, 221–233.

Kassin, S. M., & Gudjonsson, G. H. (2004). The psychology of confessions: A review of the literature and issues. *Psychological Science in the Public Interest, 5*(2), 33–67.

Kassin, S. M., & Norwick, R. J. (2004). Why people waive their Miranda rights: The power of innocence. *Law and Human Behavior, 28*(2), 211–221.

Kebbell, M. R., Hatton, C., Johnson, S. D., & O'Kelly, C. M. (2001). People with learning disabilities as witnesses in court: What questions should lawyers ask? *British Journal of Learning Disabilities, 29*(3), 98–102.

Klein, A. (2003, June 15). Lord of the flies. *The Washington Post*, p. W06.

Kleinke, C. L. (1986). Gaze and eye contact: A research review. *Psychological Bulletin, 100*(1), 78–100.

Koehn, D. (1997). Trust and business: Barriers and bridges. *Business and Professional Ethics Journal, 16*(1), 7–28.

Kohnken, G. (2004). Statement validity analysis and the 'detection of the truth'. In P. A. Granhag, & L. Stromwall (Eds.), *The detection of deception in forensic context* (pp. 41–63). New York, NY: Cambridge University Press.

Kohnken, G., Schimossek, E., Aschermann, E., & Hofer, E. (1995). The cognitive interview and the assessment of the credibility of adults' statements. *Journal of Applied Psychology, 80*(6), 671–684.

Koning, L., van Dijk, E., van Beest, I., & Steinel, W. (2010). An instrumental account of deception and reactions to deceit in bargaining. *Business Ethics Quarterly, 20*(1), 57–73.

Krauss, R. M., Apple, W., Morency, N., Wenzel, C., & Winton, W. (1981). Verbal, vocal, and visible factors in judgments of another's affect. *Journal of Personality and Social Psychology, 40*(2), 312–320.

Kraut, R. E., & Poe, D. B. (1980). Behavioral roots of person perception: The deception judgments of customs inspectors and laymen. *Journal of Personality and Social Psychology, 39*(5), 784–798.

Landstrom, S., & Granhag, P. A. (2008). Children's truthful and deceptive testimonies: How camera perspective affects adult observers' perception and assessment. *Psychology, Crime and Law*, *14*(5), 381–396.

Landstrom, S., Granhag, P. A., & Hartwig, M. (2005). Witnesses appearing live versus on video: Effects on observers' perception, veracity assessments and memory. *Applied Cognitive Psychology: The Official Journal of the Society for Applied Research in Memory and Cognition*, *19*(7), 913–933.

Leonardelli, G. J., Gu, J., McRuer, G., Medvec, V., & Galinksy, A. D. (2019). Multiple equivalent simultaneous offers (MESOs) reduce the negotiator dilemma: How a choice of first offers increases economic and relational outcomes. *Organizational Behavior and Human Decision Processes*, *152*, 64–82.

Levine, T. R., Kim, R. K., & Blair, J. P. (2010). (In)accuracy at detecting true and false confessions and denials: An initial test of a projected motive model of veracity judgments. *Human Communication Research*, *36*, 81–101.

Levine, T. R., Kim, R. K., Park, H. S., & Hughes, M. (2006). Deception detection accuracy is a predictable linear function of message veracity base-rate: A formal test of Park and Levine's probability model. *Communication Monographs*, *73*, 243–260.

Lewicki, P. (1983). Self-image bias in person perception. *Journal of Personality and Social Psychology*, *45*(2), 384–393.

Lewicki, R. J., & Robinson, R. J. (1998). Ethical and unethical bargaining tactics: An empirical study. *Journal of Business Ethics*, *17*(6), 211–228.

Lewicki, R., & Stark, N. (1996). What is ethically appropriate in negotiations: An empirical examination of bargaining tactics. *Social Justice Research*, *9*, 69–95.

Lewis, M., & Saarni, C. (1993). *Lying and deception in everyday life*. New York, NY: Guilford Press.

Lykken, D. T. (1998). *A tremor in the blood: Uses and abuses of the lie detector*. New York, NY: Plenum Press.

Mackey, C., & Miller, G. (2004). *The Interrogators: Inside the secret war against al Qaeda*. Hachette UK: Little, Brown & Co.

Malhotra, D., & Bazerman, M. (2007). *Negotiation genius. How to overcome obstacles and achieve brilliant results at the bargaining table and beyond*. New York: Bantam.

Mann, S., Vrij, A., & Bull, R. (2004, February). Detecting true lies: Police officers' ability to detect suspects' lies. *Journal of Applied Psychology*, *89*(1), 137–149.

Matarazzo, J. D., Wiens, A. N., Jackson, R. H., & Manaugh, T. S. (1970). Interviewee speech behavior under conditions of endogenously-present and exogenously-induced motivational states. *Journal of Clinical Psychology*, *26*(2), 141–148.

Michelman, J. H. (1983, November). Deception in commercial negotiation. *Journal of Business Ethics*, *2*(4), 255–262.

Nasher, J. (2015). *Entlarvt! Techniken der Wahrheitsfindung*. Frankfurt, Germany: Campus.

O'Connor, K. M., & Carnevale, P. J. (1997). A nasty but effective negotiation strategy: Misrepresentation of a common-value issue. *Personality and Social Psychology Bulletin*, *23*(5), 504–515.

Olekalns, M., & Smith, P. L. (2009, March). Mutually dependent: Power, trust, affect and the use of deception in negotiation. *Journal of Business Ethics*, *85*(3), 347–365.

O'Sullivan, M., Ekman, P., & Friesen, W. V. (1988, September). The effect of comparisons on detecting deceit. *Journal of Nonverbal Behavior*, *12*(3), 203–215.

Park, H. S., & Levine, T. R. (2001). A probability model of accuracy in deception detection experiments. *Communication Monographs*, *68*, 201–210.

Podlesny, A. J., & Raskin, C. D. (1977). Physiological measures and the detection of deception. *Psychological Bulletin*, *84*, 782–799.

Raskin, D. C., & Honts, C. R. (2002). The comparison question test. In D. C. Raskin, & C. R. Honts, *Handbook of polygraph testing* (pp. 1–47). San Deigo, CA: Academic Press.

Rogers, T., & Norton, M. I. (2011). The artful dodger; Answerting the wrong question the right way. *Journal of Experimental Psychology: Applied, 17*(2), 139–147.

Ruedy, N. E., Moore, C., Gino, F., & Schweitzer, M. E. (2013). The cheater's high: The unexpected affective benefits of unethical behavior. *Journal of Personality and Social Psychology, 105*(4), 531–548.

Ryan, S., Grazer, B., Nevins, D., Voll, D., Baum, S., Sackheim, D., ... Fain, S. (2009–2011). Lie to me. Imagine Television: 20th Century Fox Television.

Schmidt, N. B., Richey, J. A., & Maner, J. K. (2009). Exploring human freeze responses to a threat stressor. *Journal of Behavior Therapy and Experimental Psychiatry, 39*, 292–304.

Schweitzer, M. E., & Croson, R. T. (1999). Curtailing deception: The impact of direct questions on lies and omissions. *The International Journal of Conflict Management, 10*, 225–248.

Shell, G. R. (1991). When is it legal to lie in negotiation? *MIT Sloan Managment Review, 32*(3), 93–101.

Sigurdsson, J. F., & Gudjonsson, G. H. (1994). Alcohol and drug intoxication during police interrogation and the reasons why suspects confess to the police. *Addiction, 89*(8), 985–997.

Smith, N. (2001). *Reading between the lines: An evaluation of the scientific content analysis technique.* Police Research Series Paper 135, UK Home office, Research, Development, and Statistics Directorate, London.

Sporer, S. L., & Schwandt, B. (2006). Paraverbal indicators of deception: A meta-analytic synthesis. *Applied Cognitive Psychology, 20*(4), 421–446.

Spranca, M., Minsk, E., & Baron, J. (1991). Omission and commission in judgment and choice. *Journal of Experimental Social Psychology, 27*, 76–105.

Steller, M., & Kohnken, G. (1989). Criteria-based statement analysis. Credibility assessment of children's statements in sexual abuse cases. In D. C. Raskin (Ed.), *Psychological methods for investigation and evidence* (pp. 217–245). New York: Springer.

Stiff, J. B., & Miller, G. R. (1986). "Come to think of it ... " Interrogative probes, deceptive communication, and deception detection. *Human Communication Research, 12*(3), 339–357.

Stromwall, L. A., Hartwig, M., & Granhag, P. A. (2006). To act truthfully: Nonverbal behaviour and strategies during a police interrogation. *Psychology, Crime and Law, 12*(2), 207–219.

Stromwall, L., Granhag, P. A., & Landstrom, S. (2007). Children's prepared and unprepared lies: Can adults see through their strategies? *Applied Cognitive Psychology, 21*, 457–471.

Thompson, L. L. (1991, March). Information exchange in negotiation. *Journal of Experimental Social Psychology, 27*(2), 161–179.

Thompson, L. L. (2020). *The Mind and Heart of the Negotiator* (7th ed.). Hoboken, NJ: Prentice Hall.

Van Dijk, E., Van Kleef, G., Steinel, W., & Van Beest, I. (2008). A social functional approach to emotions in bargaining: When communicating anger pays and when it backfires. *Journal of Personality and Social Psychology, 94*, 600–614.

Varelius, J. (2006). Autonomy, well-being, and the case of the refusing patient. *Medicine, Health Care, and Philosophy, 9*, 117–125.

Vij, M. (2005). The determinants of country risk analysis and empirical approach. *Journal of Management Research, 5*(1), 20–31.

Volkema, R. J. (2004). Demographic, cultural, and economic predictors of perceived ethicality of negotiation behavior: A nine-country analysis. *Journal of Business Research, 57*, 69–78.

Vrij, A. (2000). *Detecting lies and deceit: The psychology of lying and implications for professional practice.* Chichester, UK: John Wiley and Sons.

Vrij, A. (2008). *Detecting lies and deceit: Pitfalls and opportunities.* Chichester, England: John C. Wiley.

Vrij, A., & Mann, S. (2001). Telling and detecting lies in a high-stake situation: The case of a convicted murderer. *Applied Cognitive Psychology*, *15*, 187–203.

Vrij, A., & Mann, S. (2004, January). Detecting deception: The benfit of looking at a combination of behavioral, auditory and speech content related cues in a systematic manner. *Group Decision and Negotiation*, *13*, 61–79.

Vrij, A., & Mann, S. (2006). Criteria-based content analysis: An empirical test of its underlying processes. *Psychology, Crime and Law*, *12*, 337–349.

Vrij, A., & Semin, G. R. (1996). Lie experts' beliefs about nonverbal indicators of deception. *Journal of Nonverbal Behavior*, *20*(1), 65–80.

Vrij, A., Edward, K., & Bull, R. (2001). Stereotypical verbal and nonverbal responses while deceiving others. *Personality and Social Psychology Bulletin*, *27*, 899–909.

Vrij, A., Edward, K., Roberts, K. P., & Bull, R. (2000). Detecting deceit via analysis of verbal and nonverbal behavior. *Journal of Nonverbal Behavior*, *24*, 239–263.

Vrij, A., Granhag, P., & Porter, S. (2010). Pitfalls and opportunities in nonverbal and verbal lie detection. *Psychological Science in the Public Interest*, *11*(3), 89–121.

Vrij, A., Mann, S., & Fisher, R. (2006a). An empirical test of the behavior analysis interview. *Law and Human Behavior*, *30*, 329–345.

Vrij, A., Mann, S., & Fisher, R. (2006b). Information-gathering versus accusatory interview style: Individual differences in respondents' experiences. *Personality and Individual Differences*, *41*, 589–599.

Walczyk, J. J., Roper, K. S., Seemann, E., & Humphrey, A. M. (2003, November). Cognitive mechanisms underlying lying to questions: Response time as a cue to deception. *Applied Cognitive Psychology*, *17*(7), 755–774.

Walczyk, J. J., Schwartz, J. P., Clifton, R., Adams, B., Wei, M., & Zha, P. (2005). Lying person-to-person about live events: A cognitive framework for lie detection. *Personnel Psychology*, *58*, 141–170.

Warren, G., Schertler, E., & Bull, P. (2009). Detecting deception from emotional and unemotional cues. *Journal of Nonverbal Behavior*, *33*(1), 59–69.

White, C. H., & Burgoon, J. K. (2001). Adaptation and communicative design: Patterns of interaction in truthful and deceptive conversations. *Human Communication Research*, *27*, 9–37.

Barbara Sunderland Manousso
Chapter 16
The HearT of Mediation

Abstract: Conflict in the workplace, known as organizational conflict, erodes productivity, creates displaced stress, tension, and absenteeism, impacts financial growth,
and profits, and promotes astronomical legal fees. It can also be a light in the dark-
ness. The successful organizational mediator acts replete with inspiring communication, neutrality, and practical solutions. Well managed companies also are mindful of
managing conflict proactively and professionally, to mitigate the conflicts that might
emerge. Conflict theory suggests that conflict is an integral part of life and organizations and not always with negative impact, once addressed. Conflict can arise
between the differing perspectives of more than one person. A person can even have
intra-personal conflict: Eat that piece of cake; no do not eat any more sweets. Conflict
and how it is handled can be a productive experience, as through the lens of SOS-Semantics of Self in Conflict TM that informs theoretically and practically on how conflict is viewed in organizations and can provide healthy solutions. This chapter is for
practitioners, organizational leaders, conflict parties, and mediators who need to
refresh and understand the dynamics of proper intent of the HearT of the mediation
process and why these dynamics are important to uphold the strength, benefits, and
integrity of genuine conflict management.

Keywords: mediation, best practice, ethics, theory of conflict, negotiation, organizational mediation, workplace, sos-semantics of self in conflict

The costs and yearly financial losses in companies are estimated up to two billion
a year in Canada and up to $359 billion in American companies due to the erosive
effects of organizational conflicts because of employee diminished work performance, low morale, and compromised loss of revenue (Picincu, 2019). For the workplace bottom-line, mediation is tailored for employees to design and personalize a
written blueprint that opens their communication and results in less stress, closes
gaps in cultural diversity, and is a timely means to learn to work together and move
forward in a collaborative, comfortable, and restorative way.

Workplace mediation cases between employees or among one or more employees
and their employer falls under the moniker of organizational conflict management.
When conflict arises in the workplace, a well-designed conversation and process,
such as mediation, offers an attainable, amicable, structured process, a communication boost. A skilled mediator orchestrates this process. A strength of this process is
that the parties do the essential work and become the architects of their solutions. At
the HearT of the process is the opportunity for all parties involved in the dynamics of
the conflict to speak, be heard, and to listen. As a result, professional mediators can

https://doi.org/10.1515/9783110746365-016

bring out the best of the mediation process by employing mediation skills, framed by ethical standards and honed communication. HearT reflects the lifeline of mediation since it includes within the word the ear to hear.

From an organizational perspective, mediation in the workplace thwarts litigation, restores productivity, and is cost-effective. In addition, it alleviates employees' negative health such as anxiety, depression, poor sleep, body pain, and displaced social interaction (Picincu, 2019). There are potent ingredients that contribute to organizational mediation's best practice. The organizational mediation process doesn't differ greatly from most mediations, but there are ways to address the relational aspect and sensitivities of the workplace and skills that can be used to clarify conflict attributes of the parties and to help them be mindful of their larger perspective of career sustainability and the ripple effect of the workplace community.

Best conflict organizational management is a balanced-triad of the ethical standards, professional mediator skills, and the organization's best judgement to know the difference. The guiding HearT for best practice of skills is set forth to provide mutual safe, neutral space to speak without interruption, and to be heard.

What is the Intent and Strength of Organizational Mediation?

Mediation is not a new tool for resolving conflict. It has been around as long as there have been conflicts, whether addressed by a chief, group elder, or an informal agreement of a third party. The Bible mentions mediation and mediators in Job 9:33, Galations 3:19, 1 Timothy 2:5, Hebrews 8:6, 9:15, 12:24, as examples. In the nineteen seventies, mediation began being used by courts to lessen the burden of court dockets. By 1982, Texas codified into statute the actual business practice of mediation for civil and family cases. Other states took notice and incorporated similar statutes and conventions of use. As the use and practice of mediation grew, it became clear that it was not just a skill set and practice option for attorneys to offer, but a separate business track for many qualified candidates from the fields of human resources, psychology, medicine, clergy, and education; the list of occupations and people who were willing to learn communication skills specific to conflict management emerged. Mediation as a field of study and practice was seen as a complement to negotiation and a problem-solving tool through facilitative, narrative, and transformative skills. The concept of mediation is that it is a conversation between parties who are the architects of their solution, guided by a mediator shepherding the process, while encouraging and providing a safe space for the parties to speak and to be heard.

The mediator is an impartial, third party neutral, who should never have any vested interest in the outcome. For the parties, mediation is a wonderful opportunity and vehicle for conflict to be addressed, aired, examined, and usually resolved.

Sometimes, if the conflict is a breach of law, attorneys might be attending with and representing the clients to provide legal explanation and advocacy. In many cases of organizational mediation, the parties do not need or want legal representation. This is important as a contrast from other genres of mediation where *pro se* parties would greatly benefit from legal guidance.

When a conflict is resolved through mediation, the parties have the control and option to work out a plan that becomes a legally binding contract, memorialized into a Mediation Settlement Agreement (MSA). Sometimes in the workplace, the final agreement, still a binding agreement, is also called a Memorandum of Understanding (MOU). They are the same document and serve the same purpose with the forward path that supports how the parties will work together, or not.

In civil court appointed cases, this MSA is filed with the court. All family MSA are always filed with the family court for the integrity and protection of children. In organizational mediation, since the basis of the disputes often do not rise to the level of lawsuit, and attorneys may or may not be representing the parties involved, the boss or someone in the hierarchy of management who might have engaged the mediation process for the benefit of the company's productivity might be the person to receive the MSA, so that the party's adherence to the MSA is monitored. On occasion, human resources might be the repository of the MSA, but less typical, so that there is no open human resource case on file. Once a conflict is under the umbrella of human resources, confidentiality of the issue is more apt to be compromised.

As in all professional mediations, the process is recognized as more than a mere reprimanding counseling session or casual conversation. Therefore, the formality of all parties signing The Agreement to Mediate and Confidentiality documents by all the parties and their legal representatives, should they have attorneys, signal the start of the mediation, as a binding process. This informs that the parties agree voluntarily to the mediation process and terms of commitment and that what is said in the process must remain confidential. The content of the mediation process or how it was accomplished is not to be shared with the water cooler gang or with anyone, even outside of the company structure. The content is never shared, but the outcome, MSA, might be needed to go to management, but this is previously agreed by the parties or is required by a ruling authority within the company, known before the mediation.

The confidentiality of mediation is a strength of the process. The court room is a public venue that allows anyone to observe cases, in addition to the attention and attendance of jurors, if the determination is given a trial. Legal matters have civil procedure that compels parties to participate and can extend the clock into months or years. Anything said in the proceeding is said for all the court to hear.

In mediation, the parties are not compelled to participate, unless it has become part of a lawsuit, and it is court ordered. Therefore, when workplace parties do not have attorneys or a conflict defined or framed by law, they cannot be required to attend the mediation, so they are considered voluntary participants. In reality, in organizational mediation, the parties are often sent by their boss, upper-level manager, or human resources. The parties' jobs are probably at stake, so parties are sent to mediation with a push and shove to maintain their income and career path. They can volunteer to continue with the company or resign.

Organizational Mediation: HearT of Best Practice

Even though organizational mediation is big business for attorneys, half of the cases of workplace conflict do not rise to the level of legal standing as previously mentioned, so they are not legally represented. Therefore, there are probably double or triple the reported discrimination and workplace cases. The mediation process is the same arch for all genres, but there are a few aspects for skill consideration that a mediator can use that differ in organizational mediation from family or civil cases.

In the organizational mediation process, it is helpful for the mediator to meet with each party prior to the mediation conference, sometimes a few times. This is an opportunity for the mediator to provide a dedicated ear and build rapport with each party without any interruption. The mediator remains neutral to each party, but the caucuses allow each party to vent and reinvent before participating in the mediation. The mediator is one hundred percent within the structure of mediation, and not an advocate for either party, which would be the ombuds role, but this meeting is optimal for the mediator to determine if all the proper parties will be present at the mediation table and can assess the parties conflict behaviors and contributions to the conflict.

In a quality mediation, the parties are in conference to be able to hear and be heard, and the HearT and strength of mediation is the framework provided by the national and local ethical standards and quality alternative dispute resolution (ADR) skills. If the mediator is an attorney, the attorney must disclose that they are mediating ONLY and will not be in the capacity of legal representation to avoid dual practice. If the mediator is also a mental health professional, they must disclose that they are not there to "fix" the parties, but to provide a process and skill set for a quality conversation.

However, there are attorneys who breech the covenant of mediator's ethical standards and overstep. Unfortunately, the mediation process can be exploited and undermined by unskilled mediators and attorney or mental health professionals/ mediators who pretend to mediate, but do not uphold the premise and strength of the mediation process. When mediation is used as a ploy to **pretend to hold** an authentic mediation, the process is not beneficial and is used without respect or relevance. This happens when the parties are not allowed to interact and are sent to separate rooms, eliminating direct communication between the parties to hear or be heard.

There has become a deceitful trend of mediators running between rooms as a messenger, calling themselves mediators, but they are really doing negotiated settlement with a legal push. Their parties think that they are in mediation because that is what they are paying for, but the parties often come away angry after paying their attorneys and the mediator to sit in a room alone for hours while the mediator is supposedly talking with the other party yet might be conducting another case's mediation or handling other office tasks at the cost of the unsuspecting mediation clients. This style of practice does not lend itself to organizational mediation, or any professional mediation ethical standard.

A few years ago, an attorney mediator was sanctioned for holding three mediations at once and just floating among the six rooms! Each case thought that she/he was working with the other party in their case. This was a direct breech of ethical standards and misrepresentation. If a mediator is being paid to mediate, clients should not be paying for a mediator's time working on another case!

Conference style mediation prevents abuse, highlights skilled, professional mediators, and provides communication between and among the parties in an empathic, transparent way that gives the lotus of control to the parties, not the mediator. Meeting only in caucus prevents the parties from relating to each other and hearing detail that might support the request of an offer humanizing the process. Mediation is not a numbers game. It is about people's needs and interests in full transparency and the value of the mediation experience allowing open communication. At the HearT of mediation is the empowerment of the parties all being heard, as well as being able to listen and speak to each other that cannot be achieved if the parties are muzzled by their attorney and, worse, their mediator. If negotiated settlement is employed, the only one empowered is the mediator who becomes a messenger. However, the messages brought by the mediator lose the impact from the delivery of the conflicting parties. Without the reason behind a number or idea, the communication package and semantics is incomplete and empty, often not transparent.

The intent of the mediation process lends itself to encourage the parties to learn and incorporate new communication and conflict management skills by feeling empathy, offering an apology, and to being actively engaged in their process.

Ethical Framework and Expectations for Mediators: The Model Standards

Skilled, professional mediators worldwide are taught a process that is guided by a proscribed curriculum and ethical framework for the mediators and the parties' best interest and best practice. In most of the world, forty hours of certificate training in civil mediation is the gold standard. Most states have their own statutes as a guide for their state's mediation processes, based on The American Bar Association (ABA), published in 2005 on their website. Here's the link > https://www.americanbar.org/groups/dispute_resolution/

Mediation, being a dynamic process, can have many forms and practical, user-friendly, and viable functions to assure the parties' success and mediator's transparency. The hallmark and competence of the process is universally consistent and well-structured by statute and the ethical considerations.

Almost daily, I receive calls from parties who did not feel that they received a proper mediation or a mediation at all. Sadly, often, after hearing of their experience, they have NOT experienced mediation. It was negotiated settlement, facilitation, or a misrepresentation of settlement forced on them.

In spite of these outliers, mediation is universally recognized as the opportunity for the parties to be the architects of their solution and resolution. The mediator's role is not to direct, encourage, or admonish the parties into what the mediator feels is the best solution. The mediator is the shepherd of the process, an impartial neutral.

One of the tenants around the world, with a few exceptions, is that the professional background and educational levels of mediators be varied. Mediation is not just another lawyer's skill. For many lawyers who swing sword, the practice of mediation doesn't easily fit within their honed advocacy skills. In practice, the nuances of mediation are far bigger and broader than the expectations of court ordered mediation. Lawyers are most often within the bubble of court ordered mediation with their cases that rise to the content of court pleadings and points of law. So, when in the role of mediator, lawyers approach chasms of legal juncture that compromises professional ethics.

Lawyer mediators are often surprised, philosophically challenged, and maybe financially threatened that mediation beyond the court system is quite a huge market. Mediation, when done correctly and effectively through the process, is an empowering tool for employment issues, community programs, like the police department, as well as federal, county, city, and local boards who use the mediation vehicle to find clarity and correct miscommunication and misconceptions like those that might be impairing the workplace, organizational structures.

At the heart of mediation is the ability and consideration of the parties to listen to each other and to be heard, – HearT. When anger is in the head and heart of a party, their need to tell someone what is weighing them down with anger and frustration is paramount to moving away from what happened to moving forward with a solution. Venting in mediation is healthy and at the HearT of the process. As one well-known theorist, Joe Folger, the co-founder of transformative mediation and co-author of The *Promise of Mediation* stated that, "if you are going to be a mediator, do not be afraid of conflict."

In a proper mediation, the mediator establishes their credentials and authority to conduct the process. The mediator explains their role and the process to the parties as an impartial and neutral facilitator and the expectations, initiative, and opportunities of the parties to control the content. Mediation is empowering for the parties when they realize that they will shape the solution themselves by looking at the dispute maybe from the perspective of their opponent, may be privy to new information, or receive enlightenment that they had never heard before or knew yet could not digest at the time. Information in a safe, private, neutral space and within a proscribed process assists the parties more clearly through a new lens, exposed to an impartial voice.

If a case goes to trial or before a judge, the solution might be a bandage for what erroneously appears to be the correct solution with little regard for hidden issues, personality dysfunction, future relationships, or insecure perceptions. In mediation, with a skilled mediator, these are all thoughtful and examined considerations that guide the parties through a process that gives them the role of a rudder with a sail full of wind.

In employment cases, disputes between employees can cost a company thousands of dollars if employees divide the office into camps, undermine formally productive relationships, or employees feel unsatisfied and not heard. Many times, employment disputes stem from a lack of communication, professional jealousy, or misguided managers who throw their employees under a bus. The issue that caused the conflict might be from a lack or omission of clear expectations or just plain mismanagement. As issues collide and conflicts emerge, and if management sidesteps their responsibility, the conflict migrates down the chain of command with disputes and threats and compromise to workplace harmony and civility.

The flow of conflict and the way it moves through a company was studied by this author through long-term care and health facilities. The theory of SOS-Semantics of Self in Conflict™ emerged and was measured to demonstrate that the head of a company creates the conflict management tone for the organization from the top through to the bottom the staff. The SOS is the alert |that announces there is a conflicting event on the horizon. Many conflicts are evident and noted by observers, but not regarded by the parties consciously or deliberately at the time.

The Theory of Conflict Influences the Mediator's Role in Organizational Conflict

SOS-Semantics of Self in Conflict™ embraces a variety of theorists who explore the impact of conflict in organizations and the staffs within them. As is often reflected in workplaces, as well as in ongoing relationships, conflicts develop on many levels between employees, as well as their associates, peers, and clients they serve. Good leaders are mindful of the cost of personnel capital and provide prophylactic training programs on conflict management and encourage their management teams to be alert to tensions within the company. Personal communication is stifled and often derailed by tension and misunderstandings.

As recognized in the literature on conflict management and healthy workplaces and within organizations in an article by Katz (2006), "[l]eaders demonstrate their responsiveness by communicating warmth and concern, listening to and respecting the aspirations of others, and giving people the resources, autonomy, and opportunity to succeed and do their job" (p. 375). This is also the honed framework of a mediation process with opportunity at different stages to engage and change the narrative to move forward productively to resolution.

Conflicts within companies can arise between economic classes, ethnic groups, young and old, male against female, or one race versus another. According to Kenneth Boulding (1990), conflicts result because of disparities in power, wealth, and prestige, as well as management miscommunication or lack of communication. It is assumed that those who hold or control desirable goods and services or who dominate situations will protect their own interests, often at the expense of others (Boulding, 1990; Monk, Kaye, & Litwin, 1984). This is especially prevalent in nursing homes and health care facilities where an administrator wants or needs to maintain their control and power over employees to maintain leadership, provide the affordable services, or protect the financial mission of the organization. Conflict theorists, such as Jeffery Rubin (1994), Dean Pruitt (1994), Erving Goffman (1974), William Ury (1995), Roger Fisher (1997, 2000), Louis Kriesberg (2003), and James Schellenberg (1996), emphasize the importance of interests over norms and values, and the ways in which the pursuit of interests generate various types of conflict as normal aspects of social life, rather than abnormal or dysfunctional occurrences. Normal aspects of social interaction seek a win-win solution where there is tolerance for differences, whether they are race, cultural, or ideological. Win-win is not always an option when there is a disparity of real or perceived power, but employee recognition, empowerment, and satisfaction can be company assets for better temperament and conflict management.

Using professional mediators or ombudsmen is a relatively new concept in managing conflict in the workplace. As Umbreit (1995) pointed out, "Informal mediation of staff conflict in human service organizations is a relatively recent development, and there is little academic or empirical research to draw upon" (p. 165). As information is more prevalent and immediate now, it is more difficult to measure all the entry points and hierarches to cover for conflict management within organizational structures by comparing their distinct cultures and diverse missions. Measuring apples with apples can be illusive.

In the workplace, being able to be flexible and to adapt to a variety of situations and people can be helpful when co-workers, subordinates, and management are comprised of a variety of personal values, experiences, beliefs, and ideologies. From close interaction, conflicts can easily arise from being incompatible. Mediators can assist the parties to hear and find clarity in these human differences.

Daily interactions in the workplace can be tested many times a day, especially when staffs come from a variety of cultural backgrounds, ages, and economic levels. This is part of the problem with long-term care and health facilities, high conflict environments because of aged and end-of-life clients. The staff might have very different cultural background from the patients, and just the reality of different age groups working closely, and the competitive nature of most long-term care workplaces can encourage conflicts (Shield & Aronson, 2003). The tone and conflict culture of a facility is set by the management style of the administrator (Monk, Kaye, & Litwin, 1984; Wood, 2004).

Besides cultural differences, the primary characteristics of conflicts are the power struggles over issues of authority, hierarchal structure, and the symbolism of the social interpersonal relationships. The authority in question is the culture of each organization versus the facility administrator's conflict behavior skills. The secondary question is personal gain versus the benefit of the group. In a long-term care or health facility, the administrator does not usually have as much patient and client contact, so issues of care arise, but the administrator might not be informed: "[o]ften the question of who is more powerful turns on who is less dependent" (Augsburger, 1992, p. 57).

In understanding a company, a mediator learns from the employees their perceptions of the company to understand their employee role. Meeting with each party a few times separately a few times before the mediation helps the mediator understand the party's narrative of the past to deconstruct and rebuild sustainable, clearer objectives and goals going forward. This is informed by structuralist theory that connects elements in the social sciences, supporting the idea that human actions are a response to the structure of their social environment, such as values, attitudes, and behaviors. Structural functionalism, known also as systems theory, equilibrium theory, or simply functionalism, refers to the concept of organizations and institutions forming the basis of a social system. A characteristic of functionalism is the concept that views of societies, as made up of component parts, whose interrelation contributes to the maintenance of the whole. Functionalism also focuses on the forces that bring cohesion, integration, explanation, and equilibrium to a society or organization (DeGeorge & DeGeorge, 1972). Functionalism emerged from the works of Auguste Comte (1798–1857), Herbert Spencer (1820–1903), and Emile Durkheim (1858–1917), and later by the American sociologist Talcott Parsons (1902–1979).

Structural functionalism seeks out the 'structural' aspects of the social system or organization under consideration, and then studies the processes that function to maintain its social structures and interactions. Parson's theory was commonly seen as a product of modern, affluent American society, where structural social conflicts had been largely eliminated or were of a transient nature, and where there appeared to be a general social cohesion and shared adherence to democratic values. Mediation gives voice to reality checking and understanding the unspoken, never heard or learned.

Sometimes, the mediator plays devil's advocate with the parties either in conference or in caucus, private meetings, which allocates equal time to the parties. In these sessions, the parties write, not just think their thoughts, which can be shared with the other party in conference. This is the only way to assure being on the same page in the same reality. According to Parsons, key requirements for organizational maintenance, which is seen to be the overriding goal of any organization, are those elements which apply to all social systems; namely, adaptation, goal attainment, integration, and pattern (or value) maintenance. In dealing with organizations, Parsons set forth need-dispositions. His objective that meshes with this study is that "there are role expectations that lead actors to give and get appropriate responses" (Ritzer & Goodman, 2004, p. 238.)

The mediator helps the parties recognize their own contributions to the organizational conflict by listening and encouraging the parties to listen and hear the dissimilarities in their perceptions. Roger Fisher called it Needs Theory and looked at the identity of individuals and their role within the group. Inter-group conflict is based primarily in social psychology theorizing, especially related to Maslow's hierarchy of needs (Hermann, 2006, p. 50). Leaders in organizations use power and authority to manage their organizations. In their minds, their role demonstrates leadership, such as with conflict behavior skills that will help them manage their facility. This is the highest need on Maslow's scale, the hierarchy of needs and self-actualization. The importance of the hierarchal need is a western mentality. If these administrators were in the east, they would place a higher value on appearing to be part of the service team, not above it as the authority voice (Avruch, 1998; Boulding, 1990; Lemert, 2004).

Kurt Lewin (1890–1947) penned field theory, "[b]ehavior, he said is always the result of a field of forces, never a matter of specific traits in the individuals or specific conditions of the environment" (Shellenberg, 1996, p. 69). This field theory is supportive of SOS-Semantics of Self in Conflict™ because the behavior that is chosen to be used by the administrator or head of an organization comes after the conflict event has unfolded and is explained by looking backward in reflection. The employees of the conflict are not always the real parties in organizational mediation, the managers and leaders might be. Sometimes the lower ranking staff are in the conflict, but the management is the one who needs to be the resolver.

Individuals within a social system have dynamic, symbiotic interactions. There is constant changing and vacillating dialogue. To facilitate the dialogue between and within each party, the mediator helps the parties explore words and labels to convey who they are and how they want to be perceived. Within a social system, the micro theorist Goffman (1974) maintained that individuals want to present a certain sense of self that will be accepted by others when they interact. Part of the symbolism and interaction among organizations, their staff, and their consumers is the "face" or persona that they want others to see and to know. In long-term and health care facilities, as well as other types of organizations, the interaction and actions result in dramaturgy, the role for communication and understanding the reality of the situation changes over the course of the mediation session. It is rare in a mediation that the attitude and personality of the parties do not change or show the range from anger, sadness, to a new realization and acceptance.

A second pivotal influence on symbolic interactionism was the philosophical perspective known as pragmatism. Its influence can be seen in the social psychological works of Cooley (1902), James (1915), Dewey (1920), Thomas (1931), and Mead (1934). In general, pragmatists use behaviors that have proven useful to them and to modify what has proven not to work. Pragmatists also have emphasized the relevance of nature, including, most important for our purposes, the social world, that of the organization, for the emergence of the individual to change their role within the workplace.

Case Study that Respects and Underscores the HearT of Mediation

Government agencies are exemplary as far as organizational mediation is concerned because they often have people who have been employed by them for great periods of time. The parties in government agencies are not only doing a job, but their personal mission is public service. When there is a conflict within an agency or between employees, the opportunity to find solutions for the employee's benefit and to uphold something that would help the public good that they are trying to represent flows to the heart of the conversation.

I was contacted by a federal agency to mediate between two employees who had been having some conflicts on and off over many years. Some of the conflicts were about program and community, but some were of the issues I learned were based on personal, gender differences. The conflicts would appear to be resolved, but much of the time, the conflicts were marginalized and suppressed, not healed at the root. When they re-emerged at another point, accumulation of anger and the past made the conflict uglier, so a proper mediation was important to the solution. In the past, they had just had conversations with their direct managers at their locations.

To build their rapport with me and for me to get some insight on them and their issues and point of conflict, I met with each party for an hour three times, once online and then the other two times in person. The key benefit at the HearT of our conversations were that they had a chance to be heard. I asked them, "What brought you to this point and what do you think will help you move forward?" Then, I didn't talk! They needed to talk!

I didn't take any notes, so I gave them my full attention to regurgitate their angst, emotions, and concern for what they both saw agency failings to understand the issues and impact on the public. In my mind, I classified their concerns in the relational, high conflict, family category. Both were well educated, articulate, and deeply crushed and concerned by the conflict. They had worked together, uncomfortably, for over ten years.

In this case, to break their cycle of conflict, I administered the Conflict Dynamic Profile-I for an individual. As I went forward, I really thought that the agency would benefit from the 360, for the whole office, but the agency was not interested. Part of the process was also giving each party a conflict dynamic profile and the conflict dynamic profile measures their behavioral attributes how are they approach conflict and anger. Using a coaching tool can be very helpful for self-analysis of the parties to be mindful of their conflict behaviors and contribution to the conflict. It helps give the parties more measurement as to perhaps why they react the way they do or when they react the way they do.

The conflict dynamic profile was developed at the Eckerd University in Florida over twenty years ago, so it is a well-honed tool that measures behavioral attributes not personality. Behavior change can be accomplished, but you can't change personality as easily. When given the conflict dynamic profile the parties usually are surprised of their behaviors that might have contributed to the conflict. This CDP tool is online for the parties to complete the 100 questions that quite accurately assess their conflict behaviors. This tool addresses the parties in a more elevated professional, caring manner. The results of their conflict dynamic profile are not shared with anybody including their boss or the other party. It is privileged information between the mediator and each party. As mediator, I am not going to fix them, but the party knows that I know their behaviors, and, more importantly, the parties now each see their personal starting points, that is usually not realized conflict behaviors. On the third time the parties met with the mediator, there was a conversation about what the results were of their conflict dynamic profile and how could they use some of their CPD-I insight to change what had happened. I let them think it through. During the third conversation with each party, after the CPD-I time and discussing their conflict dynamic profile, the parties had control over when to schedule their joint conversation, the mediation. Both parties must attend the mediation process. No lawyers were involved or needed for points of law.

When the parties met with the mediator at the mediation, which was in person, they are given the same formal dynamics again to formally sign the Agreement to Mediate and The Confidentiality Agreement, so that both of their signatures were on the same page – symbolically and actually. When this is done in person it's a lot easier and the dynamics of having the parties and their energy and anger in the same room is very important. With the necessity of zoom now you lose a lot of the anger and the negative energy that is brought to a mediation room. As in physics when you bring (use) energy, like a pendulum, energy breeds inertia (energy), so using the dynamics of physics some of that is lost on a zoom, but many parts of energy can still be somewhat regained. After each party talked about what brought them to this conversation and what they were hoping to get out of it, there were tears, apologies, forgiveness, and collaborative conversations. No monetary considerations were on the table, just a fundamental conversation on their differences in conflict behaviors that they both understood better from the private meetings and CPD-I. Their opening statements started at realistic perspectives, supporting the ideas that they generated and negotiated on together to go forward with a blueprint. They didn't have to like each other or change who they were, but they built ideas on their newly considered common ground.

Money paid to the mediator should not sway the mediator's neutrality, nor should the financial value of the outcome dictate the fees of the mediator. The important part of a mediation should be what is the understanding of the parties and what solution do they see or reject from each other, with the possibility to go forward to find a solution.

As mediator, of course, never tell the other side information learned from the other party. If the parties wish to mention private information, the mediator's role is to help the parties articulate it to the other side in the form of a proposal directly. In most mediations the mediator should never be the courier anyway. A skilled mediator helps the parties find a way to say what they need to say and make proposals to the other side that are either accepted thought about or rejected but never rejected without a counterproposal. In this case the parties came to a very satisfying solution very detailed as to how they would move forward and in what manner they would move forward.

This mediation at the table took about 10 hours over two meetings and a lot of things were said that as part of the mediated settlement agreement that one party or the other would say that didn't need to be written down. That was not allowed and every detail to the plan was memorialized. No faulty memories or denials could emerge later. And to make the MSA even stronger, the parties even said why they felt the solution would be something that they could move forward with, as a safeguard for when one of the parties reviews the outcome of it later in a different frame of mind, they cannot say why did I ever agree to that. So, the next day or the next week when they look at the agreement, they have something that's very secure to remind them what their reasoning was behind the solution that they had made at that time.

Another aspect of an organizational mediation that is very important is the location of the mediation. The location or venue for the mediation is never at the office where people can see the parties going into the mediation. The mediation should be held either at the mediator's office or in a location off company campus, a totally neutral location for both parties. There were no prying eyes or ears leaning against the walls. The parties needed to feel very free and very independent with their decisions and thoughts. So often in organizational mediation, it is the manager of the parties who actually sends the parties to the mediation who is the problem. It is very important that the parties can feel a great sense of confidentiality to speak frankly and not worry that somebody is privy to what they've said, and that the confidentiality agreement is signed by both of them right at the beginning of the mediation. The mediator reads both agreements out loud in front of both parties after the parties are informed about what the mediation process will be, because they act as a framework and the immediate reminder of what they are about to achieve, so very important to the process. Mediation is not a process that is a race to the end. It's an opportunity for the parties to work through what brought them to that point, but since the past can't be changed, to look forward for a solution that gives them both something to find pride in. The mediation is not for either party to feel rushed, pressured, or railroaded into making decisions, but where both or all parties are heard and can get to the HearT of the conflict.

Mead argued that the individual creates and transforms his or herself as well as society via the mind and the uniquely human ability uses science to induce social reform. SOS-Semantics of Self in Conflict™ offers a lens to looking at conflict behaviors reflectively from the perspective of an organic event within an event or in reaction of a previous event. When the mediator's process is comprehensive, ethical, skill based, respectful of the HearT of mediation, the transparency provides satisfying solutions for the benefit of the parties and the organizational systems and resets the culture of conflict.

References

Augsburger, D. W. (1992). *Conflict mediation across cultures: pathways and patterns*. Louisville, KY: Westminster/John Knox Press.

Avruch, K. (1998). *Culture and conflict resolution*. Washington, D.C.: United States Institute of Peace Press.

Boulding, K. E. (1990). *Three faces of power*. Newbury Park: Sage Publications. DeGeorge, R., & DeGeorge, F. (Eds.). (1972). *The structuralists from Marx to Levi-Strauss*. New York, NY: Anchor Books.

Fisher, R. (2000). "Intergroup conflict." in Deutsch, Morton, and Coleman, Peter (eds.). *The handbook of conflict resolution: Theory and practice*. San Francisco, CA: Jossey-Bass.

Fisher, R., & Ury, W. (1981). *Getting to yes: Negotiating agreement without giving in* (Second ed.). New York, NY: Penguin Books.

Fisher, R. J. (1997). *Interactive conflict resolution*. Syracuse, NY: University Press.

Goffman, E. (1974). Primary frameworks. In Gerard Delanty and Piet Strydom (eds). Philosophies of social science: The classic and contemporary readings. (pp.202–205). Philadelphia, PA: Open University Press.

Herrman, M. S. (Ed.). (2006). *Handbook of mediation: Bridging theory, research, and practice* (1st ed.). Malden, MA: Blackwell Publishing.

Katz, N. (2006). Enhancing Mediator Artistry: Multiple Frames, Spirit, and Reflection in Action. In M. S. Herrman (Ed.) *The Blackwell Handbook of Mediation: Bridging Theory, Research, and Practice (pp.374–383)*. Malden, MA: Blackwell Publishing.

Kriesberg, L. (2003). *Constructive conflicts from escalation to resolution*. Lanham, MD: Rowman & Littlefield.

Lemert, C. (2004). *Social theory: The multicultural and classic readings* (3rd ed.) Boulder, Co: Westview Press.

Monk, A., Kaye, L., & Litwin, H. (1984). *Resolving Grievances in the nursing home: A study of the ombudsman program*. New York, NY: Columbia University.

Picincu, A. 2019. The Effects of Workplace Conflict. [Online article]. Bizfluent. [Ref.16 October 2020]. Available at: https://bizfluent.com/list-5896846-effects-workplace-conflict.html

Ritzer, G., & Goodman, D. J. (2004). *Sociological theory* (sixth ed.). Boston, MA: McGraw -Hill.

Rubin, J. Z., Pruitt, D. G., & Kim, S. H. (1994). *Social conflict: Escalation, stalemate, and settlement* (2nd ed.). New York, NY: McGraw-Hill.

Schellenberg, J. A. (1996). *Conflict resolution: Theory, research, and practice*. Albany, NY: State University of New York Press.

Sheild, R. R. & Aronson, S. (2003). *Aging in Today's World: Conversations between an anthropologist and a physician*. NY: Berghahn Books.

Umbreit, M. S. (1995). *Mediating interpersonal conflicts: A pathway to peace*. West Concord, MN: CPI Publishing.

Ury, W., & Smoke, R. (1995). Anatomy of a crisis. In J. W. Breslin & J. Z. Rubin (Eds.), *Negotiation Theory and Practice* (3rd ed., pp. 47–56). Cambridge, MA: Negotiation Books.

Wood, E. (2004, July). *Long-Term Care Mediation: Making it work*. Paper presented at the University of Texas School of Nursing of Harris County for Lawyers and Mediators. Houston, TX.

Alexia Georgakopoulos, Barb Allen, Eileen Petzold-Bradley

Chapter 17
Managing Organizational Conflicts Through Innovation, Creativity, and Inclusion: Implementing a Conflict System of Shared Leadership

Abstract: The need is urgent for organizational leaders and members to transform organizational conflicts by addressing conflict that is a natural part of organizational life. Leaders must evolve their organizational systems to address underlying causes of conflict and seek solutions that serve the interests of all, irrespective of where they may reside within the organizational hierarchy. Conflict will occur anywhere there is interdependence, so this chapter provides an impetus for organizational members to be pro-active rather than reactive in addressing conflict. This chapter will examine three facets of organizational conflict resolution: 1) the need for Conflict Management Systems, 2) the role of diversity, equity, and inclusion in system design, and 3) how the practice of shared leadership in addressing conflict and system design can be realized through Liberating Structures. We first examine the critical need for leaders to design a conflict management system (CMS) within their organizations, informed and shaped from the bottom-up. The process of designing a CMS must be inclusive, transparent, and collaborative; careful to ensure all voices are heard as the system is reshaped. Organizations that have Conflict Management Systems inherently and explicitly communicate "value" for employees. CMS provide an official platform for people to safely express and address their conflicts with the goal of transforming and restoring relationships in the workplace. Invariably, as organizations become increasingly diverse, the need to address diversity, equity, and inclusion within CMS design becomes essential. While most organizations espouse the values of appreciating diversity, upholding equity, and being inclusive, far fewer can bring these values to life in people's everyday work. Lofty ideals followed by business-as-usual foments even more conflict, highlighting the necessity for all people, especially leaders, to develop competence and fluency around building a culture that truly embraces diversity. This paper concludes by introducing Liberating Structures as a practice of shared leadership. Liberating Structures offer a practical approach to radical collaboration through which people can listen, share, learn and have a higher, collective understanding of the complexities of a challenge enabling them to move towards meaningful action shaped by all. The array of diverse ideas is exponentially expanded through this shared practice, paving the way for creative and innovative solutions to previously unsolvable challenges.

https://doi.org/10.1515/9783110746365-017

Keywords: conflict management systems, cms design, culture, diversity, equity, inclusion, leadership, liberating structures, organizations

Organizational life is rife with conflict, yet conflict is a natural occurrence in organizational settings. Anytime people are interdependent and rely on one another, conflict is bound to occur, but conflict has a positive nature if it is appropriately addressed (Georgakopoulos, Storrow, and Coleman, 2017). Hansen (2021) also makes a solid case that conflict can be an opportunity to address, improve, and resolve problems in his most recent book titled *Harnessing Conflict's Potential: Turning Lighting into Light*. Imagine for a moment that conflict provides us with a struggle or obstacle, but if we had not encountered conflict, we may very well not experience innovation, growth, productivity, or progress that can follow by addressing the conflict. In this chapter, we offer concrete recommendations for managing conflicts and improving group dynamics within organizational settings.

The authors are experienced Dispute Systems Designer for multinational organizations and governmental agencies, served as lead trainers and private practitioners across diverse organizations for several years, and have real-world experiences through their established scholarly contributions. As authors collectively, we share this chapter to assist dispute systems designers in customizing Conflict Management Systems (CMS) that successfully match diverse organizations and encourage organizational members to infuse innovative processes that address conflict prevention, management, and resolution within organizational settings. First, we proceed by recommending that all organizations should have a CMS, which we describe interchangeably with what others (Amsler, Martinez and Smith, 2020) have popularly called Dispute Systems Designs (DSD). CMS or DSD call for a formal design and structure for how people should address and intervene when conflict emerges within the organizational setting. Next, we present several important challenges related to cultural inclusion and diversity within organizations and provide recommendation to tackle these challenges. We conclude with an unconventional yet refreshing perspective using Liberating Structures as a form of shared leadership that serves as an informal conflict resolution system. We will illustrate that Liberating Structures invite and leverage the latent potentialities within people which allows groups to scale to new heights.

Designing a Conflict Management System within Organizational Settings

The stakes are high for organizations to be successful; however, conflict within organizations can be very costly, and if it is not properly managed, it can impede success, productivity, and innovation. Unfortunately, many times, conflicts are addressed reactively and there is little to no attention placed on addressing conflict prevention, intervention, management, as well as resolution. Georgakopoulos, Storrow, and Coleman (2017) and Amsler, Martinez, and Smith, (2020) detail why this is a grave mistake for any organization when its members do not have a platform to address conflict through approaches that tackle all of the elements mentioned above. Designing an effective CMS is vital to the success of organizations if their organizational members and leaders wish for their organizations to not only survive but thrive in this rapidly changing era of innovation, progress, and globalization.

A CMS is a cost-effective approach to design if we consider the alternative, which is the cost of unresolved disputes that may ultimately cripple organizations. Georgakopoulos, Storrow, and Coleman (2017) present a detailed chapter on recommendations for designing a CMS with the help of conflict resolution experts who may be instrumental in assisting organizational leaders to integrate conflict resolution approaches that address conflict. They share there are a variety to models to select or draw upon within informal approaches and present a detailed example of mediation as a solid process. The objective of having an established CMS within an organization is that a CMS may provide a formidable platform to address conflict with informal processes before conflict escalates and requires formal conflict resolution interventions. These include costly lawsuits tied to long-drawn-out court proceedings or, even worse yet, aggravates hostile organizational environments that involve workplace violence, harassment, or bullying that may result as consequences of unaddressed conflict or grievances. Aside from the costly and lengthy nature of more formal approaches of litigation and court-connected processes, leveraging risk and the unpredictable outcomes that ensue from following formal approaches can cause significant psychological distress and anxiety, which often results in poor retention or ultimate termination of valuable employees and compromises the health and well-being of members within an organization. A well-designed CMS can save organizational members from the aggravation and costs related to conflict (Georgakopoulos, Storrow, and Coleman, 2017), but also can promote the well-being of members in its organization to avoid elements such as workplace bullying or harassment, to name a few adverse outcomes of not addressing conflict, which is vitally important to the success of organizations (Georgakopoulos and Kelly, 2017).

In the organizational setting, there may be a variety of approaches to tackle conflict. Specifically, mediation and facilitation are both examples of informal dispute resolution processes that can be implemented as exceptional early interventions as primary dispute resolution approaches in the CMS design. If disputes are not addressed or resolved at these informal levels, a CMS should present backups that move toward more formal processes such as arbitration or litigation. Given the unique challenges of conflict, a one size fits all approach to CMS may not be sufficient to tackle conflict, as o(1996) illustrated in their popular and classic dispute system design book. Additional resources to this classic work include several contemporary works in dispute systems design (Rogers, Bordone, Sander, and McEwen, 2019; Amsler, Martinez and Smith, 2020) that are sure to assist dispute systems designers in customizing a CMS that serves as a good match with their respective organizations and clients.

Ultimately an effective CMS should be customized and designed considering that organizations are unique, and conflicts are complex and fluid. For example, mediation applied from different models (Bush and Folger, 2005; Georgakopoulos, 2017; Moore, 2014; Winslade and Monk, 2001) may provide an optimal CMS that addresses conflict in situations that involve a few parties, whereas facilitation (Schwarz, 2017) may be valuable in addressing issues that involve a more significant number of people in groups. A CMS can include a variety of platforms to tackle conflict, which will require addressing the conflict, people, and context within its design.

Systems Thinking in Design

Offering different platforms to address conflict is imperative; moreover, every effective CMS should include a systems approach to impact the broader organization. This approach should address the parts of conflict that reveal its impacts on the whole system and show how conflicts at every level impact the overall organization. Often organizational members do not recognize the impacts of conflicts on the more global system within their organizations. Stroh (2015) presented compelling examples of building understanding and harmony using systems approaches and systems mapping as a conflict resolution approach in groups. Stroh (2015) argued that systems thinking used to solve complex problems can enable people to overcome their problems, but more sustainable and lasting result can be real social change, which is more transformative than merely resolving conflict alone. Stroh (2015) shared that systems thinking addresses change as it: (1) motivates individuals to see their influences and responsibilities in a conflict that exists, (2) allows them to see how collaborations influence the individual, as well as collective behavior, (3) encourages people to focus efforts on specific changes that are impactful and sustainable for the overall system, and (4) promotes learning from our actions and consequences of our actions, so that adapting is a key consequence of our learning. A successful CMS design should be developed with care and should be compatible with the organization (i.e., it should match the people, resources, and needs), and it should be designed with systems thinking at the center.

Design and Options in a CMS

The classic work of Costantino and Merchant (1996) provides solid design principles that are valuable and relevant to develop a solid CMS in current times: 1) the process should take into account the parties' interests, 2) parties should have realistic and cost-effective options, 3) parties should be given backup plans in case the first strategy fails, 4) parties should be informed on the procedure before it is implemented, and they should be debriefed afterward, 5) implemented methods should be ranked from low to high cost, and 6) approaches should be supplemented with incentives, reinforcement, and assistance to ensure that they are used (Costantino & Merchant, 1996). Many of these principles are underscored and reinforced by Rogers, Bordone, Sander, and McEwen (2019), but the authors further stress that design should involve targeted processes surrounding innovation, adaptation, choice, creativity, sequencing, and collaboration. Georgakopoulos, A., Coleman H. J. & Storrow, R. (2017) recommend that after considering organizational members' interests and resources, the designer should educate organizational members about the differences between conflict resolution approaches (e.g., negotiation, facilitation, mediation, arbitration ... etc.) and distinguishing characteristics within each approach so stakeholders are familiar with the processes. They suggest that the next step is for stakeholders who will be directly impacted by a CMS program to contribute and co-create the CMS, so the process involves transparency, cooperation, ownership, and buy-in which should promote sustainability and success of the program for the long term. This approach will require that leaders and managers invite employees to come to the table so they can participate in the process and contribute their ideas for the design. The value of this approach is illustrated by Cloke and Goldsmith (2002), who have argued that an inclusive approach that fosters organizational democracy exceeds expectations and results in positive outcomes.

Contemporary works have extended recommendations for dispute systems design and echoed several elements of the classic work by Costantino and Merchant (1996). For example, solid contemporary resources for dispute systems designers should include at minimum *Designing Systems and Processes for Managing Disputes* by Rogers, Bordone, Sander, and McEwen (2019), *Dispute Systems Design: Preventing, Managing, and Resolving Conflict* by Amsler, Martinez, and Smith (2020) and *The Mediation Handbook: Theory, Research, and Practice* by Georgakopoulos (2017). In combination, these resources will assist professionals with developing and customizing dispute systems designs and implementing approaches within the CMS or what has been called the Dispute Systems Design (DSD).

Along with our recommendation for organizational members to design effective CMS within organizations, addressing diversity, inclusion and equity are at the heart of intentionally building solid, quality working groups within organizations. We now turn our attention to the strength of diverse teams and the natural occurrence of conflict amid diverse work environments to provide a solid rationale for implementing CMS in organizations to address conflict within groups. We will provide recommendations on group processes that may complement organizational members in how they communicate and work with each other in organizations to harness the power of harmony in the workplace.

Facilitating and Managing Diverse Teams

Changing work environments, managing diverse workforces, and operating in agile settings are fertile ground for different organizational conflicts. Conflicts can arise anytime within and between coworkers creating constant challenges to ongoing processes. Different styles of communication and organizational culture can often lead to misunderstandings, disputes, and friction points in teams. Today we are witnessing more workplace conflict that has cultural and diversity threads that can be very challenging. Especially since the Covid-19 pandemic, organizational managers are facing culturally driven and diverse disputes in new digital environments that are complex for which they may be ill-equipped to analyze and resolve. This section will suggest some tips on establishing more inclusive workplace environments both in-person and in remote settings to help managers better navigate conflicts while encouraging a new cultural intelligence and understanding. This skill is particularly important for leaders and managers working in global and virtual teams.

Sir Vangen and Nik Winchester's (2014) "Theory of Collaborative Advantage (TCA)" is extremely useful to apply to understanding cultural dynamics in organizational settings. Sir Vangen and Nik Winchester's (2014) suggest that "culture can be paradoxical and can either help or hinder the success of team collaboration (p. 687)." In essence, managers must understand that collaborations involving members who are culturally diverse come with culturally driven "collaborative advantage" while also opening the door to culturally driven conflict (Vangen & Winchester, 2014, p. 687). Therefore, as Vangen & Winchester (2014) point out, "cultural diversity can have both positive and negative outcomes for collaborative work" (p. 687). Vangen & Winchester (2014) suggest considering a simplified three-stage process when dealing with cultural challenges in organizations which include:
1) Recognition – demonstrate awareness of the cultural friction and diagnose its source, (p. 690).
2) Research – engage in the process of cultural learning through a detailed study of practice and existing models of culture; (p. 690)
3) Reconciliation – put in place practices and structures that address the points of cultural friction (p. 690).

Diversity, Equity, and Inclusion (DEI) Approaches

Sundar Pichai, the CEO of Google on Google's diversity homepage, says *"A diverse mix of voices leads to better discussions, decisions, and outcomes for everyone" (Google, n.d.).* Like many leaders guiding teams today, fostering a collaborative culture in organizations requires the willingness and commitment of leadership to engage in collective conversations addressing the various aspects of DEI approaches. Supporting greater diversity in the workplace is becoming more important than ever for many companies in their efforts in advancing DEI approaches to new laws and require- ments. Nevertheless, Sir Vangen (2017) reminds us to consider that "there will be trade-offs and compromises in the practice of managing communication and shared understanding in culturally diverse collaborations" (p. 306). To engage is inclusivity in the workplace, the individual differences, different cultural backgrounds, abilities, and the opinions of employees need to be accepted which is more challenging task. Below are several conflict resolution approaches that we recommend being housed within your CMS design as informal regular dialogues, discussions, and/or trainings as these may assist in preventing, managing, and/or resolving workplace conflict. For the scope of this chapter, we provide you with important concepts and principles, but encourage organizational members and leaders to shape how these elements will integrated in their CMS design so they are effectively understood at a cognitive level, expressed at a skills level, and most significantly embodied at an intrinsic level with positive affective attitudes. The idea behind these processes and strategies is to address conflict pro-actively rather than reactively and to be intentionally about inclusion and equity in the CMS design to provide transformative experiences where employees improve their relationships as well as the manner in which they interact in culturally diverse environments. We want to underscore that culture can't be parceled apart from conflict thus it should be considered as a vital component that is squarely addressed in the design of a CMS.

Develop Cultural Competence and Cultural Fluency. Cultural competence, like emotional intelligence, is another critical skill for effective work performance. A more extensive definition offered by Dr. Richard T. Alpert is: "Cultural competence ability depends on awareness of one's cultural worldview, knowledge of other cultural prac- tices and worldviews, tolerant attitudes towards cultural differences, and cross-cul- tural skills" (Alpert, 2017, para. 3). Therefore, promoting cultural competence entails understanding how values, norms, and traditions "affect the way a member of a group typically perceives, thinks, interacts, behaves, and makes judgments" (Alpert, 2017, para. 2). Michele LeBaron (2003) urges that today's employees need to develop *cultural fluency* to recognize different communication styles and better understand cultural identities and differences.

Promote cultural self-awareness and diversity knowledge. As workplaces become increasingly diverse and globally connected, employees must learn to examine their cultural blind spots. Cross-cultural expert Nancy Adler (1991) points out that "some people may have *cultural blinders,* especially when may never have left their home culture or been forced to examine their general assumptions" (p. 7). When employ- ees in organizations lack cultural self-awareness, this can be a significant obstacle to conducting business. Adler (1991) further points out that "cross-cultural communica- tion continually involves misunderstandings caused by misperception, misinterpre- tations, and misevaluation" (p. 2). Adler (1991) further argues that the "most difficult skill in cross-cultural communication involves standing back from yourself, or being aware that you do not know everything, that a situation may not make sense, that your guesses may be wrong, and that the ambiguity in the situation may continue" (p. 14).

Address any problems of stereotyping and biases. Adler (2002) also describes in her research on cultural misperceptions and stereotypes that "people from different countries see, interpret, and evaluate things differently and consequently act upon them differently" (p. 77). In addition, cultural expert Anne Murphy Paul argues that we all have unconscious biases and automatic stereotyping of different people (Paul, 1998). So, we must promote cultural diversity to recognize better our emotional triggers and possible seeds of prejudices against others.

Create accountability in the workplace. It is critical to create an organizational culture where employees and project managers take ownership and responsibility for their work. It is important to assess individual, team and organizational readiness to create inclusive environments. Without accountability, this can lead to distrust and a decline in employee morale. Fostering an accountability culture includes taking the initiative, proactive communication, and accepting responsibility for all work phases. When one person does not take accountability for their errors or failures, this can lead to a delay or bottleneck in the workflow. In addition, if a team member is not adhering to their commitments, the whole team can suffer.

Provide a feedback culture. It is recommended to prepare carefully and adopt feedback mechanisms that enable employees to celebrate successes and analyze mistakes in any organization. Certain national cultures and organizations (hierarchical vs. heterarchical) may prefer direct or indirect feedback. Giving feedback should consider cultural sensitivities, but feedback should create more transparency and reduce any inconsistency.

Develop clear communication procedures guidelines and make expectations obvious. Sometimes employees experience difficulties deciding which communication method is the most appropriate to use. A vast majority of internal communication is written in many organizations today using many online communication tools.

Preparing in advance how best to foster meta communication to inclusive conversations is an important initial step. Therefore, it is necessary to standardize and simplify communication procedures and provide guidelines and perhaps even indicate an appropriate response time to streamline expectation management could be helpful. It is essential to provide clear and timely information to ensure effective teamwork and performance.

Create a mixed organizational culture. Although teams are made up of individuals, it is crucial to appreciate work well done for all team players in diverse settings. Organizational productivity relies on working well together and minimizing "silo-workers." Therefore, it is essential to create a working environment characterized by strong communication and interpersonal skills and collaboration and partnership rather than competition and internal rivalry. Effective cross-cultural team building will be required to take advantage of this diversity. Furthermore, exploring where perspectives diverge and creating shared meaning and finding common ground for discussions is critical.

Clarify notions of timing and scheduling. Often people from culturally different backgrounds tend to have different perceptions of the concepts of time. Various views of work or personal time can lead to misunderstandings in the workplace, especially regarding deadlines and project scheduling. It may be necessary to clarify what a deadline means, and the amount of time required to complete a task. To remain agile within organizations, project managers running diverse teams might require having multiple management approaches that use flexible time scheduling, multi-tasking, and adaptability.

It is essential to understand that culturally diverse teams need time to develop and mature. Avoiding workplace conflict entirely is not possible but requires open communication and transparency. Different stakeholders sometimes have competing priorities and perceptions; therefore, it is essential to create a shared vision that discuss these concepts and topics within a CMS across and among team members and departments. Cultural orientations should be considered without making general assumptions, misinterpretations, or false stereotyping. Responding to the entire team with a collaborative approach will render better results and support consensus-building. Using a systems approach, where culture and diversity are situated as significant elements within CMS will likely assist in responding and tackling culturally sensitive conflicts.

If the idea of implementing a formal CMS in your organization is daunting or too costly, we propose integrating dialogic events as an informal and accessible options that can be part of the CMS that redefines and reshapes how organizational members interact and communicate with each other. Henri Lipmanowicz and Keith McCandless developed over 33 Liberating Structures to create minimally structured yet powerfully liberating conversations that can be used in a variety of organizational settings. This section highlights how to bring the practice of shared leadership to life through dialogic events, how we can apply Liberating Structures to address cultural diversity, and we leave the readers with recommendations on how to start.

Leadership Re-Imagined

A new wave of thinking about leadership is emerging. From this perspective, leadership is not viewed as a set of attributes inherent in particularly gifted individuals, but instead, it is seen as a set of practices among those engaged together in realizing their choices (Raelin, 2015). This emerging concept of leadership involves various activities, including inviting the participation of diverse stakeholders, scanning the environment, mobilizing resources, arranging interactions across new networks, and facilitating reflection that offers feedback (p. 95). This approach will be referred to as a shared leadership approach that is brought to life through Liberating Structures.

Organizations are Conversations

As people socially interact, reality and truth are constantly created and recreated through conversations and experiences. A shared leadership approach understands organizations as conversations where people, drawing from their individual experiences, make meaning and construct reality together from their collective and emerging stories, narratives, and discussions. Therefore, to change an organization, you must change the conversations and narratives that occur within them (Ford & Ford, 2008; Shaw, 2002). Suppose your organization is not creating dedicated space and time to conduct inclusive, participative dialogic events on a regular basis. In that case, your organizational reality is deprived of access to vital information and your culture will be bereft of affirming, unifying relational experiences that can change your organization's trajectory.

Using Liberating Structures to design interactions and conversations can reduce barriers by sharing more knowledge and providing opportunities to include diverse people from all parts of the organization in the communication, problem-solving, and decision-making processes (Cloke & Goldsmith, 2002; Tourish, 2005; Stephenson, 2009; Raelin, 2012; Scharmer & Kaufer, 2013). In these environments, people can confront each other supportively, rumors are challenged and there is greater freedom within and responsibility for the organization's success (Lipmanowicz & McCandless, 2013). In addition, as everyone is pulled into these dialogic processes, less time is spent correcting misinformation, resolving conflicts, and doing damage repair from rumors and gossip (Cloke & Goldsmith, 2001).

Learning in Action

Liberating structures are learning in action. The key to building capabilities is doing it instead of sitting in a classroom learning about it. The limitations of a text-based pedagogy to leadership development become clear when leadership development aims to improve skills in practice (Gergen & Hersted, 2016). It is therefore essential to be immersed in actual practices that expose participants to opportunities for dialogic relationships. Every Liberating Structure designs experience with a specific purpose while concurrently building individual capabilities. Liberating Structures are methods of a learn-by-doing approach that enable individuals to develop greater capabilities through participation. Most people understand a workshop here or there is unlikely to change behavior overnight. However, as Liberating Structures are used over a period with consistent application of a set of principles, many of these moments build up to a point where evolved practices and mindsets become embodied (Ledwith & Springett, 2010) and transformational change occurs.

Regularly scheduled dialogic events with thoughtful, intentional design using Liberating Structures build in continuous cycles of action, reflection, and dialogue, in which diverse participants can collectively look back at the action taken and, through dialogic processes, discover together what worked well and what did not. An array of Liberating Structures can be used to design the flow of activities intended to draw out knowledge and insights, expose natural paradoxes of complex situations and provide the opportunity for collective exploration of new and creative ideas moving forward. Quick cycles of action, reflection, and dialogue with an experimental mindset that views failure as a natural part of the learning process build adaptive organizational capacity.

Building a Culture that Values Diversity, Equity, and Inclusion (DEI)

While many organizations espouse the values of diversity, equity, and inclusion, far fewer can put these lofty ideals into practice in a meaningful way that builds individual and organizational capacity. A brief outline of how to start these conversations in your organization follows.

1. Schedule a Dialogic Event. Invite a cross-section of people in your organization to a conversation. The inclusion of diverse people is imperative to walking the talk of DEI.
2. Design the Event with Someone Who Cares. Invite some co-conspirators to the design process, to design the flow of the collaborative conversation using Liberating Structures. Be very clear about the purpose of your meeting. For example, *"The two-fold purpose of this meeting is to elevate our understanding of diversity and inclusion and to strengthen our relationships with each other through meaningful conversations."*
3. Select an Appropriate Venue. Assuming you can meet in person, choose a location in which people can move around freely with no tables or other obstructions that hinder the flow of face-to-face interaction. Understanding that most meetings are held virtually, these collaborations are entirely possible with Zoom and break-out rooms.
4. Hold the Event. One great option is to start with Impromptu Networking! This is a stand-up, quick-moving face-to-face conversation between two people who have approximately 90 seconds each to share and 90 seconds to listen to a prompt. Some questions that might be asked include:
   - *"Think of a time when you felt completely accepted, comfortable and safe. What conditions made that possible? Please find someone whom you know the least and share your story and listen to theirs."*
   - *"Think of a time when you did not feel seen, heard, or respected. Share your story with someone and hear their story."*

5. Debrief each conversation. Reflection and dialogue are vital to coalescing collective understanding. There are many Liberating Structures you could use to do this, and one of the most easy-to-use and effective is 1-2-4-All. An open question as simple as, *"What stood out to you from your conversations?"* is a powerful way to elicit thoughtful responses that produce an expanded shared understanding. This Liberating Structure gives approximately 30–60 seconds for quiet individual reflection, then structures two minutes for a conversation between two people to share and listen, then structures four minutes for a conversation between four people to share and listen to each other and finally asks a spokesperson of a few of the groups to share insights with everyone.

6. Probe deeper with other Liberating Structures. Nine Whys is a relevant and meaningful Liberating Structure to go deeper. One possible question to start the conversation is, *"Why is it important that your unique attributes, traits, characteristics, skills, experience, and background are valued at work?"* Nine Whys pairs two people (dyads) in this conversation as each person is given approximately five minutes to answer this question, *" … and why is that important to you?"* asked by the partner to explore the underlying reasons to the initial question. The idea is to keep asking the why to get to the core reason. These conversations allow people to think out loud with another about what is truly important about the question. No small talk here! Again, debriefing this conversation collectively is an enlightening and unifying process.

7. Debrief the Event Itself. This essential part of the learning and adaptive organization is most often neglected, yet this is where the transformational change happens. A great Liberating Structure to use for this is an adapted version of Wise Crowds in which the participants are divided into small groups to address three questions collectively: 1) *"What part of today's meeting went particularly well?"*, 2) *"What part of today's meeting didn't work or was a thud?"*, and 3) *"What would you like to see differently at our next gathering? Do you want to help design it?"* The groups are then asked to share the insights gleaned from their conversations with leadership or the facilitator.

The questions provided in this brief outline are just examples, and the specific questions you use should intentionally serve your purpose. The idea in this section is to simply get started and trust the inclusive, participative processes that Liberating Structures unleash. Expertise is not required, only the optimistic intention to try something new. We encourage you to jump right in! We are confident you will be glad you did.

In summary, this last section described a more democratic and progressive idea of leadership as a practice and something that emerges when diverse people come together and engage in dialogue. A cultural and organizational transformation is made possible by including people from all parts of the organization to participate in dialogic events where they listen to others and contribute to the collective narrative.

Regularly scheduled dialogic events conducted with Liberating Structures have the power to open people's minds to its undeniable benefits. When time and space are made for listening, learning, and sharing, a collective narrative takes shape as people understand the bigger picture of what is going on in the organization. As people's understanding of their colleagues' work and experience evolves – what they do, as well as their successes and challenges – empathy and understanding are elevated.

Additionally, as people are invited to share their unique insights, a very strong cultural message is conveyed that they are valued by leadership. With this cultural shift that evolves over time, problems become much easier to identify, curiosity is amplified, generative ideas flow more easily, sustainable solutions are surfaced, and stronger bonds and trust between people are realized. When people from all parts of the organization are invited to talk to each other by design, silos get smashed, and one-way communication is obliterated. When undiscussables are made safe to talk about, there is little need for gossip and hearsay to fill in the blanks of corporate silence. When people from all departments and different levels in the organization are given time to engage in meaningful dialogue, the array of diverse ideas is exponentially expanded, paving the way for creative and innovative solutions to previously unsolvable challenges. As people experience the transformative power of Liberating Structures, they will likely continue to desire this form and style of interacting and communicating with members in their workplace. Expect people to step up and offer to experiment with Liberating Structures. In this way, people become self-organizing and self-correcting.

Conclusion

This chapter looked at organizational processes as essential systems for addressing conflict and ultimately creating a more unified and harmonious workplace. This chapter was divided into three parts: 1) first, we began with a discussion that recommended organizational members to design Conflict Management Systems while we discussed the benefits of implementing a design that addresses conflict prevention, management, and resolution in organizations, 2) next, we provided an overview of elements of culture, diversity, and conflict that members in organizations should intentionally address to be pro-active within the workplace, 3) finally we recommended Liberating Structures as a shared leadership practice to informally approach a CMS in the way of dialogue and problem-solving among members in the workplace.

If you are a leader in your organization with the authority to institute a formal Conflict Management System, we encourage you to have conversations with your employees and learn what would help them address conflicts that occur in the organization. Too often, we prematurely assume what people might need or want without directly asking stakeholders. Ownership, participatory decision making, and consensus are keys to successfully addressing conflict in contemporary organizations. We recommend holding one-on-one conversations, conducting focus groups, developing anonymous online surveys, asking direct supervisors, and/or developing a creative way to gather information. If you are an employee and find the topics we have discussed compelling, invite a discussion with your broader group and uppers to address dispute resolution processes, inclusion, and leadership approaches. This rich data will give organizational members a solid foundation to inform the systems that may be valuable in tackling conflict, supporting inclusion, and implementing shared leadership. Most transformational and innovative changes in organizations occur when people at all levels are invited to the table as these creative discussions can lead to vision formulation and ultimately to action implementation. These transformative changes are not idealistic when they are possible, so it is important to recognize that people have agency to shape their organizations and organizations in turn will shape people in how they address conflict.

References

Adler, N. J. (2002). *International dimensions of organizational behavior.* 4th edition. Cincinnati.

Adler, N. J. (1991). Communicating across cultures. Retrieved from: http://citeseerx.ist.psu.edu/viewdoc/download?doi=10.1.1.680.3385&rep=rep1&type=pdf

Alpert, R. (2017). Cultural diversity in the workplace, part 1. 4 Essential Skills. *Diversity Resources.* Posted: Thursday, 14 December 2017. Retrieved from http://www.diversityresources.com/cultural-diversity-workplace

Amsler, L., Martinez, J., and Smith, S. (2020). *Dispute Systems Design: Preventing, Managing, and Resolving Conflict.* Stanford, California: Stanford University Press.

Bush, R. A. B., & Folger, J. P. (2005). *The promise of mediation: The transformative approach to conflict.* San Francisco: Jossey-Bass.

Cloke, K. (2001). *Mediating dangerously, the frontiers of conflict resolution.* San Francisco, California, United States of America: Jossey-Bass.

Cloke, K., & Goldsmith, J. (2002). *The end of management and the rise of organizational democracy.* San Francisco, California, United States of America: Jossey-Bass.

Costantino, C., & Merchant, C. (1996). *Designing conflict management systems: A guide to creating productive and healthy organizations.* San Francisco, California: Jossey-Bass, A Wiley Company.

Ford, J. D., & Ford, L. W. (2008). Conversational profiles: A tool for altering the conversational pattern of change managers. *Journal of Applied Behavioral Science, 44,* 445–467.

Gergen, K. J., & Hersted, L. (2016). Developing leadership as a dialogic practice. In J. A. Raelin, *Leadership as practice: theory and application.* New York City, New York, United States of America: Routledge.

Georgakopoulos, A. (Ed.). (2017). *The mediation handbook: Research, theory, and practice.* New York, NY: Routledge; Taylor & Francis.

Georgakopoulos, A. & Allen, B. (2020). In pursuit of harmony: How a shared leadership practice works as a conflict management system. Chapter in T. Belak & L. Cook (Eds.). Chapter in *From Discord to Harmony: Making the Workplace Hum.* Information Age Publishing Inc. New York: New York.

Georgakopoulos, A., Coleman H. J. & Storrow, R. (2017). Organizational conflict management systems: The emergence of mediators as conflict resolution professionals. Chapter in Georgakopoulos, A. (Ed.). *The Mediation Handbook: Theory, research, and practice* (pp. 153–163). New York: Routledge Publishing.

Georgakopoulos, A., & Kelly, M. (2017). Tackling workplace bullying: A scholarship of engagement study of workplace wellness as a system. *International Journal of Workplace Health Management*, 10(6) pp.450–474.

Google. (n.d.). Diversity, Equity, & Inclusion. https://diversity.google/Hansen, T. (2021). Harnessing conflict's potential: Turning lighting into light. Published by Toran Hansen, U.S.

LeBaron, M. (2003). Culture and conflict. In Guy and Heidi Burgess (Eds). *Beyond Intractability*. Conflict Information Consortium, University of Colorado, Boulder. Posted: July 2003. Retrieved from http://www.beyondintractability.org/essay/culture-conflict.

Ledwith, M., & Springett, J. (2010). *Participatory practice: Community-based action for transformative change*. Bristol, United Kingdom: The Policy Press.

Lipmanowicz, H., & McCandless, K. (2013). *The surprising power of liberating structures: simple rules to unleash a culture of innovation*. Seattle, Washington, United States of America: Liberating Structures Press.

Moore, C. W. (2014). *The mediation process: Practical strategies for resolving conflicts* (4th ed.). San Francisco: Jossey-Bass.

Paul, A. M. (1998). "Where Bias Begins: The Truth About Stereotypes." *Psychology Today*. Posted: May 1, 1998. Retrieved from https://www.psychologytoday.com/us/articles/199805/where-bias-begins-the-truth-about-stereotypes

Raelin, J. A. (2012). Dialogue and deliberation as expressions of democratic leadership in participatory organizational change. *Journal of Organizational Change Mangement*, 25(1), 7–23.

Raelin, J. A. (2015, Summer). Rethinking leadership. *MIT Sloan Management Review*, 56(4).

Rogers, N., Bordone,R., Sander,F., and McEwen, C. (2019). *Designing Systems and Processes for Managing Disputes*. New York: Wolters Kluwer.

Scharmer, O., & Kaufer, K. (2013). *Leading from the emerging future*. San Francisco, California, United States of America: Berrett-Koehler Publishers, Inc.

Shaw, P. (2002). *Changing conversations in organizations*. London, United Kingdom: Routledge.

Stephenson, K. (2009). Neither hierarchy nor network: An argument for heterarchy. *People and Strategy*, 32(1), 4.

Stoh, D. P. (2015). *Systems thinking for social change: A Practical guide to soliving complex problems, avoding unintended consequesnces, and achieving lasting results*. White River Junction: Chelsea Green Publishing.

Tourish, D. (2005). Critical upward communication. *Long Range Planning*, 38, 485–503.

Vangen, S. (2017). Culturally diverse collaborations: A focus on communication and shared understanding. *Public Management Review*, 19(3), 305–325.

Vangen, S., & Winchester, N. (2014). Managing cultural diversity in collaborations: A focus on management tensions. *Public Management Review*, 16(5), 686–707.

Winslade J. & Monk G. (2001). *Narrative mediation: A new approach to conflict resolution*. San Francisco: Jossey-Bass.

Hyacinth Guy

Chapter 18
Coaching and Organisational Development: Lessons and Themes from 360 Degree Feedback

Abstract: The purpose of this chapter is to share the themes that emerged and lessons learnt from a coaching practice that has spanned fifteen years with several organisations. This practice informed a coaching typology that was applied to individuals after they completed a 360-degree feedback assessment. This chapter examines that model to ascertain whether the themes and lessons learnt extend the empirical database of coaching found in the literature. The first section gives an overview of various coaching methods described in the literature and their applicability. Next, I provide a brief historical review of my coaching practice leading up to the coaching sessions conducted in two medium sized organisations (four hundred – five hundred employees) with the leaders, managers and supervisors following a 360-degree assessment. Then, I discuss the model used, how it was applied, the themes emanating from it, where they are similar and where they vary from what is seen in the literature. Finally, I draw some conclusions and recommendations from the review.

Keywords: conflict coaching, 360-degree assessment, executive coaching; facilitation, human resource management

In my first role as a senior Human Resource Management (HRM) practitioner in the 1990s I began working with leaders, managers, and supervisors who called on the Human Resource (HR) department to help them work through performance issues they were having with staff members, or to deal with other issues that typically came under the purview of an HRM department. This role also included meeting with managers and their teams during the annual performance management process to help them set goals and key performance indicators for members of the team. It became clear to me from facilitating these sessions that many managers and persons who led teams and supervised staff, experienced great difficulty in carrying out the people management part of their jobs and their default mode was to call on the HR department to do this in their stead. I was very much aware of when my role evolved into meeting with individual managers to hold discussions on the people management aspect of their role and give guidance on how they could be more effective in that area.

I did not label it such at the time, but these early meetings were really coaching sessions with the managers. To become better at facilitating these meetings and helping managers become more effective, I pursued education, training, and certi-

https://doi.org/10.1515/9783110746365-018

fication programs that I thought would build my competencies in the area. In 2017, after leaving the corporate world, I established an HRM Consultancy with coaching, primarily for individuals, as a key offering. By that time, I was a certified LifeSuccess coach and a certified Wellness Coach. I noted though, that my approach to coaching as an internal HR practitioner had to be modified when I practiced as a consultant and external coach. In the latter situation, I did not know the persons who came to me for coaching; they were either organisation or self-referred, so discovery sessions became a key component of the coaching approach. This allowed for the client and me, the coach to build a rapport and to decide if in fact they wish to work together.

I also discovered that there were two things a client had to know to achieve success in an identified area in their life; one was where the person was presently, and the other was where did the person want to go. So, developing self-awareness in the client and setting clear goals had to be bigger components of the coaching approach than when I practiced coaching internally. Further modifications to the coaching approach for individuals were made when I began coaching individuals following 360-degree feedback assessments. The dilemma here was that the clients were being coached as individuals on the results of a 360-degree assessment; but the aims of the coaching included not only developing individual capabilities but also to support strategic organisational objectives. So, some team coaching had to be included in the coaching method utilized after 360-degree assessments and this had to be done while maintaining the confidentiality and integrity issues that were the foundation of the coaching relationship.

I completed coaching sessions with clients in one organisation and along the way I learnt what worked well and what needed to be modified both in a general way applicable to any client being coached after a 360-degree assessment, and in a specific way, to meet the need of the present client. Fundamental to this coaching approach were self-awareness, goal setting and achieving, conflict and communication coaching and understanding how people and organisations change (neuroscience).

The review is a form of action research in that as the 'researcher' I collaborated with the individuals being coached to diagnose individual problems and used information of which I was aware by virtue of interacting with all team members, to work with the individual to have him/her develop a solution to either resolve a problem, deal with an issue or conflict, develop new behaviors or to change a belief system or paradigm that no longer served them. Action research is defined as, "inquiry that is done by or with insiders to an organisation or community but never to or on them" (Herr & Anderson, 2005). The results are specific to the organisations involved; however, it is hoped that the framework used and the themes emerging resonate with other practitioners and consultants who may find applicability in similar organisational settings.

Coaching as a Profession

Grant and Cavanagh (2004) examined the maturation of the coaching industry over the years since the first published peer-reviewed paper in 1937 by C.B. Gorby. Between 1937 and 1994, they observed that only fifty papers or PhD dissertations were cited in the databases, however this number increased exponentially over the period 1995 to 2003. That period saw two significant developments in coaching; one was the advent of coaching as part of the role of the HRM practitioner and the other the emergence of professional external coaches to deal with interpersonal issues in organisations. One noticeable trend from the 1990's was the use of coaching to understand human change processes, and yet another was the emergence of coaching as an identifiable industry.

Walker (2004) reviewed the historical development of coaching noting the difficulties in obtaining information that can be considered accurate. He placed coaching as emerging around 1980 as part of the therapeutic field or personal development field, adding that as a burgeoning industry, there was need for supervision and accreditation.

Jackson (2005) looked at the definitions and approaches to coaching. In his study he sought to create coaching typologies and approaches used by UK-based practitioners to form a basis for comparative and evaluative research. He found that definitions varied and reflected the characteristics of the coaching approach utilized. This statement was made by Jackson (2005) in his paper, "How do we describe coaching . . . . ." Jackson referenced Zeus and Skiffington in his paper. May I suggest that the line read: "He stated that he could find no general typologies of coaching in the literature although Zeus and Skiffington in their 2000 paper identified three types: . . ." life skills coaching, business coaching and executive coaching. Jackson concluded that definitions "do not adequately support the processes of evaluation and research demanded by the needs of the marketplace and of an evidence-based discipline" (2005, p. 14).

Yves (2008) acknowledged the problem of inconsistent definitions in the field but noted that the discipline was benefitting from, "an infusion of ideas from diverse fields" (pg. 101). He reviewed the literature and attempted a typology, finding nine approaches and distinguishing between goal-oriented approaches and therapeutic approaches. While acknowledging variations, he argued that goal-oriented approaches had a different perspective from therapeutic perspectives in that they were strictly non-directive, solution-focused and performance-driven.

A common theme emerging from the writings above is that the industry seemed to lack some of the basic requirements to make it a true profession, notably, the low barriers to entry, not having a shared common body of knowledge and insufficient academic research. This opens the door for more evidence-based research and empirically tested models to address the variability in the definitions and the typology gap.

There are several organisations across the world that seek to provide accreditation and build the profession. The International Coaching Federation (ICF) established in 1995 is the largest such organisation. It has been seeking to fill the gaps identified by accrediting and credentialing coaches and programs and in June 2021 collaborated with McLean Hospital, a Harvard Medical School affiliate through the latter's Institute of Coaching, to support research that would enhance the quality, efficacy, and impact of the coaching field. (IOC, 2021). The ICF has a code of ethics for its members and defines coaching as "partnering with clients in a thought-provoking and creative process that inspires them to maximize their personal and professional potential" (ICF, 2022). However, there is no requirement for anyone aspiring to be a coach to become certified and the industry today continues to have low barriers to entry and to be beset by the lack of a clear typology.

There is, however, sufficient evidence for any practitioner to acknowledge that organizations have embraced the practice of coaching to grow their human capital and advance their goals and mission (DiGirolamo & Tkach, 2019). The writers mentioned herein were commissioned by the ICF to measure the impact of coaching on management employee relations. Their analyses pointed in the direction of a clear relationship between the use of coaching skills and the working relationship of the manager or leader and their team member with 85% of those who were in a coaching relationship saying that coaching did impact their performance and professions positively.

Coaching is distinct from counseling, teaching, or instructing. It is not a step or technique in a progressive discipline system, but more a process of guiding the person being coached from one level of competency to another (SHRM, 2022). This definition resonates with me as I have seen evidence of this in my coaching practice. A competency is a demonstrated and observable ability, skill, knowledge, and trait required for successful job performance. It is a combination of what one knows and how one does it. When people become aware of their competencies and how these are linked to their results, they become motivated to develop new competencies that can give them results in areas they are not getting the desired results. This leads them to reflect on their values and beliefs and to examine if there are any belief systems that are preventing them from developing the competencies they need to develop to achieve new results. In a coaching arrangement, they can become motivated to change and so choose to develop the competencies they need to set and achieve goals, resolve conflicts, and build better relationships. In short, the coaching facilitates a new level of self-awareness, and a new level of thinking which translates into behaviors.

Coaching used to be reserved for senior managers and executives but is now common practice and increasingly being made available to persons throughout the organisation. Organizations are realizing that incorporating the principles of leadership coaching into their talent development practices is a viable lever in developing and retaining talent and helping leaders work through issues that have the potential to put their own careers and the organisation at risk (Innis & Otto, 2015). The writers here identified sixteen types of coaching; some of these are executive, career, group, peer, performance, and coaching for 360-degree debriefing. They distinguish executive coaching from the other types in that it always involves a partnership among the executive, the coach and the organisation and there must be line of sight between the goals of the executive and the goals of the organisation. They also recognize three levels of learning in executive coaching: i. the tactical problem-solving level, ii. developing leadership capabilities, that is, new ways of thinking and acting that can be applied to other situations and roles and iii. developing skills and habits of self-reflection that sustain the new behaviors.

Conflict coaching was not one of the sixteen types of coaching identified by Innis and Otto of the Executive Coaching Forum; nor was it identified by Ives in his attempt to identify the approaches to coaching. Conflict coaching, also known as conflict management coaching, emerged in the 1990's to help persons manage their disputes independently or to strengthen their conflict competence in general (Noble, 2012). It is a specialized niche in the field of coaching and conflict management and is a process in which a trained coach assists a person to effectively manage their interpersonal disputes and enhance their conflict management skills. The technique may also be used to coach people to participate in mediation, negotiation, and relational conflicts more confidently. Noble sees leadership coaching as a necessary effort on the part organisations to strengthen leaders' conflict management skills. She states that this is particularly so in the light of research information at the time pointing to 43% of CEO's who believed that conflict management was the biggest area of concern for them and a development opportunity for their leaders. Noble's conflict coaching model was developed in 1999 in response to the fact that workplace and interpersonal disputes were not always about issues but more about the interaction between and among people. She identified that current alternative disputes resolution methods did not provide for one-on-one work for people who wanted to manage their disputes independently and develop skill and confidence in doing so. As a practitioner of conflict analysis and resolution, this approach resonates with me. I have not called it coaching but have trained managers, leaders, students and employees in conflict analysis and resolution for many years. The main issue in conflict coaching is what Noble refers to as the 'merry-go-round' pattern of thinking where clients keep coming back to their habitual ways of dealing with conflict. In my coaching practice, I see this as a lack of understanding of the different conflict styles and a reluctance to shift from one style to another as the need arises.

Hardy (2022) also an advocate of conflict coaching, looked at issues of unresolved conflict and how people constructed their stories and the meanings they put to them. She stated that conflict stories are typically based on incomplete information and plenty assumptions and structured around a common kind of primary story that limits our understanding and possible responses to the situation. Hardy worked with clients in conflict to coach them through the complexity of their situation and help them find a balance between being optimistic and realistic. She identified two genres of conflict coaching, that of melodrama involving injustice and suffering and tragedy, involving learning and growth. Hardy's approach although relatable, deals with specific ways people relay their stories and she has developed a technique or framework to work with them through the conflict.

In my coaching practice with leaders and managers after a 360-degree assessment, conflict issues are often raised, and many times are at the heart of an employee's workplace experience. These are generally unresolved conflicts, some of which have remained latent and some which have escalated to full blown disputes; either way the person feels some level of trauma. My observation is that while there was always a conflict story, a key issue to be resolved was the inability of the person to adjust their conflict style or their communication style, see the issue through different lens and then approach it, with a different mindset. Often, they are not aware of the different styles of conflict and where their style fits and the fact that no judgement is placed on the different styles. I was able to appreciate this as I was positioned to hear multiple stories from multiple persons on the same issues and armed with an understanding of the organisation objectives, I took a systems view of the organisation and guided a shift in the mindset of the individual encouraging them to explore different approaches for 'showing up'. It is interesting how people resist change; but when told to simply show up differently, based on new knowledge, they show willingness to try. This made a big difference in how their viewed and dealt with the conflict and is akin to what Hardy described as having a growth, rather than a fixed mindset. The individual is guided to adopt a new mindset through insightful questions, introspection, creating a safe space and encouraging self-determination and empowerment.

In this regard, the work of Rock and Page is instructive. They write when clients come to coaches they want help in effecting changes. These changes are not physical as one might change one's hairstyle but are changes geared at optimizing unrealized potential. Coaches therefore are psychosocial change agents, and the writers claim that contemporary neuroscience is beginning to provide a scientific platform to support the practice of coaching. The coach asks questions that bring the person face to face with him or herself; questions like, who are you and what do you want to do. Only when one knows where one is, can one then begin to move in the direction of where one wants to be. Noble touches on this in her book. She noted as an interdisciplinary field coaching was learning much from other fields and much has been learnt from the advances in research relating to the brain and how neural activity impacts emotions, decisions, and creativity. Having been trained in neuroscience and how the mind and brain works, I have introduced these concepts into my training approach with some success.

The review of the coaching literature must include for the purpose of this paper a brief overview of the 360-degree assessment process. Taylor (2011) describes the 360-degree feedback process as a great tool for giving managers clear feedback from their peers, employees, and direct supervisors. Unlike traditional performance appraisal, where the performance of an employee is assessed and evaluated by his or her direct supervisor only, the 360-degree assessment is a multi-rater approach to assessing performance. Ratings come from one's peers, employees, managers and sometimes, customers external to the organisation. The individual also assess himself or herself. The significant benefit in a 360-degree assessment is the post-assessment briefing and subsequent coaching to address issues. Hence, the 360-degree assessment is not a coaching approach, style, or type, but is a pre-cursor to coaching and personal and organisational development. It thus makes coaching very targeted to areas identified for development. My observation though, is that coaching following a 360-degree assessment, is never only about the areas for development identified in the assessment and a coaching recipe cannot be universally applied with the hope of achieving success or making significant change in individual and organizational performance. The coaching undertaken following a 360-degree assessment, allows the coach to have an insight into the person being coached, a holistic and systems view of the organisation, and as Innis and Otto said, helps leaders to see both "the forest and the trees".

The question can be asked, why cannot a leader or manager not simply ask peers, managers, employees, and others for feedback. The answer according to (Lloyd, 2009) is that most leaders do not ask for feedback and even if they asked and got it, feedback may not be as candid or comprehensive as it should be. I would add that feedback obtained this way would be unstructured and not be able to be compared to the behaviors required in the competencies being assessed. Hence, one may not be able to rely on the results and use these for proper decision making. The 360-degree feedback therefore is a safe way to get open and honest feedback on performance data from multiple raters across a broad spectrum of leadership competencies and behaviors. It also reduces the emotional and political barriers that people feel when providing feedback face-to-face to a boss or peer (Lloyd, 2009). A 360-degree assessment allows managers to compare the way they see themselves, with how others see them, facilitates dialogue between the individual and various raters, provides opportunities for personal development and most of all, provides increased self-awareness and motivation for personal development. It therefore is an ideal starting point for a coaching relationship.

Edelstein and Hanley (2005) describe the 360-degree review as a way for executives to get information today that possibly may have come to them some point in the future. This is usually when a characteristic or problematic behavior has reached a point where it may no longer be tolerated. A point well made in this article is that executives working in flattened organisations cannot rely on position power to get work done. Specific competencies aligned with the core values of the organisation and the role are needed to be demonstrated if a leader is to be effective. These competencies, such as persuasion skills, influencing skills, working collaboratively with others, can only be properly evaluated with feedback. They add that while the assessment reflects past management behavior, the benefits of it would only be realized through feedback and helping the executive expand his or her management behavior. This in short, is where coaching has the potential to deliver on improving individual and organisational effectiveness.

Thought must also be given to how coaching is measured and when it can be said to be successful. Johnson (2021)identifies some areas for measurement to include participation and satisfaction rates from the coaching, retention rates, business results over time, and observing the themes arising from the coaching and assessing how they feed into other organisational initiatives. For example, a coaching theme may be whether there is a correlation between the existing development programs and the actual development needs a coach observes.

Green (2002) stressed the importance of structured follow-up following a 360-degree assessment. He collected fifty-nine survey responses from nineteen observers in five large companies who had undertaken a 360-degree feedback the previous year. The results of the assessments gave the organisations a basis for seeking behavior change and in the follow up survey that was done one year later, participants reported that the feedback gave them a set of tools to work with and qualitative evidence of long-lasting benefit. Green found that the structured interventions leading to the benefit felt included higher attendance at development workshops, more self-study initiatives, increased team discussions and working with executive coaches.

This brief but succinct review of the literature on coaching shows that while the coaching field is evolving and maturing, the door continues to be open for coaches to infuse it with evidence from coaching-specific research, their own expertise and client responses. Stober, Wildflower, and Drake (2006) see the emerging profession of coaching as having the opportunity to promote the development of complementary research methods that will give practitioners useful evidence to draw on in their practices. The literature on 360-degree feedback also shows that they are mostly effective when combined with coaching programs focusing on self-awareness and behavioral change. The next sections in this paper will look at how my coaching practice evolved, the scope of the 360-degree feedback coaching I undertook in two organisations and the themes and lessons learnt from them.

From Facilitating to Coaching

I indicated in the introduction of this paper that my foray into coaching began in my role as a Human Resource Practitioner in one organisation. That role spanned developing and implementing human resource programs and managing the employee and industrial relations function. It required me to intervene and sometimes resolve issues and conflicts between managers and employees, managers and managers, managers and their supervisors and managers and employee representatives (trade unions). The role also called for working with natural teams in setting goals and objectives and with cross functional teams in planning and executing special projects for the organisation. I quickly learnt in this role that many persons in managerial roles did not have the required competencies to manage and lead and it was very difficult to get them to change behavior or try new approaches. My early attempts at coaching, which are probably better described as facilitating, created frustrations for me as I was not self-aware enough to see that I was projecting what I knew or thought I knew on other people, and expecting them, armed with that knowledge, to do what I wanted them to do.

As an example, in my early dealings with employee representatives during collective bargaining negotiations, while working under the tutelage of a senior executive, I could not understand the trade union's insistence that employees be given a pay increase in the face of an industry which was plagued by intense competition and in which the organisation was incurring losses. So, there was a desire to understand how people and organisations change beliefs and culture; in short how to connect with people. Grant and Cavanagh wrote about a phase or thrust of the literature on coaching where coaching was used as a real-life experimental methodology to understand human change (2004). In my situation it was clear that simply telling another party facts about a situation was not enough to move them to embrace my position on the issue and I wanted to understand the dynamics of that relationship and how both needs could be met.

This led me to undertake programs aimed at understanding human behavior particularly in the context of an organisation and the workplace. My study of conflict analysis and resolution was a significant contribution to building competencies in the area and I was particularly impressed with the courses on facilitation, mediation, negotiation, and communication. These spoke directly to how to engage stakeholders on matters pertaining to improving personal and organisational performance. Facilitation taught how to engage stakeholders in a change process, communication gave the language and tools to deliver the message and mediation, and negotiation laid out options to keep the communication channels open and work through organisation issues and conflicts.

I did my first formal coaching program in 2006. It was a LifeSuccess Coaching program in which I was trained to work with persons and help them to set and achieve goals, make decisions overcome fear and develop persistence. I introduced these principles into the human resource training function as personal development programs with some success. I also applied the principles when working with managers who needed assistance in dealing with employee issues, managing grievances, and dealing with conflict. This was a goal-oriented approach to coaching, but it had a humanist and behavioral perspective in that it espoused changing one's thinking to change one's results. I, however, only began to practice this aspect of coaching when I left the corporate world and after studying neuroscience was able to present this to clients in a manner that helped them understand the science behind changing mindsets and thinking.

The coaching practice evolved mainly with coaching individual executives, business owners, entrepreneurs, managers, and other persons who wanted to improve individual effectiveness, shift a behavioral pattern that they felt was not working for them or to build specific competencies in their roles. I coached one female senior executive in a large industrial organisation for a year. She came to me upon referral and in our discovery session, a session which is done prior to the coaching engagement to build rapport with the client and to both decide if we would work together, she indicated she wanted to feel empowered to participate in executive meetings and contribute in a meaningful manner at that level. While she was technically competent and valued for her knowledge and skills, she felt stressed about not being a significant contributor to the business and strategy outside of her field and she wanted to step up to that level. It was in this coaching relationship that I realized the value and importance of spending sufficient time with a client on self-awareness. In these early sessions, discussions are on life purpose, what she loved doing, what she wanted for herself and what were her core values and beliefs. In these early sessions this became more important than discussing prescriptions that would make her more effective at the executive level. We noted that she was also experiencing challenges with a subordinate staff who was not performing at an acceptable level and an ongoing conflict with a peer. We invested much time in self-discovery and I only moved on when I sensed, and she articulated that she was ready. When we did move on to discuss those issues and the other principles usually covered in the coaching program, she was armed with some increased level of self-confidence and ready to 'show up' differently and break through what she now knows to be self-imposed barriers to dealing with the issues before her.

In many of the coaching engagements I had, conflict issues were at the heart of them. On average, about 55% of the clients came to me on their own while the rest were sent by their organisations to be coached. Yet, almost all clients, had some current conflict issue in the workplace, either with a peer, a manager, or an employee. I found though, unlike Hardy, who approached the conflict by having the stories told, that the issue to be addressed was not so much how to resolve the conflict, but how to get the client to 'show up' with a different style. Clients did not understand that they had a conflict style, which influenced their communication style, or even that there were other valid conflict styles that can be demonstrated depending on the situation. One client, in response to my suggestion to show up with a collaborative style and not her natural competitive style, asked if I wanted her to pretend. I answered, 'yes' for this purpose, and that she should pretend until showing up with a different style came natural to her. Her fixed mindset about how interpersonal relationships should unfold stood in the way of allowing her to make connections at an emotional level with her peers, managers, The lesson here for me was that once new knowledge is gained, and there is a will to change, the change only comes if the client takes the first step and repeats this step until the step becomes natural to the client. Neuroscience principles help explain how new neural pathways are developed to help the client align the will to change with the actual action of changing. Repetition, then is the key to change.

This pointed me in the direction of focusing on a concept learnt in coaching which was to get the client to examine the core values and belief systems which governed the behavior and shift from a fixed to a growth mindset. The LifeSuccess coaching program teaches that as human beings we react to stimuli from our five physical senses, (what we see, hear, taste, feel and smell) and this triggers a fight or flight reaction. To shift from a fight or flight reaction to what Noble calls reflection and which I call, response, one must engage other areas of the brain and utilize intellectual faculties such as our imagination, will, intuition, memory, perception, and ability to reason to critically assess the stimuli, suppress the immediate response and then show up with a reasoned response. Techniques such as deep breathing and counting to ten after the stimuli also work in that they help to slow down to flight/fight immediate reaction, which happens in the amygdala and shift it to the pre-frontal cortex of the brain, which helps produce a more reasoned response. I tell clients, shift from reacting to responding. I then take them through a process of examining their core beliefs and values which triggered the reaction in the first place.

I had a client in a financial organisation who saw that one member of staff she supervised frequently went into the office of her manager. She said to me that she was sure they were having conversations about her because after these meetings between the subordinate and the manager, the latter would take up some issue with her which related to how she was managing the office. She, the client, saw something (the stimuli) and put a meaning to it; a meaning which was aligned with her own core values and beliefs. In our coaching sessions I asked her to think broadly about the situation, examine other possible explanations for those meetings and use her other thinking capacities such as her reasoning skills, to analyze the situation and determine if her response was the only possible one in the situation. She was guided to see that even if the situation was as she imagined it to be, she could still formulate a reasoned response and raise the issue with her manager. The lesson here for me was that clients tend to see issues through their own lens; those lenses may be tinted with their core values and beliefs which in some instances work for them and in others work against them. The client will know the difference when he/she looks at the results in a particular area of life; personal, professional, social, education, business for example. Knowing the difference and guiding clients to examine their core values and beliefs and the mindset they have in different situations, is a way to release them from a cycle of wanting different results but behaving in the same manner. This coaching is undertaken carefully, guiding the client towards what a growth mindset looks like, using as Hardy says, insightful questions and introspection. The goal is to help them think better rather than to tell them what to do (Rock, 2006).

So, while there was a general coaching framework utilized in my coaching program, this framework was more fluid than fixed and it evolved based on client needs for self-determination, respect and courtesy, boundaries, and a space to fulfil potential.

The 360-Degree Feedback Experience

Over the past five years, since 2017, I had the opportunity to work with many organisations and undertake coaching with their leaders and managers who were referred to me. In two organisations, I undertook coaching with leaders, managers, and other key personnel, following the administration of a 360-degree feedback assessment.

These were mid-sized organisations 400–500 staff members in key areas of industry in Trinidad and Tobago. I found that in my approach to coaching persons after a 360-degree assessment, I had to rethink the principles, framework, and activities that I undertook when coaching individuals who had not undergone a 360-degree feedback. In one organisation, the assessment was done on the full 12-member executive team and in the other the assessment was done on fifty-nine employees spanning, the executive team, senior managers, middle managers, and other professional level staff. I had to consider, how do I coach individually, persons who are also members of a natural team, all of whom would be guided to be open on the issues they were facing in the organisation which would have informed the results of the assessments. This opening up would surely lead me to discover areas about one person from another; and I would still have to ensure confidentiality and integrity are maintained. How would I approach it so that I address the three levels of learning, i. problem solving, ii. shifting from ways of acting and thinking that did not bring desired results and iii. learning how to be change adaptable?

While the lessons learnt from individual coaching were instructive there were more adjustments to be made and more to learn from coaching individuals post 360-degree feedback assessments. I would first outline the 360-degree process generally followed and then outline how the coaching process unfolded. The first change was that the discovery session usually done with individuals was not necessary as much of the information required to design a coaching program to suit the individual's needs was already in the 360-degree feedback assessment.

The first step in designing a 360-degree feedback assessment is to identify the competencies that the organization wishes to evaluate. In the case of the organisations with which I worked, these competencies were clearly spelt out in the core values. Some examples of these were, people management, resource management, communication, initiative, teamwork, and service focused. A questionnaire is then designed with the aim of evaluating those competencies. A Likert scale (1 to 7) is used to collect the data and there is space for assessors to make qualitative comments. The questionnaire is sent to multiple raters, persons who typically interact with the employee in the performance of duties, for example, the manager's employees, peers, and boss. The individual also completes a self-assessment. to evaluate each of these competencies. This type of feedback is more comprehensive and less prone to individual bias since there are multiple perspectives. For example, a manager may have thought over the years that his direct supervisor was being biased by rating his people management skills low. If the results of a 360-degree show a similar trend from other raters, then this is an area he may now acknowledge as having some merit and he may be moved to act on it.

Each employee at the end of the exercise, gets a report which summarizes the performance in each competency area and the scores given by the manager, peers, and employees. The report also compares the person's self-assessment with the assessments of others in the competency areas. Prior to undertaking the 360-degree feedback assessment, the organisation, through its human resource department would have held briefing sessions with staff to outline the objectives and to share how the process would unfold. Following the exercise, the organisation holds another debriefing session to discuss with persons how the report should be read and interpreted. They are also told that as part of the process they would be meeting with a coach who would discuss the report with them, hold coaching sessions with them to discuss areas of concern they may have and develop a plan of action. For transparency and objectivity, the 360-degree assessment is usually designed and administered by another consultant and I as the coach come in only after the results are released.

My scope of work as a coach involved, reviewing the 360-degree report for each manager, identify the strengths and areas for development, coach the client to help increase awareness and bridge the development gap, and link the goals and targets with the individual manager's personal development plan. In examining the scope, I asked the HR Manager to include a group meeting with all clients before the individual coaching sessions began. I had in mind that there needed to be a session where I would share with the team, the purpose of coaching, discuss the vision, mission and, core values of the organisation and create that safe space for us to interact. I also used the opportunity to do some group exercises to foster team building and gather information of conflict and communication styles. This was fun exercise and made for better understanding of the purpose and created a shared goal with the team.

The coaching sessions were then conducted with the individual members using their personalized report. Six (6) sessions were held with everyone; sometimes it was necessary to hold more. As expected, clients always want to delve into the report at the very first session and a coach must gauge this and assess if the tone it sets for the other sessions is a positive or negative one. It is not unusual for clients having read the report to become defensive, to feel hurt and disappointed and to begin to speculate who would have rated them low in certain areas. It takes a certain skill in coaching to have someone step back and look at the results objectively. It is here that I find it useful to get the client talking about themselves and enter the self-awareness phase. This was part of the learning and evolving of the coaching approach and with other clients I shifted focus from the report in the first sessions to building client self-awareness. I ask questions like, who are you in the organisation, what do you do, what do you like to do, whom do you do it for, what do they benefit when you do this, how is their organisation life enhanced when you do this. I found that by taking this approach, rather than going directly to identify areas for development, the individual developed a sense of purpose in the organisation and a feeling that he she had a role to fulfill, even in the face of areas for development in the report. At times I have encouraged clients to write a purpose statement for themselves in the organisation. One client, whose people management score was low, wrote:

I am (name). I am ethical, trustworthy, and committed to growth.

I am developing a calm disposition so I can effectively manage activities when I have limited time and so engage people effectively in the process. People feel empowered and are moved to achieve their full potential when they interact with me.

The 360-degree review had identified her strengths as ethical, trustworthy, and committed to growth. She embraced this. She then went on to stage how she would work on her weaker areas, that is "I am developing a calm disposition . . . ." She reported in later sessions and months after when I was again in the organisation for another assignment, that this was a breakthrough for her, and she was looking forward to seeing the results of the current 360-degree assessment then underway.

After one, sometimes two full sessions on self-awareness, we focus on the content of the report. In these discussions' issues of conflict, interpersonal relationships, staff performance issues emerge, and I hear stories of difficulties with bosses and employees and issues involving goal and role conflicts. The assessments completed at the group sessions are used as reference points here making conflict coaching an integral part of these sessions. I said before that I found that in dealing with conflict it was not so much the issue to be resolved but the inability of individuals to shift their conflict style and show up with another style. I found this shift particularly difficult for one client who oversaw a region. She had a low overall score, lowest being in people management and teamwork. The qualitative comments on the assessment included descriptions such as ('creates a toxic environment', "is verbally abusive", and does not know how to talk to people"). In discussions with the CEO, to whom I accounted and who had access to all the reports, I pointed out the low scores on some reports in the area of people management for some managers and the very low score for that particular manager. His response, was, yes, but she meets her targets. This proved to be a dilemma for me, and I had to craft my response carefully through astute questioning about his definition of results and success, the longevity prospects of the results and the possibility of future fallouts, such as higher turnover, absenteeism, legal claims which have a cost. I made a mental note for future reference to question, whether it was appropriate in a coaching environment to be accountable to the CEO who himself was being coached.

Conflict coaching brings the client face to face with behavior change and a key session in the program is understanding how change happens at the personal and organisational level. For the individual this is behavior change and for the organisation, this is culture change. I find this to be an integral part of the process and using evidence from the neuroscience field, clients learn that behaviors are not fixed, and that people can change habits that do not work for them. There is scientific information that shows that by linking awareness to coaching the neurons involved in sensing become active in advance of receiving the sensory input so if a manager constantly focuses on what is wrong, he/she would see more of it. One client manager had to review daily, customer response letters written by her employees. She complained that there would always be letters with errors in them and that she had to be diligent in reviewing these letters and pointing out the mistakes. It took up a significant part of her day and she resented it and resented her staff who made mistakes. We discussed her comfort level is letting the employees write and sign the letters; this was 0/10. We discussed her comfort level with having to review all the letters and sign them all; this was also 0/10. She was guided to look for the strengths in her staff and play to those strengths. Coach others who needed development in the area; we discussed the distinction between coaching as a development tool and pointing out mistakes. We also discussed giving persons time to improve; and taking decisive action when the need arose. In later sessions, she reported that she was not yet at the point of allowing all persons to do customer response letters independently, but she had set that as a goal, and she felt good about it.

Another client mentioned the issue of being late with financial reports. She felt that she could never meet the monthly timeline for submitting the reports and to submit then at the time they were required meant that they would not be accurate. I learnt that often the inputs for the financial reports came from her staff and often these were inaccurate. Rather than coaching persons on this, she undertook the task herself. She became severely overburdened and stressed. She was pressed to define 'accurate reports' and she defined this in terms of balancing the accounts. I asked her if she could accept the principle of 'done is better than perfect' in her field; her answer was no. We then discussed options for meeting the needs for timeliness and accuracy and where the line could be drawn. She produced a solution of establishing an acceptable variance level in her reports to the executive, which would be documented and made known at the time they were presented, and which would be finalized the next month the financials were presented. While she was not 100% comfortable with presenting a variance, she felt that providing the explanation to the team at the time of presentation and making the adjustments in the subsequent month when she would have had the time to do so, worked for her. Of course, we also had to discuss her approach to managing performance with her staff and she was open to that.

At the end of the coaching program, I suggested to the CEO that a debriefing session be held with all persons and lessons and themes relevant to their organization be discussed. There was agreement on this, and it is to be done. So, a 360-degree coaching dialogue will always consist of a team session, sessions to raise client's self-awareness to build practical skills in communication, conflict coaching which is shifting conflict styles, or any other need identified (I once helped a client prepare for a board presentation). Sessions are held weekly for up to one hour and clients are assigned activities to practice during the week and report on, the following week. In the coaching sessions in both organisations, I found that going directly to the strengths and areas for development areas in the report, short circuited the intent. Having gone through a 360-degree assessment and with a picture of how one is viewed from multiple raters in an organisation, clients want to do and be better . . . overall and not only in the areas identified. As a coach, I had to be open to that.

Below is the model of coaching that I use in the 360-degree coaching. Typically, at the end of a program of coaching, a successful leader would:

a. begin to identify and take steps to eliminate obstacles blocking the path to success in the areas identified.
b. become better at selecting and prioritizing goals.
c. begin to practice effective performance conversations with the team
d. identify any life-long conditioning keeping the Client from achieving goals and learn how to adjust thinking to change that conditioning.
e. become a Business Leader who has activated his/her personal power (APP), by demonstrating competence, eliciting confidence, and developing mutually beneficial relationships.
f. confidently implement transformation initiatives in the business environment

The Coaching Program

Session No.	Session Title	Session Objective/Business Outcome
1/2	Self-awareness	– Identify your life purpose and establish where and how your business and personal goals fit into this big picture – Identify and overcome paradigms and behaviors that stand in the way of success. – Identify areas for development from 360-degree assessment – Practice visioning the new you.
2	Your Personal Success Goals	– Goal setting principles; goal achieving principles – The Art of Making Decisions – Set some goals – What stands in the way of goal achievement? – Practice new behaviors with team
3	Making the Change	– The Neuroscience of Change – Understand how change works – Navigate Personal Change; Moving from here to there . . . what stands in your way – Practice new behaviors with your team.

4	Skills/ Competency Development	– Communication assessment
		– Effective Communication – tools to improve effectiveness
		  – Practice active listening
		  – Practice effective questioning
		  – Holding effective conversations with staff (and others)
		– Practice new behaviors with your team

(continued)

Session No.	Session Title	Session Objective/Business Outcome

5	Skills/ Competency Development	– The Conflict Management/Resolution Continuum
		– Conflict assessment
		  – Your Conflict style and how it works (or does not work) for you
		  – Adapting to situations:- showing up differently
		  – Practice new behaviors with your team

6	Moving through Fear Stress and Stressors	– Understanding fear; Working through fear – Develop harmony in relationships – Practice new behaviors with your team; review self-image – Understanding stress; Dealing with stress – Practice stress reducing techniques e.g., Mindfulness, breathing, meditation (*if client is open to this*) – Demonstrate new habits; review self-image.
Follow up	Unleashing Potential	– Show up and Deliver – Measurements and Metrics – Activate Personal Power (APP)

Lessons and Themes

There was a time in the history of the world that most people had successful careers by developing expertise in a technical field or by providing a professional service. Managers were looked at as the persons who had the right answers, did a job well and taught others to do the same and pronounced on their performance. This era is over. Disruptive change and the need for constant adaption are now normal and a model where managers tell others what to do is anachronistic. Managers now must guide and support rather than instruct and they have to create environments where people feel they can express their full potential. Companies are now investing in their leaders and managers so that they can show up with behaviors that are appropriate and give the results they are looking for.

The result of coaching is that people should be transformed, not only in how they behave but in how they think. Managers must be coached, and they also must coach. Coaching is more than getting agreement on what one has already decided so understanding communication and engagement are key ingredients in a coaching program. Coaches today must recognize that it would be necessary to identify competencies that managers must develop, and they must either facilitate the process or have them make their own arrangements for the activities to be undertaken. This is what sessions four and five in the program above cover.

The organisation as a client, required a coaching report for all persons who went through the program. The report I completed outlined how employees can use their strengths to improve their outcomes and how weaker areas should be addressed. It is hoped that the information would show managers where they should focus their self-improvement efforts and show their direct supervisors how best to support them in the interest of the organization. Most employees want to grow and develop their careers; this is done primarily through experience on the job with challenging job assignments, coaching from effective bosses, learning from mistakes and setbacks and with deliberate interventions to develop technical capabilities.

Some development activities that the CEO identified for himself included:

a. Become aware of the strengths and development areas of each person who reports to me by studying the 360-degree reports and the Coach's summary reports. Leverage their strengths and work with them to develop weaker areas.
b. Develop the habit of holding on-going one-on-one performance and coaching conversations with direct reports aimed at reinforcing their strengths and exploiting the learnings from mistakes and/or failures.
c. Become comfortable with the idea that on occasion, it may be necessary to escalate performance monitoring to higher levels, e.g., sanctions.
d. Create a 'safe space' for Managers to voice their views. Recognize the 'decision rights' of each team member and allow them the freedom to work within this framework.
e. Recognize the diversity (of thought, action, and behaviors) in the management team and allow freedom 'to be' within the regulatory framework of the organisation.
f. Become aware of those members of the Management team who may not be exhibiting appropriate leadership activities and act on this as per b and c above.

While the 360-degree assessment would have created self-awareness, Personal Development will happen when the Manager and Supervisor and/or Coach hold discussions on the summary report, create an action plan, incorporate it into a robust performance system, and follow up with the boss or coach to report on progress. Development accelerates when the 360 survey is repeated periodically, such as each year to measure improvement and establish an ongoing dialogue with others about personal development.

Learnings and Themes from the 360-degree Feedback Assessment

Self-awareness is an element or quality that is a core ingredient to the core meaning of coaching. It must not be skipped, short-cutted or minimized. Self-awareness is the foundation for the 'take-off'. It is likened to the GPS in a car; this needs only two cardinal points to take one to a goal, where you are and where you are going. Where you have been is immaterial. If a client cannot establish where he/she is at the starting point, it may be that other more clinical work is needed, outside of the scope of coaching for that client.

Awareness of the paradigms, which is the core values and beliefs that one holds and how this impacts results. Use concepts from neuroscience as evidence of how the brain can work to help a client achieve goals. This can start the process of shifting the client from a fixed to a growth mindset and open them up to new concepts such as:

a. Continuous progression is better than delayed perfection
b. Done is better than perfect

Repetition is the key to change and transformation. Oftentimes a new behavior is identified as the way to change. The client must be encouraged to not expect change to happen overnight; the behaviors must be repeated over time so that the neural pathways to support the change are developed. Only when the will to change is matched with the physical change in the brain that a breakthrough would be identified.

Identify competency areas for development in the coaching process. A client must come away motivated, inspired and with a higher sense of self, but they must also have tools to operationalize the change. These can be communication skills, conflict skills, or any other skills identified during the coaching or in the 360-degree assessment. Included in the final report is the need for the skills to be developed to achieve the goals of personal and organisational development.

Conclusion

Building connections is at the heart of coaching so communicate, connect, act. Contemporary organization development and change models strongly advocate communication as the key to transformation. Do conflict coaching but focus on shifting the conflict styles to suit the situation. These models overlook the need to connect with employees at an emotional level. They believe that when we communicate with employees and give them facts and other information, employees would act. This is not so. Communication is an intellectual process. There must be a connection made with employees at the emotional level. Connection happens only when employees are part of the development, transformation and change process, when they are part of the process of creating the new future. When connection happens, employees would move in the direction of the goals. Connection is at the heart and soul of coaching.

References

DiGirolamo, J. A., & Tkach, J. T. (2019). An exploration of the coaching approach to managing and leading; a white paper for managers, leaders, and professional coaches. Kentucky:InternationalCoaching Federation.

Edelstein, B., & Hanley, P. (2005). How to go 360 degree and not wind up in the same place. The International Journal of Coaching in Organisations Vol 3 Issue 4, 4–13.

Grant, A. M., & Cavanagh, M. J. (2004). Toward a profession of coaching: Sixty-five years of progress and challenges for the future. International Journal of Evidence Based Coaching and Mentoring Vol. 2, No. 1, 1–16.

Green, B. (2002). Listening to leaders: feedback on 360-degree feedback one year later. Organisational Development Journal Vol 20 No. 1, 8–16.

Hardy, S. (2022). Conflict coaching fundamentals, working with conflict stories. London: Routledge.

Herr, K., & Anderson, G. L. (2005). The Action Research Dissertation, A guide for Students and Faculty. Thousand Oaks: Sage.

ICF. (2022, March 29). International Coaching Federation. Retrieved from International Coaching Federation: https://coachfederation.org/about

Innis, S., & Otto, J. e. (2015). The executive coaching handbook – principles and guidelines for a successful coaching partnership 6th ed. Executive Coaching Forum.

IOC. (2021, August 18). Advancing the field of coaching through research. Retrieved from IOC: https://instituteofcoaching.org/press-release-advancing-field-coaching-through-research

Ives, Y. (2008). What is Coaching? An exploration of conflicting paradigms. International Journal of Evidence-Based Coaching and Mentoring Vol 6 No 2, 100–112.

Jackson, P. (2005). How do we describe coaching? An exploratory development of a typology of coaching based on accounts of UK-based practitioners. International Journal of Evidence-Based Coaching and Management, 1–53.

Johnson, D. (2021). The immediate future of coaching; making coaching more scaleable, inclusive, and affordable. CA: Red Thread Research.

Lloyd, J. (2009, July 13). 360 Degree feedback is a powerful leadership development tool. Retrieved from SHRM: https://www.shrm.org/resourcesandtools/hr-topics/employee-relations/pages/360degreeperformance.aspx

Noble, C. (2012). Conflict Management Coaching, the Cinergy Model. Canada: Cinergy Coaching.

Rock, D. (2006). Quiet Leadership, six steps to transforming performance at work. New York: Collins.

Rock, D., & Page, L. J. (2009). Coaching With the Brain in Mind, Foundations for Practice. New Jersey: Wiley.

SHRM. (2022, February 21). Coaching in a Business Environment. Retrieved from SHRM.org: file:///C:/Users/hyaci/OneDrive/Documents/1Documents%202021/2%20Coaching/Coaching%20Material/Coaching%20in%20a%20Business%20Environment.html

Stober, D., Wildflower, L., & Drake, D. (2006). Evidence-based practice: a potential approach for effective coaching. International Journal of Evidence Based Coaching and Mentoring, Vol 4, No. 1, Spring 2006.

Taylor, S. (2011, July 12). Assessing the pros and cons of 360 degree performance appraisal. Retrieved from SHRM: https://www.shrm.org/resourcesandtools/hr-topics/employee-relations/pages/360degreeperformance.aspx

Walker, S. (2004). The evolution of coaching patterns, icons, and freedom. International Journal of Evidence-Based Coaching and Mentoring Vol 2 No 2, 1–53.

Neil H. Katz, Neal J. Powless, Gayle Hardison

Chapter 19
Functions and Benefits of an Organizational Ombuds

Abstract: Interpersonal Conflicts in the workplace are often viewed as an inevitable "cost of doing business". When there are attempts to mitigate the damaging effects of ignoring workplace conflict, some organizations rely on traditionally accepted methods such as documentation, discipline, probation, or termination, often facilitated by offices of Human Resources and Legal Affairs. Furthermore, employees are often reluctant to use these offices to report issues that contribute to workplace conflict because of fear of going "on record" and possible retaliation. A more recent development within the varied menu of organizational resources to help mitigate the negative costs of workplace conflict is the Office of the Ombuds, staffed by one or more Organizational Ombuds (OO). The chapter presents a scenario of a somewhat typical workplace conflict scenario. It compares and contrasts how it was handled in an institution of higher education without an OO, and how it might have been handled if an OO was available and involved. Within this "story", readers are informed about the role and potential benefits of having an Office of the Ombuds accessible to their employees.

Keywords: workplace conflict, costs of organizational conflict, dispute settlement, conflict coaching

It had been an agonizing thirteen months for the former Chair of the Department, Dr. Garia. After coming out of semi-retirement from holding a professorship at a prestigious university, she accepted the challenge of serving as the first outside Chair of a department of twelve faculty members who had recently experienced considerable conflict and controversy. In the first two years of her service as chair, she accomplished several goals that bolstered the department's productivity and standing. However, thirteen months ago, Dean Jefferson had her "step down" as Chair. Recently, she received what appeared to be a form letter from the President of the university and the Human Resources department indicating a denial of her grievance and "no cause" for further review. This letter arrived after a panel hearing staffed by two Deans and one faculty member assessed the merit of Dr. Garia's case. As part of the hearing, she was allowed to present her reasons for the grievance to the panel for approximately ten minutes, after waiting all day for the anticipated morning phone call.

Note: The authors want to acknowledge and thank Kristal Augier and Vyata Mungur for their assistance with this chapter.

https://doi.org/10.1515/9783110746365-019

Ironically, Dr. Garia initially resisted filing a grievance with Human Resources. Her first request was to converse with Dean Jefferson, assisted by a third-party facilitator, to gain a deeper understanding for the Dean's reasons for her to step down as Chair, and to have a chance to present her view of the situation. Unfortunately, after meeting with Human Resources, the representative apprised her the only way to address the situation was to file a formal grievance and request "damages." Reluctantly, the former Chair followed the advice.

During the thirteen months' wait, Dr. Garia noticed a palpable difference in how her colleagues interacted with her. After feeling embarrassed at a faculty meeting where Dean Jefferson stated that Dr. Garia was stepping down and the Dean would be taking over the Department (serving as both the Dean of the School and Chair of the Department), she was told by a few of her friends within the college, of their concern about the Dean even seeing them engaged in conversation with the former Chair. This situation saddened and angered her to the extent that it began to impact her mental and physical health. She started to withdraw her full emotional and substantial effort from some of her duties. She spoke of her frustration with the situation to colleagues and potential students outside of the university who valued her guidance. These actions potentially cost the university tuition revenue, the benefit of outstanding graduate students, and the possibility of recruiting stellar new faculty members. Furthermore, two of her best colleagues within the department, eventually resigned from the university, at least partly because of this incident, per their report.

Commonplace or Aberration?

The situation described above may seem bizarre and rare. However, this primary author's fifty years of experience in organizations and service as a workplace conflict consultant support the belief that it contains elements of interpersonal and emotional issues that impact employees daily in many organizations. Issues of poor or blocked communication, cultural and value differences, conflict style, personality idiosyncrasies, and power differentials are just some of the factors that guarantee there will be concerns and disputes (Raines, 2019). These factors result in tangible and intangible costs to the organization in terms of time lost, voluntary resignations, productivity decline, numerous sick days, reputation damage, and detrimental psychological effects impacting health, morale, attention, and quality[1]. Organizations have traditionally attempted to address these challenges by offering town hall meetings and

---

[1] Publications, correspondence, and conversations about Ombuds have until recently referred to them as *Ombudsman* or *Ombudsmen*, or, more recently, sometimes as *Ombudsperson*. Since January 2021, The International Ombuds Association officially abided by the use of the term *Ombuds* in all of its publications. This chapter consistently reflects this recent change in the use of the term.

anonymous surveys, by expanding Human Resource departments, and establishing additional services and offices. These services and offices include Employee Assistance Programs, Sexual Harassment Officers, Equal Employment Opportunity, Legal, and, more recently, Offices of Diversity and Inclusion. The majority of these services and offices encompass the *Formal* complaint system of a university in which official paperwork is filed, and the organization is put "on notice." These complaint processes lead to time-consuming, lengthy, and expensive investigations to establish whether any official wrongdoing has occurred. In addition, they are perceived by employees as offices established to protect the university's interests, particularly their financial concerns, and employees are often worried about potential retaliation and the cost to their reputation from being labeled as a "disgruntled employee." Offices like Employee Assistance Program and Diversity and Inclusion operate fairly confidentially yet are limited to dealing only with issues that fall within their jurisdiction. Therefore, a gap exists to effectively address the more frequent concerns like the one described at the outset of this chapter.

Let us keep Dr. Garia's scenario in mind as we present some basic information to explain what an Organizational Ombuds[2] is and hypothesize how the situation might have unfolded if the university had one available to assist the employee.

---

2 In an effort to remain within the prescribed page limitation of this chapter, a detailed presentation of studies on the costs of workplace conflict is precluded. Nonetheless, readers are apprised that there are several studies and reports which attempt to approximate monetary costs of workplace conflict. These include estimates on time spent by managers/supervisors dealing with conflict (as disputants or as third parties), employee productivity and concentration distracted by conflict, significant increases in sick days and health costs, the impact of troublesome relationships to performance problems, the cost of personnel resignation and replacement, and loss of commitment from 100% effort.

One of the more interesting attempts to calculate actual costs of even ONE workplace conflict is an instrument developed by Dr. Daniel Dana (2001) and currently administered through The Mediation Training Institute at Eckerd College. If the Dana (2001) "Cost of Conflict Calculator" formula were to be applied to the conflict illustrated in this article, the tangible costs would easily reach several hundred thousand dollars in lost time of the participants in the dispute and lost effort of Dr. Garia, as well as the voluntary resignation of other affected key employees and the reputation costs of losing several potential new students and outstanding new faculty.

Unfortunately, there is a dearth of studies on the psychological costs of workplace conflict. One particularly interesting publication is a dissertation by Sosa (2019) cited and referenced in this chapter.

Some of the best resources for some of these studies and reports are cited and found in the reference section under Buss (2011), Dana (2001), Raines (2019), Ronde and Flanagan (2013), Sosa (2019), and the "White Paper on Costs of Conflict" (2015) from the Mediation Training Institute at Eckerd College.

What is an Organizational Ombuds and What Do they Do?

An Organizational Ombuds is an *independent* and *impartial* person with whom an employee can speak *confidentially* and *informally* to receive information, guidance, or discuss options about organizational-related issues, concerns, or conflicts. The types of issues which an Ombuds may address include personnel policies, physical working conditions, sexual harassment, discrimination, supervisory or personality conflicts, personal problems, and overall dispute resolution strategies (Ziegenfuss & O'Rourke, 2011, p. 21). An Ombuds can also assist an organization by surfacing potentially problematic pattern concerns from employees by serving as an "early warning function" for the organization through the identification of systemic issues for leadership.

Although the role of the Ombuds can be traced back to the seventeenth century in Sweden, the more contemporary version of an Organizational Ombuds serving employees in the United States became popular in the 1990s with the establishment of Ombuds offices in federal agencies as a requirement of government legislation. (Katz, et al., 2016). Over the last two decades there has also been a surge of Ombuds and Ombuds' offices being established within higher education institutions, state and local agencies including public school systems and healthcare facilities, non-profit organizations, and the private sector.

The primary duties of an Organizational Ombuds include working with individuals or groups within an organization to explore and assist them in determining options to address conflicts, problematic issues, or concerns without fear of retaliation or worry that raising concerns will trigger formal action prematurely. These primary duties are achieved through various activities while meeting with employees (whom most Ombuds refer to as "visitors"). Ombuds work with their visitors by listening to their concerns and helping them sort through or frame their concerns in a way that will further their understanding of the issues in dispute, and potentially enable them to navigate their way through the situation and to a solution. The Ombuds, through active listening, reflection, reframing, and feedback assists the visitor in better understanding the factors contributing to the conflict, along with assisting them in identifying potential "next steps" they can take to address their concerns. Those next steps might include moving the dispute to a more formal process by reporting to Human Resources or some other department, or it may involve the Ombuds clarifying a specific policy or procedure of the organization. Ombuds help visitors explore potential benefits or risks involved in a particular course of action. They can role-play the scenario, so the visitor is primed in having difficult conversations.

Occasionally, Ombuds may be asked to facilitate a discussion between employees or hold group meetings to address concerns without singling out a specific person or event. Ombuds may also be called on to perform shuttle diplomacy between employees or departments or conduct mediations to address issues. Moreover, as noted earlier,

Ombuds often act as an "early warning system" for an organization by identifying trends and patterns of the most frequent issues or concerns to provide leadership with "upward feedback" that can lead to systemic changes within the organization.

Ombuds Standards of Practice

Organizational Ombuds must adhere to the strict Standards of Practice established by the International Ombuds Association (IOA) to "preserve the *confidentiality* of those seeking services, to maintain a *neutral/impartial* position with respect to the concerns raised, to work in an *informal* level of the organization and to be *independent* of formal organizational structure" The four tenets of confidentiality, neutrality/impartiality, informality, and independence are at the core of what Organizational Ombuds are and do. An elucidation of the four tenets follows.

Ombuds maintain strict confidence and always safeguard visitors' identities unless imminent risk of harm to self or others is divulged. Organizational Ombuds take confidentiality very seriously. They ensure the confidentiality of their visitors by having private meetings in discreet locations, only keeping notes for themselves under lock and key, and shredding any notes taken at the end of the case. However, some coded data affecting trends, issues, policies, practices, and concerns are kept and used when reporting is necessary. Ombuds are known to use "white noise" machines or other noise-canceling devices outside their office doors to prevent accidental eavesdropping. Ombuds never reveal a visitor's identity without their express permission. Confidentiality is a privilege belonging to the Ombuds and the Ombuds office, rather than to any party or issue. No one can waive the Ombuds-visitor privilege within the organization.

The Ombuds office is accessible and non-intimidating, and Ombuds strive to create an atmosphere of rapport and relaxation by engaging the visitor in conversation. This informality helps to distinguish between interactions with more formal offices such as Human Resources or Diversity and Inclusion and the informal Office of the Ombuds. Ombuds are an "off-the-record" resource who do not make binding decisions, dictate company policies, nor adjudicate for the organization. A meeting with the Ombuds does not, in itself, preclude the visitor from pursuing other means of redress if necessary. The interaction with the Ombuds can precede taking the issue to the formal reporting channels within an organization. Furthermore, Ombuds can refer visitors to the appropriate formal channels when warranted with the understanding that their office can be complimentary or supplemental to the formal channels.

Another critical standard of practice for Ombuds is impartiality/neutrality and fairness. Ombuds do not represent or advocate for the organization or the visitor. Ombuds declare that while they are *impartial* when addressing concerns, Ombuds are *partial* to fairness, positive human interactions, and effective leadership consistent with the organization's stated values. To maintain impartiality, it is imperative that Ombuds are not structurally affiliated with any organization's compliance function and have no additional roles that might compromise their neutrality. Since Ombuds do not gain or lose from the outcome of an issue, or, as some Ombuds might say, "they have no skin in the fight", they, therefore, can consider the legitimate concerns and interests of all the individuals who may be affected by the matter under consideration. This ability to be impartial or neutral helps Ombuds surface options to resolve problems and facilitate discussions to identify the best solutions for the situation.

Lastly, Ombuds need to be independent and not beholden to supervisors or managers within the organization. Ombuds are often left off any official organizational charts and report to the highest level of the organization (i.e., President/CEO) and sometimes to the Board of Directors. In their role, Ombuds have discretion over whether or how to proceed in response to concerns and may initiate action through direct observation, if acceptable to all involved parties. Furthermore, to be effective, Ombuds must have access to any information and all individuals as permitted by law. They normally have the authority to select the Ombuds office staff and manage their budget and operations.

Although some may have concerns that an office of the Ombuds will conflict with more formal offices such as Human Resources, Diversity and Inclusion, and Employee Assistance Programs, an Ombuds office is supplemental and complimentary to those departments. The office of the Ombuds can offer support and/or refer to those offices as necessary, helping them meet the needs of employees and the organization. Ombuds, in some situations, are better suited for the type of in-depth discussions and occasional "consultations" needed to help employees manage conflicts, particularly those involving personality and/or values conflicts.

What if the University Had an Organizational Ombuds?

Circling back to the aforementioned case of Dean Jefferson and the former Chair of the Department Dr. Garia, let us see how the situation might have unraveled differently had the former Chair had access to an Ombuds.

Initially, when called to the meeting where Dean Jefferson requested that Dr. Garia resign from the position, she was caught off guard by the declaration and was inadequately prepared to ask for a thorough explanation of the reasons for the request. Nevertheless, in the days that followed, she experienced various emotions such as surprise, sadness, frustration, and anger over the thought that the Dean's assumption that she was not performing duties for the good of the Department and the College. In addition, since the request potentially put the former Chair and her faculty peers who supported her in a vulnerable position, she did not have any colleagues within her department with whom she could directly process her thoughts and feelings. She felt alone and abandoned.

If the university and college had an Ombuds office, Dr. Garia could have requested an appointment given the Ombuds office pledge of confidentiality, impartiality, informality, and independence. The conversations with the trained listening and rapport-building skills of the Ombuds would have allowed her to access the full range of her feelings which might have helped her with working through her understanding and acceptance of the changes. It would have also assisted her in uncovering why she was having such a strong emotional response to the situation.

After providing the safe space for her to work through her feelings, the Ombuds might have steered the conversation more toward how the faculty member remembered the conversation, the reasons Dean Jefferson stated for the request for the Chair to step down, and the former Chair's view of the situation. Any subsequent meetings might have had the Ombuds and the visitor consider alternative explanations for the Dean's behavior and how the former Chair might have handled things differently in their ongoing interactions, keeping in mind any cultural and conflict style differences. Once that issue was explored, the Ombuds might have shifted the conversation to discuss the multiple ways Dr. Garia could have pursued the issue – assuming she still wanted to. The Ombuds and the visitor could explore the benefits and potential risks of each course of action. Included amongst the potential paths would be moving the issue to the more formal side of the dispute resolution process, or the former Chair accepting the outcome with greater understanding yet with no further action taken.

The initial request of the Chair was a desire for a facilitated discussion between herself and Dean Jefferson along with a third-party process specialist. To accomplish this, Dr. Garia would need to decide if she would personally ask the Dean to agree to the facilitated meeting, or if she might be more comfortable asking the Ombuds to approach the Dean with the request. If the Dean agreed to the request to attend a three-part discussion, the Ombuds and Dr. Garia might have engaged in role-play scenarios before the meeting to assist her in preparing for the discussion. This "dress rehearsal" with the Ombuds would enhance the confidence and competence of the former Chair. The preparation might have also helped to mitigate her strong emotions and allow her to remain focused on the issues in dispute.

To understand how Ombuds work with "patterns" or "trends", let us postulate that in the facilitated meeting it becomes clear that Dean Jefferson insisted on near absolute loyalty from the former Chair and viewed discussions with other administrators regarding changes she would like to make as challenges to loyalty to the Dean. For illustrative purposes, let us assume the Ombuds has heard of this issue before from other faculty members and staff who report to the Dean. The Ombuds might be concerned that the impact of this strong insistence on loyalty might be detrimental to the morale of the faculty and the advancement of the department. The Ombuds might then follow up by inviting Dean Jefferson to have a conversation with the Ombuds about leadership and the possible benefits and limitations of a strong emphasis on loyalty. The Ombuds knows that they cannot enforce or demand change on their own. However, they can use their best partnership "coaching" skills to enhance employee's interpersonal and supervisory effectiveness, especially when faced with "difficult situations." This is a resource that serves as a supplement to leadership training that might be offered by other offices throughout the organization. Individual coaching from an Ombuds for leadership is always an option. It may have the added benefit of understanding what trends are under the surface within the department and how everyone is at least partly contributing to problematic patterns.

Additional Options for Organizational Ombuds

Naturally, the scenario above mentions only some of the many options for organizational Ombuds to assist in achieving the organization's mission and actualize its stated values. For instance, the Ombuds can also offer to provide group facilitated meetings and team development programming. In the case of the Chair, she felt unsupported by her peers. A faculty department meeting facilitated by the Ombuds would allow the group to process the issues and work through any personal and systemic impacts. Providing a place for group processing of issues can also create an environment that is supportive of additional conflict resolution strategies. Thus, the whole department can begin to heal from the temporary fractured relationships precipitated by the conflict. Often, with an incident such as this one, there are underlying issues that have not had the chance to surface, let alone be resolved. It takes significant effort to maneuver a shift in department dynamics that can support conflict resolution. This would all be very difficult to unpack and resolve without the ongoing support of an Organizational Ombuds. The Ombuds may also partner with other offices or groups within the organization to create team development activities designed to address some of the trust and frustration that might have lingered within the department.

Another possibility is that the Ombuds might hear from other visitors that this strong allegiance to loyalty is pervasive in other academic and even non-academic units of the university, so much so that variances in viewpoints and handling of situations are often viewed as acts of disloyalty to the existing power structure. Suppose the Ombuds suspects this is the case, and they believe it could be detrimental to the university's desire for promoting a supportive culture for all employees to thrive and succeed. In such a case, the Ombuds might report that systemic pattern or trend to the President, the Board, or to whomever the Ombuds reports. A follow-up option might be for the Ombuds to offer workshops on "Principles of Effective Leadership" or "Emotional Intelligence" or "Organizational Culture" in addition to having appropriate conflict style assessments/articles, and skill enhancement exercises available on their website.

The Case for an Organizational Ombuds

When considering whether an organization needs an Ombuds office, the organization needs to ask itself several questions:
1. How does the organization handle concerns and complaints?
2. Are they acknowledged or ignored?
3. Are they dealt with in a way that provides some degree of understanding, fairness, and acceptance to the parties involved?

Ziegenfuss and O'Rourke (2011, p. 11) note that a "good organization" is highly productive and nurtures positive working conditions. It spends a considerable amount of time and energy listening to its employees and working toward solving problems. An Organizational Ombuds is the individual who assists employees to manage and resolve concerns, potentially heading off whistleblower complaints, morale issues and expensive litigation. The informal process of an Ombuds' office can also help employees become increasingly efficient and help optimize the organization's resources. In addition, by addressing concerns with the assistance of an Ombuds, an organization can see an actual monetary cost benefit[3] considering the number of individuals involved and the time spent resolving issues if the complaint is routed to the formal dispute resolution offices. As Dana (2001, p. 30) remarks: "expensive formal disputes often escalate from informal conflict that might have been more easily and inexpensively resolved".

Thinking of the case study, one can assume that although the issue between Dean Jefferson and former Chair Garia was "settled" by a definitive ruling by the President, it initially did not necessarily result in enhanced understanding of neither party, improved communication, nor a more productive relationship. As noted, it had some tangible and intangible considerable negative costs, among those the Chair feeling frustrated with the belief that the route the university chose to pursue the issue was selected primarily to protect the university's interests and shield it from possible lawsuits. The chosen path to address the issue could have a further detrimental impact on an already struggling department, along with tarnishing the department's morale and reputation in the process. Would anyone be willing to come forward with issues in the future if this is the type of consequence they would encounter?

---

3 Although establishing the "business case" of actual cost savings and financial return on investment is not the focus of this chapter, there are several available resources containing compelling evidence for those who want to make the case. Of the ones we know, the University of Colorado (Elizabeth Hill, Ombuds, n.d.); the University of South Florida (Steven Prevaux, Ombuds, 2021), and North Carolina State University (Roy Baroff, Ombuds, 2021) have data demonstrating that *without* access to an Ombuds, eventual visitors indicated they would have either given up and remained disgruntled, filed a formal grievance, filed a lawsuit, or left the position. Each one of these options is of considerable cost to an organization, likely far exceeding the cost of an Ombuds and an Ombuds Office.

Within an Ombuds office, visitors sometimes only communicate with the Ombuds after the situation has gone awry. As an informal office, any person can come in before or after a formal process has been implemented. For the Chair, she may pursue a visit to the Ombuds even after the hearing and the President's decision to discuss what next steps are possible, which could include a formal appeal. If the visitor decides to "escalate" the issue up the formal chain, further discussion with the Ombuds might still be helpful. Dialogue about what to expect from those formal channels can be effective and prevent increased detrimental repercussions for the visitor. Other options for consideration even after a ruling might include working with the Ombuds for individualized coaching, personal reflection, and reframing of thinking; options that might help manage the fallout from the formal solutions. In the end, only the visitor knows best what path is most suitable for their effective management of the conflict. The Ombuds becomes the guide to lead them to empowered paths of action. For many, the Ombuds office becomes their only safe space to share their perspective throughout the organization. For the individual in conflict, that type of space is critically important.

Ombuds offices have the potential to manage conflict in a way that cannot exist within formal structures. For Dr. Garia, working through this issue with an Ombuds could restore faith in the Dean, the Department, and most importantly, in her own identity and self-esteem as a professor and leader. For Dean Jefferson, it could be a place for personal development and growth and the enhancement of valuable leadership skills. For the department, the opportunity for faculty and staff to process their thoughts and feelings on loyalty, trust, and empowerment may eventually lead to a healthier work environment. For the institution, there are multiple benefits including identifying negative systemic patterns that might exist throughout the institution consequently resulting in damaged reputation or costly lawsuits, as well as providing an independent and impartial voice which fosters consistency between organizational values and actions. All of these potential benefits provide ample validity to the research that states: "Institutions of Higher Learning (and other organizations) without an Ombuds are in danger of overlooking the research that procedural justice, a sense of fairness, a commitment to halting offensive behavior and psychological satisfaction are just as important to universities' bottom line as legal protection." (Byer, 2017, p. 224).

In addition to the numerous tangible benefits of an Ombuds office, organizations that utilize Organizational Ombuds send important positive symbolic messages that influence how employees think about the institution and its leadership. For instance, it has been noted that the establishment of an Ombuds "humanizes the institution by providing 'zero barrier offices' that are safe, credible, and accessible", (Rowe & Gadlin, 2017, p. 217) and "one in which the Ombuds becomes the one individual in a complex institution the constituents trust the most." (Byer, 2017, p. 236). Furthermore, Organizational Ombuds demonstrate commitment to what are usually some of the most significant *espoused values* of many institutions such as *"Caring* about our employees and their emotional/psychological well-being as well as their productivity, *Justice* with fair processes and consistent implementation, and *Excellence*, defined as a commitment of leadership for self-reflection and continuous institutional improvement." (Katz, et al., 2018, p. 14).

References

Buss, H. (2011). Controlling conflict costs: The business case of conflict management. *Journal of the International Ombudsman Association*, 4(1), pp. 54–62.

Byer, T.T. (2017). Yea, nay and everything in between: Disparities within the academic ombuds field. Harvard Negotiation Journal, 33 (3),pp. 213–238, 36–60. DOI: 10.1111/nejo. *12183*.

Dana, D. (2001). *Conflict Resolution*. NY: McGraw-Hill.

International Ombudsman Association (2021). *What are the benefits of an ombudsman office?*

Katz, N. H. et al. (2016). *A reappraisal-the need and value of ombudsmen in federal agencies. Part 2: Research report*. Administrative Conference of the United States.

Katz, N. H., Sosa, K.J & Kovack, L. N. (2018). Ombuds and conflict resolution specialists: Navigating workplace challenges in higher education. Jointly published by *Journal of International Ombuds Association*, 2018/1 and *Journal of the California Caucus of College and University Ombuds*, vol. XIV, pp. 1–41 2018.

Mediation Training Institute. (2015). *The cost of conflict* (White Paper).

NC State University. (2021). *Faculty and staff ombuds office*. https://facultyombuds.ncsu.edu/meet-the-ombuds/

Rowe, M & H. Gadlin. (2014). *The organizational ombudsman*. In W. K. Roche, P. Teague, and A. J. S. Colvin (Eds.), The Oxford handbook of conflict management in organizations, pp. 210–232. Oxford: Oxford University Press.

Runde, C., & Flanagan, T. (2013). *Becoming a conflict competent leader* (2nd ed.). San Francisco Jossey-Bass.

Raines, S (2019). *Conflict management for managers* (2nd ed.). Lanham/Boulder/NY/London Rowman and Littlefield.

Sosa, K. J. (2019). *Square peg in a round hole. An interpretative phenomenological analysis of workers' experiences with workplace conflict*. [Unpublished Dissertation] Nova Southeastern University.

University of Colorado Boulder. (n.d*.) University of Colorado Boulder ombuds office*. https://www.colorado.edu/ombuds/who-we-are

University of South Florida. (2021). *Ombuds office. Serving all USF employees*. https://www.usf.edu/ombuds/about-us/ombuds-officer.aspx

Ziegenfuss, J. & O'Rourke, P. (2011). *The ombudsman handbook: Designing and managing an effective problem-solving program*. Jefferson:Mcfarland & Company, Inc.

Teresa A. Daniel

Chapter 20
Managing Workplace Conflict: The Role of Human Resources as "Organizational Toxin Handlers"

Abstract: Workplace differences can generate intense conflict and emotional pain for employees – feelings like anger, frustration, stress, and disappointment. Some types of conflicts are caused by one-time events such as a merger or acquisition, the sudden loss of a senior leader and, most recently, worries about COVID-19-related issues connected to mandatory vaccinations, mask wearing, and return to work policies (Smith, 2021). Other sources of conflict tend to be more chronic, created by unsustainable workloads, bad managers, or reward and promotion systems that cause destructive internal competition. Toxic leaders who create an unfair work environment or who engage in frequent bullying and sexual harassment are another significant source of employee stress and workplace conflict (WBI 2021 US Workplace Bullying Study, 2021; Daniel, 2021; Society for Human Resource Management, 2019; Workhuman, 2019; Daniel & Metcalf, 2016). The unintended consequence of these problems is the creation of intense anxiety (and sometimes even paralyzing fear) among employees that causes them to lose their energy, focus, and creativity.

Keywords: toxic leaders, toxin handlers, human resource management, toxic emotions, communication, safe space

Many of these workplace events are fairly predictable – even somewhat inevitable.[1] However, if these situations are managed poorly (or worse yet, ignored and not managed at all), the chronic anger, unresolved conflict, or prolonged stress they create results in an undesirable byproduct known as *organizational toxicity*. Over time, the workplace culture becomes one in which employees feel devalued, demoralized, and often hopeless – and most assuredly not productive or actively engaged (Kulik, Creegan, Metz & Brown, 2009).

To put the matter in perspective, a large global study conducted by CPP involving 5,000 employees in nine countries reported that 85% of employees at all levels expe-

---

1 The author wishes to acknowledge the ground-breaking contributions of the late *Peter J. Frost*. His conceptual framework and ideas about the important role of the organizational toxin handler served as the spark for her interest in and continuing research on this topic. This chapter is dedicated to his memory.

In addition, the author wishes to express her appreciation to *Sullivan University* for the generous faculty research grant which provided funding for her study which is foundational to this chapter.

https://doi.org/10.1515/9783110746365-020

rience conflict to some degree and that employees working in United States companies spend approximately 2.8 hours each week involved in conflict. This amounts to around $359 billion in hours paid that are focused on dealing with conflict instead of on positive productivity (CPP Human Capital Report, 2008).

A more recent study conducted by the national Society for Human Resource Management (SHRM, 2019) estimated that the cost of productivity loss due to unplanned absences because of toxic and high-conflict workplaces is approximately $431 billion per year, with up to $86 billion per year attributed to employees calling in sick just to avoid having to deal with the negative situation at work. In addition, the SHRM report highlighted common indicators of bad workplace cultures (such as discrimination and harassment) and underscored the alarming impact that a negative workplace environment has on both employee well-being and productivity, as well as organizational profitability.

The Role of HR as "Organizational Toxin Handler"

Peter Frost first identified and coined the term for the special role some employees take on in an effort to help alleviate this toxicity for other employees – he referred to them as *"toxin handlers"* (Frost, 2003). These are the people who "voluntarily shoulder the sadness, frustration, bitterness, and the anger that are endemic to organizational life" (Frost, 2003).

In a follow up to Frost's initial work, a review of the literature was undertaken to examine HR's role in the management of conflict and emotional distress at work. Our working assumption was that many of the issues that he described about toxin handlers in general would also apply to the work of HR professionals. Many overlaps and commonalities were identified through this conceptual review suggesting that further empirical study might be of value (Daniel, 2017).

To this end, we conducted a qualitative research study during which we interviewed 26 highly-experienced HR professionals about their role dealing with difficult situations and toxic emotions at work (Daniel, 2020). We also examined the impact that this type of work has on their personal well-being, as well as its impact on organizational effectiveness. A key finding of the study was that a central aspect of HR's role is to act as an **organizational toxin handler**.

The finding from our study that came as a surprise, however, was the frequency of their involvement – 58 per cent of the participants reported helping employees deal with toxic emotions, stress, and workplace conflict on a *daily* basis! (Daniel, 2020). This result was consistent with an earlier study of more than 400 HR managers which concluded that "almost 25 percent of their time, on average, is spent on emotionally-charged problems" (Frost, 2004).

Who they are?

Toxin handlers are typically described as compassionate people with a high degree of emotional intelligence. They proactively take action to help mitigate the pain often experienced by employees at work due to conflict and stress. Their ability to pick up social and emotional cues allows them to quickly assess a situation and take appropriate action.

Recognizing that *"when people's hearts are broken, their heads do not work"* (Fox & Cowan, 2015), HR toxin handlers take time to actively listen to and work with employees to help them resolve their problems. Participants in our study cared deeply about employees and described their role in the organization as being "fixers" (Daniel, 2020). They felt a strong need to listen to and assist employees in dealing with their problems, whether personal or organizational. As one of the study participants noted:

> *I think it's the nature of HR. I think that HR is looked at as this third party that's able to come in and help fix whatever needs to be fixed, help fix whatever is broken, and help neutralize a situation.*

The fact that HR practitioners voluntarily assume this role is not really unexpected given that "caring about people" has historically been a hallmark contribution of the HR profession (Meisinger, 2005). Employees routinely seek HR's assistance because they are frequently perceived as trustworthy, empathetic, and nonjudgmental, and because employees have confidence that HR will help them resolve their problems (Kulik, et al., 2009; Frost & Robinson, 1999).

Their overarching goal is to hit the "sweet spot" of providing care and concern for employees while maintaining a sharp awareness of the need to keep the organization functioning and profitable by helping employees reduce their emotional pain and distraction and quickly get back to work (Daniel, 2020; Frost, 2003: Frost & Robinson, 1999).

What they do

The toxin handler acts much like a kidney or the immune system in a human body – by neutralizing, dissipating, and dispersing toxins that build up over time. They possess a wide-ranging repertoire of skills and competencies that help employees to better manage and cope with the pain and distress caused by workplace differences and conflicts (Frost & Robinson, 1999).

The successful resolution of employee problems can also help contain the negativity so that others in the organization are not impacted by the difficult situation. By taking the time out of their day to help others, though, their own regular responsibilities are sometimes negatively affected – most often in the form of missed deadlines or reduced productivity (Daniel, 2020; Frost, 2003).

How they Reduce Organizational Pain and Conflict

Participants in our study reported engaging in six core activities when they assisted employees deal with difficult workplace situations (Daniel, 2020). When acting as a toxin handler, their key actions included:

Listen Empathetically. Toxin handlers take the time to actively listen to an employee's pain and provide an important moment of human connection. Making sure that a person feels heard and understood can help validate feelings and give a greater sense of being valued and respected by the organization. As one study participant said:

> *So, my experience is to . . . first be a listener. When somebody comes in agitated or emotionally upset, they can't even hear anything you say until they finish speaking and getting everything out. So, I always felt it was my role to just be a listener and provide for them a safe environment where they could speak freely, and confidence was maintained.*

Suggest Solutions and Provide Resources. HR toxin handlers look for ways to help resolve the conflict and reduce or manage the emotions the employee is experiencing. This may take the form of brainstorming possible solutions, role-playing difficult conversations or simply talking about the problem in greater depth. They often have to provide solutions to both management and employees about the same situation. Providing this dual counsel can cause HR to experience significant internal conflict. In most employee situations, though, the study's participants suggested that employees mostly just needed to vent to someone who would listen.

Not all emotions that HR deals with are caused by work-related decisions, though. Employees also show up to discuss a variety of personal struggles as well – relationship issues, health problems and more. HR practitioners in the study noted that management does not consider this active listening as part of the primary role of HR, but it nevertheless requires a significant portion of HR's time:

> *People bring conflicts to work from outside of work. HR must explore ways to give them the resources needed to help them with their personal struggles.*

Work Behind the Scenes and Provide a 'Safe Space'. The work of the toxin handler most always happens behind closed doors – as a result, it is invisible to senior leaders and most of the organization. While the work is very important, it can feel thankless. Many of the HR professionals indicated that they still take on this role because they genuinely care about the well-being of their employees and the organization.

> *I've found that you have to listen, you have to make it safe [to speak freely], you have to repeat [what was said], and then you have to clarify what they're saying . . . you have to try and give them a different perspective on the situation or give them encouragement . . . whatever the case may be.*

HR also protects employees in tough situations by helping facilitate internal transfers or, in particularly intolerable situations, even helping them find a new job outside of the company.

Provide Confidential Counseling

Establishing and maintaining a sense of trust is paramount for toxin handlers when working with employees who are in a difficult situation or experiencing intense emotions. Employees must be absolutely certain that HR will keep their confidence, which can put HR professionals in a difficult situation. Although it often results in difficult role conflicts, HR supports both management and also employees. Even if the employee discusses information that may not be the most favorable to management (e.g., an employee discloses that he or she is leaving the company and wants to discuss benefits, etc.), confidentiality must still be maintained:

> *HR must honor confidentiality but help the employee to problem-solve.*

Strategize Communications and Reframe Difficult Messages

Developing a communication plan and regularly communicating news to employees – both good and bad – was viewed as a critical responsibility of the HR role. Their overriding goal was to minimize employee stress by keeping the workforce as informed as possible about difficult organizational decisions. They said reducing the unknowns was a key way HR practitioners can help make bad situations a bit more bearable.

They also felt that their job was to help "set the tone" and provide managers and supervisors with an overarching strategy about how to handle difficult messages and conflict situations, including sometimes providing them a written script and proposed questions and answers for some highly difficult situations:

> *We need to understand where trigger points for employees may lie and get ahead of the situation through communication. In this way, we can help to diffuse "hot spots" before they become terribly problematic for people. We are the liaison of those [tough] decisions. We're the "boots on the ground."*

Coach and Advise Managers

The study's participants frequently noted that a large part of their organizational role was to serve both as advisors to managers and implementers of management's decisions; however, they were careful to point out that they were not usually the final decision-makers (although, they pointed out, employees often wrongly think they are and penalize them unfairly):

> *Much of my day is spent in consultation with supervisors who are dealing with difficult employees. I'm advising them about the regulations and what steps we can take, but I'm also like a counselor because they're so frustrated. They're so fed up with this person, and they just really need somebody to vent to or somebody to talk to. I try to let them know it's not the end of the world.*

Participants reported that although they routinely assist employees, they also feel a strong responsibility to support senior leaders and help drive positive organizational outcomes. They noted that they were often involved in situations when there was a need to advocate for and protect employees while also challenging management. Navigating these competing role demands (which are often in conflict) is assuredly not easy. This duality created a great deal of stress and tension for them and was referred to numerous times as "a precarious balancing act."

The Price they Pay

Most individuals who counsel and advise people about emotional issues have had some form of professional training to give them the skills needed to do this difficult work. For HR practitioners, though, these duties are typically just an incidental part of their "real" job. The result is that they typically lack the training needed to protect their own well-being during their involvement in these difficult interpersonal situations (Daniel, 2020; Kulik, et al, 2009).

Even for experienced professionals, it is a huge challenge to remain attuned to the emotions and pain of others without taking on the toxicity encountered while trying to help. It is not surprising, then, that they are at serious risk for emotional exhaustion, burnout, and withdrawal – both psychological and professional (Frost, 2003; Frost & Robinson, 1999). While this can lead to decreased commitment and higher turnover rates, it can also take a physical toll in terms of stiff necks, nausea, and headaches rates (Frost & Robinson, 1999). At its most extreme, toxin handlers also report experiencing heart attacks and strokes as a result of the personal distress caused by these types of intense and emotion-laden situations.

It should be noted, however, that workplace conflict is not always bad. The experience of helping others can also help to generate greater meaning for the toxin handler, and result in a higher sense of self-efficacy and feelings of positive self-worth (Kulik, et al., 2009). Moreover, if managed properly, it can also help to stimulate creativity, problem-solving, as well as innovative solutions that ultimately benefit the organization (Meinert, 2017).

Why Organizations Need HR Toxin Handlers

Organizations are constantly changing and making difficult decisions that affect employees. As a result, conflict at work is inevitable. With tensions and anxieties at an all-time high due to the COVID-19 pandemic, the current political divide, and the heated national discussions about racial and gender inequality, the chances for emotional distress and workplace conflict have increased exponentially, underscoring the accelerating need for HR practitioners to engage in this work.

> . . . if you do not have that person who can sit down with people and be compassionate, be a good listener, be a good communicator, I think problems fester, they escalate, and you have huge problems in the end. So, if organizations do have people who are capable of being the toxic handlers, you're going to have a more efficient operation. You're going to have an operation who handles problems at a lower level, and they never get out of control. So, I think it [having a toxin handler] has a huge impact on an organization.

> I've had this said to me by the executives I work with that they think that the support that I give them enables them to do their jobs and to be successful in their roles. Therefore, it drives the success of the business.

By engaging in this work, HR toxin handlers enable other employees to stay focused and do their jobs. Without them, the organizational toxicity would continue to build, resulting in higher levels of turnover, increased health costs and more litigation, and reduced levels of employee morale and productivity.

Conclusions

While the work of toxin handlers is of critical importance to their organizations, it is mostly invisible to senior leaders due to the expectation that HR will maintain confidentiality and privacy for employees who seek their help. As a result, the role is not often recognized or appreciated.

Over time, engaging in this helping role tends to negatively affect the well-being of those who do it through increased levels of stress, burnout, emotional and physical exhaustion, and an increased intent to quit, making it a somewhat dangerous and mostly thankless job. As aptly described by a participant in an earlier study (Daniel, 2012):

> HR serves as a serious buffer for other employees in the organization – between management and employees. We are the "organizational shock absorbers" . . . but HR pays a heavy price for doing that.

Despite the risks, though, HR continues to voluntarily step up to help resolve difficult workplace conflicts and provide this compassionate care to employees who are in pain. Why? Because they know the work is essential in their efforts to create and sustain a humane and respectful workplace culture and they also know that not only is it the right thing to do, but it is also just good business. They are the *invisible heroes* of our workplaces – and we need them now more than ever.

References

CPP (2008, July). *CPP global human capital report: Workplace conflict and how businesses can harness it to thrive.* https://img.en25.com/Web/CPP/Conflict_report.pdf.

Daniel, T.A. (2020). *Organizational toxin handlers: The critical role of HR, OD, & coaching practitioners in managing toxic workplace situations.* New York, NY: Palgrave Macmillan.

Daniel, T.A. & Metcalf, G.S. (2016). *Stop bullying at work: Strategies and tools for HR, legal & risk management professionals* (2nd Edition). Alexandria, VA: SHRM Books.

Daniel, T.A. (2017). Managing toxic emotions at work: An examination of HR's unique role as the "organizational shock absorber". *Employment Relations Today, 43*(4), 13–19.

Daniel, T.A. (2012, Spring). Caught in the crossfire: When HR practitioners become targets of bullying. *Employment Relations Today, 39*(1),9–16.

Fox, S. & Cowan, R. L. (2015, February). Being pushed and pulled: A model of U.S. HR professionals' roles in bullying situations. *Personnel Review, 44*(1), 119–139.

Frost, P.J. (2003). *Toxic emotions at work: How compassionate managers handle pain and conflict.* Boston: Harvard Business School Press.

Frost, P.J. (2004). Handling toxic emotions: New challenges for leaders and their organizations. *Organizational Dynamics, 33*(2), 111–127.

Frost, P.J. & Robinson, S. (1999, July/August). The toxic handler: Organizational hero – and casualty. *Harvard Business Review,* 97–106. https://hbr.org/1999/07/the-toxic-handler-organizational-hero-and-casualty

Kulik, C.T., Creegan, C. Metz, I. & M. Brown (2009, September/October). HR managers as toxic handlers: The buffering effect of formalizing toxic handling. *Human Resource Management, 48*(5), 695–716.

Meinert, D. (2017, April 18). *Why workplace conflict can be healthy.* Society for Human Resource Management. https://www.shrm.org/hr-today/news/hr-magazine/0517/pages/why-workplace-conflict-can-be-healthy.aspx.

Meisinger, S.R. (2005, June). The four C's of the HR profession: Being competent, curious, courageous, and caring about people. *Human Resource Management, 44*(2), 189–194.

Smith, A. (2021, June 4). *Employers contend with conflicts over masks, vaccinations.* Society for Human Resource Management. https://www.shrm.org/resourcesandtools/legal-and-compliance/employment-law/pages/coronavirus-conflicts-over-masks-and-vaccinations.aspx.

Society for Human Resource Management (2019). *The high cost of a toxic workplace culture: How culture impacts the workforce – and the bottom line.* https://pages.shrm.org/2019culturereport?_ga=2.46299751.1379352704.1569245079-1873814319.1519658911.

Workhuman (2019, October 30). *The cost of toxic cultures.* https://www.workhuman.com/resources/globoforce-blog/the-cost-of-toxic-cultures.

Workplace Bullying Institute (WBI) 2021 US Workplace Bullying Study (2021, February 23). https://workplacebullying.org/2021-wbi-survey/.

Section 5: **Special Topics in Organizational Conflict Management**

Loraleigh Keashly, Leah P. Hollis

Chapter 21
Workplace Bullying: Not Just Another Conflict

Abstract: Workplace bullying is *most like* a prolonged, intractable, escalating destructive conflict between people with a power differential (Keashly et al., 2020a), the most difficult of conflicts to manage and resolve. It is grounded in and fueled by the organization through its policies, practices, procedures, work structure, and labor relations; in essence, workplace bullying is reflective of organizational culture and climate. Thus, while bullying may manifest at the interpersonal level, it is a systemic organizational issue. The approach for addressing bullying thus needs to recognize this embedded and progressive nature, be multi-faceted and involve a coordinated and simultaneous purposeful effort at the individual, unit/team, and organizational levels. A proactive and comprehensive approach to addressing workplace bullying is critical and urgent and a conflict management system perspective is useful in this consideration. In this chapter, we offer a brief primer on the nature and dynamics of workplace bullying. We then take an organization-level perspective on approaches for possible resolution, highlighting the critical role of policy design and implementation.

Keywords: workplace bullying, workplace mistreatment, conflict management systems, antibullying policy, organizational conflict

Bullying has been characterized as a type of workplace conflict, albeit a "unique" one (Lutgen-Sandvik & Fletcher, 2013). We have concerns about this characterization (Keashly, Minkowitz, & Nowell, 2020). While a detailed analysis is beyond the scope of this chapter, the essence of our concern is that categorizing bullying as a conflict, particularly an interpersonal conflict, may normalize or minimize something that should not be (Ferris et al., 2007). While conflict, particularly task conflict, can be creative and energizing (Jehn et al., 2008), and thus to be encouraged, workplace bullying is not. In fact, workplace bullying stifles creativity and innovation, and undercuts employee well-being and productivity (Einarsen et al, 2020). However, we recognize that a conflict perspective offers relevant insights into the dynamics, persistence, and escalatory features of bullying and, of key importance for this chapter, possible ways to prevent, intervene and remediate it (Keashly, Minkowitz & Nowell, 2020).

Applying a conflict lens, workplace bullying is *most like* a prolonged, intractable, escalating destructive conflict between people with a power differential (Keashly et al., 2020a), the most difficult of conflicts to manage and resolve. Further, it is grounded in and fueled by the organization through its policies, practices, procedures, work structure, and labor relations; in essence, workplace bullying is reflective of organizational culture and climate, which is governed and shaped by its leaders (Hollis, 2019a). Thus, while bullying may manifest at the interpersonal level, it is a systemic

https://doi.org/10.1515/9783110746365-021

organizational issue (Branch et al., 2021; Caponecchia and Wyatt, 2007; 2009; Hollis, 2019a; Illing et al, 2013; Lutgen-Sandvik & Fletcher, 2013). The approach for addressing bullying thus needs to recognize this embedded nature and be multi-faceted and involve a coordinated and simultaneous purposeful effort at the individual, unit/team, and organizational levels (Illing et al., 2013; Keashly, Tye-Williams & Jagatic, 2021; Rayner & Lewis, 2020; Salin, 2008). Currently, organizational approaches tend to be reactive, post-hoc, and piecemeal (Dollard et al., 2017; Lipsky, 2015). Treating workplace bullying as solely an interpersonal conflict and implementing only strategies designed for these types of conflicts, such as mediation, facilitation, conflict coaching, and skills training, will not be successful if the organizational fuel is not also addressed (Bozin et al., 2019; Keashly et al., 2020; Salin, 2003). A proactive and comprehensive approach to addressing workplace bullying is critical and urgent. An integrated, robust, and persons effective conflict management system (Lipsky, 2015) is an important component of this approach. To that end, we offer a brief primer on the nature and dynamics of workplace bullying and then take an organization-level perspective on approaches for possible resolution.

A Brief Primer on Workplace Bullying

Workplace bullying is the repeated and persistent hostile mistreatment of a person(s) by one or more other in the workplace, in which the person(s) becomes unable to defend themselves due to an extant or developed power imbalance (Einarsen et al., 2003). Workplace bullying not only occurs in person; it can occur through electronic means (cyberbullying) infiltrating the target's personal space through emails, cells phones, and other personal devices (Hollis, 2021; Privitera & Campbell, 2009). Regardless of the medium, workplace bullying is distinguished from occasional aggression by its repeated, enduring, and escalatory nature (Einarsen et al., 2003; Jenkins, 2011; Keashly & Jagatic, 2003; Zapf & Gross, 2001). It often begins with a triggering event, such as an unresolved or poorly managed conflict or the perception of threat (Baillien et al., 2009) and the behaviors become more frequent, more overt, and more antagonistic over time (Einarsen et al., 2011; Leymann, 1996; Keashly & Nowell, 2011). This relentless hostility demoralizes targets, undermining their capacity to defend and protect themselves, laying them open to increased trauma (Einarsen et al., 2003). Further, the longer bullying goes on unaddressed, the greater the likelihood of drawing in others in the workplace and a mobbing (multiple actor) situation develops (Zapf & Gross, 2001).

The impact of bullying is not limited to the target and actor. Bullying has an infectious, communal quality (Namie & Lutgen-Sandvik, 2009; Nekovee & Pinto, 2019). There are typically more bystanders and witnesses to the abuse than actors and direct targets (Pouwelse et al., 2021). As bullying escalates, bystanders and witnesses are pulled in as accomplices or allies, many as silent witnesses (Hollis, 2019b; Namie & Lutgen-Sandvik, 2009). Unaddressed bullying fuels unit and organizational incivility, which spirals into colleagues mistreating each other. A toxic work environment is born (Andersson & Pearson, 1999). Units with bullying and unmanaged conflicts have implications for other units and the organization as behaviors and the impact experienced by targets and witnesses spills over. When bullying takes place in an organization, everyone is affected. Thus, bullying is *never just* an interpersonal problem.

So How Big a Problem is It?

In any given year, seven to eight percent of American adults will experience workplace bullying (Keashly, 2018). Adding in those who witness bullying happening to others (25–33%), almost half of working American adults will have had some exposure to bullying at work. Using the US2019 employment information, of 153.7 million workers, 10–12 million Americans will experience bullying, and another 40–50 million will witness the mistreatment. *In a one-year period*, then, approximately 50–60 million workers are exposed to workplace bullying. Risk for exposure varies by profession and occupation (Leon-Perez et al, 2021; D'Cruz, Noronha, Keashly, & Tye-Williams, 2021). For example, academia has rates of 25% in any given year (Keashly, 2021). Hollis has found that 45% of higher education respondents are affected by workplace cyberbullying, either as the target or bystander (Hollis, 2021). And academia is not the worst (Keashly, 2021). Within professions and organizations, "being different" is a particular risk factor for being bullied, with notably higher rates reported for women, BIPOC, LGBTQA+, and those with disabilities (Carretero & Luciano, 2013; Hollis, 2021; Keashly, 2012). These are stunning and sadly reliable statistics and not unique to the US (Leon-Perez et al., 2021). Workplace bullying is a global phenomenon, discouragingly familiar to every type of organization and worker.

What are the Costs?

Being bullied harms the target, those who see it (bystanders/witnesses), those who love them (family and friends), and their organizations (Einarsen et al., 2020; D'Cruz & Noronha, 2021). It even harms those who do the bullying (Glomb, 2002). For targets, prolonged exposure negatively affects their physical health with insomnia, musculoskeletal and gastrointestinal problems, cardiovascular disorders, and substance abuse (Vignoli et al., 2015, Kivimaki et al., 2003; Nauman et al., 2019; Richman, Rospenda, Flaherty, & Freels, 2001; Rodriguez-Munoz et al. 2011; Vignoli, Guglielmi, Balducci, 2015; Xu et al., 2019). In addition, bullying has debilitating effects on mental health, including depression, anxiety, panic disorders, post-traumatic stress syndrome, and suicidal ideation (Conway et al., 2021; Gullander et al., 2014; Leach et al., 2017; Leymann & Gustafson, 1996; O'Donnell & MacIntosh, 2016; Spence Laschinger & Nosko, 2015; Tokarev et al., 2017).

Bullied employees show decreased job satisfaction and organizational commitment (Tepper, 2000), increased absenteeism (Nielsen & Einarsen, 2012), increased workplace deviance (Mitchell & Ambrose, 2007), reduced job engagement (Hollis, 2015; Merilainen et al., 2019), and turnover (Hogh, Hoel & Caneiro, 2011). Similar effects are noted for those who witness bullying (Nielsen, & Einarsen, 2013; Nielsen et al., 2020; Ng et al., 2021; Wu & Wu, 2019). In addition, the target's relationships, and support systems with coworkers and with family and friends are also disrupted (Carlson et al., 2011; Hoobler & Brass, 2006; Sperry & Duffy, 2009; Tye-Williams & Krone, 2015).

The effects on organizations are costly and include increased leaves (medical, disability and others), turnover, litigation and consultant costs, and insurance claims due to poor health, toxic work environment and organizational culture (Cowan, 2018) Without effective organizational intervention, toxicity intensifies (Cowan, 2018).

A Critically Urgent Issue

Organizational ignorance of the problem, particularly purposely not seeking information, stifles urgency- an urgency felt by targets who know and experience the impact first-hand and see the impact on work conditions, themselves, their coworkers, and the organization.

Distracted and unwilling organizations may resist discovery of this information because of its unwillingness to be accountable (Salin, 2006). The gap in urgency between the targets and the organization drives the anxiety for targets increasing the damage. Thus, organizations must understand and commit to systematically addressing the organizational conditions that fuel bullying. Developing a comprehensive and multi-faceted strategy requires an understanding of how bullying develops and is maintained, to which we now turn our attention.

So Why Does It Happen?

Bullying is a multi-causal phenomenon (Zapf, 1999). A sound conceptual model about the types of influences is the Three-Way Model of workplace bullying (Baillien et al., 2009). In brief, workplace bullying can be triggered by 1) ineffective coping and responding to frustration and strain in the work environment, where the actor projects their frustrations on to another (predatory bullying, Einarsen et al., 2003); 2) unsolved, poorly managed interpersonal conflict (dispute-related bullying, Einarsen et al., 2003) and/or 3) direct enabling or encouraging by the team and organizational cultures and processes (Salin, 2003). The personal and interpersonal processes are in a reciprocal relationship as frustrations may result in conflict between employees or with supervisors, and interpersonal conflict may lead to frustrations when conflicts are unproductive and escalating. Both of these processes can be fueled by organizational culture that support bullying as an appropriate workplace behavior (Ferris et al, 2007; Salin, 2003). Thus, from our perspective, the organizational environment is a key driver in the manifestation, and the ending of, workplace bullying.

To dig deeper into the key organizational influences, Salin's (2003) model of **enabling, motivating, and precipitating organizational processes and structures** is useful. In brief, **enabling,** or *necessary* structures are those that create an environment where bullying can flourish. These factors include perceived power imbalances (organizationally and societally, e.g., race, gender, class, ability), low perceived costs for misbehavior (no policy; lack of or inadequate responding); permissive organizational culture (Brodsky, 1976) and dissatisfaction and frustration in the work environment. **Motivating** structures are the *incentives* that encourage engaging in bullying behavior; it is "rational" to utilize bullying to achieve desired goals. Internal competition, politicized environment, reward systems (e.g., relative ranking performance systems – Samnani & Singh, 2014) and expected benefits (e.g., a promotion is achieved, productivity improves, or a deadline is met) support bullying as a way to get ahead and to produce. **Precipitating** processes are *triggering* circumstances and include downsizing and restructuring, organizational change, changes in management, or changes in the composition of the workgroup. Salin (2003) argues that "for bullying to occur, **enabling conditions must be in place,** and there must be either motivating or precipitating factors for bullying to manifest" (Salin, 2003, p. 1226). Taken together, these two models highlight organizational factors of work design, reward systems, and overall climate and thus the need to address these key drivers. For the remainder of this section, we will focus on culture and climate as the contextual variable that influences occurrence, interpretation/experience, and what happens to those who engage in bullying (Hershcovis et al., 2020).

Power of Context: Climate

A core facet of organizational climate that speaks directly to workplace bullying is Psychosocial Safety Climate (PSC). PSC is defined as a shared perception by organizational members of the administrative policies, practices, and procedures designed to protect employees' psychological safety and health (Dollard, 2007). In a robust psychosocially safe climate, employees perceive that management prioritizes their psychological well-being and will act decisively and fairly to address any risks to this well-being. Workplace bullying is one such risk. Research indicates that strong PSC is negatively related to exposure to workplace bullying (Dollard et al., 2017).

A sub-facet of PSC that is particularly relevant to workplace bullying prevention is Conflict Management Climate (CMC). CMC is defined as "employees' assessments of the organization's conflict management procedures and practices, and of how fair and predictable the interactions between leaders and followers in this regard are perceived to be" (Zahlquist et al., 2019, p. 2). To the extent that employees feel that 1) there are well-established, fair, and effective procedures to manage conflict and frustrations, 2) managers and supervisors are competent and will intervene as needed, and 3) the employees themselves can engage in active and constructive voice and action in addressing these issues, then frustrations, strains, and conflicts (and other forms of difficulties) will be addressed early on, quickly, and completely. A strong CMC *prevents* frustrations and conflicts from escalating, promotes skill development for engaging constructively with others, and builds a strong and respectful relationship among organizational members, all of which would prevent workplace bullying and other forms of workplace mistreatment from taking hold (Einarsen et al., 2018). From an organizational perspective, building and supporting a strong PSC and, specifically, a strong CCM would likely prevent much workplace bullying as key enabling processes and structures are diminished (Gazica & Spector, 2016). Further, a strong CCM reduces workplace bullying incentives as these behaviors are viewed as antithetical to collaborative, constructive, and active engagement with others in enacting effective and productive work (Desrayaud et al., 2018; Salin, 2003).

So how does one build a strong conflict management culture? Einarsen et al. (2018) suggests: 1) education about workplace bullying and about the value of effective conflict management, 2) the development of fair, effective, and accessible conflict management procedures (Rogers et al., 2018) and 3) training in conflict management skills consistent with, and necessary for, effective implementation of these conflict management procedures. An Integrated Conflict Management System (ICMS; Lipsky, 2015) is a useful framework for addressing workplace bullying and other forms of mistreatment. ICMS is grounded in a thorough assessment of the current organizational situation. This assessment involves developing a profile of the nature and pattern of conflicts and mistreatment occurring (Gazica & Spector, 2016) and identifying what procedures and mechanisms are present and how effective they are perceived to be. Based on this assessment and, in collaboration with organizational members, a mix of management and resolution procedures to address the sources of issues *early on* (prevention), when incidents occur (intervention) and coordinated sequencing of these procedures can be developed, implemented, and assessed (Lipsky, 2015).

An important consideration in addressing workplace bullying is to recognize that the situation's stage of development needs to be determined to select the appropriate initial or lead strategy (Leymann, 1996; Salin, 2006). Turning to conflict studies again, the contingency model of conflict intervention (Fisher & Keashly, 1991; Keashly et al., 2020a; Zapf & Gross, 2001) is instructive as it proposes that 1) different strategies may be appropriate and effective at different times and 2) failure of interventions may be due to inappropriate applications to the stage of the escalation (Salin,

2006). As noted in Leymann's (1996) model of bullying development, in the first phase, what Rayner et al., (2001) refer to as the "not-yet-bullied" stage, the immediate parties themselves may be able to resolve the situation with appropriate support through more informal conflict management processes such as constructive negotiation (actor and target engage directly) and facilitated discussion, mediation, and/or conflict coaching by trusted third parties, including managers and supervisors (Illing et al., 2013; Roszczynski, 2020).

However, once bullying has been established, these specific conflict management strategies may not only not be helpful but also harmful (Leon-Perez et al., 2015; Keashly et al., 2020a ; Notelaers et al., 2018). For example, mediation assumes equal capacity of parties to participate, which may not be the case in severe bullying where the target is too traumatized to participate (Bozin et al., 2019; Jenkins, 2011). Further, the confidential nature of mediation prevents an organization's ability to track patterns of bullying involving this actor and others (Keashly et al., 2020).

Another example is the use of restorative practices once it is clear bullying has occurred. A strength of this practice is the rebuilding of relationships and the broader unit community (Duncan, 2011). The challenge is that the actor(s) must accept responsibility for their behaviors and actions. If they do not, then restorative practices may backfire. Therefore, at these stages, more systemic and directive interventions are required initially, e.g., separating the target and the actor to break the harmful dynamic and then address the core causes.

Another advantage of focusing on building PSC and CCM is the value of ongoing data collection to monitor the climate. Periodic employee surveys can gauge organizational health and provide an early warning about bullying (Illing et al., 2013; Rayner & Lewis, 2020). When indicators suggest emergent problems, procedures such as skill training and third-party engagement can be activated. These strategies may include negotiation, conflict management skills, communication skills, antibullying education; coaching; facilitated discussion and mediation, and proactive restorative practices (Duncan, 2011; Isaac, 2013; Rowe & Bendersky, 2002). These aspects of an effective monitoring, responding and management system need to be *articulated in, and supported by, policy and associated procedures and organizational systems* (Ferris et al., 2021; Gardner & Cooper-Thomas, 2021)

Power of Policy

The multi-causal nature of workplace bullying requires a multi-faceted and comprehensive response, such as actions directed at the organizational and team level (e.g., culture and climate change, work redesign) **and** (not or) at the interpersonal/team and personal level (Dollard et al., 2017; Einarsen et al., 2016; Illing et al, 2013; Rayner & McIvor, 2008). At the organizational level, the evidence is strong about the critical importance of policy. Antibullying policies are related to less bullying (Baillien et al., 2014; Cooper-Thomas et al., 2013). Whether the policy is specifically anti-bullying or includes all forms of harassment or mistreatment (anti-harassment or anti-violence or dignity at work), policy is the framework within which all actions and responses regarding bullying are positioned, supported, and implemented (Ferris et al., 2021; Keashly & Wajngurt, 2016). Through policy, the organization communicates its vision for workplace relations and articulates those behaviors and processes that support it and those that undermine it (Gardner & Cooper-Thomas, 2021). Through policy, the processes of raising awareness, reporting, assessing, and responding (informal and formal) to bullying are articulated.

We noted earlier that there is a significant gap and resultant tension between targets' sense of urgency and the apparent lack of urgency by the organization as suggested by no visible action. The progressive nature of workplace bullying and the resultant urgency to address it as early as possible must be reflected in the policy and its associated procedures (Keashly et al., 2020b). Thus, policy needs to include mechanisms for prevention (reduce the risk for, and enablers of, bullying (e.g., constructive conflict management and communication skills and education; proactive restorative practice), intervention (address problem situations including negotiation, mediation, facilitation, coaching, as well as more directive strategies of party separation, discipline and termination), and remediation (in the aftermath – reactive restorative work, counselling) with a clearly articulated timeframe for activating these strategies (Ballard & Easteal, 2018; Duncan, 2011; Ferris et al.; 2021; Mawdsley & Thirwell, 2019; Rayner & Lewis, 2020).

While policy is critical in building awareness of and addressing bullying, the process by which the policy is developed is also important. The *policy development and implementation process* itself is an opportunity to engage all stakeholders and model the means of constructive engagement and dialogue that the policy and the organization want to promote (Hollis, 2018; Rayner & Lewis, 2020).

Current State of Policy: Case of Academia

We will focus on universities here for two reasons. First, universities are where much of our own scholarship and work has focused. Second, universities are unique workplaces with unique sets of workers (faculty and staff), creating a complex environment for enabling and thus addressing bullying.

Before considering specific institutional policies, it is important to briefly consider the state and federal regulation context. Federal and state laws enshrine expectations and obligations for organizations regarding working environment and health and safety and the cost of violation. Organizations respond by developing policies, procedures, and practices that address (at minimum) these obligations. While there are federal and state laws regarding mistreatment on the basis of protected class, there are no US federal laws and few state regulations regarding workplace bullying. Current state policies (California, Tennessee, Maryland, Utah, and Minnesota) make the prevention of, and accountability for, workplace bullying a suggestion rather than a requirement, with immunity built-in for employers for nominal effort. Further, employees have minimal recourse or protection from workplace bullying. Puerto Rico's territory policy, however, provides clear and enforceable guidelines for reporting, governance, and the accountability an organization may face if found responsible. Unfortunately, the Puerto Rican law does not have a prescribed time frame for an organization to respond to workplace bullying allegations, in essence, leaving it up to the organization to determine when and how to respond. Compared to federal 1964 Civil Rights laws that address harassment because of protected class status, the extant state regulations on workplace bullying do not provide strong impetus for proactive prevention or intervention and provide limited remediation. Thus, the motivation for policy must come from the organization itself.

In our time working on bullying in academic workplaces, it has been encouraging to see the increasing numbers of institutions that have policies, despite the pervasive shortfalls in state laws regarding workplace bullying. While a thorough analysis of extant policies is beyond the scope of this chapter (see Smith & Coel, 2018; Keashly & Wajgnurt, 2016 for more detail), we chose four universities whose policies, from our view, recognized the systemic and progressive nature of bullying and the need for timely and diverse ways of responding. They are: the University of South Carolina-Columbia (USC, 2019), Colorado State University (CSU, 2019), the University of California at Berkeley (UC-Berkeley, 2016) and the University of Wisconsin-Madison (UWM,) 2016. In the following list, we identified elements that were present in these policies:

- Institutional vision for a healthy, respectful, and productive working (and learning) environment
- Articulation of obligations of community members in supporting and promoting this environment
- Definition of workplace bullying and how it undermines the vision
- Articulation of roles and responsibilities of leadership, management, and community members
- Clarity on where and to whom to report bullying
- Options and processes for reporting and responding
- Timeline for initial response
- Informal resolution process in first 60 days
- Articulation of formal investigation process
  - To whom to report and what they will do when
  - Composition of review/investigatory committee
  - Provision to separate target and bully
  - Possible consequences if bullying allegations substantiated
- Provision for no retaliation

- Policy review and update every 3–4 years
- Training every two years (at minimum) for all campus members

The articulation of the institutional vision for the working and learning environment is a powerful public statement that the organization is accountable to mitigate potential compromises to the environment. As recommended by extant literature (Ballard & Easteal, 2018; Rayner & Lewis, 2020; Gardner & Cooper-Thomas, 2021), the policies clearly articulate the definition of workplace bullying. Further, the policies recognize the power differentials involved in bullying and give complainants alternative avenues to report bullying if the supervisor/dean/instructor is the problem.

Of key importance to addressing bullying, these polices emphasize the need to resolve the situation quickly and when possible, informally with formal options available. For example, the USC policy states, "Informal procedures are aimed at stopping the bullying behavior as soon as possible" (p. 3). Similarly, the UC-Berkeley policy states, "The goal of early resolution is to resolve concerns at the earliest stage possible with the cooperation of all parties involved" (p. 4). Options for informal resolution denoted in these policies include addressing behavior directly with the actor, seeking confidential advice and support from trusted colleagues and/or department, college, and university level offices such as ombuds, supervisors/chair, Human Resources/ EAP, Diversity, Equity and Inclusion offices, and unions. This support could include coaching in preparation for engaging the actor, facilitated discussion or more structured mediation. Typically, no detailed written records are maintained of these actions.

If informal resolution is unsuccessful or deemed inappropriate, these policies prescribe a formal investigation process with specific timelines for completion. UC-Berkeley states that an investigation should be completed within 90 days of the request. The UW-Madison policy stipulates an initial 30-day window for supervisors or Human Resources to meet with the grievant and provide a written decision. This grievance policy continues with a series of time-sensitive steps in 14-to-30-day increments. If the matter is not resolved, a target can appeal with the Wisconsin Relations Commission or the Board of Regents. At CSU, those who received reports of workplace bullying must forward the information to Human Resources within ten working days. A target who is not pleased with the outcome can request an administrative review with the written decision occurring within 30 working days. The USC policy details a timeline for formal investigation process that involves written notification to all involved in the complaint in 15 days and then an ad hoc investigation committee being appointed and charged in the subsequent 15 days. These timelines help address targets' and witnesses' needs for immediate communication that the institution understands the destructive nature of bullying. USC, CSU, and UC-Berkeley also have provisions to separate the parties during the investigation, and potentially as part of the final resolution. Such steps from the university provide very immediate relief for the target facing workplace bullying.

The detailed and comprehensive nature of these policies are a statement by the institution that bullying is not acceptable and is an existential threat to the community's well-being. This provides comfort and avenues for those who are exposed to bullying.

Role of Education and Training

Policy and a comprehensive and organization-wide training and education program are inextricably linked and critical to facilitating a collaborative culture, one that is antithetical to bullying and other forms of mistreatment (Berlingieri, 2015; Illing et al., 2013). Education and training are important for effective policies and procedures and for embedding the vision of a healthy and productive work environment throughout the organization, its processes and systems, and its people (Berilingieri, 2015; Gardner & Cooper-Thomas, 2021; Rayner & Lewis, 2020).

At its most basic level, organizational members need to know the policy, when to engage it, and what their roles are in the resolution. Further, organizational members need to have the capacity and competencies to carry out these responsibilities. For example, if informal resolution through negotiation (directly engaging the actor) or facilitated discussion or mediation is stipulated as an early form of action then employees, leaders, and managers need to be trained and competent to use these skills. Education and training can function preventively through increasing awareness of what bullying is and its costs and helping develop skills to manage issues as they arise. Good exemplars of this type of training are the University of California – Davis *Is it Bullying: Awareness and Strategies*, which is part of their professional development program and UW-Madison *Hostile and Intimidating Behavior Prevention Training for Faculty/Staff*. Training can also be an intervention strategy or consequence, e.g., mandating an actor for anti-bullying, conflict management or diversity training.

Conclusion

Workplace bullying is not just another type of organizational conflict. It is pernicious, contagious, and deeply destructive and thus, should have no place in an organization. However, it continues to persist. While bullying may manifest between individuals, it is fundamentally an organizational issue, embedded in and fueled by the organization's culture and reflected in its systems and processes. Thus, addressing bullying requires a recognition of its systemic nature and a willingness to transform the organizational culture to one that is collaborative and constructive. We highlight the importance of a proactive, multi-faceted and comprehensive approach with particular attention to early action, the role of conflict management approaches, and the critical importance of policy design and implementation.

References

Andersson, L. M., & Pearson, C. M. (1999). Tit for tat? The spiraling effect of incivility in the workplace. *Academy of management review, 24*(3), 452–471.

Baillien, E., Bollen, K., Euwema, M., & De Witte, H. (2014). Conflicts and conflict management styles as precursors of workplace bullying: A two-wave longitudinal study. European Journal of Work and Organizational Psychology, 23(4), 511–524.

Baillien, E., Neyens, I., De Witte, H., & De Cuyper, N. (2009). A qualitative study on the development of workplace bullying: Towards a three-way model. *Journal of Community & Applied Social Psychology, 19*(1), 1–16.

Ballard, A. J., & Easteal, P. (2018). The secret silent spaces of workplace violence: focus on bullying (and harassment). *Laws, 7*(4), 35.

Berlingieri, A. (2015). Workplace bullying: Exploring an emerging framework. *Work, Employment and Society, 29*(2), 342–353.

Bozin, D., Ballard, A. J., & Easteal, P. L. (2019). ADR: Championing the (unjust) resolution of bullying disputes? *Australasian Dispute Resolution Journal, (29)*, 162–172.

Branch, S., Shallcross, L., Barker, M., Ramsay, S., & Murray, J. P. (2021). Theoretical frameworks that have explained workplace bullying: Retracing contributions across the decades. In P. D'Cruz, E. Noronha, G. Notelaers, and C. Rayner (Eds). *Handbooks of workplace bullying, emotional abuse, and harassment. Volume 1: Concepts, Approaches and Methods*. New York Springer, p. 87–130.

Brodsky, C. M. (1976). The harassed worker. Lexington, MA: DC Heath & Co.

Carretero, N., & Luciano, J. V. (2013). Prevalence and incidence of workplace bullying among Spanish employees working with people with intellectual disability. *Disability and health Journal, 6*(4), 405–409.

Caponecchia, C., and Wyatt, A. (2007). The problem with 'workplace psychopaths. *Australian and New Zealand Journal of Occupational Health and Safety,23*(5), 403–406.

Caponecchia, C., and Wyatt, A. (2009). Distinguishing between bullying, harassmentand violence: A risk management approach. *Australia and New ZealandJournal of Occupational Health and Safety, 25*(6), 439–449.

Carlson, D. S., Ferguson, M., Perrewé, P. L., & Whitten, D. (2011). The fallout from abusive supervision: An examination of subordinates and their partners. *Personnel Psychology, 64*(4), 937–961.

Colorado State University (2019) CSU Policy : Bullying in the Workplace. http://policylibrary. colostate.edu/policy.aspx?id=729

Conway, P. M., Høgh, A., Balducci, C., & Ebbesen, D. K. (2021). Workplace bullying and mental health. In P. D'Cruz, E. Noronha, E. Baillien, B. Catley, K. Harlos, A., Hogh, & E.G. Mikkelsen (Eds). *Handbooks of workplace bullying, emotional abuse, and harassment. Volume 2: Pathways of job-related negative behaviour*. New York Springer, 101–128.

Cooper-Thomas, H., Gardner, D., O'Driscoll, M., Catley, B., Bentley, T., & Trenberth, L. (2013). Neutralizing workplace bullying: The buffering effects of contextual factors. Journal of Managerial Psychology, 28(4), 384–407.

Cowan, R. L. (2018). When workplace bullying and mobbing occur: The impact on organizations. In M. Duffy and D. Yamada (Eds). *Workplace bullying and mobbing in the United States Volume 2. Westport, CT: Praeger.*

Desrayaud, N., Dickson, F. C., & Webb, L. M. (2018). The theory of bullying conflict cultures: developing a new explanation for workplace bullying. In *The Routledge handbook of communication and bullying* (pp. 81–92). Oxfordshire, UK: Routledge.

Dollard, M. F. (2007). Psychosocial safety culture and climate; definition of a new construct. Adelaide: Work and Stress Research Group, University of South Australia.

Dollard, M. F., Dormann, C., Tuckey, M. R., & Escartín, J. (2017). Psychosocial safety climate (PSC) and enacted PSC for workplace bullying and psychological health problem reduction. *European Journal of Work and Organizational Psychology, 26*(6), 844–857.

Duffy, M., & Yamada, D. C. (2018, Eds.). *Workplace bullying and mobbing in the United* States *[2 volumes].* Westport, CT: Praeger.

Duncan, S. H. (2011). Restorative justice and bullying: A missing solution in the anti-bullying laws. *New England Journal on Criminal & Civil Confinement, 37*, 267.

Einarsen, S., Hoel, H., Zapf, D. and Cooper, C. (2003). The concept of bullying at work. In S. Einarsen, H. Hoel, D. Zapf, and C. L. Cooper (Eds.), *Bullying and emotional abuse in the workplace: International perspectives in research and practice.* Oxfordshire, UK Taylor Frances. p. 3–30.

Einarsen, S.,Hoel, H., & Zapf, D. (2011) *Bullying and harassment in the workplace: Developments in theory, research and practice* 2nd Edition. Oxfordshire, UK Taylor Francis.

Einarsen, S., Hoel, H. & Zapf, D. (2020). *Bullying and harassment in the workplace: Developments in theory, research and practice 3rd Edition.* Oxfordshire, UK Taylor Francis.

Einarsen, S., Skogstad, A., Rørvik, E., Lande, Å. B., & Nielsen, M. B. (2016). Climate for conflict management, exposure to workplace bullying and work engagement: A moderated mediation analysis. *The International Journal of Human Resource Management, 29*(3), 549–570.

Ferris, G. R., Zinko, R., Brouer, R. L., Buckley, M. R., & Harvey, M. G. (2007). Strategic bullying as a supplementary, balanced perspective on destructive leadership. *The Leadership Quarterly, 18*(3), 195–206.

Ferris, P. A., Deakin, R., & Mathieson, S. (2021). Workplace bullying policies: A review of best practices and research on effectiveness. In P. D´Cruz, E. Noronha, E. Baillien, B. Catley, K. Harlos, A. Hogh, and E.G. Mikkelsen (Eds). *Handbooks of workplace bullying, emotional abuse, and harassment. Volume 2: Pathways of job-related negative behavior,* New York: Springer 59–84.

Fisher, R. J., & Keashly, L. (1991). The potential complementarity of mediation and consultation within a contingency model of third party intervention. *Journal of Peace Research, 28*(1), 29–42.

Gardner, D., & Cooper-Thomas, H. D. (2021). Addressing workplace bullying: the role of training., In P. D´Cruz, E. Noronha, E. Baillien, B. Catley, K. Harlos, A. Hogh, and E.G. Mikkelsen (Eds). *Handbooks of workplace bullying, emotional abuse, and harassment. Volume 2: Pathways of job-related negative behavior,* New York: Springer 85–107.

Gazica, M. W., & Spector, P. E. (2016). A test of safety, violence prevention, and civility climate domain-specific relationships with relevant workplace hazards. *International Journal of Occupational and Environmental Health, 22*(1), 45–51.

Glomb, T. M. (2002). Workplace anger and aggression: informing conceptual models with data from specific encounters. *Journal of Occupational Health Psychology, 7*(1), 20.

Gullander, M., Hogh, A., Hansen, Å. M., Persson, R., Rugulies, R., Kolstad, H. A., . . . & Bonde, J. P. (2014). Exposure to workplace bullying and risk of depression. *Journal of Occupational and Environmental Medicine, 56*(12), 1258–1265.

Hershcovis, M. S., Cortina, L. M., & Robinson, S. L. (2020). Social and situational dynamics surrounding workplace mistreatment: Context matters. *Journal of Organizational Behavior*, *41*, 699–705.

Hogh, A., Hoel, H., & Caneiro, I.G. (2011). Bullying and employee turnover among healthcare workers: A three-wave prospective study. *Journal of Nursing Management*, *19 (6)*, 742–751.

Hollis, L. P. (2015). Bully university? The cost of workplace bullying and employee disengagement in American higher education. *Sage Open*, *5*(2), 2158244015589997.

Hollis, L. P. (2019a). Lessons from Bandura's Bobo Doll experiments: Leadership's deliberate indifference exacerbates workplace bullying in higher education. *Journal for the Study of Postsecondary and Tertiary Education*, *4*, 085–102.

Hollis, L. P. (2018). Bullied out of position: Black women's complex intersectionality, workplace bullying, and resulting career disruption. *Journal of Black Sexuality and Relationships*, *4*(3), 73–89.

Hollis L.P. (2019b). The abetting bully: Vicarious bullying and unethical leadership in higher education. *Journal for the Study of Postsecondary and Tertiary Education*, *3*, 1–18.

Hollis, L. P. (2021). *Human resource perspectives on workplace bullying in higher education: Understanding vulnerable employees' experiences*. London, UK: Routledge.

Hoobler, J. M., & Brass, D. J. (2006). Abusive supervision and family undermining as displaced aggression. *Journal of Applied Psychology*, *91*(5), 1125.

Illing, J. C. C. M., Carter, M., Thompson, N. J., Crampton, P. E. S., Morrow, G. M., Howse, J. H., . . . & Burford, B. C. (2013). Evidence synthesis on the occurrence, causes, consequences, prevention, and management of bullying and harassing behaviours to inform decision-making in the NHS. Project Report. London, HMSO.

Isaac, K. D. (2013). The immutable characteristic of thin skin: Exploring available remedies and assessing ADR as a viable solution for workplace bullying. Resolved: Journal of Alternative Dispute Resolution., 3, 1–41.

Jehn, K. A., Greer, L., Levine, S., & Szulanski, G. (2008). The effects of conflict types, dimensions, and emergent states on group outcomes. *Group Decision and Negotiation*, *17*(6), 465–495.

Jenkins, M. (2011). Is mediation suitable for complaints of workplace bullying? *Conflict Resolution Quarterly*, *29*(1), 25–38.

León-Pérez, J. M., Escartín, J., & Giorgi, G. (2021). The presence of workplace bullying and harassment worldwide. In P. D'Cruz, E. Noronha, L. Keashly, & S. Tye-Williams (Eds). Handbooks of workplace bullying, emotional abuse, and harassment. Volume 3: Concepts, approaches and methods, New York: Springer, p. 55–86.

Leymann, H., & Gustafsson, A. (1996). Mobbing at work and the development of post-traumatic stress disorders. *European Journal of Work and Organizational Psychology*, *5*(2), 251–275.

Lipsky, D. B. (2015). The future of conflict management systems. *Conflict Resolution Quarterly*, *33*(S1), S27-S34.

Lutgen-Sandvik, P., & Fletcher, C. V. (2013). Conflict motivations and tactics of targets, bystanders, and bullies: A thrice-told tale. In J. Oetzel & S. Ting-Toomey (Eds.) *The SAGE handbook of conflict communication: Integrating theory, research, and practice*, Thousand Oaks: Sage Publications, 349.

Keashly, L. (2012). Workplace bullying and gender: It's complicated. In S. Fox and T.R. Lituchy (Eds). *Gender and the dysfunctional workplace*. Northampton, MA Edward Elgar Publishing.

Keashly, L. (2018). Nature and prevalence of workplace bullying and mobbing in the US: What do the numbers mean? In M. Duffy and D. Yamada (Eds). *Workplace bullying and mobbing in the U.S.* Westport, CT Praeger.

Keashly, L. (2021) Workplace bullying, mobbing and harassment in academe: Faculty experience. In P. D'Cruz, E. Noronha, L. Keashly, & S. Tye-Williams (Eds). *Handbooks of workplace bullying, emotional abuse, and harassment. Volume* 4: Special topics and industries & occupations. New York Springer.

Keashly, L. & Jagatic, K (2003). By any other name: American perspectives on workplace bullying. In S. Einarsen, H. Hoel, D. Zapf., & C. Cooper (Eds.). *Bullying and emotional abuse in the workplace: International research and practice perspectives.* Oxfordshire, UK Taylor Francis, p 31–61.

Keashly, L. Minkowitz, H. & Nowell, B (2020a). Conflict, conflict resolution and workplace bullying. In S. Einarsen, H. Hoel, & D. Zapf. *Bullying and harassment in the workplace: Developments in theory, research and practice 3rd Edition.* Oxfordshire, UK Taylor Francis. p. 331–357.

Keashly, L, & Nowell, B. (2011). Workplace bullying, conflict and conflict resolution. In S. Einarsen, H. Hoel, & D. Zapf. *Bullying and harassment in the workplace: Developments in theory, research and practice* 2nd Edition. Oxfordshire, UK Taylor Francis Chapter 19 p. 423–445.

Keashly, L., Tye-Williams, S., & Jagatic, K. (2020b). By any other name: North American perspectives on workplace bullying. In S. Einarsen, H. Hoel, & D. Zapf. *Bullying and harassment in the workplace: Developments in theory, research and practice 3rd Edition.* Oxfordshire, UK Taylor Francis. p. 55–92.

Keashly, L. & Wajngurt, C. (2016). Faculty bullying in higher education. *Psychology and Education: An Interdisciplinary Journal, 53(1/2),* 79–90.

Kivimäki M., Virtanen M., Vartia, M., Elovainio, M., Vahtera, J., Keltikangas-Järvinen, L. (2003) Workplace bullying and the risk of cardiovascular disease and depression. *Occupational and Environmental Medicine, 60*(10), 779–83.

Leach, L. S., Poyser, C., & Butterworth, P. (2017). Workplace bullying and the association with suicidal ideation/thoughts and behaviour: a systematic review. *Occupational and environmental medicine, 74*(1), 72–79.

Leymann, H. (1996). The content and development of mobbing at work. *European Journal of Work and Organizational Psychology, 5*(2), 165–184.

Leon-Perez, J. M., Medina, F. J., Arenas, A. & Munduate, L. (2015). The relationship between interpersonal conflict and workplace bullying. Journal of Managerial Psychology. *30*(3), 250–263.

Mawdsley, H., & Thirlwall, A. (2019). Third-party interventions in workplace bullying: a neoliberal agenda? *Employee Relations: The International Journal. 41*(3), 506–519.

Mitchell, M. S., & Ambrose, M. L. (2007). Abusive supervision and workplace deviance and the moderating effects of negative reciprocity beliefs. *Journal of Applied Psychology, 92*(4), 1159.

Meriläinen, M., Kõiv, K., & Honkanen, A. (2019). Bullying effects on performance and engagement among academics. *Employee Relations: The International Journal. 41*(6), 1205–1223.

Namie, G., & Lutgen-Sandvik, P. E. (2010). Active and passive accomplices: The communal character of workplace bullying. *International Journal of Communication, 4,* 31.

Nauman, S., Malik, S. Z., & Jalil, F. (2019). How workplace bullying jeopardizes employees' life satisfaction: The roles of job anxiety and insomnia. *Frontiers in psychology, 10,* 2292.

Nekovee, M., & Pinto, J. (2019). Modeling the impact of organization structure and whistle-blowers on intra-organizational corruption contagion. *Physica A: Statistical Mechanics and its Applications, 522,* 339–349.

Ng, K., Niven, K., & Notelaers, G. (2021). Does bystander behavior make a difference? How passive and active bystanders in the group moderate the effects of bullying exposure. *Journal of Occupational Health Psychology* http://dx.doi.org/10.1037/ocp0000296

Nielsen, M. B., & Einarsen, S. (2012). Outcomes of exposure to workplace bullying: A meta-analytic review. *Work & Stress, 26*(4), 309–332.

Nielsen, M. B., & Einarsen, S. (2013). Can observations of workplace bullying really make you depressed? A response to Emdad et al. *International archives of occupational and environmental health, 86*(6), 717–721.

Nielsen, M. B., Mikkelsen, E. G., Persson, R., & Einarsen, S. V. (2020). Coping with bullying at work: How do targets, bullies and bystanders deal with bullying? In S. Einarsen, H. Hoel, & D. Zapf (Eds.) *Bullying and harassment in the workplace: Developments in theory, research and practice 3rd Edition*. Oxfordshire, UK Taylor Francis, p 563–591.

Notelaers, G., Van der Heijden, B., Guenter, H., Nielsen, M. B., & Einarsen, S. V. (2018). Do interpersonal conflict, aggression and bullying at the workplace overlap? A latent class modeling approach. *Frontiers in Psychology, 9*, 1743.

O'Donnell, S. M., & MacIntosh, J. A. (2016). Gender and workplace bullying: Men's experiences of surviving bullying at work. *Qualitative Health Research, 26*(3), 351–366.

Piotrowski, C. (2012). From workplace bullying to cyberbullying: The enigma of harassment in modern organizations. *Organizational Development Journal, 30*(4), 44–53

Pouwelse, M., Mulder, R., & Mikkelsen, E. G. (2021). The role of bystanders in workplace bullying: An overview of theories and empirical research. Volume 2: Pathways of job-related negative behavior *In P. D'Cruz, E. Noronha, E. Baillien, B. Catley, K. Harlos, A. Hogh, and E.G. Mikkelsen (Eds). Handbooks of workplace bullying, emotional abuse, and harassment. Volume 2: Pathways of job-related negative behavior*, 385–422.

Privitera, C., & Campbell, M. A. (2009). Cyberbullying: The new face of workplace bullying? *CyberPsychology & Behavior, 12*(4), 395–400.

Rayner, C., Hoel, H., & Cooper, C. (2001). *Workplace bullying: What we know, who is to blame and what can we do?* Boca Raton, FL. CRC Press.

Rayner, C., & Lewis, D. (2020). Managing workplace bullying: The role of policies. In S. Einarsen, H. Hoel, & D. Zapf. *Bullying and harassment in the workplace: Developments in theory, research and practice 3rd Edition*. Oxfordshire, UK Taylor Francis p. 497–519.

Rayner, C., & McIvor, K. (2008). Research report on the dignity at work project. University of Portsmouth Business School.

Richman, J. A., Rospenda, K. M., Flaherty, J. A., & Freels, S. (2001). Workplace harassment, active coping, and alcohol-related outcomes. Journal of Substance Abuse, *13*(3), 347–366.

Richman, J. A., Rospenda, K. M., Nawyn, S. J., Flaherty, J. A., Fendrich, M., Drum, M. L., & Johnson, T. P. (1999). Sexual harassment and generalized workplace abuse among university employees: prevalence and mental health correlates. *American Journal of Public Health, 89*(3), 358–363.

Rodriguez-Munoz, A., Notelaers, G., & Moreno-Jiménez, B. (2011). Workplace bullying and sleep quality: The mediating role of worry and need for recovery. *Psicología Conductual, 19*(2), 453.

Rogers, N. H., Bordone, R. C., Sander, F. E., & McEwen, C. A. (2018). *Designing systems and processes for managing disputes*. Riverwoods, IL Wolters Kluwer.

Rowe, M., & Bendersky, C. 2002. Workplace justice, zero tolerance and zero barriers: Getting people to come forward in conflict management systems. In T. Kochan & R. Locke (Eds.), *Negotiations and change: from the workplace to society*. Ithaca, NY Cornell University Press, p. 117–140

Roszczynski, L. W. (2020). *Alternative dispute resolution techniques to address workplace bullying: A modified delphi study* (Doctoral dissertation, Ashford University).

Salin, D. (2003). Ways of explaining workplace bullying: A review of enabling, motivating and precipitating structures and processes in the work environment. *Human Relations, 56*(10), 1213–1232.

Salin, D. (2006). *Organizational measures taken against workplace bullying: The case of Finnish municipalities*. Meddlanden Working Papers, Swedish School of Economic and Business Administration, Finland.

Salin, D. (2008). The prevention of workplace bullying as a question of human resource management: Measures adopted and underlying organizational factors. *Scandinavian Journal of Management, 24*(3), 221–231.

Samnani, A. K., & Singh, P. (2014). Performance-enhancing compensation practices and employee productivity: The role of workplace bullying. *Human Resource Management Review*, *24*(1), 5–16.

Smith, F. L., & Coel, C. R. (2018). Workplace bullying policies, higher education and the First Amendment: Building bridges not walls. First Amendment Studies, *52*(1–2), 96–111.

Spence Laschinger, H. K., & Nosko, A. (2015). Exposure to workplace bullying and post-traumatic stress disorder symptomology: The role of protective psychological resources. *Journal of Nursing Management*, *23*(2), 252–262.

Sperry, L., & Duffy, M. (2009). Workplace mobbing: Family dynamics and therapeutic considerations. *The American Journal of Family Therapy*, *37*(5), 433–442.

Tepper, B. J. (2000). Consequences of abusive supervision. *Academy of Management Journal*, *43*(2), 178–190.

Tokarev, A., Phillips, A. R., Hughes, D. J., & Irwing, P. (2017). Leader dark traits, workplace bullying, and employee depression: Exploring mediation and the role of the dark core. *Journal of Abnormal Psychology*, *126*(7), 911.

Tye-Williams, S., & Krone, K. J. (2015). Chaos, reports, and quests: Narrative agency and co-workers in stories of workplace bullying. *Management Communication Quarterly*, *29*(1), 3–27.

University of California Berkeley (2019). Berkeley People & Culture. Reporting Bullying Behavior. https://hr.berkeley.edu/policies/employee-relations/bullying-workplace/reporting-bullying-behavior

University of South Carolina (2019). Bullying & Harassment. https://sc.edu/about/offices_and_divisions/law_enforcement_and_safety/emergency-procedures/bullying-harassment/index.php

University of Wisconsin- Madison (2016) Hostile and intimidating behavior. https://hr.wisc.edu/hib/preventing-hib/

Vignoli, M., Guglielmi, D., Balducci, C., & Bonfiglioli, R. (2015). Workplace bullying as a risk factor for musculoskeletal disorders: the mediating role of job-related psychological strain. *BioMed research international*, https://doi.org/10.1155/2015/712642. - *open access*

Wu, S. H., & Wu, C. C. (2019). Bullying bystander reactions: A case study in the Taiwanese workplace. *Asia Pacific Journal of Human Resources*, *57*(2), 191–207.

Xu, T., Magnusson Hanson, L. L., Lange, T., Starkopf, L., Westerlund, H., Madsen, I. E., . . . & Rod, N. H. (2019). Workplace bullying and workplace violence as risk factors for cardiovascular disease: a multi-cohort study. *European Heart Journal*, *40*(14), 1124–1134.

Zahlquist, L., Hetland, J., Skogstad, A., Bakker, A. B., & Einarsen, S. V. (2019). Job demands as risk factors of exposure to bullying at work: the moderating role of team-level conflict management climate. *Frontiers in Psychology*, *10*, 2017 doi: 10.3389/fpsyg.2019.02017.

Zapf, D. (1999). Organisational, work group related and personal causes of mobbing/bullying at work. *International Journal of Manpower*. 20(1/2), 70–85.

Zapf, D., & Gross, C. (2001). Conflict escalation and coping with workplace bullying: A replication and extension. *European Journal of Work and Organizational Psychology*, *10*(4), 497–522.

Jessica Senehi, Michele Lemonius

Chapter 22
Women and Organizational Conflict Management: Promoting Human Rights and Challenging Gender Bias

Abstract: Women's experience of conflict management in organizations is shaped by social understandings of gender – that is, what it means to be a "woman." This can happen in two broad ways. First, gender-based discrimination, harassment, and violence are a violation of women's human rights; individuals, managers, and organizations need to be prepared to ensure a fair, just, and safe workplace. Second, gendered worldviews into which people have been socialized may create bias in various ways of which people may be largely unaware, and that impacts how women's behavior is seen in the workplace and even how conflicts are addressed. This chapter seeks to provide a background on women in organizational conflict management in the following ways. First, a theoretical background is provided. Next, current research on women's human rights and the role of gender in the conflict management are presented. Finally, best practices are reviewed.

Keywords: gender, social identity, human rights, bias, diversity, best practices

Gender is not about the fact of one's sex. Rather, gender refers to how a society or other collectivity makes sense of femaleness or maleness – that is, the particular roles, norms, and expectations that are assigned to females and males. While individuals, socialized into their own worldview, may apprehend these differences as quite natural, they are, in fact, socially constructed, and will differ across cultures and with social change over time. They will intersect in different ways with other socially constructed identities, such as race and class.

Gender is Socially Constructed

As Jane Mansbridge (2000) points out, gender norms can be quite arbitrary: roles such as butchering of animals may be solely the purview of men in one culture (e.g., among the Aleut of North America), but solely the purview of women in another (e.g., among the Ingalik of North America), among many other examples. However, despite these inconsistencies, Mansbridge finds that in the great majority of societies, both traditional and contemporary, values and activities associated with men are more highly valued and more highly rewarded. In an exhaustive review of research across

https://doi.org/10.1515/9783110746365-022

disciplines on gender and war, published in what was named the book of the decade by the International Studies Association, Joshua Goldstein (2001) concluded that role differences in gender are less a result of biological differences, and far more a result of tremendous cultural work in defining and maintaining these roles.

There is no essential "woman" (Fuss, 1989); what unites women is being treated according to the social norms and expectations of "woman" (de Lauretis, 1987). This is demonstrated in how the same behavior by men and women will be viewed differently. For example, within North American mainstream society, a non-smiling woman is viewed negatively whereas a non-smiling man is not (e.g., Norberg and Johansson, 2020). Hence, many women have experienced being told to smile in the workplace, which women report finding demeaning, and such statements to women are considered microaggressions (e.g., Smith, 2016).

Social Identities Encode Power Relations

Across many cultures, men's roles are accorded more status and power than women's roles. These power relations become part of culture and are embedded in social systems, including organizations, and shape perceptions and behaviors (e.g., Becker, 1999). In societies throughout the world, there has been an ongoing struggle for women's empowerment; while there are significant gains, a progression towards gender equality is ongoing (e.g., Snyder, 2017). While there is increased awareness of sexism, in many workplaces, there is an everyday, largely unconscious bias, often termed "second-generation bias" that is disempowering to women, and needs to be addressed (Ibarra et al., 2013).

People have multiple identities, the meanings of which are always socially constructed and encode power relations. Intersectionality refers to how the intersection of these identities create particular and unique sets of expectations, for example, for Black women or working-class women (Crenshaw, 1989, 2019). It is critical that support for women's human rights in organizations must also be tied to support for all human rights, for example by challenging systemic racism (e.g., Washington & Roberts, 2019) or Islamophobia (e.g., Alimahomed-Wilson, 2017). Women of color often face discrimination despite excellent work, confidence, and personal character (e.g., Hunte, 2012; Washington & Roberts, 2019).

The nature of a systemic power imbalance is that people from the disempowered group may internalize their lesser status and participate in their oppression in ways of which they are unaware (Freire, 1970). This can impact women in conflict situations when they fail to negotiate because they are loathe to be considered aggressive or are overly pessimistic about their possibility to achieve a win, especially when they are negotiating for themselves, rather than on behalf of someone else (Kolb & Williams, 2000, 2003; Kolb & Porter, 2015). Norms around silencing can lead to women speaking up less at professional conferences and in other situations, especially for their own advocacy (Tannen, 1990). Because of social disapproval of women's expressing anger, women's anger can go unrecognized even by themselves; meanwhile, anger has important information regarding when one's boundaries and values are violated, and constructive conflict management is required to maintain professional and personal wellbeing (Lerner, 1985).

Gender and Leadership

Women's conflict management styles have been often characterized as more relational than those of men (e.g., Brewer et al 2002; Brahman et al., 2004; Holt & Devore, 2005; Thomas et al., 2007). A study of school principals found that the school culture was better where principals had a more collaborative style rather than a more dominating style; and it was found that women principals were more likely to have a collaborative style (Blackburn et al., 2006). However, these findings have been inconsistent, have shown cultural and generational variation; do not always account for differences across professions; are limited by how assessments of conflict resolution style are arrived at; or may be based on studies of college students rather than management professionals (Steen and Shinkai, 2020). Further, theory and research in organizational management may encode gender biases (Runté and Mills, 2006); inequality is not outside academia or research and can unconsciously distort the production of knowledge (e.g., Harding, 1987; Haraway, 1989).

Women's management styles may be impacted by one's level within in an organization. One study found that self-reported management styles showed no differences between men and women with managerial experience, while women at lower organizational levels reported that they were more obliging and compromising in their conflict resolution styles (Korabik et al., 1993). Gender may make a greater impact on how people are perceived rather than on their behavior. Interestingly, the same study also found that subordinates evaluated female and male supervisors differently when they used similar management styles; for women, a dominating style was seen more negatively, and an obliging style was seen more positively. If this is the case, women in less powerful positions may use a more obliging style because they are accurately anticipating the reaction of others to their behavior. One way to overcome limitations of gender bias – both in terms of women's own behavior or in terms of how one interprets women's behavior – may be to learn conflict resolution skills; this is a strategy to uncover motivations and interests and increases the possibility for not relying on one style (e.g., emphasizing goals or emphasizing relationships) and for integrating management styles (Steen & Shinkai, 2020).

Promoting Human Rights

Societal gender roles contribute to varied gender biases and conflicts within organizational settings (e.g., Stamarski & Hing, 2015). These conflicts are experienced both internally, in the form of psychological pain, and externally, as expressed conflicts. Conflicts about unequal pay, harassment, racism, and being overlooked for promotion may influence a woman's fear to request fair wages in the workplace, and women continue to experience unequal pay globally and earn an average 87 percent on the dollar that men earn (U.N. Women, 2020). Socially constructed and discriminatory norms have created an even greater wage gap for marginalized women, including women of colour, Indigenous women, immigrant women, and women with children.

The motherhood pay gap has been justified by two main schools of thought: economics and sociology (Grimshaw & Rubery, 2015). Some economists argue that motherhood often leads to changes in employment to accommodate family life, and the changes in employment behaviour is evident in the depreciation of human capital, reduced commitment to employment, and being employed in less productive jobs. While these economists concern themselves with the impact on the overall market or productivity to explain the wage gap, sociologists have posited that patriarchal norms and/or assumptions have created gendered systems that promote discriminate against mothers. For example, the idea that women with children are less productive in the workplace leads to women not being hired, promoted, or paid the same as their male counterparts.

Women in the workplace continue to face insurmountable harassment. Common forms of workplace harassment include verbal abuse, humiliating behaviour, threats to person, physical violence, and unwanted sexual attention or sexual harassment. In a 2016 General Social Survey (GSS) on Canadians at Work and Home to examine experiences of workplace harassment, 19 percent of women and 13 percent of men reported that they had experienced harassment in their workplace in the past year (Hango & Moyser, 2018). Despite the pervasiveness of sexual harassment, it is under-reported because those affected by sexual harassment fear being disbelieved, blamed, and/or facing retaliation in social and professional lives (Human Rights Watch 2021).

A study on harassment and violence in the Canadian workforce found women are most likely to experience sexual harassment in the first two years of employment; 94 percent of those who reported experiencing sexual harassment were women, and women with a disability and visible minorities are over-represented among those reporting harassment (Employment and Social Development Canada, 2017). It was further found that there is a continued risk of sexual harassment when employees are unaware of reporting and grievance procedures. Such harassment in the workplace affects individuals' health, job tenure, job stability, and job satisfaction. Conflicts about gender, whether perceived or not, greatly impact the overall health of individuals, and, in turn, the productivity of organizations as a whole.

Challenging Gender Bias

Two people who have contributed a lot the discussion of women and negotiation, management, and conflict transformation in organizations are Deborah Kolb (e.g., 2013; Kolb and Williams, 2000, 2003; Kolb and Porter, 2015) and Peggy Chinn (2013). During a workshop on negotiation that Kolb was leading at the Women's Policy Institute at Harvard University's Kennedy School of Government, the women attending – all of whom were very accomplished women in their respective business fields – stated that conflict resolution teaching didn't work for them because the same behavior by a man or woman would be interpreted differently. Kolb and Judith Williams (2000) led research to learn from these women and their success in both formal and information negotiations; the findings of this research are the basis of their book *The Shadow Negotiation*. Peggy Chinn (2013), in the field of nursing, has developed a methodology of collaborative practice that is grounded by shared power and transparency. The guidance of these scholar-practitioners, grounded by the real experience of women in organizations, is reviewed below. Because this work seeks to neutralize the assumptions of gender and also to leverage the particular experiences and knowledge that women have gained on the ground, it helps mitigate the role of gender bias in organizational conflict management.

Women and Negotiation

While Kolb and her colleagues Judith Williams and Jessica Porter seek to provide guidance for women in organizations, their work is relevant to all negotiation, especially when someone is negotiating from a lesser-status position. In this way, the insights and worldview of the women they interviewed have provided a major contribution to conflict resolution knowledge in general. Kolb and Williams (2000, 2003) found that relationships of power—for example, as encoded in society's greater valuing of masculinity—create a disadvantage for women; social positioning along any lines of identity disadvantage those in a lesser-status position. Therefore, the power relationship in itself has to be negotiated as much as possible, and this is an aspect of all negotiations.

This parallel negotiation of the relationship, occurring concurrently with a negotiation about substantive issues, is termed "the shadow negotiation." Because of status inequality encoded in social systems, women may be pessimistic about negotiation, and Kolb and Williams (2000, 2003) encourage women to get out of their own way. They advise women to recognize the shadow negotiation, and provide detail and strategies for women to strengthen their negotiation efforts. They counsel negotiators to (1) take stock of everybody's interests and liabilities, and to especially recognize the value one is bringing to the negotiation; (2) gain factual information and do some scouting to learn about the particular situation; (3) develop alternatives; and (4) get a fresh perspective by seeking objective advice, tapping the experience of others, and widening one's focus. Kolb and Porter (2015) are primarily focusing on informal organization where people are negotiating within their organization for things that are important to them – what they call *small n-negotiation*.

Kolb and Williams (2000, 2003) recommend negotiators balance advocacy and connection in negotiating with others. To advocate for their interests, negotiators can draw on a repertoire of moves and turns. Strategic moves include holding out incentives, stepping up pressure, establishing authority and credibility, enlisting support, and gaining control over the process. To resist challenges, negotiators can draw on strategic turns to interrupt, name, correct, or divert the other person's move. Building connections requires appreciating the other person's situation, feelings, ideas, and face-saving. Collaboration requires ongoing work to make room for relationship-building, encourage participation, keep dialogue going, and get everyone to own the problem. While social ideas may negatively interpret women's power, this approach, grounded in the actual experience of successful women, encourage women to acknowledge, nurture, and exercise their power in effective ways.

Peggy Chinn (2013), whose writing continued from the work of the late Charlene Eldridge Wheeler (1984), provides a handbook for collaborative work developed from women's collective organizing. The ideas in *Peace and Power* (Chinn, 2013) provide detailed guidance for working with others in ways that build community, share power, create transparency, and promote collective decision-making. This approach is grounded in valuing personal and collective empowerment, awareness, cooperation, and growth.

Conclusions and Best Practices

It is a moral, legal, and financial imperative for organizations to protect women's human rights. Key approaches to address this include:

- Diversify the workforce by developing policies that outline recruitment, retention, and the development of women in all departments, including, but not limited to, women in leadership and/or decision-making positions.
- Develop organizational policies that minimize the potential for work-family conflicts and create a culture that values these policies.
- Ensure there are policies in place that reflect human rights codes and ensure that employees have a clear understanding of appropriate behavior within the organization.
- To ensure policies are followed, regular performance evaluations can be an opportunity to ensure employee understanding of the social construction of gender, gender bias, and impact; and to determine where interventions or further staff development is needed.

– Clarify how gender bias may intersect with other forms of bias and promote policies that protect the rights of all groups, for example, including visible minorities, transgender individuals, people living with disabilities, and people of diverse religious backgrounds.

The role of gender bias can negatively impact conflict management when persons are unaware about how socialization shapes their perceptions and behavior in ways that damage their own and others' effectiveness and wellbeing (e.g., Ibarra et al., 2013). To address this, organizations are encouraged to provide safe spaces for conflict management where women leaders have peer supports and coaching relationships so that they can develop their leadership skills and identity. Individuals are encouraged to develop conflict resolution and negotiation skills, especially when there is a consideration of gender (e.g., see Kolb & Williams, 2000, 2003; Chinn, 2013; Kolb & Porter, 2015).

The ethical use of power, effectiveness, and success are not zero-sum. Empowering women does not limit the effectiveness of men. The more people in society are able to fulfill their potential, the more organizations are strengthened overall, and society benefits as a whole. Considering the pervasiveness of gender, there is a need for more research to both inform and evaluate practice and policymaking.

References

Alimahomed-Wilson, S. (2017). Invisible violence, *Women, Gender, and Families of Color, 5*(1), 73–97.

Becker, M. (1999). Patriarchy and inequality. *University of Chicago Legal Forum, 1*, 21–88.

Blackburn, C. H., Martin, B. N., & Hutchinson, S. (2006). The role of gender and how it relates to conflict management style and school culture. *Journal of Women in Educational Leadership, 4*(4), 32–41.

Brahnam, S. D., Margavio, T. M., Hignite, M. A., Barrier, T. B., & Chin, J. M. (2004). A gender-based categorization for conflict resolution. *Journal of Management Development, 24*(3), 197–208.

Brewer, N., Mitchell, P., & Weber, N. (2002). Gender role, organizational status, and conflict management styles. *The International Journal of Conflict Management, 13*(1), 78–95.

Chinn, P. L. (2013). *Peace and Power*. Burlington, MA: Jones and Barlett Learning.

Crenshaw, K. (1989). Demarginalizing the intersection of race and sex. *University of Chicago Legal Forum, 1*, 139–167.

Crenshaw, K. (2019). *On Intersectionality*. New York: New Press.

de Lauretis, T. (1987). *Technologies of Gender*. Bloomington: University of Indiana Press.

Employment and Social Development Canada. (2017). *Harassment and sexual violence in the workplace – public consultation*. https://www.canada.ca/content/dam/canada/employment-social-development/services/health-safety/reports/workplace-harassment-sexual-violence-EN.pdf

Freire, P. (1970). *Pedagogy of the Oppressed*. New York: Continuum.

Fuss, D. (1989). *Essentially Speaking*. London: Routledge.

Goldstein, J. (2001). *War and Gender*. Cambridge: Cambridge University Press.

Grimshaw, D., & Rubery, J. (2015). *The motherhood pay gap*. International Labour Office. https://www.equalpayinternationalcoalition.org/wp-content/uploads/2018/08/wcms_371804.pdf

Hango, D., & Moyser, M. (2018). *Insights on Canadian Society*. Statistics Canada. https://www150.statcan.gc.ca/n1/pub/75-006-x/2018001/article/54982-eng.htm

Harding, S., ed. (1987). *Feminism and Methodology*. Bloomington: Indiana University Press.

Haraway, D. 1989. *Primate Visions*. London: Routledge.

Hold, J. L., & DeVore, C. J. (2005). Culture, gender, organizational role, and styles of conflict resolution. *International Journal of Intercultural Relations*, *29*, 165–196.

Human Rights Watch. (2021). *Gender-based violence in the workplace*. https://www.hrw.org/tag/gender-based-violence-workplace

Hunte, R. S. (2012). My walk has never been average. [Doctoral dissertation, University of Manitoba].

Ibarra, H., Ely, R. J., & Kolb, D. M. (2013, September). Women rising. *Harvard Business Review*. https://hbr.org/2013/09/women-rising-the-unseen-barriers

Kolb, D. (2013). Negotiated in the shadow of organizations. *Ohio State Journal on Dispute Resolution*, *28*(2), 241–262.

Kolb, D., and Porter, J. (2015). *Negotiating at Work*. San Francisco: Jossey-Bass.

Kolb, D., & Williams, J. (2000). *The Shadow Negotiation*. New York: Simon & Schuster.

Kolb, D., & Williams, J. (2003). *Everyday Negotiation*. San Francisco: Jossey-Bass.

Korabik, K., Baril, G. L., & Watson, C. (1993). Managers' conflict management style and leadership effectiveness. *Sex Roles*, *29*, 405–420.

Lerner, H. (1986). *The Dance of Anger*. New York: Harper & Row.

Norberg, C., & Johansson, M. (2020). "Women and 'ideal' women." *Gender Issues*, *38*, 1–24.

Runté, M., & Mills, A. J. (2006). Cold War, chilly climate. *Human Relations*, *59*(5), pp. 695–720.

Smith, R. I. (2016, October 27). *The sexism of telling a woman to smile*. The Atlantic. https://www.theatlantic.com/politics/archive/2016/10/the-sexism-of-telling-women-to-smile/623090/

Snyder, A. C. (2017). *Setting the Global Agenda for Peace*. London: Routledge.

Stamarski, C. S., Son Hing, L. S. (2015, September 16). Gender inequalities in the workplace. *Frontiers in Psychology*. https://doi.org/10.3389/fpsyg.2015.01400

Steen, A., & Shinkai, K. (2020). Understanding individual and gender differences in conflict resolution. *International Journal of Women's Dermatology*, *6*, 50–53.

Tannen, D. (1990). *You Just Do Not Understand*. New York: William Morrow.

Thomas, K. W., Thomas, G. F., & Schaubhut, N. (2007). Conflict styles of men and women at six organizational levels. *International Journal of Conflict Management*, *19*(2), 145–166.

U.N. Women. (2020, September 14). *Explainer*. https://www.unwomen.org/en/news/stories/2020/9/explainer-everything-you-need-to-know-about-equal-pay

Washington, Z, and Roberts, L. M. (2019, March 4). Women of color get less support at work. *Harvard Business Review*. https://hbr.org/2019/03/women-of-color-get-less-support-at-work-heres-how-managers-can-change-that

Wheeler, C. E. (1984). *Peace and Power*. Buffalo, NY: Margaretdaughters.

Pavel Mischenko, Neil H. Katz, Gayle Hardison

Chapter 23
Making the Invisible Visible: Uncovering the Mystery of Personality Conflicts at Work

Abstract: Conflicts are inevitable in organizations not only because of the objective differences in needs, goals, and means, but also due to individual subjective psychological differences. Those situations are often described as "personality conflicts." In this chapter we introduce a new method and approach that professionals and leaders can use to mitigate and leverage those "personality conflicts." The method, titled BOTH: Passwords to Human Minds employs powerful birth order sibling metaphors that anyone can relate to. Those metaphors, consistent with one's experience as a child among siblings, facilitate identification of typical relationship habits that develop in early life and tend to influence how we habitually respond to workplace conflicts as adults. Furthermore, The BOTH method (Birth Order Typical Habits) demonstrates how one person's typical habitual "blind spot" often unintentionally becomes a "stressor" for another, creating unnecessary "personality" conflicts. The BOTH Method provides powerful insight to lower emotional charge, and a clear situational roadmap of traditional conflict management skills.

Keywords: workplace personality conflict, relationship habits, early life programming, emotionally intelligent leader, birth order psychology, both method

An effective workplace is about being productive and constructive, yet because our workforce is still predominantly human (not robots yet), we often must deal with employees' various subjective realities. The emotional intensity that accompanies conflict sometimes creates unnecessary psychological obstacles to our business productivity. One will occasionally hear things like, "I hate his guts!" or "She is too bossy!" or "I do not want to go to work because I have to deal with so-and-so", etc. And in some instances, coworkers who are supposed to be "team players" will not like working with or even communicating with each other. Furthermore, everyone senses negative tension within the team that is ready to explode. Managers must be "practicing psychologists" to be able to deal with these types of situations.

As leaders, we are always searching for the "best practices" tools and strategies to help us manage and lead successful teams. Part of building a successful team also means being able to manage and resolve the inevitable conflicts that arise between coworkers, managers, and employees as well as between employees and the company. We know firsthand the toll that unmanaged or unaddressed conflict can have, not only on employee morale but also on productivity. When conflict is unexpressed or unre-

https://doi.org/10.1515/9783110746365-023

strained, productivity is low, but when conflict is regulated or effectively managed, productivity increases. (Hocker & Wilmot, 2018).

Unresolved conflict also has the potential to impact the bottom line of an organization when one considers the number of individuals who could be involved in attempting to resolve the conflict (i.e., employee, supervisor, human resources, legal), the number of hours needed to address the conflict, the salaries of those involved, and other costs that have a significant negative impact (Katz & Flynn, 2013; Dana, 2001).

Sometimes conflicts happen not only because of the objective differences in needs, goals, and means, but also because of the *individual subjective psychological differences* of the parties involved. Those situations are often described as *personality conflicts*, and they often happen in the Blind Spots Zone of the famous Johari Window model (Luft & Ingham, 1955), like an underwater part of our Awareness iceberg. In this chapter, we introduce a new method and approach that professionals and leaders within organizations can use to help manage and leverage those personality conflicts.

There are numerous personality assessment "tests" that one can take to not only gain insights into oneself but also to better understand the psychological makeup of others, essentially to figure out "what makes them tick." Tests such as *Myers-Briggs Type Indicator* (MBTI) measure whether someone is an extrovert (E) or introvert (I), whether they process information using their "senses" (S) vs. being intuitive (I), whether they make decisions by either thinking (T) or feeling (F), and if they do things through either a judging (J) or perceiving (P) preference. Others such as The Birkman Method help leaders understand what drives someone's behavior, and Clifton Strengths, formerly known as Strength Finders, helps individuals "discover their strengths" and begin to uncover the strengths of others to garner greater performance.

These excellent tools are widely used in management and team-building programs around the world, yet there are some disadvantages in comparison to the method we are going to discuss. First is a lack of common-sense understanding about why someone has specific profile. Since most of the known instruments measure a mixture of nurture and nature, there is no clear explanation of the mechanism for how those attitudes and behaviors developed. Another factor that potentially impacts retention and everyday use is that immediately remembering and applying theoretical concepts like MBTI letters, or as opposed to colors, etc., in practical reality is difficult without long-term practice. The BOTH model that will be offered as one of the "best practices" for conflict management in organizations provides understanding for specific interpersonal behavior formation and memorable terms that describe individual differences.

BOTH Model

BOTH is another method or tool to help leaders and individuals gain a better understanding of their individual psychological "relationship habits and the ways one partner cues another's responses" (Wood, 2017) and, as a result, handle much more effectively personality conflicts at work and at home (Mischenko, 2018, 2019). BOTH stands for *Birth Order Typical Habits*. Recent studies indicate that our early life repetitive experiences with our parents and siblings are one of the origins of certain *automatic habitual processing patterns* that are used by adults in various interpersonal situations. One of the more influential and well-researched examples could be the repetitive experiences in our childhood associated with our particular *birth order positioning* (Black, Grönqvist & Öckert, 2018; Campbell, Jeong, & Graffin, 2019). An article by Gottfredson and Reina (2020) supports the potency of those habitual actions: "It is common for leaders to non-consciously rely on . . . habitual processing patterns for their functioning and operation" (p.5). In situations of conflict and increased stress: "when a situation is 'hot,' or emotionally charged, individuals' personality systems may operate more quickly and non-consciously", (p. 4) relying on those automatic habitual processing patterns.

The BOTH method employs powerful birth order sibling metaphors that anyone can relate to. Those metaphors, consistent with one's experience as a child among siblings, facilitate identification of common communication and people management *habits* that developed early in life and that we *habitually* exercise regularly as adults in workplace relationships, especially in conflict situations. The BOTH method clearly demonstrates how one person's typical habitual "blind spot" often unintentionally becomes a stressor for another who will unconsciously activate their own blind spot. The resulting largely non-conscious interaction suddenly creates unnecessary and unproductive personality conflicts. The BOTH Method provides the necessary insight to lower emotional intensity and provides a clear roadmap for the need to utilize fundamental conflict management skills to address those personality conflict situations like reflective listening, assertion, interest-based problem-solving, etc.

The BOTH Model uses the word *habit* as a concept to describe birth order phenomena because it reflects a critically important distinction between actual (chronological) and psychological birth order that was identified by Alfred Adler (1956), who states, "It is not the child's number in the order of successive births which influences his character, but the situation into which he is born and the way he interprets it" (p. 377).

As previously noted, these developed habits that continue to influence our behavior could be considered "automatic behaviors;" an example would be the language(s) we learned to speak as children. We had no say in the language we learned; it was merely based on where we lived and the family into which we were born. An example of an "automatic" or learned behavior might be the memorization of your nation's Pledge of Allegiance or national anthem. You may not even recall how or when you learned it, but you did through repetition and with minimum effort. This idea of "automatic" behaviors highlights that we are keenly aware of how some habits were learned but unaware of how this learning happened with some others.

As discussed throughout, psychological birth order habits are some of the "automatic" behaviors which have helped us navigate the world and conflicts when they arise. Where we fall in the birth order, whether we are an *Only, Oldest/Firstborn, Middle,* or *Youngest* has influenced how we respond during stressful situations, and those responses have become our "habits" even as we have moved into the world of work and have begun to interact with other *Only, Oldest/Firstborn, Middle,* or *Youngest* "children."

Below we will provide practical examples of the specific *relationship habitual patterns* we are metaphorically describing as an *Only, Oldest, Middle,* and *Youngest,* clearly focusing on *psychological birth order* rather than on an actual (chronological) one, and how they can create unnecessary conflicts in the workplace, along with *practical guidelines* for how to effectively manage them using best practices based on this method.

Practical Applications and Guidelines

Each psychological birth order type (*Only, Oldest, Middle,* and *Youngest* described in the BOTH model) consists of seven different "relational habitual patterns". In this chapter, we will provide just one illustration for each one of those patterns.

Let's start with *Only* family programming and how unawareness of it could create personality conflict at work.

Only: "It is all about me" and "I am the most special and worthy person in the room"

We will describe here one example of the *Only* blind spots that they developed without any awareness or choice on their part by being repetitively treated by parents (and often extended family members) as the "most special" one. As a result, a specific habitual relationship pattern and expectation was born, and, of course, they carry that expectation forward into adulthood, frequently without being aware of that "family programming."

That particular "habitual pattern" could also be present in an actual chronological oldest or youngest (and rarely by middle children) due to other factors like culture, gender, parental style, etc. The BOTH model names that pattern after the *Only* because it is more pronounced for the actual only children.

Let's illustrate how these habits and patterns might be influential in creating blind spots in adulthood and personality conflicts.

A few years ago, one of the authors worked with a newly appointed branch manager of a community bank in Upstate New York. The branch manager stated that during the onboarding process, her predecessor recommended that she fire one of the tellers. The former manager described the teller as a "selfish, toxic" individual who was insubordinate and provided poor customer service. She had previously counseled the teller, and as a result, they had ongoing tension and a conflict-ridden work relationship. They just did not like each other. Was this a personality conflict that could be solved purely through psychological means?

Here is that supervisor's description of that "difficult" employee and her dealings with him:

> One of my particular challenges was my relationship with a 25-year-old employee by the name of Daniel. In fact, he insisted on being called Daniel, and I was the only one who was allowed to call him Danny. He was the kind of fellow who always referred to himself by his full name, complete with middle initial and suffix. He wore three-piece suits with cufflinks, and heavily jeweled rings, at a bank teller job in a rural area of Upstate New York that paid $10 an hour. My challenge as a manager was Daniel's low motivation – while he was very well dressed (kind of a Victorian "dandy"), he was simply lazy at work and showed obvious disgust on his face when serving certain types of clients who looked "ugly, dirty, and poor" to him. He did not mind helping gas station and bowling alley owners; though they did not look "clean", at least they were "rich." Getting Danny motivated was going to be a challenge because in my view, he was simply not a good fit for the job – I would not have hired him were it my choice. However, the problem was that he was already here and on the job.

Daniel's manager became acquainted with the BOTH model in a seminar offered by the Upstate NY Center for Financial Training and decided to use it with him. She learned about creative motivational strategies to use with a psychological *Only* child: "Keeping in mind that this only child would naturally have a feeling of being the most special person in the room." So, she tried to treat Danny that way, using a stance that his unique specialness made him the perfect person for whatever task she had at hand; for example, "Danny . . . you are right, you are the smartest one here. This is exactly why I chose you to balance these ledgers." She acknowledged his distaste for coming close to the "commoners" for fear of it "rubbing off" on him, suggesting instead that it might have a reverse effect: that his nobility would reach out and elevate the status of others.

When the new manager's predecessor visited the branch, she could not believe how much Danny's attitude and behavior had changed. This was a case of different strokes for different folks. The BOTH method helped this manager create a different and effective motivational strategy for a difficult employee and transform an unnecessary personality conflict into a productive workplace relationship. Positive rapport with that difficult employee paid off because not only did she not have to fire him, saving her bank a significant amount of money for recruitment and training of a new teller, but her efforts to apply the BOTH Method led to an increase in his engagement and later helped him to see his own blind spots and grow as a professional and a person.

> **BOTH® Model Guidelines for *Only***
>
> *If you are a psychological Only child who spent lots of time alone in their childhood*: Remember that we tend to create our own rules and expect the world to follow them. Since "the world" (parents and often grandparents) was revolving around you, you developed unrealistic expectations that you carry into adulthood that other people would automatically treat you a "very special" person.
>
> *If you work with a psychological Only*, remember they might have those "delusions of grandeur" without even being aware. Acknowledge their uniqueness while building a positive rapport through active listening and help them become grounded in reality by providing feedback about their blind spots.

Oldest: "I am not a bully!" or "They do not tell me what they really think!"

Some similar but also some quite different repetitive experiences are typical for psychological *Oldest* family-of-origin programming:

In childhood, some of us experienced repetitive situations where, in comparison to our siblings, we had the advantage of either physical or intellectual power, and sometimes both. We used that power to reinforce our desires in situations of disagreement and influence. Thus, we developed certain expectations that others would respect our power as it was our experience in childhood, and if there was an obstacle in the way of meeting our needs, we could easily use that advantage to remove the obstacle. Typically, those experiences would be most frequent for the actual (chronologically) oldest, and sometimes for actual middle siblings. In the case of chronologically middle children, they were in situations where they did not have power over their older siblings and yet might be in a powerful position toward their younger siblings. (Of course, in more rare circumstances, even actual (chronologically) youngest could have similar experiences in situations where the older sibling had some type of disability or illness that would then give "power" to the youngest.) Yet typically, actual oldest children form that relationship habit, and as adults, they appear to their team members as intensely dominant. As a result, their blind spot is their unawareness of how they are experienced by their peers and subordinates and their potential stressor is the feeling of disrespect to their position and power from others.

One of the striking examples for one of the authors was his meeting with an executive who asked for help with his team. His main complaint was that they did not tell him what they actually thought during meetings. He described a typical encounter where he would state a problem, give his analysis, and then wait to hear what they had to say. Usually, he would be met with silence. Then, with no creative group analyses, his solution would be implemented.

Many factors could be involved in this scenario, such as cross-cultural differences; the executive was an expat. Yet, it also could have been his very dominant style of speaking in a loud, intense voice and overwhelming physical presence; he was tall and husky.

He happened to be an *Oldest* in his family. In business meetings, a firstborn may not physically assault you, but their tone and intensity may cause the room to shut down.

We discussed how he could become more aware of how he overwhelmed his team with his powerful presence, and how he could change that. His dominant approach when making his proposals often sounded like "Take it, or leave it!" or "My way, or the highway!" but as soon as he recognized his blind spot behaviors, he was able to make the necessary changes to find a more inviting approach. This kind of awareness often comes as a shocking experience for an *Oldest* because, in their mind, they are being direct and honest with people about how to accomplish this or that business objective. Nothing is personal for them. They feel they have the best intentions possible for everyone.

One of our colleagues, an organizational consultant from the United Kingdom, who happens to be an *Oldest* in her family, shared a powerful insight she gained very early in her business career as a newly appointed manager. The company ran a 360-feedback assessment, and she received a report that highlighted how her team perceived her. She told us she cried for a week after receiving her feedback because her team reported that they felt intimidated by their supervisor. "I could not believe it!" she said, "So in a couple days, I called my mother and asked her if I was intimidating, and Mum said, 'Yes, you are.' That was one of the hardest realizations in my life, yet one of the most helpful."

When you discover that you have been programmed without your permission or awareness, the blind spot of someone like Charlie Munger, another brilliant *Oldest* and lifetime business partner at Berkshire Hathaway with Warren Buffett (a *Middle*), makes sense. Here's his revelation about the approach he uses in their teamwork:

> That's one of the beauties of the partnership. I am in so many activities the dominant personality. Yet (with Warren), I am particularly willing to play a secondary role. Warren's a more able man in doing what we're doing, so it's the appropriate response. It's not letting ego or jealousy, or your own personality take over.

BOTH Model Guidelines for *Oldest*

For actual Oldest and others who might share that same Oldest "psychological programming": If you had the repetitive experience of being "in a power position" for a few years in your childhood in relation to your siblings, it is important to be aware that you were programmed to behave in a "dominant" way and that you may overuse your power by exercising authority automatically without consideration for others who may wish to contribute or lead.

You may not be aware of how others perceive your exercising of authority. They experience your natural authoritative approach, which for you is based on your "being responsible and caring", as you are imposing power on them, even in situations where it is not your intention to do so.

For people who work with Oldest: Be aware that this dominance is their "blind spot", and you may need to exercise the skills of active listening and demonstrate assertion with objective data to influence them. It may also require that you raise the intensity of your nonverbal signals to get their attention, which could include a louder voice and more direct posture. Also, asking *Oldest* for help makes them more open to constructive feedback.

Next, let's consider typical psychological *Middle* childhood programming and how it impacts our workplace behavior as adults.

Middle: "I can't stand bullies and tyrants!"

When we interviewed an executive who happened to be an *Oldest* in her family of origin, we asked her, "Who is the most difficult person for you to handle?" she surprised me when she responded, "Those people who never give a straight answer, who are always too diplomatic, wishy-washy so to speak." As discussed, the *Oldest* voices their opinion forcefully and dominantly, and they naturally expect others do the same. That is not the case with psychological *Middle*. Because they are in the middle, they were conditioned to learn to see things from different perspectives. They were often stuck between the arguments of the powerful oldest sibling and the emotional youngest one. *Middle* children learn how to look at the same situation from different angles and points of view and end up mediating conflicts, working on fair and just resolutions for all. The result? They form a strong belief that although the world is not fair, they can help make it fair.

Examples of some famous *Middle* children who fought for fairness and equality were Susan B. Anthony and Martin Luther King Jr. Anthony was a prime voice in the suffrage and social reform movements of the 1800s until her death in 1920. King fought for civil rights, ultimately losing his life for his beliefs in 1968. If *Middle* children feel strongly about something, they are sometimes ready to pay the ultimate price in fighting the injustice.

While seeking equality is a positive side of the *Middle*-child habit, there is naturally a blind spot, or in this case, a huge stress button: *Middle* children stereotypically and "deep in their guts", hate and resent bullies or dominant people who say in the very beginning of the negotiations that "this is my way or the highway." *Middle* children usually activate their autopilot defensive reaction and either withdraw to avoid these people or start fighting with them in a passive-aggressive way. And by reacting defensively, they often miss the opportunity for possible win-win solutions.

Psychological *Middle* children who became more mindful of that blind spot are able to avoid this classic *personality conflict* and achieve a much more constructive outcome. The following is an example. Bill, a commercial real estate broker who always encouraged to present information he learned about the BOTH model to other real estate agents and brokers. He says that understanding the psychology of the person who you are dealing with is critical for negotiating long-term contracts. He told one of the authors that before he learned about that *Middles* have a *bully button*, he would always get angry with those "pushy" guys because they reminded him his older brother who used to tell him what to do and bullied him around. So, Bill would automatically be ready to fight until the end during negotiations, and things often ended up getting ugly. Clearly, this is personality conflict in action! But now, if someone is being pushy, he does not get triggered at all, and actually relaxes as he understands that he is probably dealing with the psychological *Oldest* who is used to applying a forceful dominant style that others can experience as bullying. Yet for the *Oldest,* that perception could be totally in their *Blind Spot Zone,* so now, Bill somewhat playfully says, "Sure, no problem, boss! Thanks for the advice. Let's go ahead with your suggestion and see if it works out to get the desired results!" Bill reported that since he started to use this approach, he had many more win-win collaborative deals with *Oldests* instead of endless rounds of fighting. He has avoided many counterproductive situations by realizing his *Middle* child blind spot and creatively working around it to achieve his collaborative goals.

And the last, we look at psychological *Youngest* habitual relationship patterns that create certain blind spots and purely subjective personality conflict at work.

BOTH® Model Guidelines for *Middle*

If you were born as a Middle: be aware that you might have this *bully button* as your blind spot stressor, take time to ask yourself why others might be acting selfish and aggressive. Try not to take it personally. Explore the possibility that others may have a significantly different perspective than yours and therefore may make decisions based on different priorities than you. Consider techniques of creative problem-solving and win-win negotiation approaches that are very effective when you are not stressed.

If you work with a stressed Middle: Reflective listening techniques are very useful. As the emotions subside, the *Middle* can rather quickly return to a resourceful state where they see things from different angles and act constructively and creatively.

Youngest: "Everybody should be playful and have fun in this life!"

Different European studies show that actual (chronologically) younger siblings are more humorous than firstborn children. (BBC News, 2005; McAteer, 2015).

Let's think about the childhood experiences for youngest-born that likely happened on a continual basis: They were typically rewarded by parents and sibling(s) for being cute and funny, and enjoyed being the center of attention and developed artistic skills or talents to "find their place" because the niches of being serious, academic-achievement oriented, etc. were typically already taken. That might have translated to the corresponding adult habits based around humor, inclusiveness, and the entertainment of others. They enjoy being the center of attention and entertaining people. They have a well-developed sense of humor, and they use humor to "break the ice", to be inclusive, and to help relieve some of the pressure in stressful situations.

Many people have made a nice and interesting living using that habit: Jerry Seinfeld, Jim Carrey, Jay Leno, Kristen Wiig, Tina Fey, Kevin Hart, and Stephen Colbert, to name a few. Besides being funny, what else do these people have in common? They are all the youngest in their families.

Of course, being funny and adding humor to charm others will help one build successful business relationships and create unique organizational cultures, like Herb Kelleher (the youngest in his family) did with Southwest Airlines.

Yet in the workplace, that behavior can result in being labeled "too playful" in some people's eyes and perhaps lead to gaining the unfortunate title of "class clown", especially if those people supervise the individual who is not aware of that particular blind spot and its negative impact. A few years ago, when one of the authors was facilitating a leadership development program for high-potential managers for one of the largest British banks in the United States, one participant – let's call him Neil – was very disappointed about receiving lower-than-expected ratings in his annual appraisal and had even started to think about leaving the bank. When questioned about the reasons for this, he mentioned feeling there was a personality conflict between him and his boss. Neil believed that this boss simply did not like him. Neil described his manager as a "very rigid, business-only" person – no jokes, no laughter in the office. By comparison, Neil believed that there is time for both hard work and a bit of fun at work. He recalled several occasions where he tried to "loosen up" his manager by telling him a joke, and instead of laughing, his boss just gave him "that look." But Neil did not give up and continued his playful ways until, to his surprise, their relationship completely deteriorated.

After Neil learned about the BOTH model, and Neil and I talked about the differences between his Birth Order Typical Habits and his manager's, which could create blind spots and stressors, their mysterious clash became clear. With that insight, Neil immediately changed his behavior – he continued to tell jokes and play around with other colleagues, but with his boss, he became strictly business only. After a three-month follow-up with supervisors, Neil's boss stated that he noticed a "significant" improvement in Neil's work attitude. He said that Neil had become "much more serious and focused", and that he was very pleased with that.

A year later, Neil reported being happy with his career after receiving a much better appraisal from this same manager as well as an offer for a very promising promotion.

This so-called personality conflict was solved by increasing Neil's self-awareness with the help of BOTH model and subsequent changes of behavior.

BOTH Guidelines for Youngest

If you were born later in your family: Remember, in the eyes of others in the workplace, you can sometime be "too playful", and others may see you as superficial or even as the "class clown", which could have a detrimental impact on your business relationships and your career. If you notice you are receiving a cold shoulder, resist your automatic temptation to tease these people more and switch to a business only approach.

> *If you work with people manifesting this particular blind spot behavior in the workplace*, it is important to be aware that behavior was programmed by childhood experiences. An empathetic appreciation coupled with listening and clear assertive feedback will help to avoid potential personality conflict.

Conclusion

Knowledge of the BOTH model can contribute to a deeper understanding of the interpersonal dynamics that often lie in the subconscious of the individuals involved in the *personality conflict* by clearly explaining the source of some behaviors that appear irrational at first glance. This increased awareness leads to lessening of destructive emotional intensity and more constructive conflict management, especially if the individuals involved are also skilled in the above-mentioned conflict management fundamental skills like reflective listening, assertion, creative problem-solving, and interest-based negotiation. (Katz et al, 2020). This model can take a well-deserved place in the toolbox of an Emotionally Intelligent Leader to be used for successful team building as well as for mediating conflicts between subordinates. (Katz et al, 2017).

References

Black, S., Grönqvist, E. &Öckert, B. (2018). Born to Lead? The Effect of Birth Order on Noncognitive Abilities. *Review of Economics and Statistics*, *100*(2),274–286.

BBC News. (2006, August 15). Younger Siblings 'More Amusing'. Retrieved from BBC News: http://news.bbc.co.uk/2/hi/health/4793463.stm

Campbell, R., Jeong, S-H., & Graffin, S. (2019). Born to take risk? The effect of CEO birth order on strategic risk taking. *The Academy of Management Journal*, *62*. 1278–1306

Dana, D. (2001). *Conflict Resolution: Mediation Tools for Everyday Worklife*. McGraw-Hill, New York, NY

Gottfredson, R.K. & Reina, C.S. (2020). Exploring why leader do what they do: An integrative review of the situation-trait approach and situation-encoding schemas. *The Leadership Quarterly*, *31*(1), 101373.

Hocker, J.L. & Wilmot, W.W. (2018). *Interpersonal Conflict*. 10th Edition. McGraw-Hill: New York, NY

Katz, N.H. & Flynn, L.T. (2013). Understanding Conflict Management Systems and Strategies in the Workplace: A Pilot Study, *Conflict Resolution Quarterly*, *30* (4): 139.

Katz, N. H., Lowe, A., & Mischenko, P. (2017). Organizational impact analysis of the training program" Birth order type habits model: Leadership and teamwork". *Obrazovanie Lichnosti*, (*1*), 41–46. Retrieved from https://www.researchgate.net/publication/316427751_Birth_Order_Type_Habits_Model_and_Organizational_Impact

Katz, N.H., et.al. (2020). *"Communication and Conflict Resolution Skills"* 3rd Edition, Kendall Hunt: Dubuque, IA.

Luft, J.; Ingham, H. (1955). "The Johari window, a graphic model of interpersonal awareness". *Proceedings of the Western Training Laboratory in Group Development*. Los Angeles: University of California, Los Angeles.

McAteer, O. (2015, January 30). The youngest sibling is the funniest, study reveals. Retrieved from
https://metro.co.uk/2015/01/27/the-youngest-sibling-is-the-funniest-study-reveals-5038620

Mischenko, P. (2018). The Birth Order Typical Habits® Model: Increasing Emotional Intelligence by
Understanding Personality Formation & Change. *Obrazovanie Lichnosti*, (*2*), 28–33. Retrieved
from https://www.researchgate.net/publication/326635108_The_Birth_Order_Typical_Habits_
Model_Increasing_Emotional_Intelligence_by_Understanding_Personality_Formation_Change

Mischenko, P. (2019). Why Your Birth Order is a Blessing and a Curse in Business [Video file].
Retrieved from https://www.udemy.com/course/a-new-breakthrough-psychological-insight-for-
leaders/

Wood, W. (2017). Habits in Personality and Social Psychology. *Personality and Social Psychology
Review*. Vol. *21*, pp. 389–403.

Haleh Karimi

Chapter 24
Organizational Conflict Management: Driving Innovation and Organizational Success Through Leadership Management and Human Connection

Abstract: Soft skills competencies have been correlated with personal, professional, and organizational success with a positive return on investment leading to growth and innovation. Human resources with soft skills competency enable organizations to innovate new products and services using their critical and analytical thinking processes to handle diversity, conflicts, and inter-cultural challenges. Emerging technologies such as big data, artificial intelligence, robotics transformed our workplace. Robots or AI cannot creatively think, manage people, resolve conflicts, innovate ideas or products; that's where having humans with soft skills competencies will be essential to have the upper hand and drive technology. Humans can use their creative mindsets and leadership skills to design new products or services, connect with humans, constructively resolve conflicts, create innovative products, lead people effectively, and manage technologies such as robots. The human connection would be essential to understand humanity to generate values through creative solutions and strategic differentiation. This chapter identifies necessary soft skills needed for the future workforce, attained through a face-to-face interview with 27 STEM business leaders. Participants shared their perceptions on what is lacking and required for the future of workforce professionals considering the emerging technologies. Business leaders perceive that soft skills competency will be essential for society to flourish and innovate, generating a win/win outcome for all stakeholders: businesses, higher educational systems, and future college graduates entering our workforce.

Keywords: management, organizational success, value creation, soft skills, innovation

In an age of never-ending connectivity, the need for soft skills is increasing. The future of the work market is projected to undergo significant technological and scientific breakthroughs, rapidly shifting the labor market with tasks performed by humans and those performed by machines and algorithms (World Economic Forum, 2018). As we enter deep into this labor market and with the rise of emerging technologies, such as artificial intelligence, machine learning, and automation entering our workforce, the future of employment will necessitate soft skills that machines cannot replace (Karimi, 2020; Wilkie, 2019). There is a significant demand for intercultural under-

https://doi.org/10.1515/9783110746365-024

standing with soft skills such as human connection, collaboration, communication, leadership, empathy, and conflict management at its core. These soft skills are considered the power skills to succeed in the future of work.

Soft skills are one of the most challenging competencies to understand and build competency. There are dozens of terms used to describe soft skill – and yet – employers, educators, and policymakers are increasingly coalescing around clear definition and classification (U. S. Chamber of Commerce Foundation, 2018).

Soft skills are considered the power skills of the future due to their reliability and connectivity to personal and organizational success. Soft Skills are skills that complement our technical skills. Technical skills are specialized or professional competencies as one attains through education or experience in various professions such as teaching, law, nursing, accounting, or engineering. While technical skills are relatively straightforward to acquire, mastering soft skills competency takes a considerable effort, time, and creativity to master soft skills competency (Spar & Dye, 2018). Soft skills are competencies more focused on one's ability to conduct or demonstrate a technical task by applying collaboration, leadership, communication, ethics, conflict management, creativity, and empathy. A healthy workforce is a collaborative culture with people working in a collaborative and harmonious environment. For this culture to be established, you need people with strong, soft skills, and conflict management is at its' core to handle diversity and cultural challenges. A well-trained individual with solid soft skills competency can use their communication, collaboration, and creativity skills to develop new ideas or help disputants resolve their conflicts.

Soft Skills Significant Driver for Success

Since the 1990s, the need for soft skills competencies in the workforce has been the subject of many studies (Bernd, 2008; Casner-Lotto & Barrington, 2006; Deming, 2015; Felder et al., 2000; Francis & Auter, 2017; Heckman, 2006; Heckman & Kautz, 2012; Livia et al., 2017; Perreault, 2004; Robles, 2012; Rosenbaum, 2001; Schulz, 2008). Due to the extensiveness of this research, there are many different explanations for the term soft skills. James Heckman, a famous winner of the 2000 Nobel prize in Economics, narrowed it down to its simplest form. He says, "soft skills predict success in life" (Cimatti, 2016, p. 100). In this publication, Heckman found a correlation between soft skills competencies and personal and professional achievements (Cinque, 2015).

Similarly, other studies conclude that soft skills are now a significant driver for academic, organizational, and life success. Individuals with soft skills competencies had a higher chance of finishing school, getting promotions, and achieving personal and professional goals (Deming, 2017; Heckman, 2019; Karimi, 2020). According to

Klaus, 75% of long-term job success depends on individuals' soft skill competency, while only 25% depends on technical skills.

Human capital can be illustrated as a two-sided coin with cognitive (technical) and non-cognitive (soft) skills at its poles. The bulk of academic programs' focus has been on developing cognitive or technical skills, which can be empirically measured or tested, unlike the non-cognitive or soft skills often neglected. Mastering non-cognitive or soft skills competency is more complicated to achieve due to its complexity. These skills range in various areas: demonstrating attentiveness to details, showing empathy with colleagues or clients, utilizing a creative mindset to solve problems, collaborating effectively with colleagues and clients, managing conflicts constructively, or incorporating cohesiveness in a teamwork environment.

These skills are harder to measure but strong predictors of success in personal and professional life. Consequently, academic programs that utilize different strategies to enhance students' familiarity with soft skills have an important place in society (Heckman & Mosso, 2014; Heckman & Kautz, 2012; Karimi, 2020; White & Shakibnia, 2019).

Importance of Soft Skills

A consensus is emerging on the importance of soft skills (Deming, 2017; Ehlers & Kellerman, 2019; Karimi, 2020; Rao, 2016; Smith & Morris, 2017; Marr, 2019; Zahler, 2019) as knowledge and familiarity with these competencies tend to set individuals apart from one another, regardless of their technical skills and experiences. This change has been epitomized in need for graduates with both technical and soft skills (Francis & Auter, 2017; Heckman, 2019; Karimi, 2020). A recent industry report indicates that 92 percent of employers emphasize soft skills than technical skills ("2019 Global Talent Trends", 2019). Similarly, a more recent study suggests 100 percent of employers are placing importance on soft skills for entry-level graduates entering the workforce (Karimi, 2020). This needs to put soft skills as number one for entry-level professionals linking to a higher level of individual and organizational success.

Essential Demand of Future Soft Skills

Soft skills are essential to demonstrate technical skills. Soft skills can be learned, but it takes time and repetition to develop and master this competency. Soft skills have been referenced as transferable skills because individuals with solid soft skills foundational competency can transfer those skills from one industry to another. As we move deeper into the future of work with the emergence of artificial intelligence, robots, and other advanced technologies, having soft skills competency will be even more essential for organizational and personal growth.

We are currently witnessing robotic surgery, robotic construction, and robotic agriculture being used in diverse organizations due to benefits such as lower operating costs and faster speed than humans doing the job. As demand is growing to use robots or artificial intelligence in our daily jobs, the demand for humans with soft skills competencies is increasing as well. Based on the workforce needs, the demand for soft skills has grown over the last decades and continues to grow in our workplaces. Soft skills competencies are essential for organizations to make end solutions and achieve organizational goals and objectives. Soft skills will be critical to getting the work done right and enabling organizations to grow and flourish creatively. The more technology enters our organizations, the more soft skills are needed to manage the technology and offer innovation and creativity while maintaining our humanity's focus. Human resources with solid soft skills competency enable organizations to innovate new products and services using their critical and analytical thinking processes.

Robots or AI cannot creatively think, manage, and resolve conflicts, innovate ideas or products, or lead people/machines/projects; that is where having humans with soft skills competencies will be essential to have the upper hand and manage technology. Humans can use their creative mindsets and leadership skills to design, create, lead, and manage people and robots.

Since 2013, employers have identified soft skills such as creativity and the capacity to innovate as essential factors in their organization's continued success; therefore, they give hiring preference to college graduates with skills that enable organizations to contribute to these goals (AAC&U, 2013). This need is still quite relevant (Spar & Dye, 2018). The survey report between July 2017 and September 2017 provided a holistic view of modern workplace learning. The result indicates that the most in-demand soft skills were leadership, communication, collaboration, and time management – regardless of industry. Furthermore, all parties agree that training for soft skills was their number one priority in 2018. A year later, a similar study determined that the top five in-demand soft skills in a candidate that companies looked for were creativity, persuasion, collaboration, adaptability, and time management (Lewis, 2018).

Given the emerging technologies entering our workforce and the recent novel Coronavirus's impact globally, we now know the higher importance of STEM skills within the healthcare industry to overcome the crippling pandemic. The STEM sector encompasses a wide array of jobs and professions, and it is essential to understand which soft skills will be in higher demand as we further enter the future of work. To uncover this need, 27 STEM employers were interviewed using semi-constructive questionnaires for hearing their voices. They expressed their detailed views on soft skills needs and demands, specifically in 2020 to 2025. They stated an inevitable soft skills gap among recent college graduates, and more work is needed to manage the soft skills gap.

Furthermore, the conversation with these employers illuminated future soft skills needed from entry-level graduates entering the workforce. Their responses are shown in Table 24.1 to illustrate the importance of soft skills competencies like leadership and human connection – both of which are respectively the highest-rated skills currently in demand.

Table 24.1: Soft Skills Employers Identified as Necessary in 2020–2025.

Soft Skills in 2020–2025	Percentage
Leadership	93
Human Connection	89
Communication (verbal, written, non-verbal)	81
Creativity	70
Collaboration	70
Critical Thinking	63
Empathy	56
Problem Solving	44
Emotional Intelligence	37
Conflict Management	30

Leadership

Leadership is defined as "the sets of activities required to articulate an organization's vision and ensure that all its stakeholders will support the vision" (Stid & Brandach, 2009, p. 36). The path to a more human-driven future of work begins with the soft skills of leadership. Leadership skills are no longer needed only at the middle or higher-level career paths, and they are an essential skill as one enters the professional world of work. It is crucial for future college graduates entering the workforce to master an array of leadership skills and become workforce-ready graduates.

According to Colburn (2018), there are two categories of soft skills: interpersonal skills (focuses between the self and others) and intrapersonal skills (focuses within oneself). Both of these categories are highly transferable across a variety of jobs. Leadership competency initiates with interpersonal skills such as self-leadership and leads to intrapersonal soft skills such as team leadership, department leadership, and ultimately organizational leadership. One employer that perceives the importance of leadership skills for future college graduates described this need for the future workforce as "Being able to lead yourself and managing your own time" (Karimi, 2020, p.149). And another employer from a fortune 500 company described this as, "At our organization, we require leadership at every level whether or not you have a leader title. Each of us is responsible for leadership. It's one of our core competencies, and what it means is that you as an individual– whether or not you need other people, you have to lead yourself. And leadership means taking the initiative, managing your time, managing expectations, making sure that you're holding yourself accountable for meeting whatever it is that you commit to . . . Whether that's to yourself, your team, the customers, or other employees– whatever that looks like. So those are kind of the key aspects of leadership for new team members entering the organization" (Karimi, p.151).

So, leadership is one essential soft skill needed throughout one's professional journey starting from the entry-level to advanced senior leadership positions. These soft skills of leadership include abilities to connect with people, lead oneself as well as team members, build relationships with colleagues, lead individuals in team-based projects, detect risks, manage conflicts constructively, create a productive team environment, make empathetic business decisions with the growth mindset, and collaborate with key stakeholders to achieve organizational goals and objectives. These soft skills under the umbrella of leadership soft skills have one thing in common: to bring success into organizations by engaging its most important asset, its human resources.

Human Connection

In an age of never-ending connectivity, human connection is one of the top soft skills required by today's business leaders for future professionals entering their workforce. Those employees who have the soft skill of leadership competency are more equipped to engage and connect with others in their organizations. The future of the STEM workforce necessitates those graduates have the ability and skills to interact with their clients, patients, or colleagues, with the ultimate aim of forming human connections. This goal is also reflected in the World Economic Forum's *Jobs of Tomorrow* report (2020), which asserts that humanity and the ability to connect with people amid the rapid development of new technologies are at the core of what tomorrow's workplace will require. In a recent study, 89 percent of interviewed employers indicated that human connection would be essential to produce insights for better client care, creative solutions/outcomes, and strategic differentiation, supporting revenue growth, personal growth, and organizational survival (Karimi, 2020).

Employers also emphasized that future graduates need soft skills competencies to help facilitate personal interactions with their internal and external stakeholders. Many of these individuals placed great value in the power of human interactions, which essentially serve as the differentiator between us – the human – and the emerging technologies characterized by the 4th industrial revolution, for instance, artificial intelligence or robotics that are entering so rapidly into our future of work environment.

Although we are still at a nascent stage of this spectrum of technological development, employers are already seeking candidates with uniquely human or soft skills (Barr, 2019). This environment inherently values this soft skill that allows us to leverage our humanity and incorporate it into other soft skills like conflict resolution, problem-solving, collaboration, conflict management, and critical thinking. These skill competencies are not only intertwined, but they are also a necessary component of the effective delivery of tasks related to technical skills.

Communication, Collaboration, Creativity, Critical Thinking

Tomorrow's other in-demand skills are the Four C's: Communication, Collaboration, Creativity, and Critical thinking. Combining these four skills can be a force multiplier by empowering employees with the skills that engender innovation and unique service offerings. Based on an employer's response explaining the need for future soft skills, "communication is at the crux of everything" (Karimi, 2020, p.148). The future workforce needs individuals who possess effective communication in all formats – face-to-face, virtual, verbal, non-verbal, email, oral, and written communication.

Creativity and collaboration are just as essential for their organizations as critical thinking. Future graduates need to foster competencies that enable them to think outside the box and collaborate to generate innovative ideas. Future graduates need to learn how to use self-realized analytical and critical thinking capabilities for assessing or facing an issue. This skill competency will enable them to solve the challenge as they arise effectively.

Empathy

Empathy is needed for the future of the work environment because it enables employees to connect and better understand their customers' needs. Empathetic employees will be more compassionate towards their customers' behaviors and more thoughtful when creating products or services for their client base. For example, a software developer creating a new app for the elderly population will understand the spectrum of needs and feelings of this sector of the people while making the app for their use. This person will have the end-user in mind when designing and creating the application software for their usage. As a result, the end product will be aligned with the specific market demand.

Empathetic employees can develop tools for achieving desired organizational outcomes by integrating their human qualities of empathy and compassion with their technical duties. These employees can draw upon their empathetic competencies, alongside their technical skills, to build trust, respect, and rapport with their customers and colleagues.

Problem-solving, Emotional Intelligence, and Conflict Management

Problem-solving will be a super key in the future, and solving problems creatively is viewed as a differentiator amid employees looking to hire entry-level graduates. Specifically, employers want entry-level graduates to have the ability to solve problems beyond searching in Google or before asking a colleague within their organization for assistance. They need to master the researching capabilities for information from various sources to find a solution. Nevertheless, employers want graduates to feel comfortable asking questions if they encounter issues while tackling these endeavors independently with proper prior research to address the problem.

Moreover, employers prefer their employees to inform problems and offer solutions simultaneously. This skill can be developed in an academic format by teaching students to leverage multiple available resources instead of solely relying on a single source such as Google. A noted example of a helpful yet untapped resource that can improve said problem-solving efforts is the wisdom of colleagues who have experienced similar problems in the past.

Future graduates need Emotional Intelligence (EI) competency and are self-aware of their feelings and emotions. Furthermore, they need to be emotionally intelligent and not heavily focused on their technical intelligence. The happy medium centers around common sense and uses it intelligently to lead their soft and technical skills.

Another future soft skill that will be needed is conflict management. Like leadership, conflict management encompasses the intrapersonal and interpersonal qualities of oneself. An effective employee starting as entry-level to a senior leadership position is in-tune internally and externally with their feelings and emotions. When the need comes to face a conflict, they can resolve it constructively to achieve a win/win outcome.

Conclusion

The entire spectrum of future soft skills focuses on the essentiality of our human strengths as we enter the work environment's future. It takes time to develop soft skills competency. So, by knowing the skills that undergraduate students will need in the high demanding STEM workforce, key stakeholders such as employers and educators will be better equipped to focus on this market demand and consequently produce workforce-ready graduates. This development process should begin with lessons about leadership, as employers suggested, starting at the freshman level. Colleges and universities should offer leadership courses to help develop their leadership soft skills. This realm of knowledge should begin the students' journey with building soft skills competencies in self-leadership, team leadership, problem-solving, communication of all types, conflict management, and critical thinking. Towards the final years of students' undergraduate journey, they should be exposed to classes that aim to provide softs skills that equip them with the knowledge and confidence to conduct their employment searches professionally. Examples of talents within this category are resume building, interviewing, and ultimately securing a job (Karimi, 2020).

Investing in future graduates' educations before they enter the workforce benefited employers that chose to invest their time and resources in fostering and developing students' soft skills competencies before they joined their organizations (Karimi, 2020). Prior research echoes this phenomenon, indicating that soft skills training directly impacts the return organizations and individuals realize from their investments (Balcar, 2016; Deming, 2017; Heckman, 2000). Heckman's timeless recommendation to educators, which was published nearly two decades ago, is to consider investing in a sustainable soft skills educational system that trains students in the art of interpersonal, professional, and leadership/management skills to help develop a successful pathway for future students. This perspective helps explain why the top skills that interviewed employers tend to value for the future of the workforce are leadership and human connection.

Soft skills will be the hard skills of the future workforce to attain personal, professional, and organizational success. More research in this space generally concludes that emerging technologies such as big data, automation, and data digitalization, robotics are transforming the workplace (Barr, 2019; Penprase, 2018). As such, soft skills play a significant role in connecting these technologies with humans (Barr, 2019). This finding correlates with what the World Economic Forum Founder and Executive Chairman Klaus Schwab have asserted. Emerging technologies are changing everything – how we relate to one another, how we work, how our economies function, and even what it means to be human (Schwab & Davis, 2018). For our society to continue to flourish and innovate, we need to establish a strong, soft skills development foundation at the core of our educational system to offer a win/win outcome for all engaged key stakeholders: businesses, higher educational systems, and future graduates entering our workforce.

References

Association of American Colleges and Universities (2013). It Takes More Than a Major: Employer Priorities for College Learning and Student Success. Retrieved from https://www.aacu.org/sites/default/files/files/LEAP/2013_EmployerSurvey.pdf

Barr, B. (2019, November 1). The 9 biggest technology trends that will transform medicine and healthcare in 2020. *Forbes*. Retrieved from https://www.forbes.com/sites/bernardmarr/2019/11/01/the-9-biggest-technology-trends-that-will-transform-medicine-and-healthcare-in-2020/#39b14d5672cd

Colburn, M. (2018). An alternative to categorizing skills as soft or hard. *OD Practitioner, 50*(4). 65–66.

Deming, D. J. (2017). The growing importance of social skills in the labor market.*The Quarterly Journal of Economics,132*(4), 1593–1640.

Francis, J. & Auter, Z. (2017, June 20). Three ways to realign higher education with today's workforce [Web blog post]. Retrieved from http://www.gallup.com/opinion/gallup/212522/ways-realign-higher-Aeducation-today-workforce.aspx

Heckman, J.J. (2019). The economics of human potential. *Heckman Equation*. Retrieved from https://heckmanequation.org/

Karimi, H. (2020). Exploring the Soft Skills Gap of Undergraduate STEM Students Entering the Healthcare Industry: Employer Perspectives and Strategies for Improvement (Doctoral dissertation, Sullivan University)

Penprase B.E. (2018) The Fourth industrial revolution and higher education. In: Gleason N. (eds) *Higher Education in the Era of the Fourth Industrial Revolution*. Singapore: Palgrave Macmillan. https://doi.org/10.1007/978-981-13-0194-0_9

Schwab, K., & Davis, N. (2018). *Shaping the Future of the Fourth Industrial Revolution. A Guide to Building A Better World*. Currency. New York.

Spar, B., and Dye, C. (2018). 2018 workplace learning report: the rise and responsibility of talent development in the new labor market. *Learning LinkedIn*. 1–80. Retrieved from https://learning.linkedin.com/content/dam/me/learning/en-us/pdfs/linkedin-learning-workplace-learning-report-2018.pdf

Stid, D., & Brandach, J. (2009). How visionary nonprofit leaders are learning to enhance management capabilities. *Emerald Group Publishing Limited, 37*(1), 35–40. doi: 10.1108/10878570910926052

U.S. Chamber of Commerce Foundation (2018). *Bridging the soft skills gap*. Retrieved http://www.globalsuccess.org/wp-content/uploads/2018/08/BridgingSoftSkillsGap_US_Chamber_of_Commerce_Foundation.pdf

White, E., & Shakibnia, A. F. (2019). State of STEM: Defining the landscape to determine high-impact pathways for the future workforce. In *Proceedings of the Interdisciplinary STEM Teaching and Learning Conference, 3*(1), pp. 4–36.

Wilkie, D. (2019). Is the 4-Year college model broken? *SHRM*. Retrieved from https://www.shrm.org/resourcesandtools/hr-topics/employee-relations/pages/is-the-4-year-college-model-broken.aspx

Woodward, B. S., Sendall, P., & Ceccucci, W. (2010). Integrating soft skill competencies through project-based learning across the information systems curriculum. *Information Systems Education Journal, 8*(8).

World Economic Forum. (2018). *Towards a reskilling revolution: A future of jobs for all*. Retrieved from http://www3.weforum.org/docs/WEF_FOW_Reskilling_Revolution.pdf

LaVena Wilkin

Chapter 25
Create a Space to Forgive: Letting Go of Blame and Anger Can Move Us from Victim to Survivor

Abstract: Organizational conflicts can result in people feeling they have been slighted or harmed in some way, and it can be difficult to move past. The resultant blame and resentment can interfere with productivity and motivation and may lead to low morale and increased turnover. Although forgiveness is not typically associated with the workplace, the benefits of forgiving those who harmed us are applicable to colleagues and may support healthier working relationships. This chapter presents a case of workplace bullying and relates that when targets were able to forgive the bully, they experienced the benefits of forgiving. Finally, it presents the model of CREATE PEACE that offers steps to forgiving others.

Keywords: forgiveness, workplace bullying, enlightened transformation, apology, condoning, reconciliation, workplace conflict

Inevitably, when people work together there are a myriad of opportunities for interpersonal conflicts to occur, and employees impacted by these events often report feeling angry and resentful. They may also blame the leaders if they believe the conflict was unmanaged or mismanaged (Wilkin, 2010). These situations often result in damaged relationships, profound pain, and emotional reactions. For the individuals involved this leads to stress-related illnesses or psychological problems. Attention is diverted from the vision, mission, and goals of the organization as employees attempt to navigate the interpersonal relationships with those who have harmed them in some way. Productivity, motivation, and morale decrease, while absenteeism and turnover intentions increase (Riek & Mania, 2012). In addition, organizations may experience loss of institutional knowledge, and damaged reputations (Heames & Harvey, 2006). Even when a conflict is resolved, the negative effects may linger long after the event is over, and the people involved may not be willing to forgive the ills perpetrated upon them.

Traditionally, forgiveness has not been associated with the workplace or as a strategy for overcoming the damaging impact conflict has on interpersonal workplace relationships. However, several studies contend that forgiveness may help employees overcome the hurt and anger they feel and begin to heal broken relationships (Butler & Mullis, 2001; Madsen, Gygi, Hammon & Plowman, 2009; Fehr & Gelfand, 2012). After all, anger, resentment, and blame are common emotional reactions when we believe we have been harmed or disrespected by someone. Unfortunately, the burden of anger and resentment creates pain, heartache, and health problems for the person experi-

https://doi.org/10.1515/9783110746365-025

encing those emotions. In fact, there is an analogy that resentment is akin to carrying a hot coal in your hand with the intention of one day throwing it at the person who hurt you. The hot coal burns and scars the hands and hearts of the person holding on to it. Forgiveness is a conscious choice to release the importance we have attached to the harmful actions, and it frees us from the downward spiral linked to negative emotions.

What is Forgiveness and Why Should We Consider It?

The first step in understanding forgiveness is clarifying what this means. Joanna North defines it as:

> "When unjustly hurt by another, we forgive when we overcome the resentment toward the offender, not by denying our right to the resentment, but instead by trying to offer the wrongdoer compassion, benevolence, and love; as we give these, we as forgivers realize that the offender does not necessarily have a right to such gifts". (Enright, 2001, p. 25)

As this definition indicates, when someone hurts us, we have the right to feel angry, and we do not need to deny that feeling. The damage comes when we pitch a tent on the altar of that anger and decide to live there. In addition, forgiveness is a gift for the person forgiving, not for the offender, who may not deserve that gift (Enright, 2001).

Enright (2001) says the real beauty of forgiveness is that it gives us back our futures. When we continue to live in the past, and tell the story of past hurts and grievances, it is as if we are carrying around a big bag of trash with us. Every now and again, just so people do not forget, we take out a piece of our smelly, slimy garbage, and show it to others, saying, "isn't this awful?" If we drive down the highway of life always looking in the rearview mirror, we will crash.

Why Forgiveness Meets with Resistance

Few of us would take drugs that we know will hurt us, yet we harbor thoughts in our minds that cause physical and emotional problems. We allow the person who hurt us to live rent free in our heads. When we let go of blame, anger, and resentment, we make room for peace and joy in our lives. So, why do we hold on to resentment; why do we resist forgiving others? In part, it is because there are some basic myths about forgiveness that many of us hold onto.

Myth #1 – Forgiveness means condoning or justifying what happened. Forgiveness is not mean that what the person did was acceptable. It does not minimize the event but acknowledges the truth of what happened (Enright, 2001).

Myth #2 – Forgiveness means forgetting. In fact, forgetting is impossible, and the relationship between remembering and forgiving is part of the forgiveness process

(Enright, 2001). To tell someone who has been abused to forgive and forget sends a message that their story is not important, and if we cannot tell our story about what happened, we cannot begin the healing process. Memory denied or ignored is like an untreated infection. It festers and threatens our physical and emotional health. And the past does not just magically go away. Remembering may not be easy but forgetting is impossible.

Myth #3 – Forgiving is as easy as saying "I forgive you". Forgiveness is work. It is a process (Schneider, 2000; Worthington, 2001).

Other reasons we resist forgiving is our monkey minds chatter away and remind us that the person really hurt us, and they do not deserve forgiveness. Remember, forgiveness is the gift we give ourselves. It benefits the forgiver, not the offender. Another reason we do not forgive is we think we are weak if we forgive. In realty, forgiveness takes great strength and courage.

There is a lot of misunderstanding about forgiveness, apology, and reconciliation. Many people think that before they can forgive a transgression, the offender must apologize. The truth of the matter is you can forgive without receiving an apology. In some cases, the person simply is not sorry or does not see how they caused any harm. Other times, the person may not still be alive, so apology is impossible. If forgiveness was dependent upon apology, you would be stuck with the anger and blame. Fortunately, that is not the case.

Another misconception is that forgiveness means reconciliation. Again, this is not the case. Although forgiveness has the power to transform relationships, forgiveness and reconciliation are two very different concepts. Forgiveness can occur without reconciliation. However, reconciliation without forgiveness is disingenuous. While resentment and anger dissipate with forgiveness, it takes trust to reconcile, and it requires a positive view of the future relationship. When someone has been in an abusive relationship or has been deeply wounded, reconciliation is not necessary.

Enlightened Transformation: Applying Forgiveness to Workplace Bullying

In 2010, I conducted research on workplace bullying in which the faculty members of a midwestern university had been bullied by their superior. Specifically, I wanted to know why some people are better able to cope with the experience of being bullied, while others are so hurt and damaged by what happened that they are broken, and they experience feelings of helplessness and hopelessness, even years after the experience. My unexpected finding was that forgiveness is a key factor in the difference between victim and survivor. As Table 25.1 indicates, there were clear differences in the behaviors and attitudes of the victims and survivors.

Table 25.1: Enlightened Transformation: Moving from victim to survivor (Wilkin, 2010).

Victims	Survivors
– Continue to search for reasons why they were targets	– Possess self-confidence
– Look to others for help	– Become an advocate for others
– Attempted to change the bullying behavior and leaders' reactions	– Changed their reaction to the situation
– Continue to blame and be angry the bully and the leaders	– Let go of blame and anger
– Seek revenge for the bully and the leaders	– Developed empathy toward the bully and the leaders

The study found that 70% of the participants stated they had forgiven the bully. The other 30% stated that they had not forgiven the bully. There were clear differences between the group of targets who forgave the bully and the ones who had not.

Targets who had not forgiven discussed wanting revenge and a desire for the bully to suffer the way they suffered; they believe the bully damaged their self-confidence and their self-esteem; they are still angry with the organizational leaders who did not address the behaviors; and they do not know how to begin forgiving the egregious acts perpetrated against them (Wilkin, 2010).

In contrast, the targets who forgave the bully all said they had empathy for the individual who hurt them; they perceived that they took something positive from the experience; they stated that forgiving the bully freed them from negative emotions and baggage they carried with them related to the events; they discussed forgiveness as a process they worked through. Forgiveness was not immediate. However, with time and through reflection, they were able to release the anger they initially felt (Wilkin, 2010).

In addition, the findings support and advance other forgiveness studies. For example, forgiveness researcher, Enright (2001), found that people who practice forgiveness often discover that they have a new purpose in life because of the negative behavior. They search for meaning in the experience and advocate for others. Likewise, Worthington's (2001) model of forgiveness determined that when people can release the negative emotions, they develop empathy for the perpetuator.

It is interesting that the targets who have not forgiven mentioned that the bully destroyed their self-esteem and self-confidence. Targets believe they have a moral responsibility to respect themselves. When they perceive self-respect and self-confidence have been stripped from them, if they forgive, they believe they are condoning the behavior. That same study found that when people have been humiliated and their self-respect has suffered, they wish that same humiliation and suffering for the perpetrator.

Layton (1998) presents a three-step model of forgiveness that begins with stunned innocence, moves on to the tortures of obsession, and culminates in transcendence. In the innocence stage, targets often search for the meaning and purpose of their pain, shame, and suffering. At this point, they ask "Why me?" or "What did I do to deserve this?" Unfortunately, when targets are unable to move past the stunned innocence stage, they continue to relieve the experience, carry anger, and blame, and suffer from the unjust behavior they have experienced. Each of the targets who forgave the bully stated it was a process. They started at the stage where they could not believe what was happening to them, and they questioned if they perceived it incorrectly.

The next stage in Layton's (1998) model, obsession, is characterized by trying to hold the person or people behind behavior accountable for their actions. In part, they look to others to help them right the unjust treatment they have experienced. In Wilkin's (2010) study, the targets who moved on advocated for others, while those who still suffered looked to the university leaders to resolve the bullying problem. The leaders' failure to do this exacerbated the feelings of helplessness and hopelessness for those who had not been able to let go of the anger and blame. In this most recent study, one person who forgave said she filed a lawsuit against the organization. One thing she wanted was for the organization to hire a human resources director, so if this happened to others, they would have a voice or a place to go. Others said they reached out to other targets and offered support or a shoulder to cry on. Her attorney thought she should ask for money; however, she just wanted to make sure others were protected (Wilkin, 2010).

When individuals reach Layton's (1998) final stage, transcendence, they look inward for the change. They recognize the transformation must come from within them. They cannot change others' behaviors; they can only change their reactions to the behavior. The targets in Wilkin's (2010) study who were able to move on recognized this, and they let go of both their desire for revenge and their anger toward the bully and the leaders who did not address the negative behavior. Targets of bullies who can forgive the bully and reach the final stage of Layton's model, transcendence, may be able to get their futures back. Overwhelming, this was the case with the targets in this study. No one said they condoned the behavior; yet they all mentioned having empathy for the bully.

The targets who were not able to forgive were still questioning why this happened to them. They said they were sad, bitter, resentful, and angry. One mentioned being in a downward spiral of hopelessness and resentment, even though the bullying occurred almost five years before. They wanted the bully to suffer. Indeed, one person said the bully was later convicted of a crime, and she went to his trial because she wanted to see him in agony. They felt their power had been stripped from them, and there was no one to help them.

The substantive theory that emerged from this study is that targets can move from victim to survivor when they are enlightened and can change their reactions to the bullying behavior, release blame and anger, and empower themselves. Prior to this occurring, they realize that they cannot change the bullying behavior, nor can they change the leaders' responses to the behavior. In fact, changing anything external to themselves is impossible. The changes come from within them (Wilkin, 2010).

Each of the targets of the bullying behavior was subjected to the same types of mistreatments. However, some targets have been able to move, while others still feel traumatized and powerless. A comparison of the faculty members who discussed being able to move on and those who say they are still suffering from the trauma revealed five key differences in the way they responded to the events. Again, every participant experienced similar behaviors, and all were initially angry that the leaders did not offer assistance. Moreover, each faculty member confronted the behavior, and then avoided the situation by either leaving the university or staying away from the bully (Wilkin, 2010).

Some participants talked about letting go of blame and anger. Others discussed their continued suffering and feelings of powerlessness, suffering, and traumatism. The survivors were self-confident; they advocated for others; they took responsibility for their own reactions; and they were not malleable. Conversely, individuals who continue to be victimized said they lacked inner strength; they looked to others to resolve the problem; they cannot forgive the university leaders or the bully; and they tried to acquiesce and do what the bully wanted (Wilkin, 2010).

Steps to Forgiving and Creating Peace

As a result of interviews with the targets of the bullying behavior and listening to the experiences of the faculty members who were able to forgive and, as a result, cope more effectively with their experiences, I created the CREATE PEACE model to help others learn to let go of blame and anger, forgive, and create more peace in their lives.

C – Choose to forgive. This is the first step in the process. Forgiveness is a choice, and the desire to forgive is the very heart of forgiveness work.

R – Remember and acknowledge the pain and the emotional distress caused by the injustice and violation; this is vital because healing cannot begin until we process the emotions. In fact, if the emotions are ignored or denied, they will manifest themselves in a continuous state of victimization.

E – Empower yourself. If we only focus on our wounded feelings, we give the person who hurt us power over our lives. Forgiveness allows you to take back your personal power.

A – Give the altruistic gift of forgiveness. It comes with no strings attached. It does not rely on apology or promises for the other person that the behavior will not be repeated.

T – Transform your life by letting go of anger, resentment, and blame. Change the story you tell. Invite love, joy, peace, and contentment into your life.

E – Expect life to change. You cannot fill your cup with peace, love, joy, and harmony if it is overflowing with anger, resentment, and bitterness. Forgiveness allows you to see the beauty in the world, and your life will become more peaceful.

P – Persist in your forgiveness practice. Forgiveness is not a one-time process. It takes time. We go through the steps over and over and over again. There is no time limit; there is just progress. Forgiveness is a process, and it requires changing your belief system. Depending on the offense, you may have lost self-confidence. Your beliefs are your reality, so keep reminding yourself that you are an amazing person with unlimited potential and a true purpose in life. Consider that your mind is like a garden, and if you do not deliberately cultivate flowers, weeds will grow without much effort. So, plant and cultivate positive thoughts. Daily affirmations are a great tool for this.

E – Empathize with the person who hurt you. Consider what happened in the person's life that made them act or treat others that way. Yes, I know, easier said than done. How does the world look through the other person's lens?

A – Advocate for others. Others in the same situation may need your emotional support. Advocate for them and offer to help them, especially if you are further along in the forgiveness process.

C – Co-create your future. Remember that you cannot change the past. The beauty and power of forgiveness is that it gives us back our futures. Transform your life and consider the joy of co-creating your future with Spirit as your constant partner.

E – Enlighten yourself. Know that you do not have to remain stuck in victimhood; know that you have the power to transform your experiences by letting go of those things that do not serve you; and embrace a life overflowing with love, peace, and joy.

Conclusion

In organizations and in life, conflicts occur, and those conflicts cause us pain and angst. Far too often, we carry the hurt with us, and the result is that holding on to blame and resentment hurts us more than it hurts the other person. If we could learn the transformative power of forgiveness, we would lead more stress-free and peaceful lives.

Forgiveness is an inside job. It is an inner process where we choose to let go of thoughts, emotions, feelings, and behaviors that are stopping us from doing all that is ours to do. Forgiveness work is not always easy, but it is freeing. When we forgive, we find our way to inner peace and happiness. The space where we held the resentment and anger creates a vacuum, and we can fill that space with love, joy, and contentment. We can CREATE PEACE.

References

Butler, D. S., & Mullis, F. (2001). Forgiveness: A Conflict Resolution Strategy in the workplace.*Journal of Individual Psychology, 57*(3),259.

Enright, R.D. (2001). *Forgiveness Is A Choice: A Step-by-step Process for Resolving Anger and Restoring Hope*. Washington, DC: American Psychological Association.

Fehr, R., & Gelfand, M. J. (2012). The forgiving organization: A multilevel model of forgiveness at work. The Academy of Management Review, 37(4), 664–688.

Heames, J. & Harvey, M. (2006). Workplace bullying: A cross-level assessment. *Management Decision, 44*(9), pp. 1214–1230.

Layton, M. (1998). The long road to forgiveness. Family Therapy Newsletter, (November- December 1998).

Madsen, S. R., Gygi, J., Hammond, S. C., & Plowman, S. F. (2009). Forgiveness as a Workplace Intervention: The Literature and a Proposed Framework. *Journal of Behavioral & Applied Management, 10*(2),246–262.

Riek, B.M., & Mania, E.W. (2012). The antecedents and consequences of interpersonal forgiveness: A meta-analytic review. *Personal Relationships, 19*(2),304–325.

Schneider, C.D. (2000, Spring). What it means to be sorry: The power of apology in mediation. *Mediation Quarterly, 17(3), 265–280.*

Wilkin, L. (2010). *Workplace bullying in academe: A Grounded theory study exploring how faculty cope with the experience of being bullied* (Doctoral dissertation). R.

Worthington, E. (2001). *Five Steps to Forgiveness: The Art and Science of Forgiving*. New York: Crown.

List of Figures

https://doi.org/10.1515/9783110746365-026

List of Tables

https://doi.org/10.1515/9783110746365-027

Index

https://doi.org/10.1515/9783110746365-028

www.ingramcontent.com/pod-product-compliance
Lightning Source LLC
Chambersburg PA
CBHW081043220326
41598CB00038B/6971